Information Technology

—— IN A ——

Global Business Environment

READINGS AND CASES

CANDACE DEANS

Thunderbird, The American Graduate School
of International Management

JAAK JURISON

Fordham University

boyd & fraser publishing company

I(T)P An International Thomson Publishing Company

Danvers • Albany • Bonn • Boston • Cincinnati • Detroit • London • Madrid • Melbourne
Mexico City • New York • Paris • San Francisco • Singapore • Tokyo • Toronto • Washington

*To the students in my first class of Global Information and Technology Management
at Thunderbird—The American Graduate School of International Management—
tomorrow's leaders in international business and information management.*

CANDACE DEANS

*To Paul Gray, who as a teacher, mentor, colleague, and friend
has been a great source of inspiration to me.*

JAAK JURISON

Executive Editor: James H. Edwards
Project Editor: Lisa Strite
Production Editor: Barbara Worth
Manufacturing Coordinator: Carol Chase
Marketing Director: William Lisowski
Composition: Rebecca Evans & Associates
Interior and Cover Design: Rebecca Evans & Associates
Cover Art: Daiji Asami

ITP The ITP™ logo is a trademark under license.

Printed in the United States of America

For more information, contact boyd & fraser publishing company:

boyd & fraser publishing company
One Corporate Place • Ferncroft Village
Danvers, Massachusetts 01923, USA

International Thomson Publishing Europe
Berkshire House 168-173
High Holborn
London, WC1V 7AA, England

Thomas Nelson Australia
102 Dodds Street
South Melbourne 3205
Victoria, Australia

Nelson Canada
1120 Birchmount Road
Scarborough, Ontario
Canada M1K 5G4

International Thomson Editores
Campose Eliseos 385, Piso 7
Col. Polanco
11560 Mexico D.F. Mexico

International Thomson Publishing GmbH
Konigswinterer Strasse 418
53227 Bonn, Germany

International Thomson Publishing Asia
221 Henderson Road
#05-10 Henderson Building
Singapore 0315

International Thomson Publishing Japan
Hirakawacho Kyowa Building, 3F
2-2-1 Hirakawacho
Chiyoda-ku, Tokyo 102, Japan

1 2 3 4 5 6 7 8 9 10 M 8 7 6 5

ISBN: 0-7895-0050-7

Contents

Preface

INFORMATION TECHNOLOGY (IT) is one of the driving forces behind globalization of markets and the reorganization of companies. This book provides a needed resource of supplementary readings and cases that integrate current information technology issues in an international context. The breadth of coverage provides a rich combination of international business and information technology topics that incorporates an added value to course material. These readings provide one means for internationalizing the core Information Technology course or a means for adding a technology dimension to the core International Business course.

This book provides a timely contribution to the currently limited curriculum resources available that address international information systems and technology issues. The idea for the book developed out of the need to supplement our courses in international IT management with additional reading material. The specific selections are based on feedback by students in previous classes.

The book is intended for use in introductory courses in information technology and international business at both the undergraduate and graduate levels. Several schools now offer a specialized course in Global Information Systems and Technology Management. This book is one of few available to meet the needs for this course. It would also be useful for a Special Topics course in business that covers a variety of issues at the intersection of global business and technology.

The articles are drawn from a variety of business and academic sources. Some articles are published here for the first time. The readings were selected with the intent to integrate both practical and theoretical issues facing managers who need to apply information technology in the global business world. Because information technology and international business environments change so rapidly, our selections come mostly from recent publications. We have also included some classic readings that provide the essential theoretical framework for understanding multinational business strategies and organizational structures. These articles are just as relevant today as they were at the time they first appeared in print.

The book is organized into six sections along the following major themes:

1. Globalization of the Marketplace

2. Globalization of the Organization

3. Global Information Systems and Technology: Planning and Strategic Implications

4. Global Connectivity and Telecommunications

5. Management of Global Information Flows

6. Integrating Technology, Systems, and People across the Globe

Each section is preceded by introductory material, written by the authors, to indicate the significance and relevance of the articles that follow. The integrating theme throughout the sections focuses on challenges for business leaders. The final section includes a set of real-world cases that provide specific examples of ways in which companies have responded to these various challenges and opportunities. These cases illustrate the role of information technology in multinational organizations and help reinforce student learning. Major challenges presented in the readings can be further expanded through the utilization of specialized class projects, guest speakers, or current case analyses.

We would like to express our thanks to the authors of the articles and publishers who gave us permission to reprint the articles. We would also like to thank Peter Keen who encouraged us to introduce this book and provided valuable guidance in the initial phase of our work. Finally, we thank the editorial staff at boyd & fraser, especially, Jim Edwards, Lisa Strite, and Barbara Worth for their encouragement and helpful suggestions.

Candace Deans
Jaak Jurison

April 1995

SECTION I

Globalization of the Marketplace

The expansion of business activity beyond the borders of one's own country has become a necessity for many companies striving to remain competitive in today's changing economic environment. Even those companies that have remained domestically focused no longer have the luxury of ignoring international business activities. The world is becoming one huge marketplace, and all players are affected in some way by new and evolving competitive forces.

The challenges can be enormous for the inexperienced company with little know-how about doing business in other parts of the world. The assumption that what works in one's home country will work anywhere else in the world has proven to be a pitfall for many companies. International business transactions and operations are more complex because of the multiplicity of languages, cultures, government regulations, legal systems, political climates, and economic variables. As business continues to become more international in scope and firms gain experience in new markets, many of these obstacles will become less burdensome.

Information technology (IT) has clearly played a significant role in the rapid expansion of business activity to all parts of the globe. Because of technology, issues commonplace in the company's domestic market—communications barriers, geographical distance, and the handling of business documents and transactions—have become concerns to be handled on an international scale. Today, IT is the essential backbone that serves as a facilitator of global information flows and the means by which to obtain a competitive advantage.

The five readings in this first section emphasize the significance of global business today and the resulting implications for corporations of the future. A paradigm shift has occurred that will continue to influence not only the business community, but society as a whole. The shift to an information age has already taken place. The consequences are yet to be fully realized.

In the first reading, Dobyns and Crawford-Mason present a broad overview of the many forces transforming business into a truly global marketplace. They quote several renowned experts who emphasize the significance of IT in this change process. The authors drive home the message that quality has replaced quantity as the key in an evolving customer-driven economy. The quality revolution will play a significant role in the transformation to a global marketplace.

In the second paper, Walter Wriston, former Chairman of Citicorp, further emphasizes the transformations occurring in the business world today. He provides examples and historical evidence to support his argument that we are experiencing a revolution as drastic and far-reaching as that represented by the shift from an agricultural age to an industrial age. Information technology has spawned an information economy in which the creation of wealth now depends on information. This change affects all aspects of our economy as well as the politics of nations. The implications for business are tremendous and are only beginning to be experienced.

Ohmae, in the third paper, stresses the importance of embracing change and thinking from a new managerial perspective. In a business world that has become borderless, managers must respond in new ways to remain effective. He argues that the need to globalize is driven primarily by customer preference. The managerial challenge of the future centers on delivering value to customers, who in turn provide the legitimacy for thinking global.

In the fourth paper, Hax focuses on three issues as the basis for future competitiveness: globalization, technology, and leadership. He discusses the profound shifts currently taking place in the economic, political, social, and technological contexts in which today's corporation operates. These evolving environments have forced companies to reevaluate corporate strategy, organizational structure and management styles. Effectively managing the change inherent in today's business environment requires a new kind of leadership. The challenges that face future leaders are discussed in the context of globalization and the increasing importance of IT to a firm's operations.

In the final paper, O'Reilly further emphasizes the significance of the global marketplace by examining changes in the workforce worldwide. He provides examples to support his contention that a fundamental shift is under way in how and when the world's work gets done. The emergence of a talented and capable global workforce is changing the dynamics of business decisions.

The papers in this section provide the reader with a foundation from which to proceed as subsequent discussions focus more specifically on the role of information technology in this evolving global marketplace. The next section examines the role of the organization and its response to changes in its international business environment.

The Global Marketplace

LLOYD DOBYNS & CLARE CRAWFORD-MASON

ON JUNE 18, 1812, President James Madison of the United States signed a declaration to start the War of 1812 against Great Britain. Two days earlier the British had repealed the maritime orders that had angered the Americans, but the war went on anyway for more than two years. On Christmas Eve, 1814, British and American negotiators concluded the Treaty of Ghent to end the war, but it ended as irrationally as it had begun. Two weeks later, the British attacked New Orleans, which was defended by a mixed bag of American regulars and volunteers commanded by General Andrew Jackson. The British suffered two thousand casualties and total defeat; the Americans had only a hundred casualties and complete victory, one of their few in the war. Jackson, widely and wildly cheered as a hero, eventually would win and serve two terms as president.

The reason the war started after the main grievance had been settled and continued after the peace treaty had been signed was communications. The only way for news to travel was by sea, and the fastest sailing ship could cross the Atlantic in two weeks, but three weeks was more normal and four weeks not unusual, so when the British attacked New Orleans, the peace treaty was still at sea.

In January 1991, a consolidated military force led by the United States attacked Iraq and Iraqi-occupied Kuwait with planes and missiles. Gary Shepard, a television reporter, saw the antiaircraft fire and bomb explosions from his hotel window in Baghdad and by telephone and satellite announced the beginning of hostilities to anyone watching *World News Tonight with Peter Jennings*. It was all but instantaneous. Until the Iraqi military stopped television broadcasts, American military leaders got bomb damage assessments from live Cable News Network (CNN) reports from Baghdad, just as the Iraqi leader Saddam Hussein had said earlier that he followed political developments in Washington and New York on CNN. Jim Hoagland, an American newspaper columnist, wrote the month before the war, "CNN is a technological and journalistic marvel that transmits not only news but an illusion of meaningful interdependence around the globe to plugged-in officials and travelers. . . . People everywhere know about the same thing at the same time. . . . anywhere is rapidly becoming everywhere."

Advances in communications technology have made as much difference to corporations as they have to countries and correspondents. Kenichi Ohmae, the managing director of McKinsey and Company in Japan, says, "One of the biggest changes that has taken place, over the last ten years particularly, is the proliferation of information. People in advanced countries receive information directly from the source through TV and [other] mass media." Thanks to satellites, fiber optics, and computers, geographical distance, so critical to communications in the War of 1812, is today inconsequential. For business purposes, every place is the same as every other place. Myron Tribus, the consultant, travels extensively and says, "Wherever you go in the world, you see Sony, you see Honda, you see Ford, you see producers distributing their things all over the world. This is an imperative because no nation can go it alone in the sense that no nation has all the resources required for survival, and in order to get the resources from others, you must trade with them." Ohmae says the old international trading rules that dated from the seventeenth-century British East India Company were that governments gave or sold private companies the right to produce and sell in their own countries; then, working together, the government and the company controlled information to consumers. No one knew what else at what price might be available somewhere else. "Now, it is completely different," he says. "People know what's best, cheapest, best quality, and, therefore, it is now the time for the consumers to choose products. . . . People have the information."

Rosabeth Moss Kanter, the Harvard professor and editor, says that information, the computer, and transportation advances caused the global market, and not only in manufacturing. "I mean," she asks, "what could be more local than the hospital down the street? Today, because of the ability to gather information, because of information technology, there are now hospitals that compete worldwide for the wealthy Arab heart patient or the wealthy European having discretionary surgery, because they can learn who those customers are, because they can spread their message, because the speed of transportation makes it easy for people to get there. There's practically nothing that's local anymore."

The "people matter, places don't" concept is one of four key elements in the modern economy faced by global companies. The others are that quality has replaced quantity as the way to measure manufacturing or service; that quality improvements are being made in some industries at a revolutionary rate, which the quality expert Joseph Juran says all firms must do if they don't want to fail; and that the economy is now customer-driven, as opposed to the days that Homer Sarasohn remembers when "the customer be damned" was a popular business opinion. "I love thinking about the consumer in the global marketplace," Kanter says, "because in essence, the consumer is what caused the political revolutions we're seeing all over the world. The falling away of the boundaries between Eastern Europe and Western Europe is all because people in Eastern Europe wanted to go shopping—they could see it on television, they could learn about it through mass media that don't respect national boundaries, and so they, too, wanted to participate." Ohmae agrees and refers to recent Russian disarmament agreements that he says were caused by "Bon Jovi and Levi Strauss, not the power of the Pentagons of this world. It's not the pressure of NATO and American military superiority that is really causing the Russian people to dismantle their hardware. I think it is the Russian people's awareness that their lifestyle . . . is not on a par with the rest of the world. . . . Ideology is not a central issue anymore. . . . people are not looking for nationalism. . . . people are looking for the good life." Power has passed to the consumer. "All over the world now," Kanter continues, "the customer has more power. Systematically, in industry after industry, power is shifting from the people who sell to the people who buy because they have more choices, because they can get it from anywhere, because there are more companies competing for their attention. . . . More competition, more choices, put more power in the hands of the customer, and that, of course, drives the need for quality."

Juergen Hubbert, a member of the Mercedes Board of Management and the head of its passenger car division, underlines that increasing competition. "It's becoming much harder," he says, "not only in the United States, where we have our competition, but even in Germany and Europe, all over the world. . . . I have a figure, which I remember, that in our field of activity [luxury automobiles], we had six competitors in 1980. In 1990, there are fifteen." The new competition came from companies in the United States, Japan, and other European countries. Even with the increased competition, Hubbert says, Mercedes still does well, even in Japan. "We had sales last year [1989] of thirty-five thousand cars," he says, "and this year we expect more than forty thousand. This means that we are number one among the imports. You can see that a high-quality and highly innovative car is even needed in Japan, in that very competitive market."

The competitive changes are all part of a natural progression of business that started with a tribal or village barter system and got increasingly complex. Two hundred years ago in the United States, there was a struggling national economy, but most of the trading that went on was local. Then, about a hundred years ago, the United States as a national economy became a region of the world economy just as Europe did. At about the same time, Japan came out of three hundred years of isolation and the government started building a modern industrial economy to compete with the West. Robert Reich, the professor of political economics at Harvard,* says, "Over the last fifty years, as transportation and communications costs have declined, the world economy has become, itself, globalized. Over the last ten years . . . you see the world economy shrinking even more. . . . Most large American companies, most large European and Japanese companies, have investments all over the world." The United States has $130 billion invested in Europe, and the twelve countries of the European Community have $190 billion in the United States. Some of that investment turns into jobs. Reich says that in 1989 "affiliates of foreign manufacturers created more jobs in the United States than American-owned manufacturing companies [and] American firms now employ 11 percent of the industrial work force in Northern Ireland." Foreign investments are not limited to the major national players.

It is likely that most Americans have never heard of a company named Unicord, but it is equally likely that those same Americans do know of Bumble Bee, the country's third-largest tuna canning company. In late 1989 Unicord, described as "an aggressive, young

*Now U.S. Secretary of Labor

Thai company," bought Bumble Bee for more than the tuna company's assets were worth. Unicord is not the only Thai company with an interest in the United States. Saha-Union, a textile and footwear company, now makes thread at a factory it opened in Georgia early in 1990, and Siam Cement, in its first American investment, has joined an Italian firm in making ceramic tiles in Tennessee.

In all three cases, it made sense for the firms to locate in the United States because it put them in one of their larger markets, and being close to your customers is almost always desirable. It also put them inside the United States should the Congress pass legislation, as some members of Congress want, to protect American companies or jobs by keeping certain foreign goods out. Japanese auto makers are already under "voluntary restraints" and can ship only a limited number of cars from Japan to the United States, which is one reason that Japan has eleven relatively new auto assembly plants in North America; no one can keep you out if you're already there. Those plants do not build vehicles exclusively for sale in the United States. Honda makes cars and motorcycles in Ohio that it exports around the world, including back to Japan. According to Reich, "by the early 1990s, when Honda annually exports fifty thousand cars to Japan from its Ohio production base, it will actually be making more cars in the United States than in Japan."

Manuel Lujon, Jr., the American secretary of the interior, told reporters that he would not own a Japanese car or any foreign car, for that matter. Some other Americans feel the same way, and there are "Buy America" campaigns aimed at persuading American consumers to buy American products to help reduce the trade deficit. That is more difficult than it sounds. What, for example, is an American car? Is it a Honda assembled in Marysville, Ohio, by American men and women, or is it a Pontiac LeMans assembled at a highly automated Korean plant, based on a design by Opel in Germany, then sold under an American name? In the auto industry, American and foreign firms now routinely engage in joint ventures and are suppliers to and customers of each other, so an American car is, in all probability, an international product. The auto industry is fairly straightforward; in other industries, figuring out what belongs to whom can get much more complicated.

Peter J. Sprague, the chairman of the American National Semiconductor Corporation, has said, "We are using Russian engineers living in Israel to design chips that are made in America and then assembled in Asia." Deming, who often says he's fond of "stupid examples," is asked how he thinks of the global marketplace. He pulls a watch from his vest pocket and the battery-powered, lighted magnifying glass he always carries from inside his jacket; peering through the glass, he reads the small print on the watch case. "Assembled in China from Swiss parts, made in Hong Kong." As he tucks the glass and watch back in their respective pockets he says, "The global marketplace."

Paul Kreisberg of the Carnegie Endowment says, "Almost all large companies are now global companies—Japanese, American, European. It's very hard to go anywhere in the world and not find companies representing every [other] country in the world in that country and often merged together in complex interrelationships. . . . You find this less frequently with Japanese companies, but American and European companies have an enormous amount of interweaving of activities and interests." Daniel Yankelovich of the Public Agenda Foundation says, "the name of the game in the future for corporations is joint ventures. It's having your R&D capability maybe in East Germany and Hungary rather than in your plant in Philadelphia. So in human terms, we're living in each other's pockets. We are making partnerships and joint ventures across national lines. Corporations are losing their national identity . . . Ten years ago, the world economy was nothing more than the sum of individual economies. There was no global economy."

To a good many people, there still isn't. Kreisberg says, "In one sense, it's all one big economy, but in terms of the entire structure of the American economy or the European economy, the global aspect of it remains a smaller part. If you take the total number of companies in the United States, many of the largest are these global companies. But if you look at all the business being done in the United States, the overwhelming proportion of the business is being done by American companies. In Europe, the overwhelming proportion of business being done is by European companies, and in Japan, business is being done by Japanese companies." That has been true for a long time, but Yankelovich doesn't think it will continue to be true. "The integration, the cross-fertilization, the joint ventures, and the breakdown of lines of culture are creating a truly global market," he says.

If joint ventures are indeed the name of the future game, the United States may be at a disadvantage. Anand Panyarachun, the executive chairman of Saha-Union Corporation, says that when a Japanese firm sets up a factory in a foreign country, it works within the cultural and legal framework of that country. "But the others," he says, meaning Americans, "when they go to a foreign country, they still think they're setting up a factory in their own territory. They want to change the rules of the game. They want to level the playing field. They want to convert that into a part of their economy." Paron Israsena, the chief executive of Siam Cement, a conglomerate and the largest company in Thailand, is involved in several joint ventures, but he tends to avoid American companies in favor of the Japanese. "The big difference," he says, "in joining with the Japanese, they have fewer lawyers. We don't go through many, many stages of the legal process, and I think the Japanese are more practical. It's easier to talk to the Japanese than to the big American corporations, because in the American corporation, there are so many levels of control." Paron's one joint venture in Europe is with Michelin in France. He says, it was difficult to reach them, but "after we contacted them once, and then we got the thing done fairly quickly, and we have become a very, very good partner of Michelin now in Paris."

Paron is not the only Asian who has noticed the incredible preponderance of lawyers in the United States. Jinnosuke Miyai, the president of the Japan Productivity Center in Tokyo, wrote a thoughtful article comparing the two economies. "Another revealing difference between Japan and America," he said, "is the number of lawyers in each country. There is one lawyer for every 10,000 people in Japan. In America, the ratio is 1 to 700. This reflects how the Japanese prize harmony, avoid differences and seek consensus." He did not add, although he could have, that Americans are the most litigious people in the world, and he may have been generous in his statistics. According to *Parade* magazine, one person in every 360 Americans is a lawyer, except in Washington, D.C., where it's one in 22. Deming tells students at his seminars to try to arrange handshake deals with honest suppliers because a legal contract "is a piece of paper that any lawyer can wriggle out of." Lawyer-bashing has become something of a sport in the United States, but in international trade, America's lawyers and lawsuits are mentioned by others as part of the overall economic problem.

When a reporter asks Josh Hammond, the president of the American Quality Foundation, "If we [Americans] don't get better, what happens?" he answers, "The question is, who's the *we*? When you look at General Motors, they're all over the world. When you look at Germany, that was viewed as a closed industry, particularly in the automotive area, but they now have joint ventures with Japan. Why? Because the Japanese are coming to Europe, and it's better to be part of them, and it's natural to be part of them, and it's logical to be part of them. So all these joint ventures with Europe and with the Japanese, the *we* is not going to have capital letters. I think it's going to be smaller. The *we* is going to be all of us. There's a remarkable thing about quality in business that I've observed, that's the willingness to share the secrets. . . . That's because, I think, there's an understanding that the *we* is all of us."

Joint ventures and other modern production techniques have also created a relatively new trade problem. What is the nationality of anything? Thomas T. Niles, the U.S. ambassador to the European Community, says governments do have a responsibility to protect their citizens and companies from unfair trading practices, then he adds, "But I think it's also important that government recognize the reality of interdependence. . . . Inevitably, that's going to happen because the problems that we're going to be dealing with in the rest of this decade and into the next century are essentially global problems. They're the problems of dealing with the environmental issues that don't respect national borders, the extraordinary flows of investment capital around the world through new trading mechanisms, and the reality that when you buy something, you won't be able to tell where it was made or where its component parts were made. It's going to be an international product. That's an important reality."

What is, for example, an import into America or an export from America? The country buys more from other countries than it sells to them—or, at least, government statistics say so. Americans are told by their political, industrial, and labor leaders that the trade deficit exists because of trade barriers to American goods in Japan and other Asian countries and barriers to American agricultural products in the European Community. The perception, and sometimes the reality, of being treated unfairly by trading partners fuels the cause in the Congress and elsewhere for protection against foreign firms. Opponents of protectionist measures say that anything Congress does against Asia, for instance, would cause Asian countries to reciprocate. To which Roger Milliken, the chief executive of Milliken & Company, says, "All of those reciprocal actions are already in place today. They've taken them long ago. There's barrier after barrier after barrier to exporting into those [Asian] countries."

Still, global companies generally fear protectionism. Edwin Artzt of Procter & Gamble says, "I know it rankles people to see foreign countries have greater access to this market [America] than we have to theirs. But, inevitably, the way to solve this problem is to establish equal access principles through multilateral trade negotiations around the world. Protectionism is not going to strengthen this country. It's a Band-Aid." Hubbert, a German, agrees. "We as a company say there will be no Fortress Europe," he says, "because only if you can and will compete in a free market can you be strong and successful." He says that when the United States imposed "voluntary restraints" on the Japanese auto makers, the only thing that happened was that the Japanese opened assembly plants in the United States and car prices went up. The American consumer had to pay. "I think we should stay with free world trade," he says, "with free competition. We want to stay in this field because more than 50 percent of our cars are exported. We need the world market."

Most global companies of whatever nationality do need the world market. Therefore, the question of what is an import and what is an export is of a great deal more than statistical or academic interest.

The U.S. trade deficit does not mean only that foreign goods are flooding the American market. What helps to make the trade deficit higher for the United States is importing goods manufactured by American firms in other countries. What helps to make the American trade deficit lower are goods manufactured by foreign firms in the United States and exported to other countries. The American goods made overseas are American imports, driving the deficit higher; the foreign goods are American exports, pulling the deficit lower. As the American novelist Joseph Heller wrote in one of his books, "Go figure."

DeAnne Julius, the chief economist at Shell International Petroleum, did precisely that. America had a trade deficit in 1986, but Julius figured that if you took into account what American companies were doing overseas and what foreign firms were doing in the United States that year, the $144 billion deficit would become a $14 billion *surplus*. Those figures would not surprise Ohmae. In *The Borderless World*, he says that global companies "are helping to create a borderless economy where trade statistics are meaningless," but backward bureaucrats in the United States and Japan "miscount the trade figures and get them wrong month after month, and in the process they provide the weapons for economic war between nations."

Reich agrees. "We are entering into a new era," he says, "in which all of these companies are becoming global. They're doing everything all around the world, including their high value-added research, development, and fabrication. They're hiring people from all over the world. They're getting capital from all over the world, and, indeed, even at the highest management levels—except for the Japanese—you find people from all over the world. There is no such thing any longer as an American multinational; it's a global multinational. . . . Digital Equipment, IBM, Coca-Cola, GM, Ford, among many other companies, made more profits outside the United States in 1989 than they made inside the United States.

"There have been for the last 350 years," Reich continues, "companies that operated around the globe. What's new is that [the location of] corporate headquarters and the nationality of ownership now matter less and less because these global companies are exporting from every country . . . Singapore's largest private employer is General Electric. . . . Taiwan [whose largest export market is the United States] counts AT&T, RCA, and Texas Instruments among its largest exporters." Ohmae says that U.S. figures show that America has an unfavorable trade balance with Mexico even though everyone recognizes that what causes it is American factories that have moved just across the border to take advantage of available Mexican labor. "So you have a trade deficit with Mexico," he says, "not because you have lost competitiveness with that country, but because you have migrated into Mexico for production." That is not a one-way street. Siemens, the German global giant, ships fuel injectors, antiskid brake solenoids, and transmission solenoids to almost every major industrial country from its factory in Newport News, Virginia. Sony and Sharp, both Japanese, export from the United States, as does Philips, a Dutch firm.

Michael E. Porter, also a Harvard professor, does not accept the Reich-Ohmae idea of a borderless world. He argued in *The Competitive Advantage of Nations* that the nationality of a company does, in fact, make a difference. "My theory," he wrote, "begins from individual industries and competitors and builds up to the economy as a whole. The particular industry . . . is where competitive advantage is either won or lost. The home nation influences the ability of its firms to succeed in particular industries. The outcome of thousands of struggles in individual industries determines the state of a nation's economy and its ability to progress."

The Economist concluded that the role of nations in the future would be about what it is today, but it used Julius's trade figures and other information to make an exception: "The one thing in which the nation-state's grip seems visibly to be loosening is the organization of economic life." George Fisher of Motorola seems to agree, but not totally. "We have to differentiate," he says, "between companies and countries. . . . Does being a successful global company headquartered in a particular country mean that country will also be successful as an economic entity? Increasingly, the answer is no. . . . I don't want to argue that companies will prosper on a global basis independent of how their home countries prosper. But the separation will grow. In Motorola's case, I hope the separation never gets so serious that it weakens the link between this company and the United States."

Artzt of Procter & Gamble says that to a certain extent, the company has a commitment to the United States because "inevitably, every company, even though it is multinational in nature or global in its business operation, has to see itself in terms of its national roots, and in that sense, we're an American company . . . We were founded in the United States. . . . We are citizens of a lot of countries, but our initial citizenship is here." Yankelovich says the nationality of corporations is confused by partnerships and joint ventures, "but they have responsibilities to their nations, and so in that fundamental respect, they are like citizens who may be diplomats and may have all kinds of entangling alliances outside the borders, but they still remain Japanese citizens or American citizens or British citizens."

Robert Galvin of Motorola does not think corporate nationality will disappear anytime soon. "In terms of the manner in which we are structurally organized and focused," he says, "there's a high quality of globalization in the larger companies. But it's not likely in the next couple of generations that we will lose the encultured, national-based makeup of most of us. I think Motorola will be an American-based company for a number of generations. I think the major Japanese companies will be looked upon as Japanese-based companies, and so for the Dutch, et cetera. But I think that we're also going to be more open-minded thinkers, individually, as we think about our roles in the other person's part of the world."

As opposed to the earlier American standard, especially in the 1960s and '70s, of insisting that all employees everywhere act like ersatz Americans, Motorola has adopted more appropriate policies. Galvin says, "We really put our feet in the shoes of the native. We try to populate our organizations with the natives to a substantial degree, and we genuinely try to understand the cultures and the tastes and the purposes of these people. There are a few things that we will not compromise, if, indeed, there happen to be varying standards, and one of those has to do with integrity. There are places in the world where standards of integrity are just different than the American standards on matters such as conflict of interest. But if you can get past that very important factor, the French or the Malaysians or the Scots or the Israelis all have much the same fundamental objectives of serving customer and having income for family. We respect the ways and means in those particular places."

That corporate attitude is no longer unusual in any country. Kunerth of Siemens says simply, "Our obligation to the different governments in the countries where we are is that in every country—and this is part of the corporate culture of Siemens—in every part of the world where we are, we want to be a good citizen of that country." Mangi Paik of the Korean Ministry of International Trade and Industry, says that global companies need to meet local needs for products around the world, and "we want the multinational firms to be more legitimate in society. They need to be good citizens, and they need to develop the local culture. At the same time, they can make money. The biggest question is how best can we harmonize those two goals." Paron of Siam Cement says that from the beginning, seventy-five years ago, the Thai company has had a four-part statement of philosophy. "And the last one," he says, "is concern for social responsibility. It is our responsibility to contribute to the society we live in, no matter if we live in Thailand or we live in Tennessee, United States. We would be a good citizen there and contribute to social responsibility, as we do a lot in Thailand. . . . We consider being a good corporate citizen a fundamental responsibility to our society. We have to be good or be useful to the community where we are operating." Tetsuo Chino, the president of Honda in North America, told the *New York Times*, "The bottom line of our company is to respect people. You have to respect the local community or you can't grow, and to do so, you have to become more American. We are trying to localize everywhere we operate. In Europe we are trying to be more European, in Brazil more Brazilian. This is a natural step for increasing business in the host country."

Artzt says that going back to the early days of this century, Procter & Gamble has operated the same way. "Our policy," he says, "has always been that we would operate as if we were citizens of the countries in which we're doing business, and that the interest of that country would be considered in all of the decisions we make. . . . At the same time, we think of ourselves as a guest in those countries. We're not in there to exploit. We're in there to develop a business, to help develop the economy of the country, to offer our employees the same kind of future that we offer our employees here [in the United States], and we do that to an extent in our own self-interest. It's a success model. We're proud of the fact that in many countries in the world, Procter & Gamble is thought of as a local company. . . . That's a direct reflection," he says, "of the way we conduct our affairs in these countries, and it's by design. . . . when a company like ours becomes thought of by the local consumers as a local company, the consumer feels more comfortable with our products."

Kanter uses Procter & Gamble as an example of one change the global marketplace has caused. "You may be doing R&D," she says, "as Procter & Gamble did for some new products jointly in Japan, Europe, and the United States, and attempting to integrate the best ideas from all of those parts of the world instead of the United States automatically dictating." She says that illustrates a critical difference between the old and new ways of doing business. "What it really means," she says, "is not that you're doing business in many countries; we've always done that. . . . What it means today to be a truly international corporation is that strategy can be set in many different parts of the world rather than just at headquarters, that there is a true local presence that takes advantage of the best of local talent, that finds a way to transfer the ideas or the output of production all over the world. . . . It's headquarters whose influence is diminishing."

The influence of American and European headquarters may be diminishing more rapidly than that of the Japanese. The Thai executive Anand says, "I think the Americans and Europeans have learned a lot in trying to train local people to take up positions of responsibility. The Japanese have a hang-up on this one. They are accused of feeling superior to local people. They will always say, 'Well, you know, the Japanese style of management is very complicated, very complex. It takes years to learn.' So when you talk about it to the Japanese, with thousands of years of culture and history, a span of ten years to them is very short. When you talk to an American, the Americans are in a hurry. They want to train people to take up managerial positions. Within five years they like to have, you know, number two man, number one man, a local man. A Japanese may talk about a generation or two."

Artzt says three things are critically important for international success, and one of them involves local people. "We have for years," he says, "been recruiting and developing and training people in countries all over the world, and in just exactly the same way that we did, and still do, here in our home base in the United States. You can't become a truly successful international company if you have to continuously export people in order to run your business. You've got to develop them." The other two ingredients for global success, he says, are "products that have a technology base that makes them appealing all over the world [and] a presence. We learned long ago that selling consumer products purely on an export basis was not a long-term recipe for success."

Tribus says that to compete in that world market takes invention, innovation, quality, and productivity. "Invention means getting the good ideas," he says, "and here we [Americans] have an advantage because of the heterogeneity of our population. . . . Innovation is the process of taking an idea and bringing it to the marketplace. . . . and the Japanese have recognized in the last ten years that innovation is the most important element for them because they already have achieved quality, and through quality you get productivity. We [Americans] had a White House Conference on Productivity. We never had a White House Conference on Quality [even though] the route to productivity is through quality."

Artzt says, "A very exciting development for us has been the realization that we don't need to alter the quality or the technology in our products from place to place in order to be successful. Consumers have very much the same value system around the world. . . . just as the world is shrinking in a lot of other ways, the evaluation of quality worldwide is coming together . . . people everywhere have the same demand, the same grading system for evaluating quality. We tend to think in terms of electronic devices, or appliances, or automobiles, or high tech equipment, but it applies to a diaper, or a bar of soap, or a sanitary napkin, or a shampoo just as well, and that is now driving our business. . . . If the toughest market in the world in terms of judging the quality and performance of a disposable diaper is Japan, develop a product that is superior and more successful in the Japanese market and sell it all over the world."

In the old economy, a producer could please the customers in one country or even one region and be successful. For a major manufacturer, customers are now everywhere, with different backgrounds, different tastes, different demands, and the product has to please them all. That makes doing business in the global marketplace a lot tougher.

Siemens, the German firm, supplies about five hundred different systems to the world's automakers, all of whom are now demanding improved quality and reasonable costs. "They are demanding more and more quality," Kunerth says, "because they have to give their customers more and more of a very good and very reliable product." He says quality was part of the 150-year-old company's first statement of purpose, but how it produces quality has changed. Siemens, like Motorola, has studied the experts around the world and developed its own system of quality to satisfy, not only its customers in the global market, but its customers' customers as well. Talking about the environmental movement, particularly in Europe and North America, Tim Leuliette, the American on the management board, says, "We've got to change the way the vehicle operates, the way the vehicle interfaces with society. We've got technology; we need to apply it to a solution the customer can afford. That is a fundamental element of how we get our business. Technology drives us." The technology, much of it, comes from the aerospace industry. "We start to be able to tell the customer what technologies are available in the future, and he starts telling us his needs, and together we start predicting what our products need to be."

As soon as Siemens produces, say, a new fuel injector for one of its customers, all the other auto companies in the world learn about it almost at once. "And if it improves the product in a cost-benefit relationship," Leuliette says, "they want it too. . . . so it's customer-driven, and there's no one customer that's the toughest. These guys feed on each other quite well, and they keep moving the standard forward." To illustrate what that means to Siemens, Leuliette talks about the fuel injector plant at Newport News. "That's a unit that in 1985 produced 30,000 fuel injectors a month, and in 1987 produced 30,000 fuel injectors a week, and today produces 30,000 a day. And [by 1992] it will be producing 30,000 a shift twice a day." That has been and is being done through quality improvement. As Galvin once said, "Quality is quantity; quality is low cost."

Kees van Ham of the European Foundation for Quality Management sees that pressure for improvement on suppliers as a "powerful mechanism" to improve quality and to make more chief executives aware of it. In 1989, the five hundred chief executives of the most important companies in Europe were asked, "What priority does quality management have in your company today?" Van Ham says 15 percent answered "highest priority," and 60 percent said "one of the highest." He says had you asked the same people the same question ten years ago, no one would have rated quality as his company's highest priority.

Internationally, there is a new cooperative effort to make quality more important. The International Productivity Service (IPS) is sponsored by the U.S. Department of Labor; the Canadian Labor Market and Productivity Center; the European Association of National Productivity Centers, representing fourteen nations; and the Japan Productivity Center. The service, a clearinghouse for information, publishes a triannual productivity journal, sponsors an international symposium every two years and organizes smaller, more frequent conferences to keep up with the latest developments.

The IPS is headed by Joji Arai, who previously headed the Japanese Productivity Center in Washington, D.C. He has lived in the United States for many years, and his father was a Japanese cowboy in the old American West. In talking about Japanese and Americans, Arai uses *we* and *they* almost interchangeably—perhaps the only man in either country who does. He says that quality improvement worldwide is more important than who produces what where. "The final goal," he says, "is to generate new wealth by utilizing the resources available and coming up with new, added value. . . . and that generation of new value directly contributes toward improving the standard of living of people. [It] has to have this ultimate goal of improving the quality of human life. . . . The only way we can keep this world in peace is by generating more value out of limited resources so that people will be able to enjoy a better life."

The Information Revolution and the New Global Market Economy

WALTER B. WRISTON

THE POLITICAL, social and economic environment in dozens of countries in which the global corporation will operate will affect the corporation in ways that are not yet fully revealed. We do know a few things. We know that in the United States thousands of manufacturing jobs that were a mainstay of our society for so many years are never going to come back, any more than we will ever see again American farms employing the twenty million people who worked there at the turn of the century. These massive historical transitions are not only disruptive, and often painful, but also upset long-held beliefs and require us to think anew—itself a painful process. The industrial age in which we all grew up is slowly fading into the information society, and as much as some may wish to do so, we can't go back again. As the journalist Mike O'Neill put it: "Today's world cannot be remodeled with yesterday's memories: there are no U-turns on the road to the future." This is the new reality and old solutions will not yield answers to new problems. Examples abound.

The information revolution has been often announced by futurists, but many of the innovations that have been predicted have never arrived. No one has yet seen the paperless society, nor a helicopter in every back yard. What we have seen instead is that information technology has demolished time and distance, but instead of increasing the power of government and thus validating Orwell's vision of Big Brother watching our every move, the proposition has been stood on its head. And we have all wound up watching Big Brother. No one who has lived through the last few years and watched on live television as the Berlin wall came down or the first protestors in Prague in 1988 chanting at the riot police: "The world sees you," can fail to understand that information technology is changing the

Wriston, Walter B. "The Information Revolution and the New Global Market Economy." Speech given at Dartmouth College in Sept. 1993 by Wriston, former chairman of Citicorp and author of "Risk and Other Four Letter Words" and "Twilight of Sovereignty."

way we think about the power of government, about the way the world works, the way we work, and indeed the nature of work itself.

The massive upheaval in the former Soviet Union is a case in point. While governments maintain elaborate intelligence gathering facilities, when a crisis arises eyes in all countries turn to the CNN monitor which is standard furniture in all government crisis management offices. The foreign minister of the former Soviet Union, Eduard A. Shevardnadze, during the Yeltsin coup put it this way: "Praise be information technology! Praise be CNN . . . Anyone who owned a parabolic antenna able to see this network's transmissions had a complete picture of what was happening."[1] And this from a senior officer of what used to be a closed and secretive society. The only ones in Moscow who did not know what was going on were the American Embassy [staff] which did not have CNN.

While historians rarely identify these sea changes when they are living through them, I would argue that the signs are unmistakable that we are now in the midst of a new revolution at least as drastic and far reaching as that which occurred in what the great historian Paul Johnson describes as the birth of the modern world society in the beginning of the 19th century. Different people see different talismans, each constructs his or her own scenario, as we are all the product of the velocity of our own experience. Social analysts observe political and social change, business people watch markets change, grow and vanish before their eyes while scientists tend to emphasize their own specialties.

The start of this revolution may perhaps be dated in this country from the passage of the G.I. Bill which made it possible for so many returning service men and women to get a college education and begin to build the base of knowledge workers. The significance of this lesson on the importance of building a stock of intellectual capital to the future of the world is not lost on the people of what used to be called the Third World. Today more than half of all the college graduates in the world are from the Third World, and indeed Mexico has more graduate engineers than France, and India more than all of Europe. By the year 2000 it is estimated that students from the developing nations will make up three fifths of all university students.[2] The idea has gotten through to large segments of the world that economic progress is largely a process of increasing the relative contribution of knowledge in the creation of wealth. Knowledge which at one time was a kind of ornament for the rich and powerful to display at conferences is now combined with management skills to produce wealth. The vast increase in knowledge in the last decade has brought with it a huge increase in our ability to manipulate matter, increasing its value by the power of the mind, generating new substances and products unlimited in nature and undreamed of a few years ago.

The world is changing not because computer operators have replaced clerk typists, but because the human struggle to survive and prosper now depends on a new source of

1   Eduard Shevardnadze, *The Future Belongs to Freedom*, New York: The Free Press, 1991, pg. 207.
2   William B. Johnston, *Global Work Force 2000: The New World Labor Market*, Harvard Business Review, March/April 1991.

wealth; it is information applied to work to create value. Information technology has created an entirely new economy, an information economy, as different from the industrial economy as the industrial was from the agricultural. And when the source of the wealth of nations changes, the politics of nations change as well.

There are many in the new administration who long for the increased regulation of all phases of our economy. Sometimes the concept is expressed as an industrial policy, and sometimes in more primitive terms. Whatever way it is phrased, it is designed to increase the power of government. In an economy whose products consist largely of information, this power erodes rapidly. As George Gilder has written: "A steel mill, the exemplary industry of the industrial age lends itself to control by governments." Its massive output is easily measured and regulated at every point by government. By contrast, the typical means of production in the new epoch is a man at a computer work station, designing microchips comparable in complexity to the entire steel facility, to be manufactured from software programs comprising a coded sequence of electronic pulses that can elude every expert control and run a production line anywhere in the world."[3] Intellectual capital is the most mobile in the world and it will go where it is wanted and it will stay where it is well treated. It will flee from manipulation or onerous regulation of its value or use and no government can restrain it for long.

The pursuit of wealth is now largely the pursuit of information. The competition for the best information is very different from the competition for the best bottom land. Today the proliferation of information technology ranging from the telephone and fax machine to fiber optic cables has flooded the world with data and information moving at near the speed of light to all corners of the world. This does not just mean more of the same as it is a well-established principle that a change of degree—if carried far enough—may eventually become a difference in kind. In biology this is how new species are created and old ones die out. Speed is what transforms a harmless lump of lead into a deadly rifle bullet. This explosion of information and the speed at which it can be transmitted has created a situation which is different in kind and not just in degree from any former time. This change affects not only the creation of wealth but also military power, the political structure of the world, and how business must be structured and run.

For thousands of years news could travel only as fast as a horse could run or a ship could sail. Military power was similarly impeded. Indeed Napoleon's armies could move no faster than those of Julius Caesar. Great national leaders were almost anonymous to all but those who had seen them in person. Today the minicam is omnipresent, but in the late 18th century there were no photographs of Washington or Jefferson, and the Tsar of Russia traveled unrecognized throughout Europe. The ability of the sovereign to keep information secret and thus a tight grip on power, began to erode with the invention of the paved road, the optical telegraph, and the newspaper. Richard Brown has observed that when "the diffusion of public information moved from face-to-face to the newspaper page,

---

3   George Gilder, *The Emancipation of the CEO*, Chief Executive, Jan./Feb. 1988

public life and the society in which politics operated shifted from a communal discipline to a market-oriented competitive regimen in which the foundation of influence changed."[4]

Government viewed all of these developments with a wary eye. In 1835 Emperor Francis I of Austria turned down a request for permission to build a steam railroad lest it carry revolution to his throne. He was more right than he knew. Years later with the advent of the telephone another sovereign saw danger in a new technology. "Leon Trotsky reportedly proposed to Stalin that a modern telephone system be built in the new Soviet State. Stalin brushed off the idea, saying I can imagine no greater instrument of counter-revolution in our time." What would he have thought if he had lived to see the Yeltsin coup which utilized an independent computer network called Relcom that links Moscow with 80 other Soviet cities and can and was plugged into similar networks in Europe and the United States to spread the news of the coup. Even more ironic was that after the KGB blocked many trunk lines, Yeltsin communicated with his greatest ally, Mayor Sobchak in Saint Petersburg via the government's own telephone network. This is in sharp contrast to the fact that it took four to six weeks for the news of Czar Nicholas' abdication to reach the people.

In America each new administration comes into office with an agenda and the 7 a.m. staff meetings in the Roosevelt room are full of optimism. After a month or two the meeting opens with "Did you see what the Post said this morning, or Brokaw said last night and what is our response?" As Jack Kennedy once remarked: "The Ship of State is the only one that leaks from the top." While one can and should argue whether this is good or bad for public policy, in the late 20th century it is reality. Professor Quinn's book brilliantly analyses what a knowledge-based business must do to keep out of the corporate graveyard—to put it mildly they have to change the way they do just about everything. Government has no such text to look to, but nevertheless will also have to learn what it can and can't do with a subsequent effect on the way business operates.

Fernard Braudel in his great historical work has written that the sovereign's first task has always been to "secure obedience, to gain for itself the monopoly of the use of force in a given society, neutralizing all the possible challenges inside it and replacing them with what Max Weber called 'legitimate violence'". In the Middle Ages, the central government took over the private armies of the feudal lords and the city states to create that monopoly of power. Today the new administration has found with the World Trade Center bombing that we are once again facing new private armies, not loyal to feudal lords, but terrorists controlled by small countries or factions within countries. No one understands information and its uses better than the modern terrorist. The terrorists who stormed the American Embassy in Teheran on November 4th, 1979, were equipped with their own television cameras and their own microwave links to Iranian TV. U.S. television networks outdid themselves to cover the event. Indeed ABC's "Nightline", now a fixture of late night television, was originally created just to cover the hostage crisis every day. They gave the

4   Richard D. Brown, Knowledge Is Power, Oxford University Press, 1989, pg. 279.

terrorists, in Margaret Thatcher's words, "the oxygen of publicity." Whatever your view of the matter, few would doubt that it presents difficult dilemmas for the sovereign. There are just some problems that are too big for any one country to handle and terrorism is one of them. Many years ago, sovereigns in many different countries came to the same conclusion about piracy, and banded together to outlaw the practice. Slavery is another case in point. The first significant international agreement was reached in 1885 at the Berlin Conference which was followed in 1890 by the Brussels Act signed by 18 countries. The security of our modern states may require similar joint treaties to outlaw terrorism. As the concept and reality of the importance of intellectual capital sinks into the world's conscience, the importance of copyright, patent, and other protections of intellectual property will also turn out to be a problem requiring similar international cooperation.

All of these events are being played out against a background of massive shifts in the political structure of the world. There are fewer and fewer dictatorships and more and more democratic regimes. At the same time that freedom is sweeping the world, old tribal values are being reasserted, and more not less nations are being formed. This is good news for the people of the world, but makes the practice of diplomacy and the formation of national security policy more difficult. Dealings between super powers is a high stakes game, but at least one knew all the players. Today new players are being created, and doubtless more are on the way.

Since the whole world is now tied together by an electronic infrastructure we now have what amounts to a continuous global conversation. The implications of the global conversation are about the same as the implications of a village conversation, which is to say enormous. In a village there is a rough sorting out of ideas, customs and practices over time. A village will quickly share news of any advantageous innovation. If anyone gets a raise or a favorable adjustment of his or her rights, everyone else will soon be pressing for the same treatment. The global conversation prompts people to ask the same questions on a global scale. To deny people human rights or democratic freedoms is no longer to deny them an abstraction articulated by the educated elite, but rather customs they have seen on their TV monitors. Once people are convinced that these things are possible in the village, an enormous burden of proof falls on those who would deny them.

Today village and indeed national borders have ceased to be boundaries. Data of all kinds move over and through them as if they did not exist. Arthur C. Clarke who first postulated the viability of a geosynchronous satellite put it this way. "Radio waves have never respected frontiers, and from an altitude of 36,000 kilometers, national boundaries are singularly inconspicuous." Satellites now peer down into every corner of a nation state, data and news are received by people within national borders on every device ranging from a hand-held transistor radio to personal computers at home and work tied into huge data networks. In short, the sovereign has totally lost control of what people can see and hear, and can no longer maintain the fiction that there are no alternate types of political structures.

The implications of all this for how business is organized, how strategy is formulated and to what end, and how and where the customers are to be served is huge. Just as the physical assets in a business are now relatively less important compared to intellectual assets, so also is the control of territory of lessening importance to nation states. Not long ago armies fought and men died for the control of the iron and steel in the Ruhr basin, because the owner of these assets conferred real economic and political power. The same was true of the rubber in Malaysia. Today these once fought over assets may be a liability. To the extent that new technology replaces once essential commodities with plastics or other synthetic materials the relative importance of these areas to the vital interest of nations is bound to change.

Just as business organizations have become flatter, less of a command and control atmosphere, more collegial in order to get the job done, so some of the old arrogance embodied in what has been called red blooded sovereignty is also changing in truly astonishing ways. The central concept of sovereignty is that the actions of the government are not subject to contradiction by any other power. While the ruler, in whatever era, could always find a political philosopher to validate his or her assertion of power, the information revolution has now given history a new reverse twist which stands conventional wisdom on its head. So great is the desire of some nations for the approval of the world that they call in outsiders to validate their own national elections. This is an extraordinary development far removed from the assertion of absolute power in conducting a nation's internal affairs. Consider the Council of Freely Elected Heads of State who Noriega called into Panama to observe the election. Former President Jimmy Carter and some European counterparts told the world in no uncertain terms that the Panama election in 1989 was dishonest and in a sense paved the way for the American military action which followed. The same group was asked to witness the Nicaraguan elections in 1990 and gave their seal of approval which started that country along the road toward a fragile democratic government. World opinion focused and illuminated by the global television net achieved what few, if any, armies could ever achieve. The same pressure is felt in the whole field of human rights which is rapidly becoming a world concern transcending national sovereignty. Today, as the chanters in Prague told the police, the world sees what is going on. The cold print in the newspaper now has a human face in living color and in real time. It makes all the difference. The Kurds, for example, have suffered from subjugation by others on and off since the Arabs conquered them in the 7th century. But it was the images of horror on CNN last year that awoke the world to their plight in Iraq. Indeed the history of the last few years has seen the growing popular support for the rights of individuals in all nations against the prerogatives of sovereigns, wherever located. To a certain extent the turmoil in corporate governance is the analogue of the political turmoil. More and more information is being demanded and with it more pressure is applied to management from pension funds and other stockholders.

Another central function of government since the rise of the nation state has been to provide for the common defense. Here again information technology has made us both more secure and more vulnerable at the same time. Weapons of war are no longer the exclusive product of the armorers' art.

It is generally estimated that computer software is about 80% of United States' weapons systems now in development. From the point of view of our enemies, attacking the software that controls or operates these weapons may be the most effective and cheapest way to cripple both our economy and our defenses. Extensive work on this possibility has been done by Scott Boorman of Yale and Paul Levitt of Boston. Software attacks, they have written, can "strike key civilian targets, such as electronic funds transfer systems . . . air traffic control systems, and even vote-tallying machinery at the heart of the democratic process . . . The so-called 'logic bomb' which was planted in the computer software of the Los Angeles Department of Water and Power in the spring of 1985 made it impossible for that utility to access its own files for a week."

In today's world, wars can be won or lost in a week. If nothing happens when the President presses the button, if our communication networks froze and our radar failed to function, our defense posture would be changed dramatically. With the story of the John Walker family fresh in our minds, it does not take much imagination to think that some software programmer might sell out to our adversaries and plant a few logic bombs to disrupt our military response. This would be a very cheap way to attack and is open to even very small countries. Lest this sound like science fiction, we should remember that in 1985 a hacker, who turned out to be in Germany, broke into the computer files in the Lawrence Berkeley Lab, to say nothing of dozens of military bases in the United States. A man called Clifford Stoll tracked the hacker to Germany where it was discovered he was selling information to the KGB. Stoll summed up the problem from the point of national security this way. "I might train an agent to speak a foreign language, fly her to a distant country, supply her with bribe money, and worry that she might be caught . . . or I could hire a dishonest computer programmer. Such a spy need never leave his home country . . . And the information returned is fresh—straight from the target's word processing system." The impact of these facts on the way we think about our national security is significant—physical security can be by-passed, and we have to devise other ways to insure military effectiveness.

Assuming that peace prevails, the intelligent enterprise operating in this new global environment has to pay more and more attention to the value of the currencies used in the different countries in which it operates or into which it sells service or products. Until recently what we call money, be it a piece of paper or a bookkeeping entry, or a physical object has been linked to a physical commodity which put some limit on a government's ability to inflate the currency. The nature of the commodity varied with the interests of the people using it. American colonists used tobacco money. American Indians favored the cowrie shells or wampum and of course the more familiar copper, gold, and silver still circulate in the world. The link between commodities and money became slowly attenuated over time. On March 6, 1933 President Franklin D. Roosevelt issued a proclamation prohibiting American citizens from holding gold. The Congress followed on June 5 that year by passing a joint resolution repudiating the gold clause in all private and public contracts. While various other actions were taken to weaken the tie to gold, the final blow was administered on August 15, 1971 when President Nixon terminated the convertibility of the dollar into gold and the era of floating exchange rates began.

In today's world, the value of a currency is determined by the price that the market will pay for it in exchange for some other currency. Indeed the market is no longer a geographic location, instead it is more than 200,000 computer screens in hundreds of trading rooms all over the world all linked together by an electronic infrastructure. The latest political joke, the newly released GDP figures or the statement of some world leader appears instantly on all screens and the traders vote by buying and selling currency. The market is a harsh disciplinarian, not only of business but also of government. When Francois Mitterand became President of France in 1981, he was elected as a committed Socialist, and almost immediately money began to flow out of the country, foreign exchange reserves were rapidly depleted, and within six months Mitterand had to reverse course and become pro-capitalist. This is not to say that governments can no longer influence the value of their currencies. They can and do, but their ability and those of their central banks readily to manipulate that value in world markets is declining. Increasingly currency values will be experienced less as a power and privilege of sovereignty than as a discipline on the economic policies of imprudent sovereigns. This new discipline is being administered by a completely new system of international finance. Unlike all prior arrangements, the new system was not built by politicians, economists, central bankers or finance ministers. No high level international conference produced a master plan. The new system was built by technology. The system is partly the accidental by-product of communication satellites and engineers learning how to use the electromagnetic spectrum up to 500 gigahertz.

The convergence of computers and telecommunications has created a new international monetary system, and even a new monetary standard by which the value of currencies is determined. The Information Standard has replaced the Gold Standard. We sit at home and watch a live broadcast of riots in a country on the other side of the earth, and a currency falls, in minutes. We hear by satellite that a leadership crisis has been resolved and a currency rises. Ten minutes after the news of the disaster at Chernobyl was received, market data showed that stocks of agricultural companies began to move up in all world markets. For the first time in history, countless investors, merchants and ordinary citizens can know almost instantly of breaking events all over the earth. And depending on how they interpret these events, their desire to hold more or less of a given currency will be inescapably translated into a rise or fall of the exchange value.

The natural first response to this claim is, it has ever been so. The pressure of events has always been a major factor in determining the value of currencies. But the speed and volume of this new global market makes it something different in kind and not just in degree. Cherished political, regulatory, and economic levers routinely used by sovereigns in the past are losing some of their power because the new Information Standard is not subject to effective political tinkering. It used to be that political and economic follies played to a local audience and their results could be in part contained. A relatively small club of central bankers and politicians representing their sovereign governments believed it could control the value of a given currency. This is no longer true, the global market makes and publishes judgments about each currency in the world every minute and every hour of the day. The forces are so powerful that government intervention can only result in expensive failure over time.

Governments do not welcome this Information Standard any more than absolute monarchs embraced universal suffrage. Politicians who wish to evade responsibility for imprudent fiscal and monetary policies correctly perceive that the Information Standard will punish them. Moreover, in contrast to former international monetary systems, there is no way for a sovereign to resign from the Information Standard.

Whatever political leaders do or say, the screens will continue to light up, traders will trade, and currency values will continue to be set not by sovereign governments but by global plebiscite on the soundness of their fiscal and monetary policies.

The whole question of how we measure things in the information age is a subject that has received little attention on the national level. The thing that is clear is that our current metrics designed for the Industrial Age are inadequate to tell us much in an information society. The Tobin Q ratio has caused some to wonder if what accountants now call goodwill may not really be a true asset. If corporate accounting is still anchored in the industrial age, government accounting is in the stone age to the point of being misleading. While efforts are being made to track and quantify the new paradigm of business, little or no effort is being made to understand how government works in the information age. Government officials resist all prudent effort to put their accounts on an accrual basis, so our six trillion dollar economy has the bookkeeping sophistication of a child's lemonade stand. No private business could survive the rigors of the marketplace with such rudimentary information. In addition to the lack of accrual accounting, everything from a ten cent pencil to Yellowstone Park is expensed. The Government has no capital accounts although the GAO has been recommending them for years.

A case in point that affects all business is the so-called balance of trade figures, even though the very phrase sounds obsolete. It can be argued that the very concept of a trade balance is an artifact of the past. As long as capital—both human and money—can move toward opportunity, trade will not balance; indeed, one will have as little reason to desire such accounting symmetry between nations as between California and New York. Commerce and production are increasingly transnational. Sometime in the mid-1980's the volume of international production exceeded the volume of international trade. That is to say, the value of goods produced within a country by a foreign owner under a global strategy was greater than trade across borders. In addition, more and more products have value added in several different countries. The dress a customer purchases at a smart store in New York may have originated with cloth woven in Korea, finished in Taiwan, and cut and sewed in India according to American design. Of course a brief stop in Milan, to pick up a "Made in Italy" label, and leave off a substantial licensing fee is *de rigueur* before the final journey to New York. Former Secretary of State George Shultz recently remarked in a speech: "A few months ago I saw a snapshot of a shipping label for some integrated circuits produced by an American firm. It said 'Made in one or more of the following countries: Korea, Hong Kong, Malaysia, Singapore, Taiwan, Mauritius, Thailand, Indonesia, Mexico, Philippines. The exact country of origin is unknown.' That label says a lot about where current trends are taking us."

Whatever the correct word for these phenomena, "trade" certainly seems an inadequate description. How does one account in the monthly trade figures for products whose "exact country of origin is unknown?" How are national governments to regulate the complexities of transnational production with anything like the firmness with which they once regulated international trade? How are politicians to whip up nationalist fervor against foreign goods when American car companies build cars in Mexico for export to Africa and pay the profits to pensioners in Chicago, and the Japanese build cars in Tennessee for export to Europe and use the income to refinance real estate in Texas? How does one assess customs duties on intellectual capital—Bill Gates, who built a Fortune 500 company with intellectual capital, can walk past any customs agent in the world with "nothing to declare." Nevertheless, if the new interventionists get their way, the global economy would be crippled.

The formation of good business and public policy is hindered by the fact that many of the terms we use today to describe the economy no longer reflect reality. This is a subset of the measurement problem. Everyone knows, for example, that all the lights would go out, all the airplanes would stop flying, and all the financial institutions and many of the factories would shut down if the computer software that runs their systems suddenly disappeared. Yet these crucial intellectual assets do not appear in any substantial way on the balance sheets of the world. Those balance sheets, however, are chock full of what in the industrial age were called tangible assets—buildings and machinery—things that can be seen and touched.

How do we measure capital formation, when much new capital is intellectual? How do we measure the productivity of knowledge workers whose product cannot be counted on our fingers? If [we] cannot do that, how can [we] track productivity growth? How do we track or control the money supply when the financial markets create new financial instruments faster than the regulators can keep track of them? And if [we] cannot do any of these things with the relative precision of simpler times, what becomes of the great mission of modern governments: controlling and manipulating the national economy? Even if some of these measurement problems are solved, as some surely will be, the phenomena they measure will be far more complex and difficult to manipulate than industrial economies of old.

These remarks today have not dwelt on the wonders of the gee-whiz technology emerging from Silicon Valley, not because they are not wondrous—they are—but because revolutions are not made by gadgets, but by a shift in the balance of power. The technology is the enabling factor, not the cause. When a system of national currencies run by central banks is transformed into a global electronic marketplace driven by private currency traders, power changes hands. When a system of national economies linked by government regulated trade is replaced—at least in part—by an increasingly integrated global economy beyond the reach of much national regulation, power changes hands. When an international telecommunications system, incorporating technologies from mobile phones to communications satellites, deprives governments of the ability to keep secrets from the world, or from their own people, power changes hands. When a microchip the size of a fingernail can turn a relatively simple and inexpensive weapon into a "Stinger" missile, enabling an illiterate tribesman to destroy a multi-million dollar armored helicopter and its highly trained crew, power changes hands. When the President picks up the phone to talk to another head of state rather than have an ambassador deliver a meticulously drafted note to the foreign ministry, power changes hands. This is not to say that sovereign power will disappear—it will not—but what it does mean is that no government, over time, can act alone not subject to contradiction. The protesters in Prague were right—the world is watching, and the power of world opinion is transmitted and focused and reported by the telcon network. The world looks and reacts and brings pressure on everything from corporate governance at the Fortune 500 companies to the destruction of the rain forest, the allegations of global warming, the disposal of toxic waste, or the violation of human rights anywhere on the planet.

This then is the kind of environment in which business will have to operate. The quick and the lean will be the survivors in tomorrow's world. The heavy-handed centralized bureaucracy will become a vanishing species. As usual, government at all levels will lag behind, clinging to the nostrums of the past, and thus complicating the management of intellect in the new world. As Susan Strange puts it: "When states do try to use their power to influence where and how international production takes place, they find they cannot direct, as with trade. They can only bargain. And the costs to themselves can be very much higher than the rather small costs of indulging in trade protection. For example, when the Brazilian government excluded all the big international computer enterprises from producing in Brazil, it imposed a very high cost on all the local enterprises needing to use the latest and best computers in order to keep up with their competitors."[5]

The process by which governments will come to terms with pluralism and the decline of red-blooded sovereignty in the information society will be slow, halting and neither smooth nor costless. We are moving, as always, into an unknown world, but one in which the management of intellectual capital will likely be the decisive factor in determining who will survive and prosper, and who will not.

5   Susan Strange, "The Name of the Game," *Sea-Changes*. Council on Foreign Relations Press, 1989, pg. 293.

Managing in a Borderless World

KENICHI OHMAE

MOST MANAGERS ARE NEARSIGHTED. Even though today's competitive landscape often stretches to a global horizon, they see best what they know best: the customers geographically closest to home. These managers may have factories or laboratories in a dozen countries. They may have joint ventures in a dozen more. They may source materials and sell in markets all over the world. But when push comes to shove, their field of vision is dominated by home-country customers and the organizational units that serve them. Everyone—and everything—else is simply part of "the rest of the world."

This nearsightedness is not intentional. No responsible manager purposefully devises or implements an astigmatic strategy. But by the same token, too few managers consciously try to set plans and build organizations as if they saw all key customers equidistant from the corporate center. Whatever the trade figures show, home markets are usually in focus; overseas markets are not.

Effective global operations require a genuine equidistance of perspective. But even with the best will in the world, managers find that kind of vision hard to develop—and harder to maintain. Not long ago, the CEO of a major Japanese capital-goods producer canceled several important meetings to attend the funeral of one of his company's local dealers. When I asked him if he would have done the same for a Belgian dealer, one who did a larger volume of business each year than his late counterpart in Japan, the unequivocal answer was no. Perhaps headquarters would have had the relevant European manager send a letter of condolence. No more than that. In Japan, however, tradition dictated the CEO's presence. But Japanese tradition isn't everything, I reminded him. After all, he was the head of a global, not just a Japanese organization. By violating the principle of equidistance, his attendance underscored distinctions among dealers. He was sending the wrong signal and reinforcing the wrong values. Poor vision has consequences.

It may be unfamiliar and awkward, but the primary rule of equidistance is to see—and to think—global first. Honda, for example, has manufacturing divisions in Japan, North America, and Europe—all three legs of the Triad—but its managers do not think or act as if the company were divided between Japanese and overseas operations. Indeed, the very word "overseas" has no place in Honda's vocabulary because the corporation sees itself as equidistant from all its key customers. At Casio, the top managers gather information directly from each of their primary markets and then sit down together once a month to lay out revised plans for global product development.

There is no single best way to avoid or overcome nearsightedness. An equidistant perspective can take many forms. However managers do it, however they get there, building a value system that emphasizes seeing and thinking globally is the bottom-line price of admission to today's borderless economy.

A GEOGRAPHY WITHOUT BORDERS

On a political map, the boundaries between countries are as clear as ever. But on a competitive map, a map showing the real flows of financial and industrial activity, those boundaries have largely disappeared. What has eaten them away is the persistent, ever speedier flow of information—information that governments previously monopolized, cooking it up as they saw fit and redistributing in forms of their own devising. Their monopoly of knowledge about things happening around the world enabled them to fool, mislead, or control the people because only the governments possessed real facts in anything like real time.

Today, of course, people everywhere are more and more able to get the information they want directly from all corners of the world. They can see for themselves what the tastes and preferences are in other countries, the styles of clothing now in fashion, the sports, the lifestyles. In Japan, for example, our leaders can no longer keep the people in substandard housing because we now know—directly—how people elsewhere live. We now travel abroad. In fact, ten million Japanese travel abroad annually these days. Or we can sit in our living rooms at home, watch CNN, and know instantaneously what is happening in the United States. During 1988, nearly 90% of all Japanese honeymooners went abroad. This kind of fact is hard to ignore. The government now seriously recognizes that it has built plants and offices but has failed to meet the needs of its young people for relaxation and recreation. So, for the first time in 2,000 years, our people are revolting against their government and telling it what it must do for them. This would have been unthinkable when only a small, official elite controlled access to all information.

In the past, there were gross inefficiencies—some purposeful, some not—in the flow of information around the world. New technologies are eliminating those inefficiencies, and, with them, the opportunity for a kind of top-down information arbitrage—that is, the ability of a government to benefit itself or powerful special interests at the expense of its people by following policies that would never win their support if they had unfettered access to all relevant information. A government could, for example, protect weak industries for fear of provoking social unrest over unemployment. That is less easy to do now, for more of its people have become cosmopolitan and have their own sources of information. They know what such a policy would cost them.

In Korea, students demonstrate in front of the American embassy because the government allows the United States to export cigarettes to Korea and thus threaten local farmers. That's what happens when per capita GNP runs in the neighborhood of $5,000 a year and governments can still control the flow of information and mislead their people. When GNP gets up to around $10,000 a year, religion becomes a declining industry. So does government.

At $26,000 a year, where Japan is now, things are really different. People want to buy the best and the cheapest products—no matter where in the world they are produced. People become genuinely global consumers. We import beef and oranges from the United States, and everyone thinks it's great. Ten years ago, however, our students would have been the ones throwing stones at the American embassy. Our leaders used to tell us American and Australian beef was too lean and too tough to chew. But we've been there and tasted it and know for ourselves that it is cheap and good.

Through this flow of information, we've become global citizens, and so must the companies that want to sell us things. Black-and-white television sets extensively penetrated households in the United States nearly a dozen years before they reached comparable numbers of viewers in Europe and Japan. With color television, the time lag fell to about five or six years for Japan and a few more for Europe. With videocassette recorders, the difference was only three or four years—but this time, Europe and Japan led the way; the United States, with its focus on cable TV, followed. With the compact disc, household penetration rates evened up after only one year. Now, with MTV available by satellite across Europe, there is no lag at all. New music, styles, and fashion reach all European youngsters almost at the same time they are reaching their counterparts in America. We all share the same information.

More than that, we are all coming to share it in a common language. Ten years ago when I would speak in English to students at Bocconi, an Italian university, most of them would listen to me through a translator. Last year, they listened to me directly in English and asked me questions in English. (They even laughed when they should at what I said, although my jokes have not improved.) This is a momentous change. The preparation for 1992 has taken place in language much sooner than it has in politics. We can all talk to each other now, understand each other, and governments cannot stop us. "Global citizenship" is no longer just a nice phrase in the lexicon of rosy futurologists. It is every bit as real and concrete as measurable changes in GNP or trade flows. It is actually coming to pass.

The same is true for corporations. In the pharmaceutical industry, for example, the critical activities of drug discovery, screening, and testing are now virtually the same among the best companies everywhere in the world. Scientists can move from one laboratory to another and start working the next day with few hesitations or problems. They will find equipment with which they are familiar, equipment they have used before, equipment that comes from the same manufacturers.

The drug companies are not alone in this. Most people, for example, believed that it would be a very long time before Korean companies could produce state-of-the-art semiconductor chips—things like 256K NMOS DRAMs. Not so. They caught up with the rest of the Triad in only a few short years. In Japan, not that long ago, a common joke among the chip-making fraternity had to do with the "Friday Express." The Japanese engineers working for different companies on Kyushu, Japan's southwestern "Silicon Island" only 100 km or so away from Korea, would catch a late flight to Korea on Friday evenings. During the weekend, they would work privately for Korean semiconductor companies. This was illegal, of course, and violated the engineers' employment agreements in Japan. Nonetheless, so many took the flight that they had a tacit gentleman's agreement not to greet or openly recognize each other on the plane. Their trip would have made no sense, however, if semiconductor-related machines, methods, software and workstations had not already become quite similar throughout the developed world.

Walk into a capital-goods factory anywhere in the developed world, and you will find the same welding machines, the same robots, the same machine tools. When information flows with relative freedom, the old geographic barriers become irrelevant. Global needs lead to global products. For managers, this universal flow of information puts a high premium on learning how to build the strategies and the organizations capable of meeting the requirements of a borderless world.

WHAT IS A UNIVERSAL PRODUCT?

Imagine that you are the CEO of a major automobile company reviewing your product plans for the years ahead. Your market data tell you that you will have to develop four dozen different models if you want to design separate cars for each distinct segment of the Triad market. But you don't have enough world-class engineers to design so many models. You don't have enough managerial talent or enough money. No one does. Worse, there is no single "global" car that will solve your problems for you. America, Europe, and Japan are quite different markets with quite different mixes of needs and preferences. Worse still, as head of a worldwide company, you cannot write off any of these Triad markets. You simply have to be in each of them—and with first-rate successful products. What do you do?

If you are the CEO of Nissan, you first look at the Triad region by region and identify each market's dominant requirements. In the United Kingdom, for example, tax policies make it essential that you develop a car suitable for corporate fleet sales. In the United States, you need a sporty "Z" model as well as a four-wheel drive family vehicle. Each of these categories is what Nissan's president, Yutaka Kume, calls a "lead-country" model—a product carefully tailored to the dominant and distinct needs of individual national markets. Once you have your short list of "lead-country" models in hand, you can ask your top managers in other parts of the Triad whether minor changes can make any of them suitable for local sales. But you start with the lead-country models.

"With this kind of thinking," says Mr. Kume, "we have been able to halve the number of basic models needed to cover the global markets and, at the same time, to cover 80% of our sales with cars designed for specific national markets. Not to miss the remaining 20%, however, we also provided each country manager with a range of additional model types that could be adapted to the needs of local segments. This approach," Mr. Kume reports, "allowed us to focus our resources on each of our largest core markets and, at the same time, provide a pool of supplemental designs that could be adapted to local preferences. We told our engineers to 'be American,' 'be European,' or 'be Japanese.' If the Japanese happened to like something we tailored for the American market, so much the better. Low-cost, incremental sales never hurt. Our main challenge, however, was to avoid the trap of pleasing no one well by trying to please everyone halfway."

Imagine, instead, if Nissan had taken its core team of engineers and designers in Japan and asked them to design only global cars, cars that would sell all over the world. Their only possible response would have been to add up all the various national preferences and divide by the number of countries. They would have had to optimize across markets by a kind of rough averaging. But when it comes to questions of taste and, especially, aesthetic preference, consumers do not like averages. They like what they like, not some mathematical compromise. Kume is emphatic about this particular point. "Our success in the U.S. with Maxima, 240 SX, and Pathfinder—all designed for the American market—shows our approach to be right!"

In high school physics, I remember learning about a phenomenon called diminishing primaries. If you mix together the primary colors of red, blue, and yellow, what you get is black. If Europe says its consumers want a product in green, let them have it. If Japan says red, let them have red. No one wants the average. No one wants the colors all mixed together. Of course it makes sense to take advantage of, say, any technological commonalities in creating the paint. But local managers close to local customers have to be able to pick the color.

When it comes to product strategy, managing in a borderless world doesn't mean managing by averages. It doesn't mean that all tastes run together into one amorphous mass of universal appeal. And it doesn't mean that the appeal of operating globally removes the obligation to localize products. The lure of a universal product is a false allure. The truth is a bit more subtle.

Although the needs and tastes of the Triad markets vary considerably, there may well be market segments of different sizes in each part of the Triad that share many of the same preferences. In the hair-care market, for instance, Japanese companies know a lot more about certain kinds of black hair, which is hard and thick, than about blond or brown hair, which is often soft and thin. As a result, they have been able to capture a few segments of the U.S. market in, say, shampoos. That makes a nice addition to their sales, of course. But it does not position them to make inroads into the mainstream segments of that market.

Back to the automobile example: there is a small but identifiable group of Japanese consumers who want a "Z" model car like the one much in demand in the United States. Fair enough. During the peak season, Nissan sells about 5,000 "Z" cars a month in the United States and only 500 in Japan. Those 500 cars make a nice addition, of course, generating additional revenue and expanding the perceived richness of a local dealer's portfolio. But they are not—and cannot be—the mainstay of such portfolios.

There is no universal "montage" car—a rear axle from Japan, a braking system from Italy, a drive train from the United States—that will quicken pulses on all continents. Remember the way the tabloids used to cover major beauty contests? They would create a composite picture using the best features from all of the most beautiful entrants—this one's nose, that one's mouth, the other one's forehead. Ironically, the portrait that emerged was never very appealing. It always seemed odd, a bit off, lacking in distinctive character. But there will always be beauty judges—and car buyers—in, say, Europe, who, though more used to continental standards, find a special attractiveness in the features of a Japanese or a Latin American. Again, so much the better.

For some kinds of products, however, the kind of globalization that Ted Levitt talks about makes excellent sense. One of the most obvious is, oddly enough, battery-powered products like cameras, watches, and pocket calculators. These are all part of the "Japan game"—that is, they come from industries dominated by Japanese electronics companies. What makes these products successful across the Triad? Popular prices, for one thing, based on aggressive cost reduction and global economies of scale. Also important, however, is the fact that many general design choices reflect an in-depth understanding of the preferences of leading consumer segments in key markets throughout the Triad. Rigid model changes during the past decade have helped educate consumers about the "fashion" aspects of these products and have led them to base their buying decisions in large measure on such fashion-related criteria.

With other products, the same electronics companies use quite different approaches. Those that make stereophonic equipment, for example, offer products based on aesthetics and product concepts that vary by region. Europeans tend to want physically small high-performance equipment that can be hidden in a closet; Americans prefer large speakers that rise from the floor of living rooms and dens like the structural columns of ancient temples. Companies that have been globally successful in white goods like kitchen appliances focus on close interaction with individual users; those that have prospered with equipment that requires installation (air conditioners, say, or elevators) focus on interactions with designers, engineers, and trade unions. To repeat: approaches to global products vary.

Another important cluster of these global products is made up of fashion-oriented, premium-priced branded goods. Gucci bags are sold around the world, unchanged from one place to another. They are marketed in virtually the same way. They appeal to an upper bracket market segment that shares a consistent set of tastes and preferences. By definition, not everyone in the United States or Europe or Japan belongs to that segment. But for those who do, the growing commonality of their tastes qualifies them as members of a genuinely cross-Triad, global segment. There is even such a segment for top-of-the-line automobiles like the Rolls-Royce and the Mercedes-Benz. You can—in fact, should—design such cars for select buyers around the globe. But you cannot do that with Nissans or Toyotas or Hondas. Truly universal products are few and far between.

INSIDERIZATION

Some may argue that my definition of universal products is unnecessarily narrow, that many such products exist that do not fit neatly into top-bracket segments: Coca-Cola, Levi's, things like that. On closer examination, however, these turn out to be very different sorts of things. Think about Coca-Cola for a moment. Before it got established in each of its markets, the company had to build up a fairly complete local infrastructure and do the groundwork to establish local demand.

Access to markets was by no means assured from day one; consumer preference was not assured from day one. In Japan, the long established preference was for carbonated lemon drinks known as saida. Unlike Gucci bags, consumer demand did not "pull" Coke into these markets; the company had to establish the infrastructure to "push" it. Today, because the company has done its homework and done it well, Coke is a universally desired brand. But it got there by a different route: local replication of an entire business system in every important market over a long period of time.

For Gucci-like products, the ready flow of information around the world stimulates consistent primary demand in top-bracket segments. For relatively undifferentiated, commodity-like products, demand expands only when corporate muscle pushes hard. If Coke is to establish a preference, it has to build it, piece by piece.

Perhaps the best way to distinguish these two kinds of global products is to think of yourself browsing in a duty-free shop. Here you are in something of an oasis. National barriers to entry do not apply. Products from all over the world lie available to you on the shelves. What do you reach for? Do you think about climbing on board your jetliner with a newly purchased six-pack of Coke? Hardly. But what about a Gucci bag? Yes, of course. In a sense, duty-free shops are the precursor to what life will be like in a genuinely borderless environment. Customer pull, shaped by images and information from around the world, determine your product choices. You want the designer handbag or the sneakers by Reebok, which are made in Korea and sold at three times the price of equivalent no-brand sneakers. And there are others like you in every corner of the Triad.

At bottom, the choice to buy Gucci or Reebok is a choice about fashion. And the information that shapes fashion-driven choices is different in kind from the information that shapes choices about commodity products. When you walk into the 7-Elevens of the world and look for a bottle of cola, the one you pick depends on its location on the shelf, its price, or perhaps the special in-store promotion going on at the moment. In other words, your preference is shaped by the effects of the cola company's complete business system in that country.

Now, to be sure, the quality of that business system will depend to some extent on the company's ability to leverage skills developed elsewhere or to exploit synergies with other parts of its operations—marketing competence, for example, or economies of scale in the production of concentrates. Even so, your choice as a consumer rests on the power with which all such functional strengths have been brought to bear in your particular local market— that is, on the company's ability to become a full-fledged insider in that local market.

With fashion-based items, where the price is relatively high and the purchase frequency low, insiderization does not matter all that much. With commodity items, however, where the price is low and the frequency of purchase high, the insiderization of functional skills is all-important. There is simply no way to be successful around the world with this latter category of products without replicating your business system in each key market.

Coke has 70% of the Japanese market for soft drinks. The reason is that Coke took the time and made the investments to build up a full range of local functional strengths, particularly in its route sales force and franchised vending machines. It is, after all, the Coke van or truck that replaces empty bottles with new ones, not the trucks of independent wholesalers or distributors. When Coke first moved into Japan, it did not understand the complex, many-layered distribution system for such products. So it used the capital of local bottlers to re-create the kind of sales force it has used so well in the United States. This represented a heavy, front-end, fixed investment, but it has paid off handsomely. Coke redefined the domestic game in Japan—and it did so, not from a distance, but with a deliberate "insiderization" of functional strengths. Once this sales force is in place, for example, once the company has become a full-fledged insider, it can move not only soft drinks but also fruit juice, sport drinks, vitamin drinks, and canned coffee through the same sales network. It can sell pretty much whatever it wants to. For Coke's competitors, foreign and domestic, the millions of dollars they are spending on advertising are like little droplets of water sprinkled over a desert. Nothing is going to bloom—at least, not if that is all they do. Not if they fail to build up their own distinctive "insider" strengths.

When global success rests on market-by-market functional strength, you have to play a series of domestic games against well-defined competitors. If the market requires a first-class sales force, you simply have to have one. If competition turns on dealer support programs, that's where you have to excel. Some occasions *do* exist when doing more better is the right, the necessary, course to follow. Still, there are usually opportunities to redefine these domestic games to your own advantage. Companies that fail to establish a strong insider position tend to mix up the strategies followed by the Cokes and the Guccis. The managers of many leading branded-goods companies are often loud in their complaints about how the Japanese market is closed to their products. Or, more mysteriously, about the inexplicable refusal of Japanese consumers to buy their products when they are obviously better than those of any competitor anywhere in the world. Instead of making the effort to understand Japanese distribution and Japanese consumers, they assume that something is wrong with the Japanese market. Instead of spending time in their plants and offices or on the ground in Japan they spend time in Washington.

Not everyone, of course. There are plenty of branded-goods companies that *are* very well represented on the Japanese retailing scene—Coke, to be sure, but also Nestlé, Schick, Wella, Vicks, Scott, Del Monte, Kraft, Campbell, Unilever (its Timotei shampoo is number one in Japan), Twinings, Kellogg, Borden, Ragu, Oscar Mayer, Hershey, and a host of others. These have all become household names in Japan. They have all become insiders.

For industrial products companies, becoming an insider often poses a different set of challenges. Because these products are chosen largely on the basis of their performance characteristics, if they cut costs or boost productivity, they stand a fair chance of being accepted anywhere in the world. Even so, however, these machines do not operate in a vacuum. Their success may have to wait until the companies that make them have developed a full range of insider functions—engineering, sales, installation, finance, service, and so on. So, as these factors become more critical, it often makes sense for the companies to link up with local operations that already have these functions in place.

Financial services have their own special characteristics. Product globalization already takes place at the institutional investor level but much less so at the retail level. Still, many retail products now originate overseas, and the money collected from them is often invested across national borders. Indeed, foreign exchange, stock markets, and other trading facilities have already made money a legitimately global product.

In all these categories, then, as distinct from premium fashion-driven products like Gucci bags, insiderization in key markets is the route to global success. Yes, some top-of-the-line tastes and preferences have become common across the Triad. In many other cases, however, creating a global product means building the capability to understand and respond to customer needs and business system requirements in each critical market.

THE HEADQUARTERS MENTALITY

By all reasonable measures, Coke's experience in Japan has been a happy one. More often than not, however, the path it took to insiderization—replicating a home-country business system in a new national market—creates many more problems than it solves. Managers back at headquarters, who have had experience with only one way to succeed, are commonly inclined to force that model on each new opportunity that arises. Of course, sometimes it will work. Sometimes it will be exactly the right answer. But chances are that the home-country reflex, the impulse to generalize globally from a sample of one, will lead efforts astray.

In the pharmaceutical industry, for example, Coke's approach would not work. Foreign entrants simply have to find ways to adapt to the Japanese distribution system. Local doctors will not accept or respond favorably to an American-style sales force. When the doctor asks a local detail man to take a moment and photocopy some articles for him, he has to be willing to run the errands. No ifs, ands, or buts.

One common problem with insiderization, then, is a misplaced home-country reflex. Another, perhaps more subtle, problem is what happens back at headquarters after initial operations in another market really start paying off. When this happens, in most companies everyone at home starts to pay close attention. Without really understanding why things have turned out as well as they have, managers at headquarters take an increasing interest in what is going on in Japan or wherever it happens to be.

Functionaries of all stripes itch to intervene. Corporate heavyweights decide they had better get into the act, monitor key decisions, ask for timely reports, take extensive tours of local activities. Every power-that-be wants a say in what has become a critical portion of the overall company's operations. When minor difficulties arise, no one is willing to let local managers continue to handle things themselves. Corporate jets fill the skies with impatient satraps eager to set things right.

We know perfectly well where all this is likely to lead. A cosmetics company, with a once enviable position in Japan, went through a series of management shake-ups at home. As a result, the Japanese operation, which had grown progressively more important, was no longer able to enjoy the rough autonomy that made its success possible. Several times, eager U.S. hands reached in to change the head of activities in Japan, and crisp memos and phone calls kept up a steady barrage of challenges to the unlucky soul who happened to be in the hot seat at the moment. Relations became antagonistic, profits fell, the intervention grew worse, and the whole thing just fell apart. Overeager and overanxious managers back at headquarters did not have the patience to learn what really worked in the Japanese market. By trying to supervise things in the regular "corporate" fashion, they destroyed a very profitable business.

This is an all-too-familiar pattern. With dizzying regularity, the local top manager changes from a Japanese national to a foreigner, to a Japanese, to a foreigner. Impatient, headquarters keeps fitfully searching for a never-never ideal "person on the spot." Persistence and perseverance are the keys to long-term survival and success. Everyone knows it. But headquarters is just not able to wait for a few years until local managers—of whatever nationality—build up the needed rapport with vendors, employees, distributors, and customers. And if, by a miracle, they do, then headquarters is likely to see them as having become too "Japanized" to represent their interests abroad. They are no longer "one of us." If they do not, then obviously they have failed to win local acceptance.

This headquarters mentality is not just a problem of bad attitude or misguided enthusiasm. Too bad, because these would be relatively easy to fix. Instead, it rests on—and is reinforced by—a company's entrenched systems, structures, and behaviors. Dividend payout ratios, for example, vary from country to country. But most global companies find it hard to accept low or no payout from investment in Japan, medium returns from Germany, and larger returns from the United States. The usual wish is to get comparable levels of return from all activities, and internal benchmarks of performance reflect that wish. This is trouble waiting to happen. Looking for 15% ROI a year from new commitments in Japan is going to sour a company on Japan very quickly. The companies that have done the best there—the Coca-Colas and the IBMs—were willing to adjust their conventional expectations and settle in for the long term.

Or, for example, when top managers rely heavily on financial statements, they can easily lose sight of the value of operating globally—because these statements usually mask the performance of activities outside the home country. Accounting and reporting systems that are parent-company dominated—and remember, genuinely consolidated statements are still the exception, not the rule—merely confirm the lukewarm commitment of many managers to global competition. They may talk a lot about doing business globally, but it is just lip service. It sounds nice, and it may convince the business press to write glowing stories, but when things get tough, most of the talk turns out to be only talk.

Take a closer look at what actually happens. If a divisionalized Japanese company like Matsushita or Toshiba wants to build a plant to make widgets in Tennessee, the home-country division manager responsible for widgets often finds himself in a tough position. No doubt, the CEO will tell him to get that Tennessee facility up and running as soon as possible. But the division manager knows that, when the plant does come on-stream, his own operations are going to look worse on paper. At a minimum, his division is not going to get credit for American sales that he used to make by export from Japan. Those are now going to come out of Tennessee. The CEO tells him to collaborate, to help out, but he is afraid that the better the job he does, the worse it will be for him—and with good reason!

This is crazy. Why not change company systems? Have the Tennessee plant report directly to him, and consolidate all widget-making activities at the divisional level. Easier said than done. Most companies use accounting systems that consolidate at the corporate, not the divisional, level. That's traditional corporate practice. And every staff person since the time of Homer comes fully equipped with a thousand reasons not to make exceptions to time-honored institutional procedures. As a result, the division manager is going to drag his feet. The moment Tennessee comes on-line, he sees his numbers go down, he has to lay off people, and he has to worry about excess capacity. Who is going to remember his fine efforts in getting Tennessee started up? More to the point, who is going to care—when his Japanese numbers look so bad?

If you want to operate globally, you have to think and act globally, and that means challenging entrenched systems that work against comforts. Say our widget maker has a change of heart and goes to a division-level consolidation of accounts. This helps, but the problems are just beginning. The American managers of a sister division that uses these widgets look at the Tennessee plant as just another vendor, perhaps even a troublesome one because it is new and not entirely reliable. Their inclination is to treat the new plant as a problem, ignore it if possible, and to continue to buy from Japan where quality is high and delivery guaranteed. They are not going to do anything to help the new plant come on-stream or to plan for long-term capital investment. They are not going to supply technical assistance or design help or anything. All it represents is fairly unattractive marginal capacity.

If we solve this problem by having the plant head report to the division manager, then we are back where we started. If we do nothing, then this new plant is just going to struggle along. Clearly, what we need is to move toward a system of double counting of credits—so that both the American manager *and* the division head in Japan have strong reasons to make the new facility work. But this runs afoul of our entrenched systems, and they are very hard to change. If our commitment to acting globally is not terribly strong, we are not going to be inclined to make the painful efforts needed to make it work.

Under normal circumstances, these kinds of entrepreneurial decisions are hard enough to reach anyway. It is no surprise that many of the most globally successful Japanese companies—Honda, Sony, Matsushita, Canon, and the like—have been led by a strong owner-founder for at least a decade. They can override bureaucratic inertia; they can tear down institutional barriers. In practice, the managerial decision to tackle wrenching organizational and systems changes is made even more difficult by the way in which problems become visible. Usually, a global systems problem first comes into view in the form of explicitly local symptoms. Rarely do global problems show up where the real underlying causes are.

Troubled CEOs may say that their Japanese operations are not doing well, that the money being spent on advertising is just not paying off as expected. They will not say that their problems are really back at headquarters with its superficial understanding of what it takes to market effectively in Japan. They will not say that it lies in the design of their financial reporting systems. They will not say that it is part and parcel of their own reluctance to make long-term front-end capital investments in new markets. They will not say that it lies in their failure to do well the central job of any headquarters operation: the development of good people at the local level. Or at least they are not likely to. They will diagnose the problems as local problems and try to fix them.

THINKING GLOBAL

Top managers are always slow to point the finger of responsibility at headquarters or at themselves. When global faults have local symptoms, they will be slower still. When taking corrective action means a full, zero-based review of all systems, skills, and structures, their speed will decrease even further. And when their commitment to acting globally is itself far from complete, it is a wonder there is any motion at all. Headquarters mentality is the prime expression of managerial nearsightedness, the sworn enemy of a genuinely equidistant perspective on global markets.

In the early days of global business, experts like Raymond Vernon of the Harvard Business School proposed, in effect, a United Nations model of globalization. Companies with aspirations to diversify and expand throughout the Triad were to do so by cloning the parent company in each new country of operation. If successful, they would create a mini-U.N. of clonelike subsidiaries repatriating profits to the parent company, which remained the dominant force at the center. We know that successful companies enter fewer countries but penetrate each of them more deeply. That is why this model gave way by the early 1980s to a competitor-focused approach to globalization. By this logic, if we were a European producer of medical electronics equipment, we had to take on General Electric in the United States so that it would not come over here and attack us on our home ground. Today, however, the pressure for globalization is driven not so much by diversification or competition as by the needs and preferences of customers. Their needs have globalized, and the fixed costs of meeting them have soared. That is why we must globalize.

Managing effectively in this new borderless environment does not mean building pyramids of cash flow by focusing on the discovery of new places to invest. Nor does it mean tracking your competitors to their lair and preemptively undercutting them in their own home market. Nor does it mean blindly trying to replicate home-country business systems in new colonial territories. Instead, it means paying central attention to delivering value to customers—and to developing an equidistant view of who they are and what they want. Before everything else comes the need to see your customers clearly. They—and only they—can provide legitimate reasons for thinking global.

Building the Firm of the Future

ARNOLDO C. HAX

THERE IS A GROWING CONVICTION in academic circles that profound changes are taking place in the economic, political, social, and technological environments within which the firm operates. The discontinuities that these changes cause make it necessary to thoroughly review the firm's strategy, structure, administrative processes, and management style.

The current discontinuities are the product of two extremely powerful forces: the tendency toward the globalization of the major industrial and consumer markets, and the increasing importance of technology in the firm's activities. This paper attempts to explore the nature and intensity of these two forces, as well as the demands they place on business leaders. Understanding and handling these forces correctly will require a new type of leadership, the creation of which poses an enormous challenge to all the institutions of this country, but especially to the university, the government, and the firm.

THE IMPACT OF INDUSTRIAL GLOBALIZATION

Without any doubt the success or failure of the firm of the future will take place in a global setting. Almost all the major industries have global markets, competitors, and suppliers. Between 1962 and 1986, worldwide exports increased from 12 percent to 30 percent, totaling $2.48 trillion in 1987.[1]

Rapid technological advances in transportation and communications, the convertibility of the world's major currencies, the liberalization of credit policies, the tariff reduction sponsored by the General Agreement on Tariffs and Trade (GATT), and the integration of capital markets have collectively made the world richer and more interdependent. By the end of this decade, it is forecast, there will be one billion telephones in the world, all interconnected and able to dial each other directly.[2] This network offers unparalleled worldwide voice, data, and image communication capabilities.

Hax, Arnoldo C. "Building the Firm of the Future," *Sloan Management Review* (Spring 1989), 75–82.

The U.S. economy used to be fairly immune to the economies of other countries and the policies of other governments. U.S. economists used to assume that the United States had a closed economy. For half a century, and until as recently as 1975, the U.S. balance of payments was very close to zero and, indeed, the rest of the world did not seem to affect the U.S. economy very much. Today the situation is completely different. International trade currently accounts for more than 11 percent of the U.S. gross national product,[3] and in 1987 the balance of payments was $160 billion in the red.[4]

The balance of payment deficit accounts for both a serious deficit in the balance of trade and for increasing interest obligations of the United States as a result of its enormous accumulated debt. The deficit has been growing steadily during the 1980s, in spite of a fall in the U.S. dollar against the German mark and the Japanese yen by about 50 percent since February 1985.

The 1987 deficit represents a contribution by the United States of more than four million jobs distributed more or less evenly among Japan, Europe, and the rest of the world. Devastating economic consequences would be unleashed in those countries if the United States were to raise protectionist barriers that substantially limited their imports. Nonetheless, we know that the current situation is not sustainable, and that eventually the U.S. trade deficit will have to disappear.

The recent trends in U.S. global industrial competitiveness present an extraordinarily gloomy picture. The last decade has seen a U.S. decline in worldwide market shares in most major international markets including, recently, agriculture and high-technology products—sectors in which U.S. predominance was once well established. This lack of competitiveness resulted from consistent declines in productivity growth rates and from weak rates of savings and investment in real assets compared with most of our critical international competitors, particularly Japan and West Germany. Consequently, since 1973 the United States has seen an erosion in real wages. The United States, that once-greatest lending nation, has become the world's greatest debtor. This situation imposes an enormous threat not only to the U.S. economy, but to the overall global economy.

Within this context, "triadic thinking" has emerged. The triad is composed of the three advanced world economies—the United States, Japan, and Western Europe—where 85 to 90 percent of all the high-value-added high-technology products are manufactured and consumed.[5] Latin American countries are thought to be loosely allied with the United States, other Asian countries with Japan, and African countries with Europe. The triad has become the critical framework for thinking about global competition. It is equally relevant for the managers of a firm trying to pursue a global strategy and for the political leaders of the free world trying to establish more fair and effective trade policies than those now prescribed by GATT. The general prediction is that as the European Economic Community (EEC) countries move toward being a single, integrated political and economic entity by 1992, trading among the countries within each triad area will intensify, but trading across areas will be more limited. The future peace and prosperity of the world depend on the way these issues are resolved.

In the meantime, signs of globalization are appearing in all areas of economic activity. The preferences, desires, and needs of customers all over the world are becoming more homogeneous. This tendency has led Ted Levitt, an eminent professor of marketing, to affirm the vindication of the Model T: "If a company forces costs and prices down and pushes quality and reliability up—while maintaining reasonable concern for suitability— customers will prefer its world-standardized products"[6]

Industry after industry has adopted global standards in consumer goods such as video-recorders, cameras, watches, soft drinks, televisions, motorcycles, and cars, as well as in industrial goods such as photocopiers, computers, telephone switching systems, semiconductors, chemicals, and aerospace products. Even more important, new industries such as video- and radio-cassettes, compact discs, satellite networks, robots, and fiber optics are globally standardized from day one.[7]

To make the situation even more complicated, the economic imperatives pushing the firm to achieve large economies of scale by worldwide product standardization coexist with political imperatives pushing them in a different direction. Governments and customers in each country want the firm to respond more adequately to local needs.

The search for an appropriate balance between economic and political imperatives is the essence of a global strategy. Firms taking part in world markets have evolved from a *multinational* (or multidomestic) strategy—serving the multiple needs of national markets through relatively independent local organizations—toward a *global* strategy—supplying standardized products to the world markets by means of global-scale operations—and finally toward what has been called the *transnational* strategy—maximizing global economies while being responsive to the restrictions imposed by the various countries in which the firm operates.

In the words of Chris Bartlett, who coined the term, a transnational organization distinguishes itself from its multinational or global counterparts because: "(1) it builds and legitimizes multiple diverse internal perspectives able to sense the complex environmental demands and opportunities; (2) its physical assets and management capabilities are distributed internationally but are interdependent; and (3) it requires a robust and flexible international integrative process."[8]

What requirements does this global picture impose on the firm of the future?

First, no country can remain indifferent to the challenge involved in developing competitive advantages in world markets. To refuse to respond would require either raising protectionist barriers to prevent the free flow of goods or accepting a position of mediocrity within the international context. Both alternatives would lead to standards of living below those to which citizens legitimately aspire.

Second, the success or failure of the firm in a global context will be determined by its managerial capabilities, not by comparative advantages based on factors of production such as labor and natural resources. This fact has been demonstrated repeatedly by Asian countries such as Japan, Korea, Taiwan, Hong Kong, and Singapore; these nations do not have natural resources worth speaking about, yet they have managed to establish an enormous superiority in major industrial sectors. As the share of direct labor in total costs decreases, and natural resources are delegated to industries in developing countries, the basic factor for attaining competitive supremacy will be management competence and leadership quality.

Thus managers of the future must fully understand the critical international issues and have sufficient knowledge of languages and history to grasp the different cultures they encounter. This aspect of executive training has been neglected in the United States, where a person can receive the highest academic degrees without being able to speak a foreign language and without having learned any history apart from that which is related to the United States. I believe this gap in the U.S. manager's education is giving rise to serious competitive disadvantages that must be remedied in the country's elementary schools, high schools, and universities.

The lack of foreign language capabilities on the part of most U.S. managers is a controversial issue. Many believe it is not an important weakness, since English is the accepted business language throughout the world. Why bother to learn another language? In my opinion this question entirely misses the point. It is impossible to penetrate another culture—to comprehend the differences in values and beliefs—without knowing the culture's language. If this effort is not made, narrow parochialism is likely to replace the sophistication needed to operate in the international setting.

Most top managers of American firms now understand this point. John Opel, former chairman of IBM, stated in a recent visit to the MIT Sloan School of Management that his most important strategic concern had been to convert IBM into a truly global company. He added that his goal could not become a reality unless all key managers had a rich, deep understanding of the world's problems and opportunities. Opel declared that IBM would not promote its managers beyond a certain level unless they had acquired substantial international experience. Similarly, in some units of Citicorp (ones that work with international financial institutions), executives are not promoted until they are fluent in more than one language.

These examples are not isolated; they reveal the new emphasis modern corporations place on international education.

THE GROWING IMPORTANCE OF TECHNOLOGY

Developing internationally sophisticated managers is just one of the challenges we must accept in order to regain global competitiveness. The second, equally demanding task is to accelerate the speed at which innovations in new products and technological processes are translated into profitable commercial ventures. These two concerns point to the crucial task of the firm: to succeed in global markets where technology increasingly plays the dominant role.

The driving force behind high technology today is the computer and all that is related to it: semiconductors, chips, robots, and telecommunications. This multitude of technologies provides unlimited opportunities—as well as potentially devastating risks. Charles Brown, former chairman of the board of AT&T, stated in a talk given at MIT that there were three "killing" technologies: microprocessors, fiber optics (and optical waveguides), and software technology. If AT&T does not handle each of these efficiently, then its competitors may gain a lethal advantage. If used wisely and in a timely fashion, these technologies can introduce discontinuities into the marketplace that provide insurmountable advantages. They *must* be monitored and managed.

Fortunately for us, as the world becomes increasingly complex, technology enables us to gain access to this complexity, even by using desktop computers.

During the last decade, technology has also dramatically affected the firm's production capabilities. A set of technologies—known collectively as programmable automation—has allowed managers to respond to ever-rising consumer expectations regarding quality, diversity, delivery, price, and rate of new product introduction. These technologies include computer-aided design, computer-aided manufacturing, computer-aided engineering, flexible manufacturing systems, robotics, and computer-integrated manufacturing.

Making these technologies work requires much more than major capital investments. Technological systems now connect not only the firm's key operations; they also link the plant with customers, suppliers, and procurement officers. Those connections often call for substantial changes in the managerial infrastructure. Thus these technologies bring not only enormous potential for improvement, but also managerial challenges that make conventional business management obsolete.[9]

How is the U.S. doing in the technology arena? A report from the Council on Competitiveness, chaired by John Young of Hewlett-Packard, was particularly critical of our inability to commercialize technology rapidly.[10] For example, American share of the market in consumer electronics dropped from nearly 100 percent in 1970 to an insignificant 5 percent now. Key industries, such as pharmaceuticals and semiconductors, are being challenged by foreign competitors. The percentage of U.S. patents granted to foreign investors went from 35 percent in 1975 to 46.6 percent in 1987. The reasons behind this decline include our relative slowness in getting innovations into the marketplace, an insufficient focus on manufacturing and quality, and improper tradeoffs between short- and long-term goals.

A survey organized by Japan's Ministry for International Trade and Industry (MITI) covering 189 technologies in 43 product lines showed that the United States was superior or equal to Japan in 80 percent of the product technologies surveyed. Japan was superior or equal in 80 percent of the process technologies. Unfortunately for the United States, product innovations are rapidly duplicable, while process innovations are the result of a know-how that is much more difficult to transfer. Consequently, this process superiority gives Japan a greater sustainable competitive advantage.[11]

The United States is also behind Japan in the deployment of robots and flexible manufacturing systems. According to Ramchandran Jaikumar at Harvard, in the last five years Japan has invested more than twice as much in automation as the United States. During this time, 55 percent of the machine tools introduced in Japan were computer numerically controlled (CNC), which is the most advanced technology in this field. In the United States, the figure was only 18 percent. More than 40 percent of all CNC machines in the world are in Japan.

In the Japanese companies Jaikumar studied, more than 40 percent of the workforce were college-graduate engineers. All had been trained to use CNC machines. In the United States, only 8 percent of the workers were engineers, and less than 25 percent had been trained on CNC machines. The Japanese engineers' training took three times as long as the U.S. training. Japanese plants had on average 2.5 times more CNC machines than U.S. plants, four times as many engineers, and four times as many people trained in the use of the machines.[12]

In the face of these figures, it is not surprising that the United States is consistently losing competitive capacity to Japan. What implications does all this have for the firm of the future?

Undoubtedly, we must improve our technological capabilities. Investment in education, research and development, and production technology must play a major role. If we are to rebuild U.S. competitiveness, the firm, the university, and the government must make integral and cooperative efforts in these areas.

- *The first item on the agenda is to invest in every facet of the U.S. educational system.* World statistics once again paint a bleak picture for the United States. Consider these facts.[13]

The U.S. educational system is unable to produce the number of engineers and scientists needed to obtain technological leadership. It is estimated that a deficit of more than 500,000 scientists and engineers will exist by 2010.

There are also significant deficiencies in the *quality* of science and engineering education. Elementary and secondary schools suffer from severe shortages of qualified math and science teachers, and the system is doing little to attract and develop them. Bill Aldridge, executive director of the National Science Teachers Association, recently stated that 30 percent of the science teachers in the United States are unfit to teach those subjects and that the level of unfitness is increasing. American children attend school on average only 180 days in the year; their Japanese counterparts, 240. Elementary and high-school teachers in the U.S. are notoriously poorly paid—although they are responsible for carrying out one of the most important tasks in our society. In contrast, Japan pays high-school teachers salaries equivalent to those of middle managers.

American students take fewer courses in science and math than students in most industrialized nations. Not surprisingly, they are among the poorest performers in achievement tests on geometry, algebra, calculus, biology, physics, and chemistry.

Japan, whose population is approximately half that of the United States, produces the same number of engineers that we do every year. It is hardly surprising, then, that with twice the engineering capacity per capita, Japanese products are better designed and manu-factured.

Another unsettling fact is that foreign students represent about 40 percent of the graduate students in U.S. engineering schools. More than half the U.S. engineering doc-torates go to foreign students.

- *The second item on the agenda for strengthening our technological capability is to develop a coherent policy that will improve the private sector's ability to develop and apply technology. The federal government must play a key role in this effort.*

During the 1950s, 1960s, and 1970s, federal investments in U.S. universities enabled major new industries to be formed in the biotechnology and aerospace fields and in basic parts of the electronics industry. But during the 1980s, the Reagan administration signifi-cantly reduced support for basic research. To make matters worse, 70 percent of federal expenditures went into military research; before Reagan took office, there had been a fifty-fifty split between military and civil research. R&D outlay in current dollars for defense and space-related purposes increased from $18.2 billion in 1980 to an estimated $48.5 billion in 1987.[14]

The Council on Competitiveness report criticizes the federal government's recent role in facilitating the commercial application of technology. Its findings include the following.[15]

- The federal government has not focused on the commercial application of technology as a public policy issue. As a result, current government policies and procedures tend to inhibit rather than accelerate rapid commercialization.

- Large federal budget deficits in a low savings society drive up the cost of capital and hinder commercialization of technology.

- Federal government mechanisms for determining science and technology priorities and for coordinating policies across agencies are insufficient.

- Federal investments in the education, facilities, and equipment that make up the nation's science and technology infrastructure are inadequate.

- Inconsistent government R&D incentives undermine private sector efforts to make long-term research and development investments.

- There is no consensus on the scope, mission, and relevance of the federal laboratories to the needs of the country over the next twenty years.

- In serving as a contractor and regulator of economic activity, the federal government has too often assumed an adversarial role in its relationship with industry.

- In too many instances, promising science and technology initiatives have not been implemented.

Taken together, these findings generate an urgent challenge: the federal government needs to implement a sound policy for American technological development.

- *This challenge leads us to the third item on our agenda for recapturing technological prominence, which is to establish the conditions that allow U.S. manufacturers to cooperate as well as to compete in the international setting.* Three key words summarize this need for change: alliances, networking, and flexibility.

Alliances are coalitions between two or more companies; this category includes, for example, joint ventures, licensing agreements, and supply agreements. The reasons for these alliances are varied. They include technology acquisition; economics of scale; access to new markets, materials, or components; pressure from local governments; and global standardization of a product.[16]

Philips, the electronic consumer goods producer, provides a good example of how alliances are changing the way we compete. Philips has been responsible for major innovations and was one of the first companies to develop audio cassettes, compact disks, and digital cassettes. In the case of audio cassettes, Philips enjoyed an enormous economic success mainly because it produced a globally standardized product. As a result, the firm went through the early stages of compact disk and digital cassette development cooperating openly with Sony and Matsushita. (In this industry, approximately ten people in the world need to agree in order to achieve complete standardization.) Philips, Sony, and Matsushita cooperated fully, without payment of mutual licenses, in the initial product development stages, until the final product specifications were written. From then on, in the production and marketing phases, the three companies competed aggressively in all markets. This initial cooperation and subsequent competition brought advantages to all three manufacturers, as well as to consumers, who benefit from lower prices and the accessibility of interchanging products.

In the United States, alliances between national competing companies have been prohibited by antitrust legislation, forcing U.S. firms to seek alliances with foreign companies. This is the case in the automobile industry, where General Motors has worked with Toyota and Isuzu, Ford with Toyo Kogyo, Chrysler with Mitsubishi, and American Motors with Renault.

One of the first national cooperative efforts in the U.S. was the formation of MCC (Microelectronics and Computer Technology Corporation), which is a private initiative grouping twenty-one leading companies; its aim is to finance technological research efforts jointly. Its existence sets a major precedent in the United States in that the Department of Justice approved the corporation, on the condition that it end as soon as the research generates a marketable product.

The European Economic Community has overtaken the United States in establishing major technological cooperative projects among a large number of companies; these include ESPRIT and EUREKA.[17] These efforts are accelerating as the EEC becomes more integrated.

The United States must recognize the need not just to permit, but to encourage, constructive cooperative arrangements. In most industrial countries, the government actively initiates and promotes these ventures. Denying U.S. managers this flexibility prevents them from playing the global business game according to the rules other countries use. This statement should not be heard as a call to relax ethical and moral standards; I simply mean that cooperation is now a proper and intelligent way to conduct worldwide business.

It is vital that more creative alignments be encouraged among government, business, and academic institutions. Traditional structures and relationships must be reviewed. Neither a purist adherence to the notion of a free market nor the adoption of a totally controlled economy provides a useful answer. Centrally planned economies, in addition to not responding to democratic aspirations, have also not produced the results their countries' leaders had hoped for. At the same time, economic systems are full of imperfections that contradict the hypothesis of an efficient market operated without government intervention.

President Reagan railed publicly against government intervention in the economy, but in practice he helped create one of the biggest Keynesian stimuli in our history by accumulating $2.132 trillion in debt.[18] The stimulus was so large that it preserved the prosperity of the American people—at least temporarily—in the face of high interest rates and record budget deficits. However, there is no doubt that this trend cannot continue for much longer. Perhaps it would make more sense to develop a structure that facilitated intelligent communication between corporations and the government—one that would, in certain cases, permit business alliances to be established, as frequently occurs in some Asian and European countries.

Networking is another key concept for the firm of the future. It represents the development of lateral relationships inside and outside the firm and the country. The corporate structure is becoming more compact. Information that was once collected and presented to top management by middle managers is now gathered and presented by computers and communications networks. As a result, the middle levels in the management hierarchy are contracting, structures are becoming more compact, and the workforce is getting more diverse and enterprising.[19]

Tom Malone, a computer scientist and organizational psychologist at MIT, is developing a field that he calls "coordination theory"; its purpose is to study the impact of information on organizations. One major impact is that networks are beginning to replace the conventional managerial hierarchy. The traditional roles of boss and subordinate, with the associated flow of vertical communication, are being replaced by networking and group work. *Lateral* networks are becoming more crucial than the managerial hierarchy, which may become either invisible or irrelevant.[20]

One experiment that should be monitored closely is the creation of Saturn Corporation within General Motors. Saturn is the first corporation founded by GM since the era of

Alfred P. Sloan. As has been amply documented, U.S. manufacturers have had a cost disadvantage of about $2,500 with respect to a Japanese car sold in Detroit. General Motors executives believed it would be practically impossible to close this gap within existing organizational frameworks. Consequently, they established a new management organization. At Saturn, GM is attempting to build the firm of the future within the confines of a huge and very conventional American corporation. Doing this means redesigning not only the firm's traditional *functions* (technology, production, marketing, sales, distribution, services, etc.) but also its *organizational structure* and *decision-making processes*.

The formulas used in the past to organize and administer firms have not produced acceptable results in the last decade. The firm of the future might have to be built according to a completely novel framework, demanding an extraordinary amount of creativity.

Finally, global firms must develop *flexible*, multidimensional decision-making processes capable of responding to a rapidly changing environment. Headquarters is no longer the locus of decision making. Rather, the locus changes from one decision to the next, moving from worldwide product managers to country and functional managers, depending on whether product, geographic, or functional expertise is most relevant. The old question of centralization versus decentralization is an anachronism. What is important is the decision-making process, not its structure. The process must be flexible and it must depend on appropriate global networking as its key coordination mechanism.[21]

TOWARD A NEW FORM OF LEADERSHIP

I have argued that the competitive pressures resulting from globalization and technological progress are changing how we manage a firm. These two forces also require a new form of leadership. Tomorrow's leader must be a charismatic, inspirational force in a new world: one characterized by an ever-increasing rate of change, realigned social and cultural values, and dramatic changes in workforce composition and demographic trends.

The firm of the future will need managers who can lead. At the heart of leadership is the creation, development, and retention of power, exercised in a wise and ethical manner. Bertrand Russell has said that power is the fundamental concept in social science, just as energy is the fundamental concept in physics. Not surprisingly, therefore, leadership is equated with the proper use of power.[22] Leadership is, among other things, the ability to create a vision, communicate it, and seek consensus and commitment. Incidentally, consensus does not mean accepting the lowest common denominator. On the contrary, it means giving everybody the right to defend a different point of view, to challenge directions, and to disagree. But after every opinion has been expressed, a common direction is agreed upon—strongly influenced by the leader's vision—and then everyone makes a commitment to its pursuit.

We need what J.M. Burns refers to as a transformational leader—as opposed to a transactional leader—someone able to make not incremental but decisive changes, and to motivate people to do more than they originally expected to.[23] Kay R. Whitmore, president of Eastman Kodak, said in a recent speech at MIT that tomorrow's leaders will have three vital responsibilities.

First, they must have a clear vision of what they intend to accomplish in both the long and short term. This vision may be supported by numbers and data, but it will also be based on intuition, customer experience, and business judgment. The vision will recognize the necessity of organizational and technological transformation.

Second, leaders must have a strong sense of renewal; they must be eager to create opportunities using an entrepreneurial approach.

Third, leaders must have a readiness to communicate, cope with controversy, encourage trust, and respond to an increasingly diverse workforce.

The tasks confronting the firm of the future are not easy ones, but the promises are exciting and the rewards immeasurable.

REFERENCES

This paper was originally written in Spanish. The author wishes to acknowledge the help of Marcelo Larraguibel and Felipe Guardiola in translating it into English.

1. L.C. Thurow, "America, Europe and Japan—A Time to Dismantle the World Economy," *The Economist*, 9 November 1985, pp. 21–26; Statistical Abstract of the U.S., U.S. Bureau of the Census 1988, Table No. 1373, World Summary.
2. K.R. Whitmore, "A Common Agenda for an Uncommon Future." MIT Management (formerly Sloan), Summer 1987, pp. 5–9.
3. For an interesting analysis of the importance of overseas trade and the competitive position of the United States in the international context, see S. Cohen et al., "Global Competition—The New Reality" (Berkeley, CA: University of California, working paper of the President's Commission on Industrial Competitiveness, 8 November 1984); and P. Morici, "Reassessing American Competitiveness" (Washington, DC: National Planning Association, 1988).
4. Survey of Current Business (Washington, DC: U.S. Department of Commerce, July 1988), p. 69.
5. K. Ohmae, "The Triad World View," Journal of Business Strategy, Spring 1987, pp. 8–19.
6. T. Levitt, "The Globalization of Markets," *Harvard Business Review*, May-June 1983, pp. 92–102.
7. H. Takeuchi and M.E. Porter. "Three Roles of International Marketing in Global Strategy" in *Competition in Global Industries*, ed. M.E. Porter (Boston: Harvard Business School Press, 1986), pp. 111–146.
8. For a good discussion of global strategy see C.A. Bartlett, "Building and Managing the Transnational: The New Organizational Challenge." in *Competition in Global Industries*, ed. M.E. Porter (Boston: Harvard Business School Press, 1986); and C. Prahalad and Y.L. Doz, *The Multinational Mission—Balancing Local Demands and Global Vision* (New York: The Free Press, 1987).
9. R.H. Hayes and R. Jaikumar, "Manufacturing's Crisis: New Technologies, Obsolete Organization," *Harvard Business Review*, September-October 1988, pp. 77–85.
10. Council on Competitiveness, "Picking up the Pace: The Commercial Challenge to American Innovation," undated report.
11. Morici (1988).
12. R. Jaikumar, "Postindustrial Manufacturing," *Harvard Business Review*, November-December 1986, pp. 69–76.

13. These figures appear in K.R. Whitmore (Summer 1987); G. Bylinski, "The High-Tech Race—Who's Ahead?" Special Report, *Fortune*, 13 October 1986, pp. 26–57; and "Changing America: The New Face of Science and Engineering" (Washington, DC; Interim Report of the Task Force on Women, Minorities, and the Handicapped in Science and Technology, 1988).

14. Statistical Abstract of the U.S., U.S. Bureau of the Census, 1988, Table No. 948. R&D Outlay.

15. Council on Competitiveness (undated report).

16. For a more detailed consideration of alliances, see M.E. Porter et al., "Coalitions and Global Strategy" *Competition in Global Industries*, ed. M.E. Porter (Boston: Harvard Business School Press, 1986); R. Harrigan, *Managing for Joint Venture Success* (Lexington, MA: Lexington Books, 1986); and E.B. Roberts and C.A. Berry, "Entering New Businesses: Selecting Strategies for Success," *Sloan Management Review*, Spring 1985, pp. 3–17.

17. For an analysis of technological strategy in Europe, see P. Nueno and Oosterveld, "The Status of Strategy in Europe," *Technology in the Modern Corporation*, ed. M. Horwitch (New York: Pergamon Press, 1986).

18. Thurow (1985); and Statistical Abstract of the U.S., U.S. Bureau of the Census 1988, Table No. 668, GNP in constant (1982) dollars.

19. K.R. Whitmore (Summer 1987).

20. For a discussion of coordination theory and its managerial implications, see T.W. Malone, J. Yates, and R.I. Benjamin, "Electronic Markets and Electronic Hierarchies," *Communication of the ACM* 30 (1987): 484–497; T.W. Malone and S. Smith, "Modeling the Performance of Organizational Structures," *Operation Research* 36 (May–June 1988): 421–436; and E.H. Schein, "Reassessing the 'Divine Rights' of Managers," *Sloan Management Review*, Winter 1989, pp. 63–68.

21. Bartlett (1987).

22. A significant amount of academic work has been oriented in this direction. See J.P. Kotter, *Power and Influence—Beyond Formal Authority* (New York: The Free Press, 1985); and H. Mintzberg, *Power in and around Organizations* (Englewood Cliffs, NJ: Prentice-Hall, 1983).

23. For more on leadership in the firm, see B.M. Bass, *Leadership and Performance beyond Expectations* (New York: The Free Press, 1985); W. Bennis and B. Nanus, *Leaders: The Strategies of Taking Charge* (New York: Harper & Row, 1985); J.B. Burns, *Leadership* (New York: Harper & Row, 1968); R.M. Kanter, *The Change Masters: Innovation and Entrepreneurship in the American Corporations* (New York: Simon & Schuster, 1983); E.H. Schein, *Organizational Culture and Leadership: A Dynamic View* (San Francisco: Jossey-Bass, 1985); and N.M. Tichy and M.A. Devanna, *The Transformational Leader* (New York: John Wiley & Sons, 1986).

Your New Global Workforce

BRIAN O'REILLY

A FUNDAMENTAL SHIFT is under way in how and where the world's work gets done—with potentially ominous consequences for wealthy, industrialized nations. The key to this change: the emergence of a truly global labor force, talented and capable of accomplishing just about anything, anywhere. Says Larry Irving, an executive of Daniel Industries who moved from Houston to run a factory that his company bought in eastern Germany: "The average American doesn't realize that there is a truly competitive work force out there that is vying for their jobs. The rest of the world is catching up."

Just what is driving U.S. companies—and some from Europe and Japan—to locate that new plant not in Waltham, Massachusetts, or Tucson, Arizona, but instead in Bangalore, India, where 3M makes tapes, chemicals, and electrical parts, or Guadalajara, Mexico, where Hewlett-Packard assembles computers and designs computer memory boards? It isn't only the search for cheap labor. Corporations also want to establish sophisticated manufacturing and service operations in markets that promise the most growth, often emerging nations. The migration of jobs to new lands isn't a straightforward one-for-one proposition either, one job gained there for every one lost to an industrialized country. New technology and the continuing drive for higher productivity push companies to build in undeveloped countries plants and offices that require only a fraction of the manpower that used to be needed in factories back home. In part because of this, the statistics on the number of foreign workers employed by multinational companies don't adequately reflect the shift of work abroad.

It is far from clear what form the new world of work will ultimately take. But there's already plenty to be concerned about, and excited by, in the transition taking place.

What happens when the corporate drive for greater efficiency collides with the expansion of the supply of labor available around the globe? Will there be enough jobs to go around? Some experts aren't so sure. Says Percy Barnevik, CEO of ABB Asea Brown Boveri, the $29-billion-a-year Swiss-Swedish builder of transportation and electric generation systems: "It is a fallacy to think that industry will increase employment overall in the Western world, at least in our industry."

Barnevik foresees "a massive move from the Western world. We already have 25,000 employees in former communist countries. They will do the job that was done in Western Europe before." More jobs will shift to Asia, he says. ABB, which employed only 100 workers in Thailand in 1980, has 2,000 there now, and will have more than 7,000 by the end of the century. Put it all together, and Barnevik's forecast borders on the apocalyptic: "Western European and American employment will just shrink and shrink in an orderly way. Like farming at the turn of the century."

A. Gary Shilling, an economist in Springfield, New Jersey, predicts the overhang of workers will hold down wages all over the developed world. "Four years ago people were talking about a shortage of labor" in the U.S., he says. "But with the push for productivity in the West and Japan, and the rise of the newly industrialized countries and Mexico and Indonesia, we will have a surplus." Technology and capital move easily around the world, he observes, and the only things likely to stay put are locally produced services, like hair-cutting. "Unless you have labor that is uniquely suited to what you're doing, there is no assurance the entire process won't move to another place."

The trend unfolding is likely to be more complex, uneven, and subtle than Shilling and Barnevik paint it. Interviews with executives around the globe reveal that increasingly sophisticated work is indeed being parceled out to faraway nations, whose labor forces are exceedingly capable. Says a top executive at Siemens, the giant German industrial and electronics company: "Thirty years ago they could barely spell 'steam turbine' in India. Now we are building the biggest ones in the world there."

The move toward a global work force takes many forms and consists of far more than a stampede to backward low-wage countries. For example, American direct foreign investment still appears to be creating jobs at factories and operations in high-wage countries, primarily Canada and Europe. In 1990, the latest year for which U.S. Commerce Department data are available, American companies employed 2.8 million people in Western Europe, up 4% from the previous year. That was a bigger jump than the 2% rise, to 1.5 million, in Asian workers they employed, or a similar 2% increase in Latin American employees, to 1.3 million. The explanation, in part, is that up until now most direct foreign investment has been aimed at expanding a company's presence in relatively affluent markets.

When work does move to less developed lands, it's by no means automatic that the shift will bring Western levels of employment and prosperity to new host countries. Martin Anderson, a vice president specializing in global manufacturing for the Gemini Consulting firm in Morristown, New Jersey, notes that new factories abroad, even in low-wage countries, tend to be far more labor efficient than their counterparts in the company's home country. That's one reason why counting noses is not a good guide to the value of goods and services produced offshore. "Some of the most Japanese-looking American plants are going up in Brazil," he observes. Not only is the number of blue-collar workers reduced, says Anderson, but staff and managerial employees are as well. Says David Hewitt, another consultant at Gemini: "If companies reduce one million jobs at home through re-engineering their work, they may add 100,000 overseas."

The other reason figures on foreign employment don't fully reflect the dispersal of work abroad: Unlike ten or 15 years ago when companies were more vertically integrated, factories abroad owned by Americans, Europeans, and Japanese are increasingly likely to outsource—to contract for parts and labor from independent local suppliers. Outsourcing requires no bricks-and-mortar investment, nor does it add to the employment tallies of the corporation buying the goods or services. Subramanian Rangan, a doctoral student in political economy at Harvard who has studied the phenomenon, says outsourcing is difficult to measure but already large enough to amount to "new channels of trade." Anderson calculates that at least half the value of goods shipped from American-owned electronics factories abroad was actually added at independently owned plants.

How difficult is it to find so-called sourcers abroad? No trouble at all in some industries. Charles Komar, president of a big clothing company in New York that bears his name, says agents for foreign factories prowl through department stores studying the labels in clothing. "I get calls all the time from people saying they know of a factory in Turkey that can sew the clothes for less than I'm paying now."

Janet Palmer, a professor at New York City's Lehman College specializing in the movement of office work abroad, was called by a consultant from California looking for a cheap place to have text and numbers typed into a computer. She told him of typing mills in the Philippines that would do it for 50 cents per 10,000—characters approximately five pages, double spaced. A few days later the man called back and announced he had found an outfit in China charging only 20 cents.

Those foreign sourcers are becoming increasingly capable. An example: For years, Ron Ahfers was an industrial designer for J.C. Penney. His job included designing the control panels on the private-label microwave ovens that Penney bought from Samsung Group in Korea to make them easy to use and consistent across several models. One year a while back, when Samsung engineers came to New York to see Ahlers's work, they were embarrassed by how much better his designs were than the ones they created for their own brand-name appliances. Ahlers and his colleagues were astonished when one of them said, "The designer will be punished." The proposal from Korea in the next model year was much better. Penney, in fact, soon began shifting microwave design to Samsung. Eventually the U.S. company shut down its entire in-house design office.

Visits to the global labor force in places like Eastern Europe, India, and Jamaica reveal just how ready these folks are to handle complex work, but they also suggest the looming oversupply of workers. Says Anderson of Gemini Consulting: "Sit in any boardroom and it is absolutely clear that those countries are the kinds of places in competition for capital. Smart companies see they have to keep technology and capital fluid, and move them to where they can make best use of the advances countries achieve."

"Look out the window from any tall building here, and what do you see?" asks Larry Irving, a Texan, in his not-so-tall office in Potsdam, a town a few miles south of Berlin in what used to be East Germany. "Smokestacks!" That's good news for Irving's company, Daniel Industries, which makes meters that measure the flow of natural gas through pipelines. The smokestacks exist because most of Eastern Europe relied on coal for heating and electricity, and Irving figures there will soon be rapid construction of new pipelines throughout the region—and a market for his meters. That new market looks all the more attractive in light of a slowdown in the company's business back home.

U.S. Direct Investment in Millions of U.S. Dollars

	1975	1980	1985	1991	
Britain	$13,927	$28,605	$33,024	$68,261	
China	N.A.	N.A.	N.A.	$350	
Germany*	$8,726	$15,418	$16,764	$32,942	
India	$367	$398	$383	$533	
Ireland	$664	$2,319	$3,693	$7,450	
Jamaica	$654	$407	$122	$667	
Japan	$3,339	$6,243	$9,235	$22,918	
Mexico	$3,200	$5,989	$5,088	$11,570	
Singapore	$485	$1,204	$1,874	$4,313	
Thailand	$260	$361	$1,074	$1,787	

Source: Commerce Department

*East & West Germany combined for 1991.

Up until now, most of the $450 billion that America has invested in factories and offices abroad has gone to Western countries, but the flow of money—last year, $26 billion—is likely to shift toward emerging countries that have skilled work forces. Figures reflect cumulative investment.

Employees of U.S. Multinationals in Thousands

	1977	1982	1985	1990	
Britain	1,069.3	830.7	809.5	846.7	
China	N.A.	N.A.	N.A.	14.4	
Germany*	587.4	541.3	541.1	590.5	
India	94.6	75.2	71.8	38.3	
Ireland	27.6	38.4	35.2	45.5	
Jamaica	N.A.	8.8	6.2	8.7	
Japan	389.1	302.0	331.0	407.8	
Mexico	370.1	470.3	466.0	551.6	
Singapore	44.2	46.1	49.0	85.8	
Thailand	27.3	29.4	29.1	64.4	

Source: Commerce Department

*East & West Germany combined for 1990.

The number of foreign workers employed by U.S. companies declined in the early Eighties as conglomerates sold off acquisitions made earlier, but rose by half a million between 1986 and 1990 to 6.7 million. U.S. firms withdrew from India when it imposed investment controls, but are coming back.

Daniel Industries debated setting up a factory in West Germany, but the cost of land, labor, and buildings was too high. Instead, early this year the company bought the assets of Messtechnik Babelsberg, a measuring-instrument firm that was formerly part of a huge state-run conglomerate in East Germany. Irving is dazzled by the skills and training of the East German workers he inherited. They underwent years of demanding apprenticeship, much like West German workers, before entering the work force. Though not up to speed on the use of computerized technology in the factory or the final product, they are so well grounded in engineering that they are easily trained. Not least, they cost about half as much as West German workers.

But foreign investment can't repair all the problems of the former East Germany fast enough to avoid painful dislocations. Three years ago the plant Daniel Industries acquired employed 600 workers. Bringing in better technology, Daniel needed only a fraction of them to make the meters it expects to sell next year. So despite their impressive skills, the company kept only 60 of the 600. Their low wages have not eliminated the need for large and continuing capital improvements to stay competitive. The company is installing a million-dollar computerized machining tool that will do the work of many workers. Across eastern Germany the actual unemployment rate is approaching 40%. "If you include workers who were forced into early retirement or who will be unable to get work when current training programs end, it is that high," says Hermann Wagner, an executive at Treuhandanstalt, the German agency that is privatizing East German factories.

Hourly Compensation in U.S. Dollars for Workers in Manufacturing

	1975	1980	1985	1991
Britain	$3.32	$7.83	$6.19	$19.42
China	$0.17	$0.30	$0.24	$0.26 [3]
Germany*	$6.35	$12.33	$9.57	$22.17
India	$0.19	$0.44	$0.35	$0.39 [2]
Ireland	$3.03	$5.95	$5.92	$11.90
Jamaica[1]	N.A.	N.A.	$1.44	$1.61 [3]
Japan	$3.05	$5.61	$6.43	$14.41
Mexico	N.A.	N.A.	$1.60	$2.17
Singapore	$0.84	$1.49	$2.47	$4.38
Thailand	N.A.	N.A.	$0.53	$0.68 [3]
U.S.	$6.36	$9.87	$13.01	$15.45

Source: BLS

*East & West Germany combined for 1991.   [1] ILO data.   [2] 1986.   [3] 1990.

The strong dollar made American workers overpriced in the mid–Eighties, but now they are one of the best bargains in the industrialized world. A shortage of workers is helping boost wages in Singapore. In most cases, compensation includes benefits.

Unemployment as a Percent of Labor Force

	1975	1980	1985	1991	1993 *(proj.)*
Britain	3.3%	5.6%	11.5%	8.3%	9.7%
China	N.A.	4.9%	1.8%	2.3%	N.A.
Germany*	4.7%	3.2%	8.0%	4.7%	4.8%
India	N.A.	N.A.	N.A.	20.0% [1]	N.A.
Ireland	8.3%	7.3%	17.4%	15.8%	16.6%
Jamaica	20.5%	27.4%	25.0%	15.7% [3]	N.A.
Japan	1.9%	2.0%	2.8%	2.1%	2.3%
Mexico	7.2%	6.9% [1]	4.4%	2.6%	N.A.
Singapore	4.5%	3.1%	4.1%	1.9%	N.A.
Thailand	0.4%	0.8%	2.6%	3.1% [2]	N.A.
U.S.	8.5%	7.0%	7.1%	7.1%	6.5%

Source: OECD and ILO

* East & West Germany combined for 1991 & 1993. [1] 1988. [2] 1988. [3] 1990.
[4] CIA estimate for 1990.

Governments vary in how they report unemployment figures, and some numbers are rough estimates, but trends show that growing investment in Singapore and Mexico is helping to reduce unemployment. Thailand's apparently rising unemployment actually reflects a shift away from agriculture and improved reporting methods.

In Hungary, General Electric saw an opportunity to acquire a recognized brand name and existing lines of distribution to West and East European markets when in 1990 it bought Tungsram, a big Budapest light bulb maker. What GE also got in the bargain turned out to be a work force that was one of the best in the world at designing and making advanced lighting fixtures. Hungarian engineers are excellent, says Peter Harper, acting finance director at the Tungsram plant. "Give them a concept and they will go out and develop it." The Budapest plant makes automotive lamps used in cars built in Japan and Europe. A Tungsram factory in Nagykanizsa, Hungary, has become GE's leading center for making advanced compact fluorescent bulbs, with many of the bulbs now going to the United States. Tungsram managers are understandably weak in marketing and financial management, but GE has replicated there the executive training programs it offers in the U.S. "With their analytical background as engineers, they handle it very well," concludes Harper.

But Hungary too is suffering an insufficiency of jobs for skilled workers. The official unemployment rate, less than 1% three years ago, is now at 12% and will probably go higher. Tungsram employed 18,600 workers when it was acquired, but a third have been let go.

If you thought your job was immune from globalization because you were in a service business, don't go back to sleep. Recent advances in telecommunications technology and aggressive efforts by out-of-the-way nations to boost their educational systems have put wings on everything from insurance work to engineering and computer programming.

In Jamaica, 3,500 people work at office parks connected to the U.S. by satellite dishes. There they make airline reservations and process tickets, handle calls to toll-free numbers, and do data entry. More than 25,000 documents a day, including credit card applications, are scanned electronically in the U.S. and copies transmitted to Montego Bay and Kingston for handling.

More sophisticated service work travels even farther. A New Yorker calling Quarterdeck Office Systems, a California-based software company, with a question about how to work a particular program will often detect a brogue on the answerer's voice. Beginning at four in the morning, New York time, before Californians are at work, the calls are routed to Dublin, where Quarterdeck has its second phone-answering operation. At the same place, scores of multilingual workers take calls from all over Europe. That would have been almost impossible a few years ago, until the Irish government spent billions to upgrade the country's phone system. It did so expressly to turn the island into a telecommunications-based service center.

Quarterdeck originally used Ireland as a center for translating instruction manuals and software for use in Europe. It gradually came to realize the Irish schools were turning out impressive numbers of technically trained graduates. Increasingly complex software chores were assigned there, and Irish nationals were sent to California to develop original programs. Quarterdeck eventually leased special high-quality telephone lines to link offices in Dublin and Santa Monica, California. Once that connection was in place, it was a small step and little added cost to use the line to reroute customer calls from the U.S.

All across Ireland are dozens of offices devoted to handling complex service work from the U.S. In the village of Fermoy, in County Cork, 150 Metropolitan Life workers analyze medical insurance claims to determine if they are eligible for reimbursement. This is not grunt work. It demands considerable knowledge of medicine, the American medical system, and the insurance business. Met Life's Irish workers also review new policies sold by salesmen in the U.S. for gaps and errors.

Near Limerick, workers at another U.S. insurance company monitor the movement of money in and out of American corporate clients' employee pension accounts to make sure they comply with American laws. The job is far more complex, insists the office manager—who doesn't want to be identified—than mere medical claims processing.

Why do companies relocate work to Ireland? In part because it is cheaper. Operating costs are about 30% to 35% less than in the U.S., says Frank Verminski, head of the Met Life office. And the Irish Development Authority provides generous tax and other incentives worth about a year's pay for each new job created.

Even more important, there appears to be a strong work ethic intensified by a serious shortage of jobs in Ireland. In a nation with only 1.1 million jobs for a population of 3.5

million, Irish men and women consider themselves very fortunate to get a "permanent and pensionable position." The Met Life job requires 18 weeks of training. What is the annual turnover rate in Ireland? "About 1%," says Verminski. "We've lost three people in three years." The manager of the insurance office handling pensions says the work was sent to Ireland in part because workers in Hartford goofed off so much that managers gave up trying to improve productivity there. Now, she says, "we think all the time of what other work could be handled here."

Ireland is one of those countries that believe the notion that educating your work force will solve all your economic problems. It sends over a quarter of its 18-year-olds off to college—far more than most European countries. But as in India and the Philippines, there are political, cultural, and unfathomable reasons why some nations simply fail to create or attract a lot of industry. In such places, college grads too often end up twiddling their thumbs. Smart managers recognize the opportunity such underemployed grads represent: a big and growing supply of hypereducated workers they can tap into. Some workers may even be willing, or eager, to relocate for a job. Recently a recruiter for Philips, the Dutch electronics company, marched into Trinity College in Dublin and guaranteed a job in Holland to every computer science graduate of the class.

Don't scoff just because you never heard of the University of Limerick or the Indian Institute of Science in Bangalore. Corporate recruiters have, and they are often impressed. Says Stuart Reeves, senior vice president for Dallas-based EDS, the information technology management company: "If you're hiring college types, there isn't a lot of difference in quality across nations. The difference among college graduates by countries is a lot less than the difference among day laborers and high-schoolers. And there's a lot of pent-up talent out there."

In the mid-Eighties, Texas Instruments started setting up an impressive software programming operation in Bangalore, a city of four million in southern India. "We came because of the amount of talent that was available here," says Richard Gall, managing director of TI in India. "We couldn't hire enough software designers in Europe to meet demand, and India was producing more than it could use." And even though TI had to install its own electrical generators and satellite dishes to operate efficiently, wages are low enough that work still gets done for half what it costs in the U.S.

Since TI's arrival, 30 more companies including Motorola and IBM have set up software programming offices in the area, on a cool plateau west of Madras. The 3M company created a software writing operation in Bangalore several years ago. Based in part on the managerial and technical talent it found, 3M began expanding its manufacturing operations, which are pictured on FORTUNE'S cover. Its new plant employs 120 people and makes electrical connectors, chemicals, and pressure-sensitive tapes.

Indian-owned software companies like Infosys, with 350 programmers, have sprung up too and are performing work for General Electric, among others. Are Indian programmers any good? "They are less expensive, but that's not why we went there," says Albert

Hoser, president of Siemens's U.S. subsidiary, whose parent company uses them. "They do some of the best work in the world."

The potential for a further shift of programming to offshore sites is considerable. Software programming accounts for a third or more of the R&D budgets at many high-tech companies. Says Gall: "As designs and software get more complex, the cost advantage of India becomes greater. We've only scratched the surface of what could happen here."

In the face of what some see as a worldwide glut of skilled workers, a few nations actually experience a shortage of labor. But their drive to boost their own prosperity, by keeping good jobs at home and shipping lower-wage work to neighbors, has the effect of expanding the world labor supply. Japan, for example, uses neighboring countries as a place to offload messy and unpleasant work, such as painting and building construction, that it can afford to disdain.

Singapore is helping to make Asian labor markets more accessible to Western companies. That small country (pop.: 2.7 million) has done such a good job of attracting foreign investment that it began running out of semiskilled workers. AT&T decided to make telephones there in 1985. "The operation was successful beyond our wildest dreams," says Jeff Inselmann, vice president for AT&T's manufacturing in Singapore. Hundreds of other companies similarly set up plants in Singapore. The result: Managerial and technical skills flowed rapidly to the city-state, hastened by special tax breaks to companies that establish regional headquarters there.

But foreigners wouldn't keep expanding operations and assigning more complex and high-wage work to Singapore if the place ran out of factory workers. So the government recently persuaded Indonesia to turn a chain of that nation's islands 12 miles across the Strait of Malacca from Singapore into industrial parks. With a population of 181 million underemployed people crammed mostly on the island of Java, Indonesia was happy to cooperate. In less than two years, more than 40 companies, including AT&T, Thomson, and Sumitomo Electric Industries, have established factories in the new parks, chiefly on Batam Island, two-thirds the size of Singapore.

Batam is still mostly raw jungle, criss-crossed by roads carved out of the bright red earth and dotted with factories, dormitories, and radio towers. Labor shortage? AT&T set up its factories and recruited 700 workers from Java and Sumatra in eight months. Their pay is a third the cost of comparable labor in Singapore. Batam's population is expected to grow sixfold, to 700,000 by the end of the decade.

Which leaves Singapore free to do what it does very well: design and manage, often for American and European corporations, and help them make efficient use of local labor and talent. Hewlett-Packard's new portable inkjet printer business is run from Singapore—design, manufacture, and profit responsibility. Singaporeans designed and manufacture two popular pagers for Motorola—one accepts voice messages, the other is the size of a credit card. Originally meant for Asian markets, they have proved so popular that Motorola is beginning to ship them to the U.S.

Though the bulk of Motorola's research is still done in the U.S., the company is expanding the amount of R&D work performed in Southeast Asia. AT&T Bell Laboratories already has researchers there. Should American engineers be panicked that their jobs could go abroad? Says William Terry, executive vice president at Hewlett-Packard: "Panicked? No. America will always be an attractive market. People will want to buy things designed and made in the U.S. But worried? Yes."

What happens when these deep, heretofore inaccessible pools of labor and talent are plumbed by the rest of the industrialized world? That will depend in part on the pace of change. Will wealthy nations and companies have the time and the wits to adapt their skills and organizations to take advantage of the change, perhaps moving on to some new, higher form of economic activity? Will prosperity come fast enough to countries long denied it that workers won't riot in a revolution of rising expectations?

It's clear that there is something almost incomprehensibly vast going on—a realignment perhaps, as Percy Barnevik suggests, on the order of the end of the agricultural era in Western nations, when people moved off the land and into cities for factory work. Says Gemini's Anderson: "It's some sort of shift from the industrial age to an information age. But it's not that simple. People will still need cars and refrigerators, and people will have to make them. I'm not sure I know exactly what it is."

In the face of such change, whatever form it eventually takes, one should keep in mind a few emerging verities: More than ever before, work will flow to the places best equipped to perform it most economically and efficiently. For one thing, the speed and thoroughness of information delivery in the Nineties guarantee that managers will now *know* where work can best be done.

To try to restrict the flow of work in the name of saving jobs in this country or that is futile, certainly in the long run. Some nations may succeed at it for a short time, but the cost will be punishing dislocations. It would, for example, be ridiculous and dangerous for the U.S. to try to "stanch the flow of jobs to Mexico," as protectionists might describe it. True, open trade with Mexico will mean that some jobs in the U.S. may disappear, but they wouldn't have lasted long anyway, given the pressures of foreign competition. And with U.S. exports likely to go up substantially, many more jobs will be created—on both sides of the border.

As in the past, countries will do well economically if they concentrate on doing what they do best, pursuing policies that will enhance those industries and services in which they can add the most value. Their particular competence may change over time; consider the example of Singapore. But the prize will consistently go to those countries eager to embrace the new.

SECTION II

Globalization
of the Organization

As the external business environment evolves into a truly global network of corporations, organizations are responding with strategies and organizational structures that enable them to better meet the challenges of an increasingly competitive global marketplace. New strategies require new thought processes and sometimes even a transformation of corporate culture. Information technology will play a key role in this process as companies face the challenge of creating an infrastructure for coordination while at the same time recognizing local autonomy.

The readings in this section provide a broad background that encompasses many issues faced by organizations in their efforts to remain successful players in global markets. Organizations will be challenged to change and find new ways of doing business.

In the first paper, Porter describes the changing patterns of international competition and the resulting implications for corporations and their leaders. This work summarizes Porter's contributions in the area of global strategy and competitive advantage. Porter's well-established concept of value-chain activities provides a foundation from which to discuss the key dimensions of international strategy and a means by which to evaluate a firm's strategic posture.

In the two subsequent papers, Bartlett and Ghoshal provide some specific recommendations for corporations as they face the challenge of redefining corporate strategy and organizational structures to meet the new requirements of a borderless world. First, the authors argue that companies must now optimize efficiency, responsiveness, and learning simultaneously in their worldwide operations if they are to remain competitive. In order to achieve these objectives, new strategies and organizational changes are required. The authors suggest that the development of a transnational organization is the necessary means for coping with the increasing complexities of the international business environment.

In the final paper, Bartlett and Ghoshal describe the new managerial capability necessary to support the characteristics of the trans-national company. The authors argue that the true universal manager is not a global manager, but rather a network of specialists representing business, national, and functional perspectives that balance one another.

The papers in this section and Section I lay the groundwork for addressing more specific topics relevant to the role of information technology. How a firm's IT strategy supports its evolving corporate strategies is a key issue for future success. The next section focuses on these issues from the IT perspective.

Changing Patterns of
International Competition

MICHAEL E. PORTER

WHEN EXAMINING THE ENVIRONMENTAL CHANGES facing firms today, it is a rare observer who will conclude that international competition is not high on the list. The growing importance of international competition is well recognized both in the business and academic communities, for reasons that are fairly obvious when one looks at just about any data set that exists on international trade or investment. Exhibit 1, for example, compares world trade and world GNP. Something interesting started happening around the mid-1950s, when the growth in world trade began to significantly exceed the growth in world GNP. Foreign direct investment by firms in developing countries began to grow rapidly a few years later, about 1963.[1] This period marked the beginning of a fundamental change in the international competitive environment that by now has come to be widely recognized. It is a trend that is causing sleepless nights for many business managers.

There is a substantial literature on international competition, because the subject is far from a new one. A large body of literature has investigated the many implications of the Heckscher-Ohlin model and other models of international trade which are rooted in the principle of comparative advantage.[2] The unit of analysis in this literature is the country. There is also considerable literature on the multinational firm, reflecting the growing importance of the multinational since the turn of the century. In examining the reasons for the multinational, I think it is fair to characterize this literature as resting heavily on the multinational's ability to exploit intangible assets.[3] The work of Hymer and Caves among others has stressed the role of the multinational in transferring know-how and expertise gained in one country market to others at low cost, and thereby offsetting the unavoidable extra costs of doing business in a foreign country. A more recent stream of literature

This article grows out of the seventh lecture in a series of lectures on Strategy and Organization for Individual Innovation and Renewal, sponsored by the Transamerica Chair, School of Business Administration, University of California at Berkeley. March 15, 1985.

EXHIBIT 1   Growth of World Trade

Source: United Nations. *Statistical Yearbooks.*

extends this by emphasizing how the multinational firm internalizes transactions to circumvent imperfections in various intermediate markets, most importantly the market for knowledge.

There is also a related literature on the problems of entry into foreign markets and the life cycle of how a firm competes abroad, beginning with export or licensing and ultimately moving to the establishment of foreign subsidiaries. Vernon's product cycle of international trade combines a view of how products mature with the evolution in a firm's international activities to predict the patterns of trade and investment in developed and developing countries.[4] Finally, many of the functional fields in business administration research have their branch of literature about international issues—e.g., international marketing, international finance. This literature concentrates, by and large, on the problems of doing business in a foreign country.

As rich as it is, however, I think it is fair to characterize the literature on international competition as being limited when it comes to the choice of a firm's international strategy. Though the literature provides some guidance for considering incremental investment decisions to enter a new country, it provides at best a partial view of how to characterize a firm's overall international strategy and how such strategy should be selected. Put another way, the literature focuses more on the problem of becoming a multinational than on strategies for established multinationals. Although the distinction between domestic firms and multinationals is seminal in a literature focused on the problems of doing business abroad, the fact that a firm is multinational says little if anything about its international strategy except that it operates in several countries.

Broadly stated, my research has been seeking to answer the question: what does international competition mean for competitive strategy? In particular, what are the distinctive questions for competitive strategy that are raised by international as opposed to domestic competition? Many of the strategy issues for a company competing internationally are very much the same as for one competing domestically. A firm must still analyze its industry structure and competitors, understand its buyer and the sources of buyer value, diagnose its relative cost position, and seek to establish a sustainable competitive advantage within some competitive scope, whether it be across-the-board or in an industry segment. These are subjects I have written about extensively.[5] But there are some questions for strategy that are peculiar to international competition, and that add to rather than replace those listed earlier. These questions all revolve, in one way or another, around how a firm's activities in one country affect or are affected by what is going on in other countries—the connectedness among country competition. It is this connectedness that is the focus of this article and of a broader stream of research recently conducted under the auspices of the Harvard Business School.[6]

PATTERNS OF INTERNATIONAL COMPETITION

The appropriate unit of analysis in setting international strategy is the industry, because the industry is the arena in which competitive advantage is won or lost. The starting point for understanding international competition is the observation that its pattern differs markedly from industry to industry. At one end of the spectrum are industries that I call *multidomestic*, in which competition in each country (or small group of countries) is essentially independent of competition in other countries. A multidomestic industry is one that is present in many countries (e.g., there is a consumer banking industry in Sri Lanka, one in France, and one in the U.S.), but in which competition occurs on a country-by-country basis. In a multidomestic industry, a multinational firm may enjoy a competitive advantage from the one-time transfer of know-how from its home base to foreign countries. However, the firm modifies and adapts its intangible assets to employ them in each country and the outcome is determined by conditions in each country. The competitive advantages of the firm, then, are largely specific to each country. The international industry becomes a collection of essentially domestic industries—hence the term "multidomestic." Industries where competition has traditionally exhibited this pattern include retailing, consumer packaged goods, distribution, insurance, consumer finance, and caustic chemicals.

At the other end of the spectrum are what I term *global* industries. The term global—like the word "strategy"—has become overused and perhaps under-understood. The definition of a global industry employed here is an industry in which a firm's competitive position in one country is significantly influenced by its position in other countries.[7] Therefore, the international industry is not merely a collection of domestic industries but a series of linked domestic industries in which the rivals compete against each other on a truly worldwide basis. Industries exhibiting the global pattern today include commercial aircraft, TV sets, semiconductors, copiers, automobiles, and watches.

The implications for strategy of the distinction between multidomestic and global industries are quite profound. In a multidomestic industry, a firm can and should manage its international activities like a portfolio. Its subsidiaries or other operations around the world should each control all the important activities necessary to do business in the industry and should enjoy a high degree of autonomy. The firm's strategy in a country should be determined largely by the circumstances in that country; the firm's international strategy is then what I term a "country-centered strategy."

In a multidomestic industry, competing internationally is discretionary. A firm can choose to remain domestic or can expand internationally if it has some advantage that allows it to overcome the extra costs of entering and competing in foreign markets. The important competitors in multidomestic industries will either be domestic companies or multinationals with stand-alone operations abroad—this is the situation in each of the multidomestic industries listed earlier. In a multidomestic industry, then, international strategy collapses to a series of domestic strategies. The issues that are uniquely international revolve around how to do business abroad, how to select good countries in which to compete (or assess country risk), and mechanisms to achieve the one-time transfer of know-how. These are questions that are relatively well developed in the literature.

In a global industry, however, managing international activities like a portfolio will undermine the possibility of achieving competitive advantage. In a global industry, a firm must in some way integrate its activities on a worldwide basis to capture the linkages among countries. This will require more than transferring intangible assets among countries, though it will include it. A firm may choose to compete with a country-centered strategy, focusing on specific market segments or countries when it can carve out a niche by responding to whatever local country differences are present. However, it does so at some considerable risk from competitors with global strategies. All the important competitors in the global industries listed earlier compete worldwide with coordinated strategies.

In international competition, a firm always has to perform some functions in each of the countries in which it competes. Even though a global competitor must view its international activities as an overall system, it has still to maintain some country perspective. It is the balancing of these two perspectives that becomes one of the essential questions in global strategy.[8]

CAUSES OF GLOBALIZATION

If we accept the distinction between multidomestic and global industries as an important taxonomy of patterns of international competition, a number of crucial questions arise.

When does an industry globalize? What exactly do we mean by a global strategy, and is there more than one kind? What determines the type of international strategy to select in a particular industry?

An industry is global if there is some competitive advantage to integrating activities on a worldwide basis. To make this statement operational, however, we must be very precise about what we mean by "activities" and also what we mean by "integrating." To diagnose the sources of competitive advantage in any context, whether it be domestic or international, it is necessary to adopt a disaggregated view of the firm. In my newest book, *Competitive Advantage,* I have developed a framework for doing so, called the value chain.[9] Every firm is a collection of discrete activities performed to do business that occur within the scope of the firm—I call them value activities. The activities performed by a firm include such things as salespeople selling the product, service technicians performing repairs, scientists in the laboratory designing process techniques, and accountants keeping the books. Such activities are technologically and in most cases physically distinct. It is only at the level of discrete activities, rather than the firm as a whole, that competitive advantage can be truly understood.

A firm may possess two types of competitive advantage: low relative cost or differentiation—its ability to perform the activities in its value chain either at lower cost or in a unique way relative to its competitors. The ultimate value a firm creates is what buyers are willing to pay for what the firm provides, which includes the physical product as well as any ancillary services or benefits. Profit results if the value created through performing the required activities exceeds the collective cost of performing them. Competitive advantage is a function of either providing comparable buyer value to competitors but performing activities efficiently (low cost), or of performing activities at comparable cost but in unique ways that create greater buyer value than competitors and, hence, command a premium price (differentiation).

The value chain, shown in Figure 1, provides a systematic means of displaying and categorizing activities. The activities performed by a firm in any industry can be grouped into the nine generic categories shown. The labels may differ based on industry convention, but every firm performs these basic categories of activities in some way or another. Within each category of activities, a firm typically performs a number of discrete activities which are particular to the industry and to the firm's strategy. In service, for example, firms typically perform such discrete activities as installation, repair, parts distribution, and upgrading.

The generic categories of activities can be grouped into two broad types. Along the bottom are what I call *primary* activities, which are those involved in the physical creation of the product or service, its delivery and marketing to the buyer, and its support after sale. Across the top are what I call *support* activities, which provide inputs or infrastructure that allow the primary activities to take place on an ongoing basis.

Procurement is the obtaining of purchased inputs, whether they be raw materials, purchased services, machinery, or so on. Procurement stretches across the entire value

FIGURE 1   The Value Chain

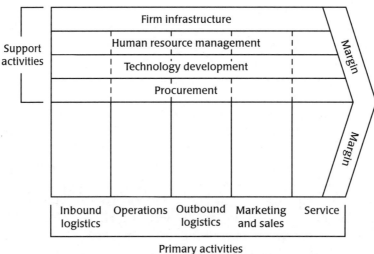

chain because it supports every activity—every activity uses purchased inputs of some kind. There are typically many different discrete procurement activities within a firm, often performed by different people. Technology development encompasses the activities involved in designing the product as well as in creating and improving the way the various activities in the value chain are performed. We tend to think of technology in terms of the product or manufacturing process. In fact, every activity a firm performs involves a technology or technologies which may be mundane or sophisticated, and a firm has a stock of know-how about how to perform each activity. Technology development typically involves a variety of different discrete activities, some performed outside the R&D department.

Human resource management is the recruiting, training, and development of personnel. Every activity involves human resources, and thus human resource management activities cut across the entire chain. Finally, firm infrastructure includes activities such as general management, accounting, legal finance, strategic planning, and all the other activities decoupled from specific primary or support activities but that are essential to enable the entire chain's operation.

Activities in a firm's value chain are not independent, but are connected through what I call linkages. The way one activity is performed frequently affects the cost or effectiveness of other activities. If more is spent on the purchase of a raw material, for example, a firm may lower its cost of fabrication or assembly. There are many linkages that connect activities, not only within the firm but also with the activities of its suppliers, channels, and ultimately its buyers. The firm's value chain resides in a larger stream of activities that I term the value system. Suppliers have value chains that provide the purchased inputs to the firm's chain; channels have value chains through which the firm's product or service passes; buyers have value chains in which the firm's product or service is employed. The connections among activities in this vertical system also become essential to competitive advantage.

A final important building block in value chain theory, necessary for our purposes here, is the notion of *competitive scope*. Competitive scope is the breadth of activities the firm employs together in competing in an industry. There are four basic dimensions of competitive scope:

- *segment* scope, or the range of segments the firm serves (e.g., product varieties, customer types);

- *industry* scope, or the range of industries the firm competes in with a coordinated strategy;

- *vertical* scope, or what activities are performed by the firm versus suppliers and channels; and

- *geographic* scope, or the geographic regions the firm operates in with a coordinated strategy.

Competitive scope is vital to competitive advantage because it shapes the configuration of the value chain, how activities are performed, and whether activities are shared among units. International strategy is an issue of geographic scope, and can be analyzed quite similarly to the question of whether and how a firm should compete locally, regionally, or nationally within a country. In the international context, government tends to have a greater involvement in competition and there are more significant variations among geographic regions in buyer needs, although these differences are matters of degree.

International Configuration and Coordination of Activities

A firm that competes internationally must decide how to spread the activities in the value chain among countries. A distinction immediately arises between the activities labeled downstream on Figure 2, and those labeled upstream activities and support activities. The location of downstream activities, those more related to the buyer, is usually tied to where the buyer is located. If a firm is going to sell in Japan, for example, it usually must provide service in Japan and it must have salespeople stationed in Japan. In some industries it is possible to have a single sales force that travels to the buyer's country and back again; some other specific downstream activities such as the production of advertising copy can also sometimes be done centrally. More typically, however, the firm must locate the capability to perform downstream activities in each of the countries in which it operates. Upstream activities and support activities, conversely, can at least conceptually be decoupled from where the buyer is located.

FIGURE 2   Upstream and Downstream Activities

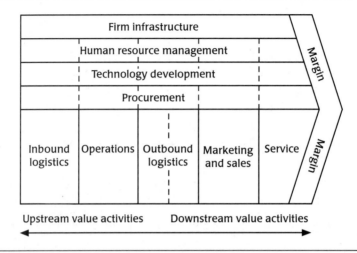

This distinction carries some interesting implications. The first is that downstream activities create competitive advantages that are largely country-specific: a firm's reputation, brand name, and service network in a country grow out of a firm's activities in that country and create entry/mobility barriers largely in that country alone. Competitive advantage in upstream and support activities often grows more out of the entire system of countries in which a firm competes than from its position in any one country, however.

A second implication is that in industries where downstream activities or buyer-tied activities are vital to competitive advantage, there tends to be a more multidomestic pattern of international competition. In industries where upstream and support activities (such as technology development and operations) are crucial to competitive advantage, global competition is more common. In global competition, the location and scale of these potentially footloose activities is optimized from a worldwide perspective.[10]

The distinctive issues in international, as contrasted to domestic, strategy can be summarized in two key dimensions of how a firm competes internationally. The first is what I term the *configuration* of a firm's activities worldwide, or where in the world each activity in the value chain is performed, including in how many places. The second dimension is what I term *coordination*, which refers to how like activities performed in different countries are coordinated with each other. If, for example, there are three plants—one in Germany, one in Japan, and one in the U.S.—how do the activities in those plants relate to each other?

A firm faces an array of options in both configuration and coordination for each activity. Configuration options range from concentrated (performing an activity in one location and serving the world from it—e.g., one R&D lab, one large plant) to dispersed (performing every activity in each country). In the latter case, each country would have

FIGURE 3   Configuration and Coordination Issues by Category of Activity

Value Activity	Configuration Issues	Coordination Issues
Operations	Location of production facilities for components and end products	Networking of international plants Transferring process technology and production know-how among plants
Marketing and sales	Product line selection Country (market selection)	Commonality of brand name worldwide Coordination of sales to multi-national accounts Similarity of channels and product positioning worldwide Coordination of pricing in different countries
Service	Location of service organization	Similarity of organization service standards and procedures worldwide
Technology development	Number and location of R&D centers	Interchange among dispersed R&D centers Developing products responsive to market needs in many countries Sequence of product introductions around the world
Procurement	Location of the purchasing function	Managing suppliers located in different countries Transferring market knowledge Coordinating purchases of common items

a complete value chain. Coordination options range from none to very high. For example, if a firm produces its product in three plants, it could, at one extreme, allow each plant to operate with full autonomy—e.g., different product standards and features, different steps in the production process, different raw materials, different part numbers. At the other extreme, the plants could be tightly coordinated by employing the same information system, the same production process, the same parts, and so forth. Options for coordination in an activity are typically more numerous than the configuration options because there are many possible levels of coordination and many different facets of the way the activity is performed.

Figure 3 lists some of the configuration issues and coordination issues for several important categories of value activities. In technology development, for example, the configuration issue is where R&D is performed: one location? two locations? and in what countries? The coordination issues have to do with such things as the extent of interchange among R&D centers and the location and sequence of product introduction around the world. There are configuration issues and coordination issues for every activity.

FIGURE 4   The Dimensions of International Strategy

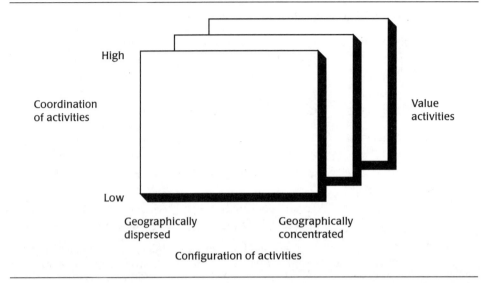

Figure 4 is a way of summarizing these basic choices in international strategy on a single diagram, with coordination of activities on the vertical axis and configuration of activities on the horizontal axis. The firm has to make a set of choices for each activity. If a firm employs a very dispersed configuration—placing an entire value chain in every country (or small group of contiguous countries) in which it operates, coordinating little or not at all among them—then the firm is competing with a country-centered strategy. The domestic firm that only operates in one country is the extreme case of a firm with a country-centered strategy. As we move from the lower left-hand corner of the diagram up or to the right, we have strategies that are increasingly global

Figure 5 illustrates some of the possible variations in international strategy. The purest global strategy is to concentrate as many activities as possible in one country, serve the world from this home base, and tightly coordinate those activities that must inherently be performed near the buyer. This is the pattern adopted by many Japanese firms in the 1960s and 1970s, such as Toyota. However, Figures 4 and 5 make it clear that there is no such thing as one global strategy. There are many different kinds of global strategies, depending on a firm's choices about configuration and coordination throughout the value chain. In copiers, for example, Xerox has until recently concentrated R&D in the U.S. but dispersed other activities, in some cases using joint-venture partners to perform them. On dispersed activities, however, coordination has been quite high. The Xerox brand, marketing approach, and servicing procedures have been quite standardized worldwide. Canon, on the other hand, has had a much more concentrated configuration of activities and

FIGURE 5   Types of International Strategy

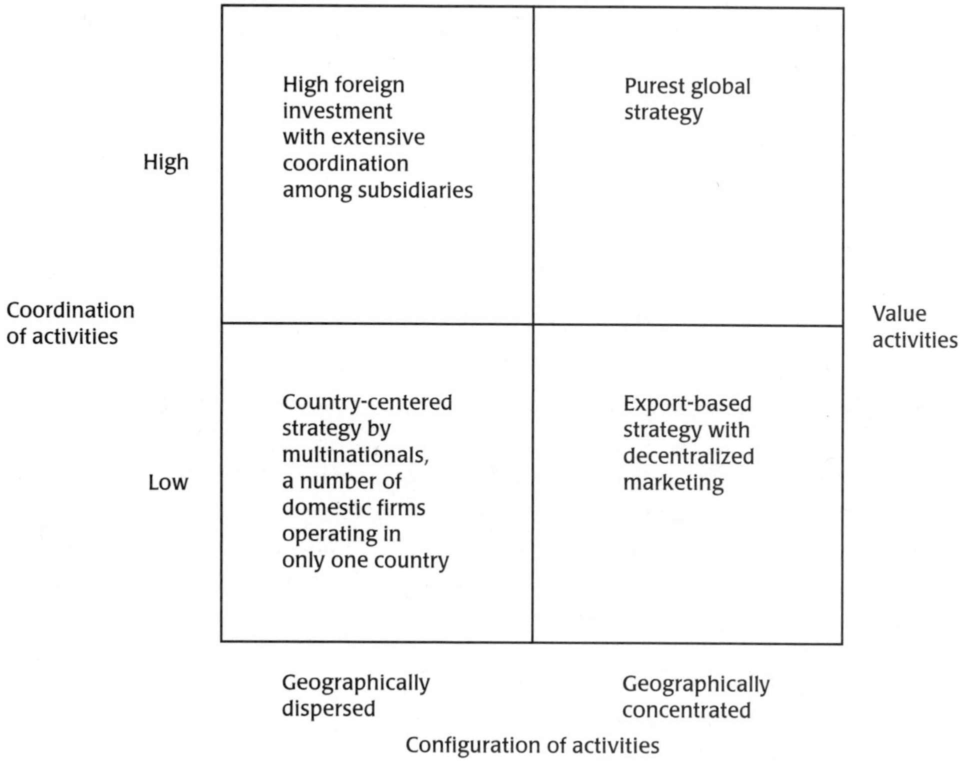

	Geographically dispersed	Geographically concentrated
High	High foreign investment with extensive coordination among subsidiaries	Purest global strategy
Low	Country-centered strategy by multinationals, a number of domestic firms operating in only one country	Export-based strategy with decentralized marketing

Coordination of activities

Value activities

Configuration of activities

somewhat less coordination of dispersed activities. The vast majority of support activities and manufacturing of copiers have been performed in Japan. Aside from using the Canon brand, however, local marketing subsidiaries have been given quite a bit of latitude in each region of the world.

A global strategy can now be defined more precisely as one in which a firm seeks to gain competitive advantage from its international presence through either concentrating configuration, coordination among dispersed activities, or both. Measuring the presence of a global industry empirically must reflect both dimensions and not just one. Market presence in many countries and some export and import of components and end products are characteristic of most global industries. High levels of foreign investment or the mere presence of multinational firms are not reliable measures, however, because firms may be managing foreign units like a portfolio.

Configuration/Coordination and Competitive Advantage

Understanding the competitive advantages of a global strategy and, in turn, the causes of industry globalization requires specifying the conditions in which concentrating activities globally and coordinating dispersed activities leads to either cost advantage or differentiation. In each case, there are structural characteristics of an industry that work for and against globalization.

The factors that favor concentrating an activity in one or a few locations to serve the world are as follows:

- economies of scale in the activity;

- a proprietary learning curve in the activity;

- comparative advantage in where the activity is performed; and

- coordination advantages of co-locating linked activities such as R&D and production.

The first two factors relate to *how many* sites an activity is performed at, while the last two relate to *where* these sites are. Comparative advantage can apply to any activity, not just production. For example, there may be some locations in the world that are better places than others to do research on medical technology or to perform software development. Government can promote the concentration of activities by providing subsidies or other incentives to use a particular country as an export base, in effect altering comparative advantage—a role many governments are playing today.

There are also structural characteristics that favor dispersion of an activity to many countries, which represent concentration costs. Local product needs may differ, nullifying the advantages of scale or learning from one-site operation of an activity. Locating a range of activities in a country may facilitate marketing in that country by signaling commitment to local buyers and/or providing greater responsiveness. Transport, communication, and storage costs may make it inefficient to concentrate the activity in one location. Government is also frequently a powerful force for dispersing activities. Governments typically want firms to locate the entire value chain in their country, because this creates benefits and spillovers to the country that often go beyond local content. Dispersion is also encouraged by the risks of performing an activity in one place: exchange-rate risks, political risks, and so on. The balance between the advantages of concentrating and dispersing an activity normally differ for each activity (and industry). The best configuration for R&D is different from that for component fabrication, and this is different from that for assembly, installation, advertising, and procurement.[11]

The desirability of coordinating like activities that are dispersed involves a similar balance of structural factors. Coordination potentially allows the sharing of know-how among dispersed activities. If a firm learns how to operate the production process better in Germany, transferring that learning may make the process run better in plants in the United States and Japan. Differing countries, with their inevitably differing conditions, provide a fertile basis for comparison as well as opportunities for arbitraging knowledge, obtained in different places about different aspects of the business. Coordination among dispersed activities also potentially improves the ability to reap economies of scale in activities if subtasks are allocated among locations to allow some specialization—e.g., each R&D center has a different area of focus. While there is a fine line between such forms of coordination and what I have termed configuration, it does illustrate how the way a network of foreign locations is managed can have a great influence on the ability to reap the benefits of any given configuration of activities. Viewed another way, close coordination is frequently a partial offset to dispersing an activity.

Coordination may also allow a firm to respond to shifting comparative advantage, where shifts in exchange rates and factor costs are hard to forecast. Incrementally increasing the production volume at the location currently enjoying favorable exchange rates, for example, can lower overall costs. Coordination can reinforce a firm's brand reputation with buyers (and hence lead to differentiation) through ensuring a consistent image and approach to doing business on a worldwide basis. This is particularly likely if buyers are mobile or information about the industry flows freely around the world. Coordination may also differentiate the firm with multinational buyers if it allows the firm to serve them anywhere and in a consistent way. Coordination (and a global approach to configuration) enhances leverage with local governments if the firm is able to grow or shrink activities in one country at the expense of others. Finally, coordination yields flexibility in responding to competitors, by allowing the firm to differentially respond across countries and to respond in one country to a challenge in another.

Coordination of dispersed activities usually involves costs that differ by form of coordination and industry. Local conditions may vary in ways that may make a common approach across countries suboptimal. If every plant in the world is required to use the same raw material, for example, the firm pays a penalty in countries where the raw material is expensive relative to satisfactory substitutes. Business practices, marketing systems, raw material sources, local infrastructures, and a variety of other factors may differ across countries as well, often in ways that may mitigate the advantages of a common approach or of the sharing of learning. Governments may restrain the flow of information required for coordination or may impose other barriers to it. The transaction costs of coordination, which have recently received increased attention in domestic competition, are vitally important in international strategy.[12] International coordination involves long distances, language problems, and cultural barriers to communication. In some industries, these factors may mean that coordination is not optimal. They also suggest that forms of coordination which involve relatively infrequent decisions will enjoy advantages over forms of coordination involving on-going interchange.

There are also substantial organizational difficulties involved in achieving cooperation among subsidiaries, which are due to the difficulty in aligning subsidiary managers' interests with those of the firm as a whole. The Germans do not necessarily want to tell the Americans about their latest breakthroughs on the production line because it may make it harder for them to outdo the Americans in the annual comparison of operating efficiency among plants. These vexing organizational problems mean that country subsidiaries often view each other more as competitors than collaborators.[13] As with configuration, a firm must make an activity-by-activity choice about where there is net competitive advantage from coordinating in various ways.

Coordination in some activities may be necessary to reap the advantages of configuration in others. The use of common raw materials in each plant, for example, allows worldwide purchasing. Moreover, tailoring some activities to countries may allow concentration and standardization of other activities. For example, tailored marketing in each country may allow the same product to be positioned differently and hence sold successfully in many countries, unlocking possibilities for reaping economies of scale in production and R&D. Thus coordination and configuration interact.

Configuration/Coordination and the Pattern of International Competition

When benefits of configuring and/or coordinating globally exceed the costs, an industry will globalize in a way that reflects the net benefits by value activity. The activities in which global competitors gain competitive advantage will differ correspondingly. Configuration/ coordination determines the ongoing competitive advantages of a global strategy which are additive to competitive advantages a firm derives/possesses from its domestic market positions. An initial transfer of knowledge from the home base to subsidiaries is one, but by no means the most important, advantage of a global competitor.[14]

An industry such as commercial aircraft represents an extreme case of a global industry (in the upper right-hand corner of Figure 4). The three major competitors in this industry— Boeing, McDonnell Douglas, and Airbus—all have global strategies. In activities important to cost and differentiation in the industry, there are compelling net advantages to concentrating most activities and coordinating the dispersed activities extensively.[15] In R&D, there is a large fixed cost of developing an aircraft model ($1 billion or more) which requires worldwide sales to amortize. There are significant economies of scale in production, a steep learning curve in assembly (the learning curve was born out of research in this industry), and apparently significant advantages of locating R&D and production together. Sales of commercial aircraft are infrequent (via a highly skilled sales force), so that even the sales force can be partially concentrated in the home country and travel to buyers.

The costs of a concentrated configuration are relatively low in commercial aircraft. Product needs are homogenous, and there are the low transport costs of delivering the product to the buyer. Finally, worldwide coordination of the one dispersed activity, service, is very important—obviously standardized parts and repair advice have to be available wherever the plane lands.

As in every industry, there are structural features which work against a global strategy in commercial aircraft. These are all related to government, a not atypical circumstance. Government has a particular interest in commercial aircraft because of its large trade potential, the technological sophistication of the industry, its spillover effects to other industries, and its implications for national defense. Government also has an unusual degree of leverage in the industry: in many instances, it is the buyer. Many airlines are government owned, and a government official or appointee is head of the airline.

The competitive advantages of a global strategy are so great that all the successful aircraft producers have sought to achieve and preserve them. In addition, the power of government to intervene has been mitigated by the fact the there are few viable worldwide competitors and that there are the enormous barriers to entry created in part by the advantages of a global strategy. The result has been that firms have sought to assuage government through procurement. Boeing, for example, is very careful about where it buys components. In countries that are large potential customers, Boeing seeks to develop suppliers. This requires a great deal of extra effort by Boeing both to transfer technology and to work with suppliers to assure that they meet its standards. Boeing realizes that this is preferable to compromising the competitive advantage of its strongly integrated worldwide strategy. It is willing to employ one value activity (procurement) where the advantages of concentration are modest to help preserve the benefits of concentration in other activities. Recently, commercial aircraft competitors have entered into joint ventures and other coalition arrangements with foreign suppliers to achieve the same effect, as well as to spread the risk of huge development costs.

The extent and location of advantages from a global strategy vary among industries. In some industries, the competitive advantage from a global strategy comes in technology development, although firms gain little advantage in the primary activities so that these are dispersed around the world to minimize concentration costs. In other industries such as cameras or videocassette recorders, a firm cannot succeed without concentrating production to achieve economies of scale, but instead it gives subsidiaries much local autonomy in sales and marketing. In some industries, there is no net advantage to a global strategy and country-centered strategies dominate—the industry is multidomestic.

Segments or stages of an industry frequently vary in their pattern of globalization. In aluminum, the upstream (alumina and ingot) stages of the industry are global businesses. The downstream stage, semifabrication, is a group of multidomestic businesses because product needs vary by country, transport costs are high and intensive local customer service is required. Scale economies in the value chain are modest. In lubricants, automotive oil tends to be a country-centered business while marine motor oil is a global business. In automotive oil, countries have varying driving standards, weather conditions, and local laws. Production involves blending various kinds of crude oils and additives, and is subject to few economies of scale but high shipping costs. Country-centered competitors such as Castrol and Quaker State are leaders in most countries. In the marine segment, conversely, ships move freely around the world and require the same oil everywhere. Successful competitors are global.

The ultimate leaders in global industries are often first movers—the first firm to perceive the possibilities for a global strategy. Boeing was the first global competitor in aircraft, for example, as was Honda in motorcycles, and Becton Dickinson in disposable syringes. First movers gain scale and learning advantages which are difficult to overcome. First mover effects are particularly important in global industries because of the association between globalization and economies of scale and learning achieved through worldwide configuration/coordination. Global leadership shifts if industry structural change provides opportunities for leapfrogging to new products or new technologies that nullify past leaders' scale and learning—again, the first mover to the new generation/technology often wins.

Global leaders often begin with some advantage at home, whether it be low labor cost or a product or marketing advantage. They use this as a lever to enter foreign markets. Once there, however, the global competitor converts the initial home advantage into competitive advantages that grow out of its overall worldwide system, such as production scale or ability to amortize R&D costs. While the initial advantage may have been hard to sustain, the global strategy creates new advantages which can be much more durable.

International strategy has often been characterized as a choice between worldwide standardization and local tailoring, or as the tension between the economic imperative (large-scale efficient facilities) and the political imperative (local content, local production). It should be clear from the discussion so far that neither characterization captures the richness of a firm's international strategy choices. A firm's choice of international strategy involves a search for competitive advantage from configuration/coordination throughout the value chain. A firm may standardize (concentrate) some activities and tailor (disperse) others. It may also be able to standardize and tailor at the same time through the coordination of dispersed activities, or use local tailoring of some activities (e.g., different product positioning in each country) to allow standardization of others (e.g., production). Similarly, the economic imperative is not always for a global strategy—in some industries a country-centered strategy is the economic imperative. Conversely, the political imperative is to concentrate activities in some industries where governments provide strong export incentives and locational subsidies.

Global Strategy vs. Comparative Advantage

Given the importance of trade theory to the study of international competition, it is useful to pause and reflect on the relationship to the framework I have presented to the notion of comparative advantage. Is there a difference? The traditional concept of comparative advantage is that factor-cost or factor-quality differences among countries lead to production of products in countries with an advantage which export them elsewhere in the world. Competitive advantage in this view, then, grows out of *where* a firm performs activities. The location of activities is clearly one source of potential advantage in a global firm. The global competitor can locate activities wherever comparative advantage lies, decoupling comparative advantage from its home base or country of ownership.

Indeed, the framework presented here suggests that the comparative advantage story is richer than typically told, because it not only involves production activities (the usual focus of discussions) but also applies to other activities in the value chain such as R&D, processing orders, or designing advertisements. Comparative advantage is specific to the *activity* and not the location of the value chain as a whole.[16] One of the potent advantages of the global firm is that it can spread activities among locations to reflect different preferred locations for different activities, something a domestic or country-centered competitor does not do. Thus components can be made in Taiwan, software written in India and basic R&D performed in Silicon Valley, for example. This international specialization of activities within the firm is made possible by the growing ability to coordinate and configure globally.

At the same time as our framework suggests a richer view of comparative advantage, however, it also suggests that many forms of competitive advantage for the global competitor derive less from *where* the firm performs activities than from *how* it performs them on a worldwide basis; economies of scale, proprietary learning, and differentiation with multinational buyers are not tied to countries but to the configuration and coordination of the firm's worldwide system. Traditional sources of comparative advantage can be very elusive and slippery sources of competitive advantage for an international competitor today, because comparative advantage frequently shifts. A country with the lowest labor cost is overtaken within a few years by some other country—facilities located in the first country then face a disadvantage. Moreover, falling direct labor as a percentage of total costs, increasing global markets for raw materials and other inputs, and freer flowing technology have diminished the role of traditional sources of comparative advantage.

My research on a broad cross-section of industries suggests that the achievement of sustainable world market leadership follows a more complex pattern than the exploitation of comparative advantage per se. A competitor often starts with a comparative advantage-related edge that provides the basis for penetrating foreign markets, but this edge is rapidly translated into a broader array of advantages that arise from a global approach to configuration and coordination as described earlier. Japanese firms, for example, have done a masterful job of converting temporary labor-cost advantages into durable systemwide advantages due to scale and proprietary know-how. Ultimately, the systemwide advantages are further reinforced with country-specific advantages such as brand identity as well as distribution channel access. Many Japanese firms were fortunate enough to make their transitions from country-based comparative advantage to global competitive advantage at a time when nobody paid much attention to them and there was a buoyant world economy. European and American competitors were willing to cede market share in "less desirable" segments such as the low end of the producer line, or so they thought. The Japanese translated these beachheads into world leadership by broadening their lines and reaping advantages in scale and proprietary technology. The Koreans and Taiwanese, the latest low labor cost entrants to a number of industries, may have a hard time replicating Japan's success, given slower growth, standardized products, and now alert competitors.

Global Platforms

The interaction of the home-country conditions and competitive advantages from a global strategy that transcend the country suggest a more complex role of the country in firm success than implied by the theory of comparative advantage. To understand this more complex role of the country, I define the concept of a *global platform*. A country is a desirable global platform in an industry if it provides an environment yielding firms domiciled in that country an advantage in competing globally in that particular industry.[17] An essential element of this definition is that it hinges on success *outside* the country, and not merely country conditions which allow firms to successfully master domestic competition. In global competition, a country must be viewed as a platform and not as the place where all a firm's activities are performed.

There are two determinants of a good global platform in an industry, which I have explored in more detail elsewhere.[18] The first is comparative advantage, or the factor endowment of the country as a site to perform particular activities in the industry. Today, simple factors such as low-cost unskilled labor and natural resources are increasingly less important to global competition compared to complex factors such as skilled scientific and technical personnel and advanced infrastructure. Direct labor is a minor proportion of cost in many manufactured goods and automation of non-production activities is shrinking it further, while markets for resources are increasingly global and technology has widened the number of sources of many resources. A country's factor endowment is partly exogenous and partly the result of attention and investment in the country.

The second determinant of the attractiveness of a country as a global platform in an industry are the characteristics of a country's demand. A country's demand conditions include the size and timing of its demand in an industry, factors recognized as important by authors such as Linder and Vernon.[19] They also include the sophistication and power of buyers and channels and the product features and attributes demanded. Local demand conditions provide two potentially powerful sources of competitive advantage to a global competitor based in that country. The first is *first-mover advantages* in perceiving and implementing the appropriate global strategy. Pressing local needs, particularly peculiar ones, lead firms to embark early to solve local problems and gain proprietary know-how. This is then translated into scale and learning advantages as firms move early to compete globally. The other potential benefit of local demand conditions is a baseload of demand for product varieties that will be sought after in international markets. These two roles of the country in the success of a global firm reflect the interaction between conditions of local supply, the composition and timing of country demand, and economies of scale and learning in shaping international success.

The two determinants interact in important and sometimes counterintuitive ways. Local demand and needs frequently influence private and social investment in endogenous factors of production. A nation with oceans as borders and dependence on sea trade, for example, is more prone to have universities and scientific centers dedicated to oceanographic education and research. Similarly, factor endowment seems to influence local demand. The per capita consumption of wine is highest in wine-growing regions, for example.

Comparative disadvantage in some factors of production can be an advantage in global competition when combined with pressing local demand. Poor growing conditions have led Israeli farmers to innovate in irrigation and cultivation techniques, for example. The shrinking role in competition of simple factors of production relative to complex factors such as technical personnel seem to be enhancing the frequency and importance of such circumstances. What is important today is unleashing innovation in the proper direction, instead of passive exploitation of static cost advantages in a country which can shift rapidly and be overcome. International success today is a dynamic process resulting from continued development of products and processes. The forces which guide firms to undertake such activity thus become central to international competition.

A good example of the interplay among these factors is the television set industry. In the U.S., early demand was in large screen console sets because television sets were initially luxury items kept in the living room. As buyers began to purchase second and third sets, sets became smaller and more portable. They were used increasingly in the bedroom, the kitchen, the car, and elsewhere. As the television set industry matured, table model and portable sets became the universal product variety. Japanese firms, because of the small size of Japanese homes, cut their teeth on small sets. They dedicated most of their R&D to developing small picture tubes and to making sets more compact. In the process of naturally serving the needs of their home market, then, Japanese firms gained early experience and scale in segments of the industry that came to dominate world demand. U.S. firms, conversely, cut their teeth on large-screen console sets with fine furniture cabinets. As the industry matured, the experience base of U.S. firms was in a segment that was small and isolated to a few countries, notably the U.S. Japanese firms were able to penetrate world markets in a segment that was both uninteresting to foreign firms and in which they had initial scale, learning, and labor cost advantages. Ultimately the low-cost advantage disappeared as production was automated, but global scale and learning economies took over as the Japanese advanced product and process technology at a rapid pace.

The two broad-determinants of a good global platform rest on the interaction between country characteristics and firms' strategies. The literature on comparative advantage, through focusing on country factor endowments, ignoring the demand side, and suppressing the individual firm is most appropriate in industries where there are few economies of scale, little proprietary technology or technological change, or few possibilities for product differentiation.[20] While these industry characteristics are those of many traditionally traded goods, they describe few of today's important global industries.

THE EVOLUTION OF INTERNATIONAL COMPETITION

Having established a framework for understanding the globalization of industries, we are now in a position to view the phenomenon in historical perspective. If one goes back far enough, relatively few industries were global. Around 1880, most industries were local or regional in scope.[21] The reasons are rather self-evident in the context of our framework. There were few economies of scale in production until fuel-powered machines and assembly-line techniques emerged. There were heterogeneous product needs among regions within countries, much less among countries. There were few if any national media—the *Saturday Evening Post* was the first important national magazine in the U.S. and developed in the teens and twenties. Communicating between regions was difficult before the telegraph and telephone, and transportation was slow until the railroad system became well developed.

These structural conditions created little impetus for the widespread globalization of industry. Those industries that were global reflected classic comparative advantage considerations—goods were simply unavailable in some countries (who then imported them from others) or differences in the availability of land, resources, or skilled labor made some countries desirable suppliers to others. Export of local production was the form of global strategy adapted. There was little role or need for widespread government barriers to international trade during this period, although trade barriers were quite high in some countries for some commodities.

Around the 1880s, however, were the beginnings of what today has blossomed into the globalization of many industries. The first wave of modern global competitors grew up in the late 1800s and early 1900s. Many industries went from local (or regional) to national in scope, and some began globalizing. Firms such as Ford, Singer, Gillette, National Cash Register, Otis, and Western Electric had commanding world market shares by the teens, and operated with integrated worldwide strategies. Early global competitors were principally American and European companies.

During this first wave of modern globalization were rising production scale economies due to advancements in technology that outpaced the growth of the world economy. Product needs also became more homogenized in different countries as knowledge and industrialization diffused. Transport improved, first through the railroad and steamships and later in trucking. Communication became easier with the telegraph, then the telephone. At the same time, trade barriers were either modest or overwhelmed by the advantages of the new large-scale firms.

The burst of globalization soon slowed, however. Most of the few industries that were global moved increasingly towards a multidomestic pattern—multinationals remained, but between the 1920s and 1950 they often evolved towards federations of autonomous subsidiaries. The principal reason was a strong wave of nationalism and resulting high tariff barriers, partly caused by the world economic crisis and world wars. Another barrier to global strategies, chronicled by Chandler,[22] was a growing web of cartels and other interfirm contractual agreements. These limited the geographic spread of firms.

The early global competitors began rapidly dispersing their value chains. The situation of Ford Motor Company was no exception. While in 1925 Ford had almost no production outside the U.S., by World War II its overseas production had risen sharply. Firms that became multinationals during the interwar period tended to adopt country-centered strategies. European multinationals, operating in a setting where there were many sovereign countries within a relatively small geographical area, were quick to establish self-contained and quite autonomous subsidiaries in many countries. A more tolerant regulatory environment also encouraged European firms to form cartels and other cooperative agreements among themselves, which limited their foreign market entry.

Between the 1950s and the late 1970s, however, there was a strong reversal of the interwar trends. As Exhibit 1 illustrated, there have been very strong underlying forces driving the globalization of industries. The important reasons can be understood using the configuration/coordination dichotomy. The competitive advantage of competing world-wide from concentrated activities rose sharply, while concentration costs fell. There was a renewed rise in scale economies in many activities due to advancing technology. The minimum efficient scale of an auto assembly plant more than tripled between 1960 and 1975, for example, while the average cost of developing a new drug more than quadrupled.[23] The pace of technological change has increased, creating more incentive to amortize R&D costs against worldwide sales.

Product needs have continued to homogenize among countries, as income differences have narrowed, information and communication has flowed more freely around the world, and travel has increased.[24] Growing similarities in business practices and marketing systems (e.g., chain stores) in different countries have also been a facilitating factor in homogenizing needs. Within countries there has been a parallel trend towards greater market segmentation, which some observers see as contradictory to the view that product needs in different countries are becoming similar. However, segments today seem based less on country differences and more on buyer differences that transcend country boundaries, such as demographic, user industry, or income groups. Many firms successfully employ global focus strategies in which they serve a narrow segment of an industry worldwide, as do Daimler-Benz and Rolex.

Another driver of post-World War II globalization has been a sharp reduction in the real costs of transportation. This has occurred through innovations in transportation technology including increasingly large bulk carriers, container ships, and larger, more efficient aircraft. At the same time, government impediments to global configuration/coordination have been falling in the postwar period. Tariff barriers have gone down, international cartels and patent-sharing agreements have disappeared, and regional economic pacts such as the European Community have emerged to facilitate trade and investment, albeit imperfectly.

The ability to coordinate globally has also risen markedly in the postwar period. Perhaps the most striking reason is falling communication costs (in voice and data) and reduced travel time for individuals. The ability to coordinate activities in different countries has also been facilitated by growing similarities among countries in marketing systems, business practices, and infrastructure—country after country has developed supermarkets and mass distributors, television advertising, and so on. Greater international mobility of buyers and information has raised the payout to coordinating how a firm does business around the world. The increasing number of firms who are multinational has created growing possibilities for differentiation by suppliers who are global.

The forces underlying globalization have been self-reinforcing. The globalization of firms' strategies has contributed to the homogenization of buyer needs and business practices. Early global competitors must frequently stimulate the demand for uniform global varieties; for example, as Becton Dickinson did in disposable syringes and Honda did in motorcycles. Similarly, globalization of industries begets globalization of supplier industries—the increasing globalization of automotive component suppliers is a good example. Pioneering global competitors also stimulate the development and growth of international telecommunication infrastructure as well as the creation of global advertising media—e.g., *The Economist* and *The Wall Street Journal*.

STRATEGIC IMPLICATIONS OF GLOBALIZATION

When the pattern of international competition shifts from multidomestic to global, there are many implications for the strategy of international firms. While a full treatment is beyond the scope of this paper, I will sketch some of the implications here.[25]

At the broadest level, globalization casts new light on many issues that have long been of interest to students of international business. In areas such as international finance, marketing, and business-government relations, the emphasis in the literature has been on the unique problems of adapting to local conditions and ways of doing business in a foreign country in a foreign currency. In a global industry, these concerns must be supplemented with an overriding focus on the ways and means of international configuration and coordination. In government relations, for example, the focus must shift from stand-alone negotiations with host countries (appropriate in multidomestic competition) to a recognition that negotiations in one country will both affect other countries and be shaped by possibilities for performing activities in other countries. In finance, measuring the performance of subsidiaries must be modified to reflect the contribution of one subsidiary to another's cost position or differentiation in a global strategy, instead of viewing each subsidiary as a stand-alone unit. In battling with global competitors, it may be appropriate in some countries to accept low profits indefinitely—in multidomestic competition this would be unjustified.[26] In global industries, the overall system matters as much or more than the country.

Of the many other implications of globalization for the firm, there are two of such significance that they deserve some treatment here. The first is the role of *coalitions* in global strategy. A coalition is a long-term agreement linking firms but falling short of merger. I use the term coalition to encompass a whole variety of arrangements that include joint ventures, licenses, supply agreements, and many other kinds of interfirm relationships. Such interfirm agreements have been receiving more attention in the academic literature, although each form of agreement has been looked at separately and the focus has been largely domestic.[27] International coalitions, linking firms in the same industry based in different countries, have become an even more important part of international strategy in the past decade.

International coalitions are a way of configuring activities in the value chain on a worldwide basis jointly with a partner. International coalitions are proliferating rapidly and are present in many industries.[28] There is a particularly high incidence in automobiles, aircraft, aircraft engines, robotics, consumer electronics, semiconductors and pharmaceuticals. While international coalitions have long been present, their character has been changing. Historically, a firm from a developed country formed a coalition with a firm in a lesser-developed country to perform marketing activities in that country. Today, we observe more and more coalitions in which two firms from developed countries are teaming up to serve the world, as well as coalitions that extend beyond marketing activities to encompass activities throughout the value chain.[29] Production and R&D coalitions are very common, for example.

Coalitions are a natural consequence of globalization and the need for an integrated worldwide strategy. The same forces that lead to globalization will prompt the formation of coalitions as firms confront the barriers to establishing a global strategy of their own. The difficulties of gaining access to foreign markets and in surmounting scale and learning thresholds in production, technology development, and other activities have led many firms to team up with others. In many industries, coalitions can be a transitional state in the adjustment of firms to globalization, reflecting the need of firms to catch up in technology, cure short-term imbalances between their global production networks and exchange rates, and accelerate the process of foreign market entry. Many coalitions are likely to persist in some form, however.

There are benefits and costs of coalitions as well as difficult implementation problems in making them succeed (which I have discussed elsewhere). How to choose and manage coalitions is among the most interesting questions in international strategy today. When one speaks to managers about coalitions, almost all have tales of disaster which vividly illustrate that coalitions often do not succeed. Also, there is the added burden of coordinating global strategy with a coalition partner because the partner often wants to do things its own way. Yet, in the face of copious corporate experience that coalitions do not work and a growing economics literature on transaction costs and contractual failures, we see a proliferation of coalitions today of the most difficult kind—those between companies in different countries.[30] There is a great need for researching in both the academic community and in the corporate world about coalitions and how to manage them. They are increasingly being forced on firms today by new competitive circumstances.

A second area where globalization carries particular importance is in *organizational structure*. The need to configure and coordinate globally in complex ways creates some obvious organizational challenges.[31] Any organization structure for competing internationally has to balance two dimensions; there has to be a *country* dimension (because some activities are inherently performed in the country) and there has to be a *global* dimension (because the advantages of global configuration/coordination must be achieved). In a global industry, the ultimate authority must represent the global dimension if a global strategy is to prevail. However, within any international firm, once it disperses any activities there are tremendous pressures to disperse more. Moreover, forces are unleashed which lead subsidiaries to seek growing autonomy. Local country managers will have a natural tendency to emphasize how different their country is and the consequent need for local tailoring and control over more activities in the value chain. Country managers will be loath to give up control over activities or how they are performed to outside forces. They will also frequently paint an ominous picture of host government concerns about local content and requirements for local presence. Corporate incentive systems frequently encourage such behavior by linking incentives narrowly to subsidiary results.

In successful global competitors, an environment is created in which the local managers seek to exploit similarities across countries rather than emphasize differences. They view the firms's global presence as an advantage to be tapped for their local gain. Adept global competitors often go to great lengths to devise ways of circumventing or adapting to local differences while preserving the advantages of the similarities. A good example is Canon's personal copier. In Japan, the typical paper size is bigger than American legal size and the standard European size. Canon's personal copier will not handle this size—a Japanese company introduced a product that did not meet its home market needs in the world's largest market for small copiers! Canon gathered its marketing managers from around the world and cataloged market needs in each country. They found that capacity to copy the large Japanese paper was only needed in Japan. In consultation with design and manufacturing engineers, it was determined that building this feature into the personal copier would significantly increase its complexity and cost. The decision was made to omit the feature because the price elasticity of demand for the personal copier was judged to be high. But this was not the end of the deliberations. Canon's management then set out to find a way to make the personal copier saleable in Japan. The answer that emerged was to add another feature to the copier—the ability to copy business cards—which both added little cost and was particularly valuable in Japan. This case illustrates the principle of looking for the similarities in needs among countries and in finding ways of creating similarities, not emphasizing the differences.

Such a change in orientation is something that typically occurs only grudgingly in a multinational company, particularly if it has historically operated in a country-centered mode (as has been the case with early U.S. and European multinationals). Achieving such a reorientation requires first that managers recognize that competitive success demands exploiting the advantages of a global strategy. Regular contact and discussion among subsidiary managers seems to be a prerequisite, as are information systems that allow operations in different countries to be compared.[32] This can be followed by programs for exchanging information and sharing know-how and then by more complex forms of coordination. Ultimately, the reconfiguring of activities globally may then be accepted, even though subsidiaries may have to give up control over some activities in the process.

THE FUTURE OF INTERNATIONAL COMPETITION

Since the late 1970s, there have been some gradual but significant changes in the pattern of international competition which carry important implications for international strategy. Our framework provides a template with which we can examine these changes and

FIGURE 6   Future Trends in International Competition

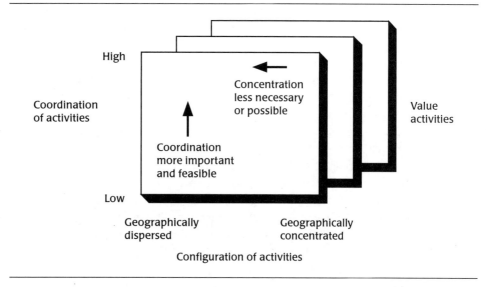

probe their significance. The factors shaping the global configuration of activities by firms are developing in ways which contrast with the trends of the previous thirty years. Homogenization of product needs among countries appears to be continuing, though segmentation within countries is as well. As a result, consumer packaged goods are becoming increasingly prone toward globalization, though they have long been characterized by multidomestic competition. There are also signs of globalization in some service industries as the introduction of information technology creates scale economies in support activities and facilitates coordination in primary activities. Global service firms are reaping advantages in hardware and software development as well as procurement.

In many industries, however, limits have been reached in the scale economies that have been driving the concentration of activities. These limits grow out of classic diseconomies of scale that arise in very large facilities, as well as out of new, more flexible technology in manufacturing and other activities that is often not as scale sensitive as previous methods. At the same time, though, flexible manufacturing allows the production of multiple varieties (to serve different countries) in a single plant. This may encourage new movement towards globalization in industries in which product differences among countries have remained significant and have blocked globalization in the past.

There also appear to be some limits to further decline in transport costs, as innovations such as containerization, bulk ships, and larger aircraft have run their course. However, a parallel trend toward smaller, lighter products and components may keep some downward pressure on transport costs. The biggest change in the benefits and costs of concentrated configuration has been the sharp rise in protectionism in recent years and the resulting rise in nontariff barriers, harkening back to the 1920s. As a group, these factors point to less need and less opportunity for highly concentrated configurations of activities.

When we examine the coordination dimension, the picture looks starkly different. Communication and coordination costs are dropping sharply, driven by breathtaking advances in information systems and telecommunication technology. We have just seen the beginning of developments in this area, which are spreading throughout the value chain.[33] Boeing, for example, is employing computer-aided design technology to jointly design components on-line with foreign suppliers. Engineers in different countries are communicating via computer screens. Marketing systems and business practices continue to homogenize, facilitating the coordination of activities in different countries. The mobility of buyers and information is also growing rapidly, greasing the international spread of brand reputations and enhancing the importance of consistency in the way activities are performed worldwide. Increasing numbers of multinational and global firms are begetting globalization by their suppliers. There is also a sharp rise in the computerization of manufacturing as well as other activities throughout the value chain, which greatly facilitates coordination among dispersed sites.

The imperative of global strategy is shifting, then, in ways that will require a rebalancing of configuration and coordination. Concentrating activities is less necessary in economic terms, and less possible as governments force more dispersion. At the same time, the ability to coordinate globally throughout the value chain is increasing dramatically through modern technology. The need to coordinate is also rising to offset greater dispersion and to respond to buyer needs.

Thus, today's game of global strategy seems increasingly to be a game of coordination— getting more and more dispersed production facilities, R&D laboratories, and marketing activities to truly work together. Yet, widespread coordination is the exception rather than the rule today in many multinationals, as I have noted. The imperative for coordination raises many questions for organizational structure, and is complicated even more when the firm has built its global system using coalitions with independent firms.

Japan has clearly been the winner in the postwar globalization of competition. Japan's firms not only had an initial labor cost advantage but the orientation and skills to translate this into more durable competitive advantages such as scale and proprietary technology. The Japanese context also offered an excellent platform for globalization in many industries, given postwar environmental and technological trends. With home market conditions favoring compactness, a lead in coping with high energy costs, and a national conviction to raise quality, Japan has proved a fertile incubator of global leaders. Japanese multinationals had the advantage of embarking on international strategies in the 1950s and 1960s when the imperatives for a global approach to strategy were beginning to accelerate, but without the legacy of past international investments and modes of behavior.[34] Japanese firms also had an orientation towards highly concentrated activities that fit the strategic imperative of the time. Most European and American multinationals, conversely, were well established internationally before the war. They had legacies of local subsidiary autonomy that reflected the interwar environment. As Japanese firms spread internationally, they dispersed activities only grudgingly and engaged in extensive global coordination. European and country-centered American companies struggled to rationalize overly dispersed configurations of activities and to boost the level of global coordination among foreign units. They found their decentralized organization structures—so fashionable in the 1960s and 1970s—to be a hindrance to doing so.

As today's international firms contemplate the future, Japanese firms are rapidly dispersing activities, due largely to protectionist pressures but also because of the changing economic factors I have described. They will have to learn the lessons of managing overseas activities that many European and American firms learned long ago. However, Japanese firms enjoy an organizational style that is supportive of coordination and a strong commitment to introducing new technologies such as information systems that facilitate it. European firms must still overcome their country-centered heritage. Many still do not compete with truly global strategies and lack modern technology. Moreover, the large number of coalitions formed by European firms must overcome the barriers to coordination if they are not to prove ultimately limiting. The European advantage may well be in exploiting an acute and well-developed sensitivity to local market conditions as well as a superior ability to work with host governments. By using modern flexible manufacturing technology and computerizing elsewhere in the value chain, European firms may be able to serve global segments and better differentiate products.

Many American firms tend to fall somewhere in between the European and Japanese situations. Their awareness of international competition has risen dramatically in recent years, and efforts at creating global strategies are more widespread. The American challenge is to catch the Japanese in a variety of technologies, as well as to learn how to gain the benefits of coordinating among dispersed units instead of becoming trapped by the myths of decentralization. The changing pattern of international competition is creating an environment in which no competitor can afford to allow country parochialism to impede its ability to turn a worldwide position into a competitive edge.

REFERENCES

1. United Nations Center on Transnational Corporations. *Salient Features and Trends in Foreign Direct Investment* (New York, NY: United Nations, 1984).
2. For a survey, see R.E. Caves and Ronald W. Jones, *World Trade and Payments*, 4th ed. (Boston, MA: Little, Brown, 1985).
3. There are many books on the theory and management of the multinational, which are too numerous to cite here. For an excellent survey of the literature, see R.E. Caves, *Multinational Enterprise and Economic Analysis* (Cambridge, England: Cambridge University Press, 1982).
4. Raymond Vernon, "International Investment and International Trade in the Product Cycle," *Quarterly Journal of Economics*, Vol. 80 (May 1966):190–207. Vernon himself, among others, has raised questions about how general the product cycle pattern is today.

5. Michael E. Porter, *Competitive Strategy: Techniques for Analyzing Industries and Competitors* (New York, NY: The Free Press, 1980); Michael E. Porter, "Beyond Comparative Advantage," Working Paper, Harvard Graduate School of Business Administration, August 1985.

6. For a description of this research, see Michael E. Porter, ed., *Competition in Global Industries* (Boston, MA: Harvard Business School Press).

7. The distinction between multidomestic and global competition and some of its strategic implications were described in T. Hout, Michael E. Porter, and E. Rudden, "How Global Companies Win Out," *Harvard Business Review* (September/October 1982), pp. 98–108.

8. Howard V. Perlmutter, "The Tortuous Evolution of the Multinational Corporation." *Columbia Journal of World Business* (January/February 1969), pp. 9–18. Perlmutter's concept of ethnocentric, polycentric, and geocentric multinationals takes the *firm* not the industry as the unit of analysis and is decoupled from industry structure. It focuses on management attitudes, the nationality of executives, and other aspects of organization. Perlmutter presents ethnocentric, polycentric, and geocentric as stages of an organization's development as a multinational, with geocentric as stages of an organization's development as a multinational, with geocentric as the goal. A later paper (Yoram Wind, Susan P. Douglas, and Howard V. Perlmutter, "Guidelines for Developing International Marketing Strategies," *Journal of Marketing*, Vol. 37 (April 1973: 14–23) tempers this conclusion based on the fact that some companies may not have the required sophistication in marketing to attempt a geocentric strategy. Products embedded in the lifestyle or culture of a country are also identified as less susceptible to geocentrism. The Perlmutter et al. view does not link management orientation to industry structure and strategy. International strategy should grow out of the net competitive advantage in a global industry of different types of worldwide coordination. In some industries, a country-centered strategy, roughly analogous to Perlmutter's polycentric idea may be the best strategy irrespective of company size and international experience. Conversely, a global strategy may be imperative given the competitive advantage that accrues from it. Industry and strategy should define the organization approach, not vice versa.

9. Michael E. Porter, *Competitive Advantage: Creating and Sustaining Superior Performance* (New York, NY: The Free Press, 1985).

10. Buzzell (Robert D. Buzzell, "Can You Standardize Multinational Marketing," *Harvard Business Review* [November/December 1980], pp. 102–113); Pryor (Millard H. Pryor, "Planning in a World-Wide Business," *Harvard Business Review*, Vol. 23 [January/February 1965]); and Wind, Douglas, and Perlmutter (op. cit.) point out that national differences are in most cases more critical with respect to marketing than with production and finance. This generalization reflects the fact that marketing activities are often inherently country-based. However, this generalization is not reliable because in many industries, production and other activities are widely dispersed.

11. A number of authors have framed the globalization of industries in terms of the balance between imperatives for global integration and imperatives for national responsiveness, a useful distinction. See, C.K. Prahalad, "The Strategic Process in a Multinational Corporation," unpublished DBA dissertation, Harvard Graduate School of Business Administration, 1975; Yves Doz, "National Policies and Multinational Management," an unpublished DBA dissertation, Harvard Graduate School of Business Administration, 1976; and Christopher A. Bartlett, "Multinational Structural Evolution: The Changing Environment in the International Division" unpublished DBA dissertation. Harvard Graduate School of Business Administration, 1979. I link the distinction here to where and how a firm performs the activities in the value chain internationally.

12. See, for example, Oliver Williamson, *Markets and Hierarchies* (New York, NY: The Free Press, 1975). For an international application, see Mark C. Casson, "Transaction Costs and the Theory of the Multinational Enterprise," in Alan Rugman, ed., *New Theories of the Multinational Enterprise* (London:

Croom Helm, 1982): David J. Teece, "Transaction Cost Economics and the Multinational Enterprise: An Assessment," *Journal of Economic Behavior and Organization*.

13. The difficulties in coordinating are internationally parallel to those in coordinating across business units competing in different industries with the diversified firm. See Michael E. Porter, *Competitive Advantage: Creating and Sustaining Superior Performance* (New York, NY: The Free Press, 1985). Chapter 11.

14. Empirical research has found a strong correlation between R&D and advertising intensity and the extent of foreign direct investment (for a survey, see Caves, 1982, op cit.). Both these factors have a place in our model of the determinants of globalization, but for quite different reasons. R&D intensity suggests scale advantages for the global competitor in developing products or processes that are manufactured abroad either due to low production scale economies or government pressures, or which require investments in service infrastructure. Advertising intensity, however, is much closer to the classic transfer of marketing knowledge to foreign subsidiaries. High advertising industries are also frequently those where local tastes differ and manufacturing scale economies are modest, both reasons to disperse many activities.

15. For an interesting description of the industry, see the paper by Michael Yoshino in Porter, ed., op. cit.

16. It has been recognized that comparative advantage in different stages in a vertically integrated industry sector such as aluminum can reside in different countries. Bauxite mining will take place in resource-rich countries, for example, while smelting will take place in countries with low power cost. See R.E. Caves and Ronald W. Jones, op. cit. The argument here extends this thinking *within* the value chain of any stage and suggests that the optimal location for performing individual activities may vary as well.

17. The firm need not necessarily be owned by investors in the country, but the country is its home base for competing in a country.

18. See Porter, *Competitive Advantage*, op. cit.

19. See S. Linder, *An Essay on Trade and Transformation* (New York, NY: John Wiley, 1961); Vernon, op. cit. (1966); W. Gruber, D. Mehta, and R. Vernon, "R&D Factor in International Trade and International Investment of United States Industries," *Journal of Political Economics*, 76/1 (1967):20–37.

20. Where it does recognize scale economies, trade theory views them narrowly as arising from production in one country.

21. See Alfred Chandler in Porter, ed., op. cit., for a penetrating history of the origins of the large industrial firm and its expansion abroad, which is consistent with the discussion here.

22. Ibid.

23. For data on auto assembly, see "Note on the World Auto Industry in Transition," Harvard Business School Case Services (#9-382-122).

24. For a supporting view, see Theodore Levitt, "The Globalization of Markets," *Harvard Business Review* (May/June 1983). pp. 92–102.

25. The implications of the shift from multidomestic to global competition were the theme of a series of papers on each functional area of the firm prepared for the Business School Colloquium on Competition in Global Industries. See Porter, ed., op. cit.

26. For a discussion, see Hout, Porter, and Rudden, op. cit. For a recent treatment, see Gary Hamel and C.K. Prahalad, "Do You Really Have a Global Strategy," *Harvard Business Review* (July/August 1985), pp. 139–148.

27. David J. Teece, "Firm Boundaries, Technological Innovation, and Strategic Planning," in L.G. Thomas, ed., *Economics of Strategic Planning* (Lexington, MA: Lexington Books, 1985).

28. For a treatment of coalitions from this perspective, see Porter, Fuller, and Rawlinson, in Porter, ed., op. cit.

29. Hladik's recent study of international joint ventures provides supporting evidence. See K. Hladik, "International Joint Ventures: An Empirical Investigation into the Characteristics of Recent U.S.-Foreign

Joint Venture Partnerships," unpublished Doctoral dissertation, Business Economics Program, Harvard University, 1984.

30. For the seminal work on contractual failures, see Williamson, op. cit.

31. For a thorough and sophisticated treatment, see Christopher A. Bartlett's paper in Porter, ed., op. cit.

32. For a good discussion of the mechanisms for facilitating international coordination in operations and technology development, see M.T. Flaherty in Porter, ed., op. cit., (forthcoming). Flaherty stresses the importance of information systems and the many dimensions that valuable coordination can take.

33. For a discussion, see Michael E. Porter and Victor Millar, "How Information Gives You Competitive Advantage." *Harvard Business Review* (July/August 1985), pp. 149–160.

34. Prewar international sales enjoyed by Japanese firms were handled largely through trading companies. See Chandler, op. cit.

Managing Across Borders:
New Strategic Requirements

CHRISTOPHER A. BARTLETT & SUMANTRA GHOSHAL

THE DEMANDS OF MANAGING in an international operating environment changed considerably over the past decade. In an increasing number of industries, the benefits of exploiting global economies of scale and scope enhanced the need for integration and co-ordination of activities. At the same time, volatile exchange rates, industrial policies of host governments, resistance of consumers to standardized global products, and the changing economies of flexible manufacturing technologies increased the value of more nationally responsive differentiated approaches.[1] And with the emergence of competitive battles among a few large firms with comparable resources and skills in global-scale efficiency *and* nationally responsive strategies, the ability to learn—to transfer knowledge and expertise from one part of the organization to others worldwide—became more important in building durable competitive advantage. Managers of multinational companies (MNCs) are now faced with the task of optimizing efficiency, responsiveness, and learning *simultaneously* in their worldwide operations—which suggests new strategic and organizational challenges.

This is the first of two articles that explore this new situation; they are based on a research project that involved extensive discussions with more than 250 managers in nine of the world's largest multinational companies.[2] In this article we will describe the strategic challenges these companies faced because of increasing complexity of environmental demands, and the ways in which they tried to respond to those challenges. Our analysis suggests that, for most MNCs, limited organizational capability (rather than lack of analysis or insight) represents the most critical constraint in responding to new strategic demands. In the follow-up article, we will describe how companies are trying to overcome this constraint by building a very different kind of multinational organization, one that can cope with the increasing complexity of the international environment.

Bartlett, Christopher A., and Ghoshal, Sumantra. "Managing across Borders: New Strategic Requirements." *Sloan Management Review* (Fall 1987), 7–17.

NEW CHALLENGES: MIXED RESPONSES

The international operations of all the companies we studied were in a state of transition. The 1980s brought new demands and pressures that forced them to question their world-wide strategic approach and to adapt their organizational capabilities. Some seemed to be managing the transitions successfully, others were simply surviving, and a few were encountering major difficulties.

In the branded packaged goods industry, both Unilever and Procter & Gamble responded to the need for greater scale efficiency and more globally integrated marketing strategies and technology development by providing better coordination and control over their world-wide operations. Kao, the leading Japanese consumer chemicals company, was able to use its formidable technological capabilities, scale-efficient plants, and marketing creativity to score major victories against both those competitors in its home market, yet it was unable to leverage those skills worldwide. Despite significant investments and substantial management effort, the company's internationalization thrust stalled out in the small developing markets of neighboring East Asia.

Turbulence in the consumer electronics industry led both Philips and Matsushita to make major readjustments over the past decade. Philips made heroic changes to its historically decentralized organization to achieve greater global-scale efficiency. More recently, Matsushita has begun to reconfigure its operations to make them more localized and responsive to host country pressures. But for General Electric, the once-cherished dream of becoming a leading player in the global consumer electronics industry was abandoned in favor of the more modest goal of defending its home-market position in televisions, radios, and other such products, based on an outsourcing strategy.

Over the past decade, Japan's NEC used the technological changes and political upheaval in the telecommunications switching business to build a strong presence in the global marketplace. In the same period, the Swedish electronics company L.M. Ericsson successfully adapted its strategic approach and realigned its worldwide organization to protect, then build, its global-market position in telecommunications. ITT, meanwhile, floundered in this business. Despite being the second largest supplier of telecommunications equipment in the world in the late 1970s, and the leading company outside the U.S., and despite a staggering investment of over $1 billion in new switching technology, ITT was forced to abandon its attempt to enter the U.S. switching market. And it finally had to sell the crown jewel, its formidable Europe telecommunications business.

Why was it that some companies fell behind while others adapted to the international industry's competitive environment in the 1980s? The inability of certain businesses within Kao, GE, and ITT to adjust to important new demands is not presented as an example of strategic incompetence or managerial ineptitude. Indeed, all three companies are frequently cited as examples of corporate excellence. To understand the source of their problems, one must first analyze the changes occurring in the international environment, and how they affect each of these companies differently. Then it is important to study how each organization adjusted in order to understand why results have been so different from one company to the next.

TRADITIONAL STRATEGIC DEMANDS

Trying to distill the key strategic tasks in large and complex industries is a hazardous venture but, at the risk of oversimplification, one can make the case that until recently most worldwide industries presented relatively unidimensional strategic requirements. In each industry, a particular set of forces dominated the environment and the success of firms that possessed a particular set of corresponding competencies.

Rewarding Efficiency in Global Industries

Bell Laboratories' development of the transistor in 1947 paved the way for global efficiency in the consumer electronics industry. Transistors led to printed circuit boards, and then to integrated circuits, which made mass production feasible by reducing both the amount and skill level of labor required for assembly. The automation of component insertion, in-line testing, materials handling, final assembly, and packaging further reduced manufacturing costs and increased product quality. As a result of all these developments, the efficient scale for production of color televisions went from 50,000 sets per annum in the early 1960s to 500,000 sets by the late 1970s.

Meanwhile, scale economies in R&D and marketing were also increasing. State-of-the-art skills in micromechanics, micro-optics, and electronics could not be supported by revenues from a single market. Funding from global volume was essential to support the breadth and depth of expertise required by the three diverse technologies.

Furthermore, the emergence of giant chain stores caused increasing concentration in distribution channels worldwide and raised the need for marketing economies. The resulting shift in bargaining power from manufacturers to researchers changed the rules of the distribution game. Instead of delivering small lot sizes to single-store operators and recovering fairly large marketing overheads, manufacturers could ship large lot-size deliveries to giant chain outlets, but also had to operate within very low margins. Because these outlets sold on price, manufacturers could no longer rely on knowledgeable store personnel to move their merchandise. To educate the consumer and communicate product benefits, they had to invest heavily in advertising, and this too raised break-even volumes. Finally, local service capability, once an entry barrier to global firms, also became less important as increased product reliability reduced the need for service, and as the development of replaceable service boards practically eliminated the need for skilled service technicians.

According to some industry members, by the late 1970s the new manufacturing, research, and marketing economies meant that a global player in the color TV business needed to produce at least 2.0 or 2.5 million sets annually—forty to fifty times the mini-mum efficient scale in the early 1960s.

In an environment characterized by incrementally changing technologies, failing transportation and communication costs, relatively low tariffs and other protectionist barriers, and increasing homogenization of national markets, these huge scale economies progressively increased the benefits of global efficiency in the consumer electronics busi-ness. The industry gradually assumed the attributes of a classic *global industry*—one in which important characteristics like consumer needs, minimum efficient scale, and con-text of competitive strategy were defined not by individual national environments, but by the global economy.

Firms like Matsushita were ideally placed to exploit the emerging global-industry demands. Having expanded internationally much later than their American and European counterparts, they were able to capitalize on highly centralized scale-intensive manufac-turing and R&D operations, and leverage them through worldwide exports of standardized global products. Such *global strategies* fit the emerging industry characteristics far better than the more tailored country-by-country approach that companies like Philips and GE had been forced to adopt in an earlier era of high trade barriers, differences in consumer preferences, and pretransistor technological and economic characteristics.[3]

Building Responsiveness in Multinational Industries

If global efficiency was the dominant strategic demand in the consumer electronics indus-try, the consumer packaged goods business represented an interesting contrast. Tradition-ally, global integration of activities offered this industry few benefits. Instead, national responsiveness appeared to be the key strategic requirement.

In laundry detergents, for example, there was very little scope for standardizing products within Europe, let alone worldwide. As late as 1980, washing machine penetration varied from less than 30 percent of all households in the U.K. to over 85 percent in Germany. Washing practices varied from northern European countries, where "boil washing" had long been standard, to Mediterranean countries, where hand washing in cold water rep-resented an important demand segment. Differences in water hardness, perfume prefer-ence, fabric mix, and phosphate legislation made product differentiation from country to country a strategic requirement.

Not only product attributes, but even marketing strategies, had to be responsive to the different conditions in different national markets. Concentration in distribution channels varied greatly—five chains controlled 65 percent of the market in Germany, but no chain controlled even 2 percent of the retail market in neighboring Italy. The possibility of using advertising and promotional tools also varied by market. In Holland, for example, each brand was allowed a maximum number of minutes of commercial television air time per annum, while in Germany the use of coupons, refunds, and similar forms of promotion was virtually blocked by national laws.

Against this strong need for differentiated approaches to each national market, global scale offered few benefits. In R&D, most of the consumer chemical companies were involved only in formulating the final products; basic research for developing the ingredients was carried out by the chemical manufacturers. Similarly, the relatively simple operations of soap making could be carried out efficiently at a scale that could support a separate plant for all but the smallest markets. In any case, with raw material purchases accounting for 40 to 50 percent of costs, and advertising and marketing accounting for another 20 percent, development and production represented only a modest part of total costs.

This and many other industries with similar characteristics were what we call *multinational industries*—worldwide businesses in which the need for local differentiation made multiple national industry structures flourish. In such an environment, Unilever's *multinational strategy* was a natural fit—the company had a long history of building strong national companies that were sensitive to local needs and opportunities, then allowing them the freedom to manage their local businesses entrepreneurially, with minimal direction from headquarters. It took Procter & Gamble time to learn that transferring the parent company's products and marketing approaches abroad would not guarantee success, but the company was able to adapt. At Kao, subsidiaries were almost totally dependent on efficient, but highly centralized, operations. This proved to be an even less appropriate fit, and prevented the company from responding to the dominant industry requirements.

Exploiting Learning in International Industries

Unlike the consumer electronics industry, which was dominated by the need for efficiency, or the branded packaged goods industry, where responsiveness was the key strategic task, the telecommunications switching industry traditionally required a more multidimensional strategic capability. Monopoly purchasing in most countries by a government-owned post, telegraph, and telephone authority created a demand for responsiveness—a demand enhanced by the strategic importance almost all governments accord to developing local manufacturers of telecom equipment. Significant scale economies in production, and the need to arrange complex credit facilities for buyers through multinational lending agencies, required global integration and activity coordination. However, the most critical task for the manufacturers of telecom switching equipment was the ability to develop and harness new technologies and to exploit them worldwide. The ability to learn and to appropriate the benefits of learning in multiple national markets differentiated the winners from the losers in this highly complex business.

The historical diffusion of telecommunications switching technologies followed the classic international product cycle described by Vernon.[4] In most cases, new products were developed in one of the advanced Western economies, often because of the powerful research capabilities of AT&T's Bell Labs in North America. Next, they were adopted in other developed countries, typically in European countries first, then in Japan. Once the new technology was understood, and the product design was standardized, companies in the developed nations began to export to countries using earlier-generation products. Exports were usually replaced quickly by local manufacturing in response to host government demands. After the local subsidiary developed adequate understanding of the technology, it was allowed to develop and adapt the product locally, to suit unique attributes of the local markets or to help local vendors. By this time, the next new product—an augmented version based on the same technology, or built on an altogether new technology—would be ready for transfer, and the same cycle would be repeated.

We call industries such as this one, where the key to success lies in one's ability to transfer knowledge (particularly technology) to overseas units and to manage the product life-cycle efficiently and flexibly, *international industries*. This name reflects the importance of the international product cycle that lies at the core of the industry's strategic demands.

Recognizing that its small home market could not support the R&D efforts required to survive, L.M. Ericsson built its strategy around an ability to transfer and adapt its innovative product and process technologies to international markets. Its *international strategy*—sequential diffusion of innovation developed in the home market—fit the industry's requirements much better than ITT's multinational approach or NEC's global posture.

STRATEGIC CHALLENGE OF THE 1980S: TRANSITION TO TRANSNATIONALITY

Our portrayal of these industries' strategic demands in the late 1970s is clearly oversimplified. Different tasks in the value-added chains of the different businesses required different levels of efficiency, responsiveness, and learning capabilities. We have charted what appeared to us to be the "center of gravity" of these activities—the environmental forces that had the most significant impact on the industry's strategic task demands.

In the 1980s, each of these industries underwent some major transitions. In all three, the earlier dominance of a single set of environmental forces was replaced by a much more complex set of environmental forces. Increasingly, firms must respond simultaneously to diverse and often conflicting strategic needs. Today, it is more difficult for a firm to succeed with a relatively unidimensional strategic capability that emphasizes only efficiency, or responsiveness, or learning. To win, it must now achieve all three goals at one time.

Need for Multidimensional Strategic Capabilities

In the consumer electronics industry, the trends of increasing scale economies in manufacturing, R&D, and marketing persisted, and the need for global efficiency, if anything, increased. But the very success of efficient competitors contributed to a counterbalancing set of strategic influences that heightened the need for national differentiation and responsiveness. Most noticeably, host governments reacted strongly when the trickle of imported consumer electronics became a flood that upset the trade balances and threatened local industries. In the United States and Europe, antidumping suits, orderly marketing agreements, and political pressures fragmented the manufacturing operations of global companies by forcing almost all companies to set up local plants.

Consumers also reacted to an overdose of standardized global products by showing a renewed preference for differentiated products; the advent of flexible manufacturing processes fed the trend. Amstrad, the fast-growing British computer and electronics company, got its start by recognizing and responding to this local consumer need. It captured a major share of the high-end audio market in the U.K. by moving away from the standardized inexpensive "music centers" marketed by the global firms, and offering customers a product more reminiscent of the old "hi-fi" systems. Their product was encased in teak rather than metal cabinets with a control panel tailor-made to appeal to the British consumers' preferences. Largely because of localized challenges such as Amstrad's, Matsushita has had to reverse its earlier bias toward standardized global designs and place more emphasis on differentiation of products. From fifteen models in its portable audio product range in 1980, the company increased the line to thirty in 1985; it also doubled the number of tape recorder models it produces, while sales per model have declined 60 percent.

The major industry shakeout of the past twenty years has left only a handful of viable competitors, all roughly equivalent in their potential to capture scale economies and develop responsive strategies. In the emerging environment, it is increasingly important for these companies to capture and interpret information, and to use the resulting knowledge and skills on a global basis. The growing sophistication of global competitive strategies means that knowledge gained about a competitor, and skills developed in response to its activities in one market, may be of vital importance for company units elsewhere in the world. Furthermore, with more sophisticated markets worldwide, rapidly changing technology, and shorter product life cycles, rich rewards are accruing to companies that can develop and diffuse successful innovations. In brief, a company's worldwide organizational learning capability is fast becoming an essential strategic asset.

In the branded packaged goods industry, similarly, responsiveness continues to be a critical task, but both efficiency and worldwide learning have become more important. In the detergent business, for example, product standardization has become more and more feasible because of standardization in the washing machine industry. Growing penetration of washing machines has also contributed, as has the increasing share of synthetic textiles, which narrows the differences in washing practices across countries. But the biggest impetus toward globalization has come from the firms themselves. Managers at P&G, Unilever, Henkel, and Colgate faced sharply rising input prices caused by the oil crisis of the mid-1970s, and the simultaneous recession in demand that made passing increased costs on to customers impossible. They found that developing standard brands, formulas, and packages created some economies in the production process. Further savings were made possible by developing common advertising and promotion approaches.

Innovations made jointly by a company's headquarters and a number of national organizations have been the most important instrument for creating standardized products that satisfied the diverse demands of customers at acceptable cost levels. For example, P&G sells a heavy duty liquid detergent called Tide in the United States, Ariel in Europe, and Cheer in Japan. The product was truly global in its development: It incorporated surfactant technology, developed in the country's international technical coordination group to respond to cold water washing in Japan, water softening technology, developed at the European Technical Center to respond to the hardness of washing water in most European countries; and builder technology, developed in the United States to combat the higher soil content in dirty clothes. At the same time, however, the existence of regional development groups ensured that the detergent satisfied primary requirements of customers in each country. Such successes have stimulated other global competitors and have broadened the competitive game from one based primarily on national marketing capability to a much more complex one where local responsiveness, global efficiency, and worldwide innovation and learning are all part of the rules.

Similarly, the new digital technology, at one stroke, enhanced the need for efficiency, responsiveness, and learning in the telecommunications switching business. The increasing need for efficiency and integration is driven by soaring R&D costs that can only be supported through global volume and higher scale economies in component production. The magnitude of skills and resources required to create a new digital switch is difficult for most companies to assemble in one organizational unit, and this has made global innovations essential. At the same time, the growing strategic importance of the switch— it is now the core of a country's information infrastructure—has enhanced its importance to national governments, thereby enhancing the need for companies to be responsive to local demands.

These transitions were not unique to the three industries we have described. Many other industries, from heavy earth-moving equipment and automobiles to photocopiers and power tools, have confronted similar environmental changes. In the emerging international environment, therefore, there are fewer and fewer examples of industries that are pure global, textbook multinational, or classic international. Instead, more and more businesses are being driven by *simultaneous* demands for global efficiency, responsiveness, and worldwide learning. These are the characteristics of what we call a *transnational industry*.

This is not to suggest that the strategic challenges facing companies in the branded packaged goods business are the same as those confronting global competitors in the consumer electronics industry. The nature, the strength, and the mix of the three broad demands obviously vary widely. But it is true that companies in both these businesses— and many others besides—will find it increasingly difficult to defend a competitive position based on only one dominant capability. They will need to develop their strategy to a point where they can manage efficiency, responsiveness, and learning on a worldwide basis.

Responding to the Challenge: Toward Transnational Capabilities

These new demands had a profound impact on all the companies we studied. Firms whose key competencies had previously fit the dominant industry requirement found they needed to develop entirely new capabilities. Those whose strategic posture was an industry mismatch in the era of unidimensional strategic demands also faced the challenge of developing multidimensional capabilities. For many, however, there was the incentive of being able to leverage previously inappropriate organizational capabilities.

Companies like Philips, Unilever, and ITT, which had traditionally operated in a multi-national strategic mode (with responsiveness as their dominant posture), faced the challenge of developing global efficiency and improving their ability to develop knowledge and skills worldwide and diffuse it throughout the organization. Firms such as Kao, NEC, and Matsushita, on the other hand, had traditionally adopted a global strategic posture with efficiency as their trump card, and confronted the need for more national responsiveness and improved access to worldwide innovative resources and stimuli. GE, Procter & Gamble, and L.M. Ericsson had been exponents of the international product cycle model, efficiency transferring domestic innovations and expertise to worldwide operations. They faced the challenge of expanding their capability to create more global innovations while ensuring that their international operations retained the appropriate balance of responsiveness and efficiency.

THE ORGANIZATIONAL CONSTRAINT

One thing was clear. In all the companies we studied, there was either an explicit or an implicit recognition of the changing strategic task demands we have described. Even in those organizations that were lagging in their adaptation to the new demands, or that had abandoned their attempts to adjust, the issue was not a poor understanding of environmental forces or inappropriate strategic intent. Without exception, they knew *what* they had; their difficulties lay in *how* to achieve the necessary changes.

• Kao had been trying unsuccessfully since the late 1960s to establish a foothold in the European and North American markets. Management recognized that a lack of responsiveness to the very different customer preferences and market structures was limiting the company's potential outside Japan. Emulating the practices of Unilever and P&G, the company created regional headquarters in Asia, America, and Europe. It also undertook a personnel development program to upgrade the skills and organizational status of its overseas groups, and to internationalize the perspectives of managers at headquarters.

However, functional managers at headquarters—the dominant group in this traditionally centralized company—saw the localization thrust as a signal to become more directly involved in overseas operations. The company failed to develop the national responsiveness it was seeking, since its established processes reinforced the strong direct control of headquarters functional staff and prevented regional and country managers from significantly influencing product development or even local product-market strategies.

• Many GE managers foresaw that superior global efficiency of its Japanese competitors would erode the company's competitive position in the consumer electronics business. It was manifest to them that GE's philosophy of building autonomous mini-GEs in each country had become inappropriate; greater integration and coordination of activities were necessary. Plans were made to develop more globally efficient operations by shifting production to Southeast Asia and developing specialized internal sourcing plants.

But, in an organization that had historically considered foreign subsidiaries appendages to a dominant home country operation, the importance and urgency of these plans were lost. It was a case of too little too late, and the company could not reverse the traditional role of international operations as sales outlets dependent on the parent. By this stage, the Japanese competitors had developed insurmountable leads in the battle for low-cost position, and GE had lost the opportunity to develop a global presence.

• Soon after Rand Araskog took over as ITT's chief executive, he committed himself to selling off many of its diverse businesses to provide the resources and management focus that would be necessary to make the company a leader in the changing battle for domination of global telecommunications. He also recognized that ITT would have to change the way it managed its business. In particular, there was an urgent need to change the company's product development process in response to the emerging digital technology. All but the smallest national subsidiaries of the company had traditionally developed their own products in cooperation with their local post, telegraph, and telephone authorities. While this had generated multiple standards and a plethora of product varieties, the company had reaped considerable political rewards from being able to present a locally designed product to each government.

But the resources and technological capabilities required to develop a digital switch were clearly beyond the ability of any single country unit. At the same time, the trend toward deregulation had reduced the rewards of local differentiation. As a result, integrating the technological capabilities and financial resources of different national entities to design a standard global product had become a strategic imperative.

However, despite its best efforts, ITT's management failed to persuade the different national units to cooperate with each other in building a standard switch. Conditioned by a long history of local autonomy, and driven by systems that measured performance on a local basis, national units strongly resisted joint efforts and common standards. Fierce turf protection led to constant duplication of efforts and divergence of specifications; total development costs ballooned to over $1 billion. The biggest problem appeared when the company decided to take the System 12 switch to the U.S. market. In true ITT tradition, the U.S. group asserted its right to develop its own product and launched a major new R&D effort, despite concerns from the company's chief technological officer that they risked developing what he called System 13. After years of effort and hundreds of millions of dollars in additional development costs, the product was still not ready for the market. Ultimately, it was this failure to create an integrated process for global product development that led to ITT's withdrawal from the telecommunications switching business.

The problems these companies faced were not caused by a lack of strategic analysis or insight, but instead by the limitations and biases in their own organizations that prevented the development of required strategic competencies. While the consequences were somewhat extreme in their cases, all the other companies we surveyed faced basically the same kind of organizational constraints in developing the multidimensional strategic capability that the environment of the 1980s required.

The Critical Role of Administrative Heritage

Managers of all these companies have since learned that while strategic plans can be scrapped and redrawn overnight, a company's organizational capability is much more durable and difficult to restructure. There is no such thing as a zero-based organization. A company's organizational capability develops over many years and is tied to a number of attributes: a configuration of organizational assets and capabilities that are built up over decades; a distribution of managerial responsibilities and influence that cannot be shifted quickly; and an ongoing set of relationships that endure long after any structural change has been made. Collectively, these factors constitute a company's *administrative heritage*. It can be, at the same time, one of the company's greatest assets—the underlying source of its key competencies—and also one of its most significant liabilities, since it resists change and thereby prevents realignment or broadening of strategic capabilities.

A company's administrative heritage is shaped by many factors. Strong leaders often leave indelible impressions on their organizations, as Kenosuke Matsushita has in the company that bears his name, and as Harold Geneen has in a company that still reflects his philosophies.

• Geneen is best known for strengthening the corporate controller's function in ITT, but he also built up a strong tradition that headquarters managers could not interfere with either the strategic autonomy or the day-to-day operating decisions of national management in subsidiaries. He resisted the development of a central research function in the telecommunications business, and instead ensured that the national units controlled almost all the key resources and technological expertise of the company. He also placed the strongest managers in different national units, and held them fully accountable for their performance. This led to a distribution of resources and power that was strongly biased in favor of this administrative heritage that resisted subsequent efforts to achieve global integration.

Home country culture and social systems also have significant influences on a company's administrative heritage. For example, the more important roles that owners and bankers play in corporate level decision making in many European companies led to an internal culture quite different from that of their American counterparts. These companies tended to emphasize personal relationships rather than formal structures, and financial controls rather than coordination of technical or operational detail.[5] This management style led companies like Unilever to develop highly autonomous national subsidiaries that were managed like a portfolio of offshore investments, rather than like a single worldwide business. In contrast, Japanese cultural norms that emphasized group decision making and commitment to long-term welfare of employees led to highly centralized management processes that resisted the growth in the resources and influence of foreign units.[6]

• Decision-making processes based on *nemawashi* and *ringi* require close face-to-face contact among participating managers. These processes lay at the core of Kao's management systems and obstructed management's efforts to give foreign subsidiaries greater access, legitimacy, and influence. Further, a commitment to maintain and increase domestic employment impeded the company's ability to expand the activities and resources of the offshore units.

Finally, the internationalization history of a firm also influences its administrative heritage.[7] Expanding in the pre-Second World War period of rising tariffs and discriminatory legislation, many European companies were forced to transfer most value adding activities to their foreign subsidiaries. High tariff barriers in the 1920s and 1930s forced Philips to decentralize not only assembly but even component production; the dangers of German occupation of Holland led to decentralization of R&D; and, finally, the postwar boom further strengthened the roots of decentralization, since the war-ravished headquarters did not have the capability to coordinate the company's rapidly growing international operations. Japanese companies faced quite the opposite situation. Making their main international thrust in the 1970s—the era of falling tariffs and transport costs, and increasing homogenization of national markets—their centrally controlled, export-based internalization strategy represented a perfect fit with the external environment, besides being consistent with their own cultural norms and internal management processes. American companies, many of which enjoyed their fastest international expansion in the 1950s and 1960s, grew primarily on the strength of new technologies and management processes that they had developed during the war.[8] The creation of new products and technologies at home, and their exploitation abroad, became the core of internationalization strategies.

• While delegating most application engineering, manufacturing, sourcing, and marketing responsibilities to its foreign subsidiaries, GE kept basic research tightly centralized at home. The assumption was that a domestic operation could create new products that would then be available to foreign units for adoption and adaptation. This parent-company-as-leader mentality proved a major impediment to building a worldwide manufacturing function. It compromised the willingness of the U.S. company to rely on offshore sources, and kept it from recognizing the need to tap into the multiple centers of technological excellence that had emerged in different parts of the world.

In developing the capabilities required to cope with the complex demands of transnational industries, each of the companies we studied was confronted with the limiting constraints of its administrative heritage. Yet such limitations were not always immediately recognized. The more normal approach was to respond to new demands by emulating those competitors that were most successful in dealing with the situation. Philips's initial reaction to the growing competitive challenge from Japan was to pull product decisions and sourcing control to headquarters. This step was intended to replicate (and therefore, enable Philips to compete with) companies like Matsushita, whose global efficiency was dependent on standardized products and centralized production. Meanwhile, managers at Matsushita were extremely aware of the growing need for responsiveness, and launched a localization program aimed at enhancing the self-sufficiency and entrepreneurship of the worldwide subsidiary companies—attributes of Philips's national organizations that were greatly admired and envied in Osaka.

Initially, both approaches not only failed, but also had unfortunate consequences, primarily because they did not take into account the powerful administrative heritage of the organization that had to implement the changes. At Philips, the national subsidiaries were not only the main sources of international knowledge and skill, but also the entrepreneurial spark plugs that fired many strategic initiatives. Denying their traditional roles and diminishing their influence damaged their motivation and deprived corporate management the benefits of their considerable resources. Instead of improving global efficiency, the action jeopardized the company's key organizational asset. Philips has since recognized that, while global efficiency has to be achieved, it must be done in a way that is consistent with its administrative heritage and that protects and indeed builds on the formidable strengths of its national organizations. Facing limited success in its localization program, Matsushita has also learned that the way to build national responsiveness is not to weaken central management, but to leverage the strengths of its centralized culture-bound systems.

Philips and Matsushita (and many of the other companies we studied) eventually recognized the importance of both harnessing and offsetting the powerful influence of their administrative heritage as they adapted to new strategic demands. (In the companion article, we will describe some of the ways in which these companies were able to do so.) In contrast, as the earlier examples showed, the companies that were slow to adapt to the new environment never seemed to recognize the importance of their administrative heritage, and were therefore unable to leverage its strengths while counterbalancing its limitations.

ORGANIZATIONAL CAPABILITY AS KEY COMPETENCE

The ability of a company to survive and succeed in today's turbulent international environment depends on two factors: The fit between its strategic posture and the dominant industry characteristics, and its ability to adapt that posture to the multidimensional task demands shaping the current competitive environment. Kao's inability to succeed internationally stemmed from a poor fit between its centralized scale and technology-driven strategy in an industry that demanded a more differentiated and market-responsive approach. ITT's problems, on the other hand, were due more to an inability to adapt strongly focused organizational norms and behaviors, shaped by its unique administrative heritage, to the fast-changing, multidimensional demands of today's telecommunications industry. And GE experienced both fit and adaptation problems.

Despite the very different tasks facing the other companies in our study, in broad terms they are all moving toward a common goal, though from diverse directions. In the terminology we have adopted, they are making the transition from being multinational, international, or global companies to being transnational corporations. Obviously, these companies are not adopting a common strategy—the differences in their industry characteristics and administrative heritages prevent that. Indeed, neither a particular competitive posture nor a specific organizational form characterizes these companies. What *is* emerging as common to all of them is a new set of beliefs about managing across borders.[9] Fundamental to this new mentality is the awareness of the importance of administrative heritage both as an asset to protect and as a constraint to overcome. To respond to the complexity, diversity and dynamism of the external environment, and to build the multidimensional strategic postures that are required, each of these companies has to overcome the unidimensional bias shaped by its administrative heritage. To become a transnational, each must build a multidimensional organization capable of developing new strategic competencies while protecting the existing strengths. What are the key attributes of such an organization? How can managers develop those attributes? How should such an organization be managed once it is built? These are some of the questions that we will address in the following article.

REFERENCES

1. The tension between the strategic requirement for integration and differentiation has a long intellectual history, but is perhaps best captured in the classic Lawrence and Lorsch study [P. Lawrence and J. Lorsch, *Organization and Environment* (Boston: Harvard Business School Press, 1967)]. Their differentiation-integration framework was first applied to the international organization task by Prahalad [C.K. Prahalad, "The Strategic Process in a Multinational Corporation," (Boston: unpublished doctoral dissertation, Harvard Graduate School of Business Administration, 1976)], and subsequently adapted by others, including Doz and Bartlett, [*see* Y. Doz, *National Policies and Multinational Strategic Management* (New York: Praeger, 1979)] and C.A. Bartlett, "Multinational Structural Evolution: The Changing Decision Environment" (Boston: unpublished doctoral dissertation, Harvard Graduate School of Business Administration, 1979)].

2. This research project consisted of three phases. The first aimed at identifying and describing the key challenges faced by managers of worldwide companies and documenting "leading practice" in coping with these challenges. That was also the hypothesis-generating phase, and the sample was selected to represent the greatest variety of strategic and organizational situations. In the consumer electronics industry, globalization offered the greatest benefits; in the consumer packaged products business, the forces of national responsiveness were especially strong, and in the telecommunications switching industry both global and local forces were very important. Within each industry, we selected a group of firms that represented the greatest variety of administrative heritages, including differences in nationality, internationalization history, and corporate culture. The research sites we chose were Philips, Matsushita, and GE in consumer electronics, Kao, Procter & Gamble, and Unilever in consumer chemicals, and ITT, NEC, and L.M. Ericsson in telecommunications switching.

In each of these companies, we interviewed a great many managers in the corporate headquarters and also in a number of national organizations in the U.S., Brazil, U.K., Germany, France, Italy, Taiwan, Singapore, Japan, and Australia. In addition, we studied company documents, and also collected information about the industries and the companies from a range of external sources. This two-article series is written primarily on the basis of data collected in this first phase of the project.

In the next stage, we conducted detailed questionnaire surveys in three of these nine companies. The principal objective of the survey was to carry out a preliminary test of some hypotheses generated during the first phase of clinical research to define the hypotheses more precisely, and to develop suitable instruments for testing them more rigorously. Approximately 100 managers each from NEC, Matsushita, and Philips participated in the survey.

Finally, in the third phase of the study, the hypotheses were tested through a large-sample mailed questionnaire survey that yielded data on 720 cases of headquarters-subsidiary relations in sixty-six of the largest U.S. and European multinational corporations.

The overall findings of the project are being reported in our forthcoming book, tentatively entitled *Managing across Borders: The Transnational Solution,* to be published by the Harvard Business School Press.

3. The term "global," applied to industries, companies, and strategies, has been subject to widely differing definition and usage. For further discussion, see M.E. Porter, "Competition in Global Industries: A Conceptual Framework," in M.E. Porter, ed., *Competition in Global Industries* (Boston: Harvard Business School Press, 1986). We will use the term *global strategy* in its purest sense—one that defines product, manufacturing scale, technology, sourcing patterns, and competitive strategy on the assumption of a unified world market. It is the classic standardized product exported from a centralized global-scale plant and distributed according to a centrally managed global strategy.

4. See R. Vernon, "International Investment and International Trade in the Product Cycle." *Quarterly Journal of Economics,* May 1966. pp. 190–207.

5. The internationalization process and accompanying organizational attributes of many European multinationals have been described by L.G. Franko, *The European Multinationals* (Stanford, CA: Graylock, 1976).

6. For a detailed discussion of the management process in Japanese firms and their impact on strategy, see M.Y. Yoshino, *Japan's Managerial System: Tradition and Innovation* (Cambridge: MIT Press, 1968).

7. Readers with a particular interest in the history of international business will find a far richer historical analysis in A.D. Chandler, "The Evolution of Modern Global Enterprise," in *Competition in Global Industries,* ed. M.E. Porter (Boston: Harvard Business School Press, 1986).

8. Documenting the postwar expansion of U.S.-based companies, Jean Jacques Servan-Schreiber attributed the Americans' success to their technological and managerial abilities. See J.J. Servan-Schreiber, *The American Challenge* (New York: Atheneum, 1968).

9. The issue of a management mind-set being critical to the task of managing MNCs was highlighted almost two decades ago by Perlmutter. See H.V. Perlmutter, "The Tortuous Evolution of the Multinational Corporation," *Columbia Journal of World Business,* January-February 1969, pp. 9–18.

Managing Across Borders:
New Organizational Responses

CHRISTOPHER A. BARTLETT & SUMANTRA GHOSHAL

IN A COMPANION ARTICLE we described how recent changes in the international operating environment have forced companies to optimize *efficiency*, *responsiveness*, and *learning* simultaneously in their worldwide operations. To companies that previously concentrated on developing and managing one of these capabilities, this new challenge implied not only a total strategic reorientation but a major change in organizational capability, as well.

Implementing such a complex, three-pronged strategic objective would be difficult under any circumstances, but in a worldwide company the task is complicated even further. The very act of "going international" multiplies a company's organizational complexity. Typically, doing so requires adding a third dimension to the existing business-and-function-oriented management structure. It is difficult enough balancing product divisions that bring efficiency and focus to domestic product-market strategies with corporate staffs whose functional expertise allows them to play an important counterbalance and control role. The thought of adding capable, geographically oriented management—and maintaining a three-way balance of organizational perspectives and capabilities among product, function, and area—is intimidating to most managers. The difficulty is increased because the resolution of tensions among product, function, and area managers must be accomplished in an organization whose operating units are often divided by distance and time and whose key members are separated by culture and language.

From Unidimensional to Multidimensional Capabilities

Faced with the task of building multiple strategic capabilities in highly complex organizations, managers in almost every company we studied made the simplifying assumption that they were faced with a series of dichotomous choices.[1] They discussed the relative merits of pursuing a strategy of national responsiveness as opposed to one based on global

Bartlett, Christopher A., and Ghoshal, Sumantra. "Managing Across Borders: New Organization Responses." *Sloan Mangement Review* (Fall 1987), 43–53.

integration; they considered whether key assets and resources should be centralized or decentralized and they debated the need for strong central control versus greater subsidiary autonomy. How a company resolved these dilemmas typically reflected influences exerted and choices made during its historical development. In telecommunications, ITT's need to develop an organization responsive to national political demands and local specification differences was as important to its survival in the pre- and post-World War II era as was NEC's need to build its highly centralized technological manufacturing and marketing skills and resources in order to expand abroad in the same industry in the 1960s and 1970s.

When new competitive challenges emerged, however, such unidimensional biases became strategically limiting. As ITT demonstrated by its outstanding historic success and NEC showed by its more delayed international expansion, *strong geographic management* is essential for development of dispersed responsiveness. Geographic management allows world-wide companies to sense, analyze and respond to the needs of different national markets.

Effective competitors also need to build strong *business management* with global prod-uct responsibilities if they are to achieve global efficiency and integration. These managers act as champions of manufacturing rationalization, product standardization, and low-cost global sourcing. (As the telecommunications switching industry globalized, NEC's organizational capability in this area gave it major competitive advantage.) Unencumbered by either territorial or functional loyalties, central product groups remain sensitive to overall competitiveness issues and become agents to facilitate changes that, though pain-ful, are necessary for competitive viability.

Finally, a strong worldwide *functional management* allows an organization to build and transfer its core competencies—a capability vital to world-wide learning. Links between functional managers allow the company to accumulate specialized knowledge and skills and to apply them wherever they are required in the worldwide operations. Functional management acts as the repository of organizational learning and as the prime mover for its consolidation and circulation within the company. It was for want of a strongly linked research and technical function across subsidiaries that ITT failed in its attempt to coordi-nate the development and diffusion of its System 12 digital switch.

Thus, to respond to the needs for efficiency, responsiveness, and learning *simultane-ously*, the company must develop a multidimensional organization in which the effective-ness of each management group is maintained *and* in which each group is prevented from dominating the others. As we saw in company after company, the most difficult challenge for managers trying to respond to broad, emerging strategic demands was to develop the new elements of multidimensional organization without eroding the effectiveness of their current unidimensional capability.

Overcoming Simplifying Assumptions

For all nine companies at the core of our study, the challenge of breaking down biases and building a truly multidimensional organization proved difficult. Behind the pervasive either/or mentality that led to the development of unidimensional capabilities, we identified three simplifying assumptions that blocked the necessary organizational development. The need to reduce organizational and strategic complexity has made these assumptions almost universal in worldwide companies, regardless of industry, national origin, or management culture.

- There is a widespread, often implicit assumption that roles of different organizational units are uniform and symmetrical; different businesses should be managed in the same way, as should different functions and national operations.

- Most companies, some consciously, most unconsciously, create internal interunit relationships on clear patterns of dependence or independence, on the assumption that such relationships *should* be clear and unambiguous.

- Finally, there is the assumption that one of corporate management's principal tasks is to institutionalize clearly understood mechanisms for decision making and to implement simple means of exercising control.

Those companies most successful in developing truly multidimensional organizations were the ones that challenged these assumptions and replaced them with some very different attitudes and norms. Instead of treating different businesses, functions, and subsidiaries similarly, they systematically *differentiated* tasks and responsibilities. Instead of seeking organizational clarity by basing relationships on dependence or independence, they built and managed *interdependence* among the different units of the companies. And instead of considering control their key task, corporate managers searched for complex mechanisms to *coordinate and coopt* the differentiated and interdependent organizational units into sharing a vision of the company's strategic tasks. These are the central organizational characteristics of what we described in the earlier article as transnational corporations—those most effective in managing across borders in today's environment of intense competition and rapid, often discontinuous change.

FROM SYMMETRY TO DIFFERENTIATION

Like many other companies we studied, Unilever built its international operations under an implicit assumption of organizational symmetry. Managers of diverse local operating companies in products ranging from packaged foods to chemicals and detergents all reported to strongly independent national managers, who in turn reported through regional directors to the board. In the post–World War II era, the company began to recognize a need to supplement this geographically dominated structure with an organizational ability to capture potential economies and to transfer learning across national boundaries. To meet this need, a few product-coordination groups were formed at the corporate center. But the assumption of organizational symmetry ensured that all businesses were similarly managed, and the number of coordination groups grew from three in 1962 to six in 1969 and to ten by 1977.

By the mid-1970s, however, the entrenched organizational symmetry was being threatened. Global economic disruption caused by the oil crisis dramatically highlighted the very substantial differences in the company's businesses and markets and forced management to recognize the need to differentiate its organizational structures and administrative processes. While standardization, coordination, and integration paid high dividends in the chemical and detergent businesses, for example, important differences in local tastes and national cultures impeded the same degree of coordination in foods. As a result, the roles, responsibilities, and powers of the central product-coordination groups eventually began to diverge as the company tried to shake off the constraint of the symmetry assumption.

But as Unilever tackled the challenge of managing some businesses in a more globally coordinated manner, it was confronted with the question of what to coordinate. Historically, the company's philosophy of decentralized capabilities and delegated responsibilities resulted in most national subsidiaries' becoming fully integrated, self-sufficient operations. While they were free to draw on product technology, manufacturing capabilities, and marketing expertise developed at the center, they were not required to do so, and most units chose to develop, manufacture, and market products as they thought appropriate. Thus functions, too, tended to be managed symmetrically.

Over time, decentralization of all functional responsibilities became increasingly difficult to support. In the 1970s, for example, when arch-competitor Procter & Gamble's subsidiaries were launching a new generation of laundry detergents based on the rape seed formula created by the parent company, most of Unilever's national detergent companies responded with their own products. The cost of developing thirteen different formulations was extremely high, and management soon recognized that not one was as good as P&G's centrally developed product. For the sake of cost control and competitive effectiveness, Unilever had to break with tradition and begin centralizing European product development. The company has since created a system in which central coordination is more normal, although very different for different functions such as basic research, product development, manufacturing, marketing, and sales.

Just as they saw the need to change symmetrical structures and homogeneous processes imposed on different businesses and functions, most companies we observed eventually recognized the importance of differentiating the management of diverse geographic operations. Despite the fact that various national subsidiaries operated with very different external environments and internal constraints, they all traditionally reported through the same channels, operated under similar planning and control systems, and worked under a set of common and generalized mandates.

Increasingly, however, managers recognized that such symmetrical treatment can constrain strategic capabilities. At Unilever, for example, it became clear that Europe's highly competitive markets and closely linked economies meant that its operating companies in that region required more coordination and control than those in, say, Latin America. Little by little, management increased the product-coordination groups' role in Europe until they had direct line responsibility for all operating companies in their businesses. Elsewhere,

FIGURE 1   Unilever's Differentiated Organization

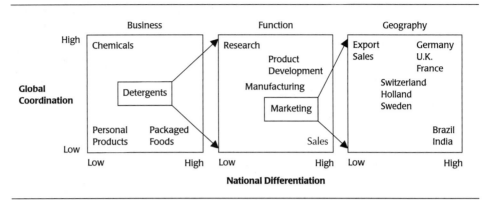

however, national management maintained its historic line management role, and product coordinators acted only as advisers. Unilever has thus moved in sequence from a symmetrical organization to a much more differentiated one: differentiating by product, then by function and finally by geography.

Recently, within Europe, differentiation by national units has proceeded even further. Operations in "key countries" such as France, Germany, and the United Kingdom are allowed to retain considerably more autonomy than those in "receiver countries" such as Switzerland, Sweden, Holland and Denmark. While the company's overall commitment to decentralization is maintained, "receiver countries" have gradually become more dependent on the center for direction and support, particularly in the areas of product development and competitive strategy.

Figure 1 is a schematic representation of the different ways in which Unilever manages its diverse businesses, functions, and markets.[2] The vertical axis represents the level of global integration, and hence of central coordination; the horizontal axis represents the extent of national differentiation, and consequently of the desired influence of subsidiaries in strategic and operational decisions.

The detergent business must be managed in a more globally integrated manner than packaged foods, but also needs a more nationally differentiated strategy than the chemicals business. But not all tasks need to be managed in this differentiated yet coordinated manner: there is little need for national differentiation in research or for global coordination of sales management. And even those functions such as marketing that exhibit the more complex simultaneous demands need not be managed in this way in all national markets. Marketing strategy for export sales can be highly coordinated, while approaches taken in closed markets like India and Brazil can be managed locally. Only in key strategic markets like Germany, the U.K., and France is there a need for differentiated yet coordinated marketing strategies. This flexible and differentiated management approach stands in marked contrast to the standardized, symmetrical approach implied in Unilever's earlier blanket commitment to decentralized responsibility.

But Unilever is far from unique. In all of the companies we studied, senior management was working to differentiate its organizational structure and processes in increasingly sophisticated ways.[3] For example, Philips' consumer electronics division began experimenting with an organization differentiated by product life-cycle stage—high-tech products like CD players being managed with very different strategies and organization processes from those for stable high-volume products like color TVs, which, in turn, were managed differently from mature and declining products like portable radios. Procter & Gamble is differentiating the roles of its subsidiaries by giving some of them responsibilities as "lead countries" in product strategy development, then rotating that leadership role from product to product.[4] Matsushita differentiates the way it manages its worldwide operations not on the basis of geography, but on the unit's strategic role. (Single-product, wholly owned manufacturing units, the A Group, are managed differently from multiproduct, multifunction companies, the B Group, and from simple sales and marketing subs, the C Group.) L.M. Ericsson, which had centralized most of the basic research on its digital switch, is now decentralizing development and applications responsibilities to a few key country subsidiaries that have the capability to contribute.[5]

Thus, instead of deciding the overall roles of product, functional, and geographic management on the basis of simplistic dichotomies such as global versus domestic businesses or centralized versus decentralized organizations, many companies are creating different levels of influence for different groups as they perform different activities. Doing this allows the relatively underdeveloped management perspectives to be built in a gradual, complementary manner rather than in the sudden, adversarial environment often associated with either/or choices. Internal heterogeneity has made the change from unidimensional to multidimensional organization easier by breaking the problem up into many small, differentiated parts and by allowing for a step-by-step process of organizational change.

FROM DEPENDENCE OR INDEPENDENCE TO INTERDEPENDENCE

The limitations of the assumption of clarity in organizational relationships eventually confronted top managers in the Japanese soap and detergent company Kao. In the early 1980s they began to recognize that their foreign subsidiaries' strong dependence on the parent company provided significant benefits of global efficiency only at the cost of less sensitivity and responsiveness to local market needs. For example, when investigating the reason for the company's slow penetration of the shampoo market in Thailand despite offering a technologically superior product, headquarters managers found that the subsidiary had adopted the product positioning, packaging, and pricing policies developed for the Japanese domestic market. Since local management had been unable to make the necessary local adaptations, managers were brought in from headquarters to identify the source of the problem and to make necessary changes in the marketing mix.

In other companies we studied—Unilever and ITT, for example—clarity of organizational relationships was achieved by giving foreign subsidiaries substantial independence.

But, as our earlier discussion of Unilever illustrated, such organizational clarity was achieved at the cost of substantial inefficiency; individual subsidiaries often reinvented the wheel or operated at suboptimal scale.

New strategic demands make organizational models of simple interunit dependence *or* independence inappropriate. The reality of today's worldwide competitive environment demands collaborative information sharing and problem solving, cooperative support and resource sharing, and collective action and implementation. Independent units risk being picked off one-by-one by competitors whose coordinated global approach gives them two important strategic advantages—the ability to integrate research, manufacturing, and other scale-efficient operations, and the opportunity to cross-subsidize the losses from battles in one market with funds generated by profitable operations in home markets or protected environments.[6] The desire to capture such strategic benefits was one of Philip's main motivations as it attempted to coordinate the competitive responses of historically independent national organizations.

On the other hand, foreign operations totally dependent on a central unit must deal with problems reaching beyond the loss of local market responsiveness described in the Kao example. They also risk being unable to respond effectively to strong national competitors or to sense potentially important local market or technical intelligence. This was the problem Procter & Gamble's Japan subsidiary faced in an environment where local competitors began challenging P&G's previously secure position with successive, innovative product changes and novel market strategies, particularly in the disposable diapers business. After suffering major losses in market share, management recognized that a local operation focused primarily on implementing the company's classic marketing strategy was no longer sufficient; the Japanese subsidiary needed the freedom and incentive to be more innovative. Not only to ensure the viability of the Japanese subsidiary, but also to protect its global strategic position, P&G realized it had to expand the role of the local unit and change its relationship with the parent company to enhance two-way learning and mutual support.

But it is not easy to change relationships of dependence or independence that have been built up over a long history. Many companies have tried to address the increasing need for interunit collaboration by adding layer upon layer of administrative mechanisms to foster greater cooperation. Top managers have extolled the virtues of teamwork and have even created special departments to audit management response to this need. In most cases these efforts to obtain cooperation by fiat or by administrative mechanisms have been disappointing. The independent units have feigned compliance while fiercely protecting their independence. The dependent units have found that the new cooperative spirit implies little more than the right to agree with those on whom they depend.

Yet some companies have gradually developed the capability to achieve such cooperation and to build what Rosabeth Kanter calls an "integrative organization."[7] Of the companies we studied, the most successful did so not by creating new units, but by changing the basis of the relationships among product, functional, and geographic management groups.

From relations based on dependence or independence, they moved to relations based on formidable levels of explicit, genuine interdependence. In essence, they made integration and collaboration self-enforcing by making it necessary for each group to cooperate in order to achieve its own interests. Companies were able to create such interdependencies in many ways, as two brief examples will illustrate.

- NEC has developed reciprocal relationships among different parts of its organizations by creating a series of internal quasi markets. It builds cooperation between the R&D function and the different product groups by allocating only a part of the R&D budget directly to the company's several central laboratories. This portion is used to support basic and applied research in core technologies of potential value to the corporation as a whole. The remaining funds are allocated to the product groups to support research programs that reflect their priorities. In response to the product divisions' proposed projects, each research group puts forward proposals that it feels will lead to the desired product or process improvements. What follows is a negotiation process that results in the product divisions' "buying" some of the proposals put up by the laboratories, while different R&D groups adopt some of the projects demanded by the product managers. In other words, NEC has created an internal market for ensuring that research is relevant to market needs. (A similar process seems to have had comparable success at Matsushita.)[8]

- Procter & Gamble employs an entirely different approach to creating and managing interdependencies. In Europe, for example, it formed a number of Eurobrand teams for developing product market strategies for different product lines.[9] Each team is headed by the general manager of a subsidiary that has a particularly well-developed competence in that business. It also includes the appropriate product and advertising managers from the other subsidiaries and relevant functional managers from the company's European headquarters. Each team's effectiveness clearly depends on the involvement and support provided by its members and, more important, by the organizational units they represent. Historically, the company's various subsidiaries had little incentive to cooperate. Now, however, the success of each team—and the reputation of the general manager heading it—depends on the support of other subsidiaries; this has made co-operation self-enforcing. Each general manager is aware that the level of support and commitment he can expect from the other members of the Eurobrand team depends on the support and contribution the product managers from his subsidiaries provide to the other teams. The interdependencies of these Eurobrand teams were able to foster teamwork driven by individual interests.

In observing many such examples of companies building and extending interdepend-ence among units, we were able to identify three important flows that seem to be at the center of the emerging organizational relationships. Most fundamental was the product interdependence that most companies were building as they specialized and integrated their worldwide manufacturing operations to achieve greater efficiency, while retaining sourcing flexibility and sensitivity to host country interests.[10] The resulting *flow of parts, components, and finished goods* increased the interdependence of the worldwide operations in an obvious and fundamental manner.

We also observed companies developing a resource interdependence that often contrasted sharply with earlier policies that had either encouraged local self-sufficiency or required the centralization of all surplus resources. Systems such as NEC's internal quasi markets were designed to develop a greater *flow of funds, skills, and other scarce resources* among organizational units.

Finally, the worldwide diffusion of technology, the development of international markets, and the globalization of competitive strategies have meant that vital strategic information now exists in many different locations worldwide. Furthermore, the growing dispersion of assets and delegation of responsibilities to foreign operations have resulted in the development of local knowledge and expertise that has implications for the broader organization. With these changes, the need to manage the *flow of intelligence, ideas, and knowledge* has become central to the learning process and has reinforced the growing interdependence of worldwide operations, as P&G's Eurobrand teams illustrate.

It is important to emphasize that the relationships we are highlighting are different from the interdependencies commonly observed in multiunit organizations. Traditionally, MNC managers have attempted to highlight what has been called "pooled interdependence" to make subunit managers responsive to global rather than local interests. (Before the Euroteam approach, for instance, P&G's European vice president often tried to convince independent-minded subsidiary managers to transfer surplus generated funds to other more needy subsidiaries, in the overall corporate interest, arguing that, "Someday when you're in need they might be able to fund a major product launch for you.")

As the example illustrates, pooled interdependence is often too broad and amorphous to affect day-to-day management behavior. The interdependencies we described earlier are more clearly reciprocal, and each unit's ability to achieve its goals is made conditional upon its willingness to help other units achieve their own goals. Such interdependencies more effectively promote the organization's ability to share the perspectives and link the resources of different components, and thereby to expand its organizational capabilities.[11]

FROM CONTROL TO COORDINATION AND COOPTION

The simplifying assumptions of organizational symmetry and dependence (or independence) had allowed the management processes in many companies to be dominated by simple controls—tight operational controls in subsidiaries dependent on the center, and a looser system of administrative or financial controls in decentralized units.[12] When companies began to challenge the assumptions underlying organizational relationships, however, they found they also had to adapt their management processes. The growing interdependence of organizational units strained the simple control-dominated systems and underlined the need to supplement existing processes with more sophisticated ones. Furthermore, the differentiation of organizational tasks and roles amplified the diversity of management perspectives and capabilities and forced management to differentiate management processes.

As organizations became, at the same time, more diverse and more interdependent, there was an explosion in the number of issues that had to be linked, reconciled, or integrated. The rapidly increasing flows of goods, resources, and information among organizational units increased the need for *coordination* as a central management function. But the costs of coordination are high, both in financial and human terms, and coordinating capabilities are always limited. Most companies, though, tended to concentrate on a primary means of coordination and control—"the company's way of doing things" (At ITT it was through "the system," as Harold Green used to call his sophisticated set of controls, while at Kao it was primarily through centralization of decisions.) Clearly, there was a need to develop multiple means of coordination, to rank the demands for coordination, and to allocate the scarce coordinating resources. The way in which one of our sample companies developed its portfolio of coordinative processes illustrates the point well.

During the late 1970s and early 1980s, Philips had gradually developed some sophisticated means of coordination. This greatly helped the company shape its historically evolved, nationally centered organization into the kind of multidimensional organization it needed to be in the 1980s. Coordinating the flow of goods in a global sourcing network is a highly complex logistical task, but one that can often be formalized and delegated to middle and lower-level management. By standardizing product specifications and rationalizing sourcing patterns through designating certain plants as international production centers (IPCs), Philips facilitated goods–flow coordination. By making these flows reasonably constant and forecastable, the company could manage them almost entirely through formal systems and processes. These became the main coordination mechanisms in the company's attempt to increase the integration of worldwide sourcing of products and components.

Coordinating the flow of financial, technical, and human resources, however, was not so easily routinized. Philips saw the allocation of these scarce resources as a reflection of key strategic choices and therefore managed the coordination process by centralizing many decisions. The board became heavily involved in major capital budgeting decisions; the product divisions reasserted control over product development, a process once jealously guarded by the national organizations; and the influential corporate staff bureau played a major role in personnel assignments and transfers.

But while goods flows could be coordinated through formalization, and resource flows through centralization, critical information flows were much more difficult to manage. The rapid globalization of the consumer electronics industry in the 1970s forced Philips to recognize the need to move strategic information and proprietary knowledge around the company much more quickly. While some routine data could be transferred through normal information systems, much of the information was so diverse and changeable that establishing formal processes was impossible. While some core knowledge had to be stored and transferred through corporate management, the sheer volume and complexity of information—and the need for its rapid diffusion—limited the ability to coordinate through centralization. Philips found that the most effective way to manage complex flows of information and knowledge was through various socialization processes: the transfer of people, the encouragement of informal communication channels that fostered information exchange, or the creation of forums that facilitated interunit learning.

Perhaps most well known is the company's constant worldwide transfer and rotation of a group of senior managers (once referred to internally as the "Dutch Mafia," but today a more international group) as a means of transferring critical knowledge and experience throughout the organization. Philips also made more extensive use of committees and task forces than any other company we studied. Although the frequent meetings and constant travel were expensive, the company benefitted not only from information exchange but also from the development of personal contacts that grew into vital information channels.

In other companies, we saw a similar broadening of administrative processes as managers learned to operate with previously underutilized means of coordination. Unilever's heavy reliance on the socialization of managers to provide the coordinational "glue" was supplemented by the growing role of the central product-coordination departments. In contrast, NEC reduced central management's coordination role by developing formal systems and social processes in a way that created a more robust and flexible coordinative capability.

Having developed diverse new means of coordination, management's main task is to carefully ration their usage and application. As the Philips example illustrates, it is important to distinguish where tasks can be formalized and managed through systems, where social linkages can be fostered to encourage informal agreements and cooperation, and where the coordination task is so vital or sensitive that it must use the scarce resource of central management arbitration.[13]

While the growing interdependence of organizational units forces the development of more complex administrative processes, the differentiation of roles and responsibilities forces management to change the way it uses the new coordination and control mechanisms. Even though they recognize the growing diversity of tasks facing them, a surprising number of companies have had great difficulty in differentiating the way they manage products, functions, or geographic units. The simplicity of applying a single planning and control system across businesses and the political acceptability of defining uniform job descriptions for all subsidiary heads were often allowed to outweigh the clear evidence that the relevant business characteristics and subsidiary roles were vastly different.

We have described briefly how companies began to remedy this situation by differentiating roles and responsibilities within the organization. Depending on their internal capabilities and on the strategic importance of their external environments, organizational units might be asked to take on roles ranging from that of strategic leader with primary corporatewide responsibility for a particular business or function, to simple implementer responsibility only for executing strategies and decisions developed elsewhere.

Clearly, these roles must be managed in quite different ways. The unit with strategic leadership responsibility must be given freedom to develop responsibility in an entrepreneurial fashion, yet must also be strongly supported by headquarters. For this unit, operating controls may be light and quite routine, but coordination of information and resource flows to and from the unit will probably require intensive involvement from senior management. In contrast, units with implementation responsibility might be managed through tight operating controls, with standardized systems used to handle much of the coordination—primarily of goods flows. Because the tasks are more routine, the use of scarce coordinating resources could be minimized.

Differentiating organizational roles and management processes can have a fragmenting and sometimes demotivating effect, however. Nowhere was this more clearly illustrated than in the many companies that unquestioningly assigned units the "dog" and "cash cow" roles defined by the Boston Consulting Group's growth-share matrix in the 1970s.[14] Their experience showed that there is another equally important corporate management task that complements and facilitates coordination effectiveness. We call this task *cooption:* the process of uniting the organization with a common understanding of, identification with, and commitment to the corporation's objectives, priorities, and values.

A clear example of the importance of cooption was provided by the contrast between ITT and NEC managers. At ITT, corporate objectives were communicated more in financial than in strategic terms, and the company's national entities identified almost exclusively with their local environment. When corporate management tried to superimpose a more unified and integrated global strategy, its local subsidiaries neither understood nor accepted the need to do so. For years they resisted giving up their autonomy, and management was unable to replace the interunit rivalry with a more cooperative and collaborative process.

In contrast, NEC developed an explicitly defined and clearly communicated global strategy enshrined in the company's "C&C" motto—a corporatewide dedication to building business and basing competitive strategy on the strong link between computers and communications. For over a decade, the C&C philosophy was constantly interpreted, refined, elaborated, and eventually institutionalized in organizational units dedicated to various C&C missions (e.g., the C&C Systems Research Laboratories, the C&C Corporate Planning Committee, and eventually the C&C Systems Division). Top management recognized that one of its major tasks was to inculcate the worldwide organization with an understanding of the C&C strategy and philosophy and to raise managers' consciousness about the global implications of competing in these converging businesses. By the mid-1980s, the company was confident that every NEC employee in every operating unit had a clear understanding of NEC's global strategy as well as of his or her role in it. Indeed, it was this homogeneity that allowed the company to begin the successful decentralization of its strategic tasks and the differentiation of its management processes.

Thus the management process that distinguished transnational organizations from simpler unidimensional forms was one in which control was made less dominant by the increased importance of interunit integration and collaboration. These new processes required corporate management to supplement its control role with the more subtle tasks of coordination and cooption, giving rise to a much more complex and sophisticated management process.

SUSTAINING A DYNAMIC BALANCE: ROLE OF THE "MIND MATRIX"

Developing multidimensional perspectives and capabilities does not mean that product, function, and geographic management must have the same level of influence on all key decisions. Quite the contrary. It means that the organization must possess a differentiated influence structure—one in which different groups have different roles for different activities. These roles cannot be fixed but must change continually to respond to new environmental demands and evolving industry characteristics. Not only is it necessary to prevent any one perspective from dominating the others, it is equally important not to be locked into a mode of operation that prevents reassignment of responsibilities, realignment of relationships, and rebalancing of power distribution. This ability to manage the multidimensional organization capability in a flexible manner is the hallmark of a transnational company.

In the change processes we have described, managers were clearly employing some powerful organizational tools to create and control the desired flexible management process. They used the classic tool of formal structure to strengthen, weaken, or shift roles and responsibilities over time, and they employed management systems effectively to redirect corporate resources and to channel information in a way that shifted the balance of power. By controlling the ebb and flow of responsibilities, and by rebalancing power relationships, they were able to prevent any of the multidimensional perspectives from atrophying. Simultaneously, they prevented the establishment of entrenched power bases.

But the most successful companies had an additional element at the core of their management processes. We were always conscious that a substantial amount of senior management attention focused on the *individual* members of the organization. NEC's continual efforts to inculcate all corporate members with a common vision of goals and priorities; P&G's careful assignment of managers to teams and task forces to broaden their perspectives; Philips's frequent use of conferences and meetings as forums to reconcile differences; and Unilever's extensive use of training as a powerful socialization process and its well-planned career path management that provided diverse experience across businesses, functions, and geographic locations—all are examples of companies trying to develop multidimensional perspectives and flexible approaches at the level of the individual manager.

What is critical, then, is not just the structure, but also the mentality of those who constitute the structure. The common thread that holds together the diverse tasks we have described is a managerial mindset that understands the need for multiple strategic capabilities, that is able to view problems from both local and global perspectives, and that accepts the importance of a flexible approach. This pattern suggests that managers should resist the temptation to view their task in the traditional terms of building a formal global matrix structure—an organizational form that in practice has proven extraordinarily difficult to manage in the international environment. They might be better guided by the perspective of one top manager who described the challenge as "creating a matrix in the minds of managers."

Our study has led us to conclude that a company's ability to develop transnational organizational capability and management mentality will be the key factor that separates the winners from the mere survivors in the emerging international environment.

REFERENCES

1. The findings presented in this article are based on a three-year research project on the organization and management of multinational corporations. A description of the three-phase study and of the nine American, European, and Japanese MNCs that made up the core of the clinical research stage is contained in the companion article, "Managing across Borders: New Strategic Requirements" (Summer 1987). Complete findings will be presented in the forthcoming book, *Managing across Borders: The Transnational Solution* (Boston: Harvard Business School Press, forthcoming).

2. This global integration/national responsiveness framework was first applied to the analysis of MNC tasks by Prahalad. See C.K. Prahalad, "The Strategic Process in a Multinational Corporation" (Boston: Harvard Business School, unpublished doctoral dissertation, 1976).

3. Working with a group of Swedish companies, Hedlund has come to similar conclusions. He describes MNCs with dispersed capabilities and differentiated operations as "heterarchies." See G. Hedlund, "The Hypermodern MNC—A Heterarchy?" *Human Resource Management*, Spring 1986, pp. 9–35.

4. Rugman and Poynter have observed a similar phenomenon in the trend toward assigning mature national subsidiaries worldwide responsibility for products with worldwide markets. See A.M. Rugman and T.A. Poynter, "World Product Mandates: How Will Multinationals Respond?" *Business Quarterly*, October 1982, pp. 54–61.

5. This issue of differentiation in the roles and responsibilities of MNC subsidiaries has been discussed and a normative framework for creating such differentiation has been proposed in C.A. Bartlett and S. Ghoshal, "Tap Your Subsidiaries for Global Reach," *Harvard Business Review*, November-December 1986, pp. 87–94.

6. Such global competitive strategies have been described extensively by many authors. See, for example, T. Hout, M.E. Porter, and E. Rudden, "How Global Companies Win Out," Harvard Business Review, September-October 1982, pp. 98–108, and G. Hamel and C.K. Prahalad, "Do You Really Have a Global Strategy?" *Harvard Business Review*, July-August 1985, pp. 139–148.

7. See R.M. Kanter, *The Change Masters* (New York: Simon & Schuster, 1983).

8. The use of such internal quasi market mechanisms as a means of managing interdependencies has been richly described by Westney and Sakakibara. See D.E. Westney and K. Sakakibara, "The Role of Japan-Based R&D in Global Technology Strategy" *Technology in Society* (1985): 315–330.

9. For a full description of the development of Eurobrand in P&G, See C.A. Bartlett, "Procter & Gamble Europe: Vizir Launch" (Boston: Harvard Business School, Case Services #9-384-139).

10. Kogut provides an excellent discussion on how multinational corporations can develop operational flexibility using a worldwide configuration of specialized resource capabilities linked through an integrated management system. See B. Kogut, "Designing Global Strategies: Profiting from Operational Flexibility," *Sloan Management Review*, Fall 1985, pp. 27–38.

11. The distinction among sequential, reciprocal, and pooled interdependencies has been made in J.D. Thompson, *Organizations in Action* (New York: McGraw-Hill, 1967).

12. The role of headquarters management in establishing control over worldwide operations and the means by which it is done have been richly described in Y.L. Doz and C.K. Prahalad, "Headquarters Influence and Strategic Control in MNCs," *Sloan Management Review*, Fall 1981, pp. 15–30.

13. The use of centralization, formalization, and socialization as means of coordination has been discussed by many authors, including P.M. Blau and R.A. Schoenherr, *The Structure of Organizations* (New York:

Basic Books, 1971); and W.G. Ouchi, "Markets, Bureaucracies, and Clans," *Administrative Science Quarterly 25* (March 1980): 129–141. In the specific context of the multinational corporation, the process implications of these mechanisms were described by Bartlett in a model that distinguished "substantive decision management," "temporary coalition management," and "decision context management" as alternative management process modes in MNCs. See C.A. Bartlett, "Multinational Structural Evolution: The Changing Decision Environments" (Boston: Harvard Business School, unpublished doctoral dissertation, 1979).

See also the contributions of G. Hedlund, T. Kogono, and L. Leksell in *The Management of Headquarters—Subsidiary Relationships in MNCs*, ed. L. Otterbeck (London: Gower Publishing, 1981); and Doz and Prahalad (Fall 1981).

14. See P. Haspeslagh, "Portfolio Planning: Uses and Limits," *Harvard Business Review*, January-February 1982, pp. 58–73.

What Is a Global Manager?

CHRISTOPHER A. BARTLETT & SUMANTRA GHOSHAL

IN THE EARLY STAGES of its drive overseas, Corning Glass hired an American ex-ambassador to head up its international division. He had excellent contacts in the governments of many nations and could converse in several languages, but he was less familiar with Corning and its businesses. In contrast, ITT decided to set up a massive educational program to "globalize" all managers responsible for its worldwide telecommunications business—in essence, to replace its national specialists with global generalists.

Corning and ITT eventually realized they had taken wrong turns. Like many other companies organizing for worldwide operations in recent years, they found that an elite of jet-setters was often difficult to integrate into the corporate mainstream; nor did they need an international team of big-picture overseers to the exclusion of focused experts.

Success in today's international climate—a far cry from only a decade ago—demands highly specialized yet closely linked groups of global business managers, country or regional managers, and world-wide functional managers. This kind of organization characterizes a *transnational* rather than an old-line multinational, international, or global company. Transnationals integrate assets, resources, and diverse people in operating units around the world. Through a flexible management process, in which business, country, and functional managers form a triad of different perspectives that balance one another, transnational companies can build three strategic capabilities:

- global-scale efficiency and competitiveness;
- national-level responsiveness and flexibility; and
- cross-market capacity to leverage learning on a worldwide basis.

While traditional organizations, structured along product or geographic lines, can hone one or another of these capabilities, they cannot cope with the challenge of all three at once. But an emerging group of transnational companies has begun to transform the classic hierarchy of headquarters-subsidiary relationships into an integrated network of specialized yet interdependent units. For many, the greatest constraint in creating such an organization is a severe shortage of executives with the skills, knowledge, and sophistication to operate in a more tightly linked and less classically hierarchical network.

In fact, in the volatile world of transnational corporations, there is no such thing as a universal global manager. Rather, there are three groups of specialists: business managers, country managers, and functional managers. And there are the top executives at corporate headquarters, the leaders who manage the complex interactions between the three—and can identify and develop the talented executives a successful transnational requires.

To build such talent, top management must understand the strategic importance of each specialist. The careers of Leif Johansson of Electrolux, Howard Gottlieb of NEC, and Wahib Zaki of Procter & Gamble vividly exemplify the specialized yet interdependent roles the three types of global managers play.

THE BUSINESS MANAGER: STRATEGIST + ARCHITECT + COORDINATOR

Global business or product-division managers have one overriding responsibility: to further the company's global-scale efficiency and competitiveness. This task requires not only the perspective to recognize opportunities and risks across national and functional boundaries but also the skill to coordinate activities and link capabilities across those barriers. The global business manager's overall goal is to capture the full benefit of integrated worldwide operations.

To be effective, the three roles at the core of a business manager's job are to serve as the strategist for his or her organization, the architect of its worldwide asset and resource configuration, and the coordinator of transactions across national borders. Leif Johansson, now president of Electrolux, the Swedish-based company, played all three roles successfully in his earlier position as head of the household appliance division.

In 1983, when 32-year-old Johansson assumed responsibility for the division, he took over a business that had been built up through more than 100 acquisitions over the previous eight years. By the late 1980s, Electrolux's portfolio included more than 20 brands sold in some 40 countries, with acquisitions continuing throughout the decade. Zanussi, for example, the big Italian manufacturer acquired by Electrolux in 1984, had built a strong market presence based on its reputation for innovation in household and commercial appliances. In addition, Arthur Martin in France and Zoppas in Norway had strong local brand positions but limited innovative capability.

As a result of these acquisitions, Electrolux had accumulated a patchwork quilt of companies, each with a different product portfolio, market position, and competitive situation. Johansson soon recognized the need for an overall strategy to coordinate and integrate his dispersed operations.

Talks with national marketing managers quickly convinced him that dropping local brands and standardizing around a few high-volume regional and global products would be unwise. He agreed with the local managers that their national brands were vital to maintaining consumer loyalty, distribution leverage, and competitive flexibility in markets that they saw fragmenting into more and more segments. But Johansson also understood the views of his division staff members, who pointed to the many similarities in product characteristics and consumer needs in the various markets. The division staff was certain Electrolux could use this advantage to cut across markets and increase competitiveness.

Johansson led a strategy review with a task force of product-division staff and national marketing managers. While the task force confirmed the marketing managers' notion of growing segmentation, its broader perspective enabled Johansson to see a convergence of segments across national markets. Their closer analysis also refined management's understanding of local market needs, concluding that consumers perceived "localness" mainly in terms of how a product was sold (distribution through local channels, promotion in local media, use of local brand names) instead of how it was designed or what features it offered.

From this analysis, Johansson fashioned a product-market strategy that identified two full-line regional brands to be promoted and supported in all European markets. He positioned the Electrolux brand to respond to the cross-market segment for high prestige (customers characterized as "conservatives"), while the Zanussi brand would fill the segment where innovative products were key (for "trendsetters").

The local brands were clustered in the other two market segments pinpointed in the analysis: "yuppies" ("young and aggressive" urban professionals) and "environmentalists" ("warm and friendly" people interested in basic value products). The new strategy provided Electrolux with localized brands that responded to the needs of these consumer groups. At the same time, the company captured the efficiencies possible by standardizing the basic chassis and components of these local-brand products, turning them out in high volume in specialized regional plants.

So, by tracking product and market trends across borders, Leif Johansson captured valuable global-scale efficiencies while reaping the benefits of a flexible response to national market fragmentation. What's more, though he took on the leadership role as a strategist, Johansson never assumed he alone had the understanding or the ability to form a global appliance strategy; he relied heavily on both corporate and local managers. Indeed, Johansson continued to solicit guidance on strategy through a council of country managers called the 1992 Group and through a set of product councils made up of functional managers.

In fact, the global business manager's responsibility for the distribution of crucial assets and resources is closely tied to shaping an integrated strategy. While he or she often relies on the input of regional and functional heads, the business manager is still the architect who usually initiates and leads the debate on where major plants, technical centers, and sales offices should be located—and which facilities should be closed.

The obvious political delicacy of such debates is not the only factor that makes simple economic analysis inadequate. Within every operating unit there exists a pool of skills and capabilities that may have taken a lot of time and investment to build up. The global business manager has to achieve the most efficient distribution of assets and resources while protecting and leveraging the competence at hand. Electrolux's household appliance division had more than 200 plants and a bewildering array of technical centers and development groups in many countries. It was clear to Johansson that he had to rationalize this infrastructure.

He began by setting a policy for the household appliance division that would avoid concentration of facilities in one country or region, even in its Scandinavian home base. At the same time, Johansson wanted to specialize the division's development and manufacturing infrastructure on a "one product, one facility" basis. He was determined to allocate important development and manufacturing tasks to each of the company's major markets. In trying to optimize robustness and flexibility in the long term rather than minimize short-term costs, Johansson recognized that a specialized yet dispersed system would be less vulnerable to exchange-rate fluctuations and political uncertainties. This setup also tapped local managerial and technical resources, thereby reducing dependence on the small pool of skilled labor and management in Sweden.

Instead of closing old plants, Johansson insisted on upgrading and tailoring existing facilities, whenever possible. In addition to averting political fallout and organizational trauma, Electrolux would then retain valuable know-how and bypass the startup problems of building from scratch. An outstanding example of this approach is Zanussi's Porcia plant in Italy, which Electrolux turned into the world's largest washing machine plant. After a massive $150-million investment, the Porcia plant now produces 1.5 million units a year.

Although acquisition-fueled growth often leads to redundancy and overcapacity, it can also bring new resources and strengths. Instead of wiping out the division's diversity through homogenization or centralization, Johansson decided to leverage it by matching each unit's responsibilities with its particular competence. Because of the Scandinavian flair for modular design, he assigned the integrated kitchen-system business to Electrolux's Swedish and Finnish units. He acknowledged Porcia's experience in component production by consolidating design and production of compressors there. Johansson's reshaping of assets and resources not only enhanced scale economies and operational flexibility but also boosted morale by giving operating units the opportunity to leverage their distinctive competences beyond their local markets.

Newly developed business strategies obviously need coordination. In practice, the specialization of assets and resources swells the flow of products and components among national units, requiring a firm hand to synchronize and control that flow. For organizations whose operations have become more dispersed and specialized at the same time that their strategies have become more connected and integrated, coordination across borders is a tough challenge. Business managers must fashion a repertoire of approaches and tools, from simple centralized control to management of exceptions identified through formal policies to indirect management via informal communication channels.

Leif Johansson coordinated product flow—across his 35 national sales units and 29 regional sourcing facilities—by establishing broad sourcing policies and transfer-pricing ranges that set limits but left negotiations to internal suppliers and customers. For instance, each sales unit could negotiate a transfer price with its internal source for a certain product in a set range that was usually valid for a year. If the negotiations moved outside that range, the companies had to check with headquarters. As a coordinator, Johansson led the deliberations that defined the logic and philosophy of the parameters; but he stepped back and let individual unit managers run their own organizations, except when a matter went beyond policy limits.

In contrast, coordination of business strategy in Johansson's division was managed through teams that cut across the formal hierarchy. Instead of centralizing, he relied on managers to share the responsibility for monitoring implementation and resolving problems through teams. To protect the image and positioning of his regional brands—Electrolux and Zanussi—he set up a brand-coordination group for each. Group members came from the sales companies in key countries, and the chairperson was a corporate marketing executive. Both groups were responsible for building a coherent, pan-European strategy for the brand they represented.

To rationalize the various product strategies across Europe, Johansson created product-line boards to oversee these strategies and to exploit any synergies. Each product line had its own board made up of the corporate product-line manager, who was chair, and his or her product managers. The Quattro 500 refrigerator-freezer, which was designed in Italy, built in Finland, and marketed in Sweden, was one example of how these boards could successfully integrate product strategy.

In addition, the 1992 Group periodically reviewed the division's overall results, kept an eye on its manufacturing and marketing infrastructure, and supervised major development programs and investment projects. Capturing the symbolic value of 1992 in its name, the group was chaired by Johansson himself and included business managers from Italy, the United Kingdom, Spain, the United States, France, Switzerland, and Sweden.

Indeed, coordination probably takes up more of the global business manager's time than any other aspect of the job. This role requires that a manager have great administrative and interpersonal skills to ensure that coordination and integration don't deteriorate into heavy-handed control.

Many traditional multinational companies have made the mistake of automatically anointing their home country product-division managers with the title of global business manager. Sophisticated transnational companies, however, have long since separated the notions of coordination and centralization, looking for business leadership from their best units, wherever they may be located. For example, Asea Brown Boveri, the Swiss-headquartered electrical engineering corporation, has tried to leverage the strengths of its operating companies and exploit their location in critical markets by putting its business managers wherever strategic and organizational dimensions coincide. In Asea Brown Boveri's power-transmission business, the manager for switchgear is located in Sweden, the manager for power transformers is in Germany, the manager for distribution transformers is in Norway, and the manager for electric metering is in the United States.

Even well-established multinationals with a tradition of tight central control are changing their tack. The head of IBM's telecommunications business recently moved her division headquarters to London, not only to situate the command center closer to the booming European market for computer networking but also "to give us a different perspective on all our markets."

THE COUNTRY MANAGER: SENSOR + BUILDER + CONTRIBUTOR

The building blocks for most worldwide companies are their national subsidiaries. If the global business manager's main objective is to achieve global-scale efficiency and competitiveness, the national subsidiary manager's is to be sensitive and responsive to the local market. Country managers play the pivotal role not only in meeting local customer needs but also in satisfying the host government's requirements and defending their company's market positions against local and external competitors.

The need for local flexibility often puts the country manager in conflict with the global business manager. But in a successful transnational like Electrolux, negotiation can resolve these differences. In this era of intense competition around the world, companies cannot afford to permit a subsidiary manager to defend parochial interests as "king of the country."

Nor should headquarters allow national subsidiaries to become the battleground for corporate holy wars fought in the name of globalization. In many companies, their national subsidiaries are hothouses of entrepreneurship and innovation—homes for valuable resources and capabilities that must be nurtured, not constrained or cut off. The subsidiaries of Philips, for one, have consistently led product development: in television, the company's first color TV was developed in Canada, the first stereo model in Australia, and the first teletext in the United Kingdom. Unilever's national subsidiaries have also been innovative in product marketing strategy: Germany created the campaign for Snuggle (a fabric softener); Finland developed Timotei (an herbal shampoo); and South Africa launched Impulse (a body perfume).

In fact, effective country managers play three vital roles: the sensor and interpreter of local opportunities and threats, the builder of local resources and capabilities, and the contributor to and active participant in global strategy. Howard Gottlieb's experience as general manager of NEC's switching-systems subsidiary in the United States illustrates the importance of all three tasks.

As a sensor, the country manager must be good at gathering and sifting information, interpreting the implications, and predicting a range of feasible outcomes. More important, this manager has the difficult task of conveying the importance of such intelligence to people higher up, especially those whose perceptions may be dimmed by distance or even ethnocentric bias. Today, when information gathered locally increasingly applies to other regions or even globally, communicating effectively is crucial. Consumer trends in one country often spread to another; technologies developed in a leading edge environment can have global significance; a competitor's local market testing may signal a wider strategy; and national legislative initiatives in areas like deregulation and environmental protection tend to spill across borders.

Gottlieb's contribution to NEC's understanding of changes in the telecommunications market demonstrates how a good sensor can connect local intelligence with global strategy. In the late 1980s, Gottlieb was assigned to build the U.S. market for NEAX 61, a widely acclaimed digital telecom switch designed by the parent company in Japan. Although it was technologically sophisticated, early sales didn't meet expectations.

His local-market background and contacts led Gottlieb to a quick diagnosis of the problem. NEC had designed the switch to meet the needs of NTT, the Japanese telephone monopoly, and it lacked many features U.S. customers wanted. For one thing, its software didn't incorporate the protocol conversions necessary for distributing revenues among the many U.S. companies that might handle a single long-distance phone call. Nor could the switch handle revenue-enhancing features like "call waiting" and "call forwarding," which were vital high-margin items in the competitive, deregulated American market.

In translating the needs of his U.S. division to the parent company NEC, Gottlieb had a formidable task. To convince his superiors in Japan that redesigning NEAX 61 was necessary, he had to bridge two cultures and penetrate the subtleties of the parent company's Japanese-dominated management processes. And he had to instill a sense of urgency in several corporate management groups, varying his pitches to appeal to the interests of each. For instance, Gottlieb convinced the engineering department that the NEAX 61 switch had been underdesigned for the U.S. market and the marketing department that time was short because the Bell operating companies were calling for quotes.

A transnational's greater access to the scarcest of all corporate resources, human capability, is a definite advantage when compared with strictly local companies—or old-line multinationals, for that matter. Scores of companies like IBM, Merck, and Procter & Gamble have recognized the value of harvesting advanced (and often less expensive) scientific expertise by upgrading local development labs into global centers of technical excellence.

Other companies have built up and leveraged their overseas human resources in different ways. Cummins Engine, for example, has set up its highly skilled but surprisingly low-cost Indian engineering group as a worldwide drafting resource; American Airlines's Barbados operation does much of the corporate clerical work; and Becton Dickinson, a large hospital supply company, has given its Belgian subsidiary pan-European responsibility for managing distribution and logistics.

Indeed, the burden of identifying, developing, and leveraging such national resources and capabilities falls on country managers. Howard Gottlieb, after convincing Tokyo that the United States would be an important market for NEC's global digital switch design, persuaded headquarters to permit his new engineering group to take part early on the product development of the next generation switch—the NEAX 61 E. He sent teams of engineers to Japan to work with the original designers; and, to verify his engineers' judgments,

Gottlieb invited the designers to visit his customers in the United States. These exchanges not only raised the sensitivity of NEC's Japan-based engineers to U.S. market needs but also significantly increased their respect for their American colleagues. Equally important, the U.S. unit's morale rose.

As a builder, Gottlieb used this mutual confidence as the foundation for creating a software-development capability that would become a big corporate asset. Skilled software engineers, very scarce in Japan, were widely available in the United States. Gottlieb's first move was to put together a small software team to support local projects. Though its resources were limited, the group turned out a number of innovations, including a remote software-patching capability that later became part of the 61 E switch design. The credibility he won at headquarters allowed Gottlieb to expand his design engineering group from 10 to more than 50 people within two years, supporting developments not only in North America but also eventually in Asia.

In many transnationals, access to strategically important information—and control over strategically important assets—has catapulted country managers into a much more central role. As links to local markets, they are no longer mere implementers of programs and policies shaped at headquarters; many have gained some influence over the way their organizations make important strategic and operational decisions. In most of today's truly transnational companies, country managers and their chief local subordinates often participate in new product–development committees, product marketing task forces, and global-strategy conferences. Even at the once impenetrable annual top management meetings, national subsidiary managers may present their views and defend their interests before senior corporate and domestic executives—a scenario that would have been unthinkable even a decade ago.

Of course, the historic position of most national units of worldwide companies has been that of the implementer of strategy from headquarters. Because the parent company's accepted objectives are the outcome of discussion and negotiation involving numerous units, divisions, and national subsidiaries, sometimes a country manager must carry out a strategy that directly conflicts with what he or she has lobbied for in vain.

But a diverse and dispersed worldwide organization, with subsidiaries that control many of the vital development, production, and marketing resources, can no longer allow the time-honored "king of the country" to decide how, when, and even whether his or her national unit will implement a particular strategic initiative. The decision made by the North American subsidiary of Philips to outscore its VCRs from a Japanese competitor rather than the parent company is one of the most notorious instances of how a local "king" can undermine global strategy. At NEC, Howard Gottlieb spent about 60% of his time on customer relations and probing the market and about 30% managing the Tokyo interface. His ability to understand and interpret the global strategic implications of U.S. market need—and the software development group he built from scratch—allowed him to take part in NEC's ongoing strategy debate. As a result, Gottlieb changed his division's role from implementer of corporate strategy to active contributor in designing that strategy.

THE FUNCTIONAL MANAGER: SCANNER + CROSS-POLLINATOR + CHAMPION

While global business managers and country managers have come into their own, functional specialists have yet to gain the recognition due them in many traditional multinational companies. Relegated to support-staff roles, excluded from important meetings, and even dismissed as unnecessary overhead, functional managers are often given little chance to participate in, let alone contribute to, the corporate mainstream's global activity. In some cases, top management has allowed staff functions to become a warehouse for corporate misfits or a graveyard for managerial has-beens. Yet at a time when information, knowledge, and expertise have become more specialized, an organization can gain huge benefits by linking its technical, manufacturing, marketing, human resources, and financial experts worldwide.

Given that today's transnationals face the strategic challenge of resolving the conflicts implicit in achieving global competitiveness, national responsiveness, and worldwide learning, business and country managers must take primary responsibility for the first two capabilities. But the third is the functional manager's province.

Building an organization that can use learning to create and spread innovations requires the skill to transfer specialized knowledge while also connecting scarce resources and capabilities across national borders. To achieve this important objective, functional managers must scan for specialized information worldwide, "cross-pollinate" leading-edge knowledge and best practice, and champion innovations that may offer transnational opportunities and applications.

Most innovation starts, of course, when managers perceive a particular opportunity or market threat, such as an emerging consumer trend, a revolutionary technological development, a bold competitive move, or a pending government regulation. When any of these flags pops up around the world, it may seem unimportant to corporate headquarters if viewed in isolation. But when a functional manager acts as a scanner, with the expertise and perspective to detect trends and move knowledge across boundaries, he or she can transform piecemeal information into strategic intelligence.

In sophisticated transnationals, senior functional executives serve as linchpins, connecting their areas of specialization throughout the organization. Using informal networks, they create channels for communicating specialized information and repositories for proprietary knowledge. Through such links, Electrolux marketing managers first identified the emergence of cross-market segments and NEC's technical managers were alerted to the shift from analog to digital switching technology.

In the same manner, Wahib Zaki of Procter & Gamble's European operations disapproved of P&G's high-walled organizational structures, which isolated and insulated the technical development carried out in each subsidiary's lab. When Zaki became head of R&D in Europe, he decided to break down some walls. In his new job, he was ideally placed to become a scanner and cross-pollinator. He formed European technical teams and ran a series of conferences in which like-minded experts from various countries could exchange information and build informal communication networks.

Still, Zaki needed more ammunition to combat the isolation, defensiveness, and "not invented here" attitude in each research center. He distributed staff among the European technical center in Brussels and the development groups of P&G's subsidiaries. He used his staff teams to help clarify the particular role of each national technical manager and to specialize activities that had been duplicated on a country-by-country basis with little transfer of accumulated knowledge.

In response to competitive threats from rivals Unilever, Henkel, and Colgate-Palmolive— and to a perceived consumer trend—P&G's European headquarters asked the Brussels-based research center to develop a new liquid laundry detergent. By that time, Zaki had on hand a technical team that had built up relationships among its members so that it formed a close-knit network of intelligence and product expertise.

The team drew the product profile necessary for healthy sales in multiple markets with diverse needs. In several European markets, powdered detergents contained enzymes to break down protein-based stains, and the new liquid detergent would have to accomplish the same thing. In some markets, a bleach substitute was important; in others, hard water presented the toughest challenge; while in several countries, environmental concerns limited the use of phosphates. Moreover, the new detergent had to be effective in large-capacity, top-loading machines, as well as in the small front-loading machines common in Europe.

Zaki's team developed a method that made enzymes stable in liquid form (a new technique that was later patented), a bleach substitute effective at low temperatures, a fatty acid that yielded good water-softening performance without phosphates, and a suds-suppressant that worked in front-loading machines (so bubbles wouldn't ooze out the door). By integrating resources and expertise, Zaki cross-pollinated best practice for a new product.

The R&D group was so successful that the European headquarters adopted the use of teams for its management of the new brand launch. P&G's first European brand team pooled the knowledge and expertise of brand managers from seven subsidiaries to draft a launch program and marketing strategy for the new liquid detergent Vizir, which ensured its triumphant rollout in seven countries in six months. P&G's homework enabled it to come up with a product that responded to European needs, while Colgate-Palmolive was forced to withdraw its liquid detergent brand, Axion—which had been designed in the United States and wasn't tailored for Europe—after an 18-month market test.

As a reward for his performance in Europe, Wahib Zaki was transferred to Procter & Gamble's Cincinnati corporate headquarters as a senior vice president of R&D. He found that researchers there were working on improved builders (the ingredients that break down dirt) for a new liquid laundry detergent to be launched in the United States. In addition, the international technology-coordination group was working with P&G's Japanese subsidiary to formulate a liquid detergent surfactant (the ingredient that removes greasy stains) that would be effective in the cold-water washes common in Japanese households, where laundry is often done in used bath water. Neither group had shared its findings or new ideas with the other, and neither had incorporated the numerous breakthroughs represented by Vizir—despite the evidence that consumer needs, market trends, competitive challenges, and regulatory requirements were all spreading across national borders.

Playing the role of champion, Zaki decided to use this development process to demonstrate the benefits of coordinating P&G's sensitivity and responsiveness to diverse consumer needs around the world. He formed a team drawn from three technical groups (one in Brussels and two in the United States) to turn out a world liquid laundry detergent. The team analyzed the trends, generated product specifications, and brought together dispersed technical knowledge and expertise, which culminated in one of Procter & Gamble's most successful product launches ever. Sold as Liquid Tide in the United States, Liquid Cheer in Japan, and Liquid Ariel in Europe, the product was P&G's first rollout on such a global scale.

As Zaki continued to strengthen cross-border technology links through other projects, Procter & Gamble gradually converted its far-flung sensing and response resources into an integrated learning organization. By scanning for new developments, cross-pollinating best practice, and championing innovations with transnational applications, Wahib Zaki, a superlative functional manager, helped create an organization that could both develop demonstrably better new products and roll them out at a rapid pace around the world.

THE CORPORATE MANAGER: LEADER + TALENT SCOUT + DEVELOPER

Clearly, there is no single model for the global manager. Neither the oldline international specialist nor the more recent global generalist can cope with the complexities of cross-border strategies. Indeed, the dynamism of today's marketplace calls for managers with diverse skills. Responsibility for worldwide operations belongs to senior business, country, and functional executives who focus on the intense interchanges and subtle negotiations required. In contrast, those in middle management and front-line jobs need well-defined responsibilities, a clear understanding of their organization's transnational mission, and a sense of accountability—but few of the distractions senior negotiators must shoulder.

Meanwhile, corporate managers integrate these many levels of responsibility, playing perhaps the most vital role in transnational management. The corporate manager not only leads in the broadest sense; he or she also identifies and develops talented business, country, and functional managers—and balances the negotiations among the three. It's up to corporate managers to promote strong managerial specialists like Johansson, Gottlieb, and Zaki, those individuals who can translate company strategy into effective operations around the world.

Successful corporate managers like Floris Maljers, co-chairman of Unilever, have made the recruitment, training, and development of promising executives a top priority. By the 1980s, with Maljers as chairman, Unilever had a clear policy of rotating managers through various jobs and moving them around the world, especially early in their careers. Unilever was one of the first transnationals to have a strong pool of specialized yet interdependent senior managers, drawn from throughout its diverse organization.

But while most companies require only a few truly transnational managers to implement cross-border strategies, the particular qualities necessary for such positions remain in short supply. According to Maljers, it is this limitation in human resources—not unreliable or inadequate sources of capital that has become the biggest constraint in most globalization efforts.

Locating such individuals is difficult under any circumstances, but corporate managers greatly improve the odds when their search broadens from a focus on home-country managers to incorporate the worldwide pool of executives in their organization. Because transnationals operate in many countries, they have access to a wide range of managerial talent. Yet such access—like information on local market trends or consumer needs that should cross organizational boundaries—is often an underexploited asset.

As a first step, senior executives can identify those in the organization with the potential for developing the skills and perspectives demanded of global managers. Such individuals must have a broad, nonparochial view of the company and its operations yet a deep understanding of their own business, country, or functional tasks. Obviously, even many otherwise talented managers in an organization aren't capable of such a combination of flexibility and commitment to specific interests, especially when it comes to cross-border coordination and integration. Top management may have to track the careers of promising executives over a number of years before deciding whether to give them senior responsibilities. At Unilever, for example, the company maintains four development lists that indicate both the level of each manager and his or her potential. The progress of managers on the top "A1" list is tracked by Unilever's Special Committee, which includes the two chairmen.

Once corporate managers identify the talent, they have the duty to develop it. They must provide opportunities for achievement that allow business, country, and functional managers to handle negotiations in a worldwide context. A company's ability to identify individuals with potential, legitimize their diversity, and integrate them into the organization's corporate decisions is the single clearest indicator that the corporate leader is a true global manager—and that the company itself is a true transnational.

SECTION III

Global Information Systems and Technology: Planning and Strategic Implications

Integrated information systems and information technology applications have become central to the operations of the firm and an important link to corporate strategy. This changing role of information technology represents an important challenge for top management as larger investments in technology become necessary and the risks more difficult to predict. There are many examples of ways in which companies have utilized information technology to provide a competitive advantage to the company. The opportunities are endless, while the challenges remain paramount.

In the first paper in this section, Ives, Jarvenpaa, and Mason identify seven developments in the business environment that are driven by information technology and provide the impetus for globalization. The authors argue that analysis of these global business drivers will help a firm identify its global business system requirements. The firm's overall objectives should reflect a close alignment between the global vision for the firm and its IT strategy and architecture. Appropriate alignment strategy can potentially provide a global competitive advantage that would not otherwise be possible.

In the second paper, Karimi and Konsynski contend that new organizational structures are necessary to meet the changing needs of new market structures and information systems strategies. The authors identify options for aligning business strategies and structures with a firm's IT architecture. Choosing the right strategy and structure may have profound consequences for the functionality and efficient management of the firm's resources.

Without question, the future holds many uncertainties and challenges for the transnational company. The readings in this section present some of the issues from a managerial strategic-planning perspective. The strategic plan becomes the firm's blueprint from which to make adjustments and take action even in the midst of change and uncertainty.

Global Business Drivers:
Aligning Information Technology
to Global Business Strategy

BLAKE IVES, SIRKKA L. JARVENPAA & RICHARD O. MASON

IN THE FOREFRONT of the transition of a firm to a globally coordinated and managed organization is information technology. Information technology can drive the change, be harnessed to it, or rise up as a severe impediment. The chief executive of a major corporation has suggested that "globalization is no longer an objective but an imperative, as markets and geographical barriers become increasingly blurred and even irrelevant."[1] This paper explores how the application of information technology to the transition process can result in successful firms in a global market.

Information technology (I/T) can drive a firm toward globalization in a number of ways. Using computer and communications technologies, firms can extract the information components from tangible products, or substitute knowledge for material, and then instantly transport the electronically represented information or knowledge throughout the world. Value can be added or an information-based product can be used at the most economically advantageous location. The time delays, high costs, and lack of customer responsiveness associated with transportation, reproduction, and inventory can be reduced or even eliminated. This instantaneous "world reach" produces major changes in order management, manufacturing, and marketing cycles. For example, the Society for Worldwide Interbank Financial Telecommunications (SWIFT) system electronically moves money freely and rapidly across national boundaries and toward those investments that offer the greatest return. The system allows credit transfers between some 1500 banks in approximately 70 countries. In a given day, as much as $700 billion is transmitted through the system.[2] Hamilton argues that information technology in the financial services industry has created a totally new system of world finance: "The growth of international communications, the development of the data-processing capability of the big computer and the personal desk-top facility, and the arrival of the day of the wired society have revolutionalized the way in which finance is transacted."[3] I/T is also transforming the international transport and logistics businesses.[4] Large players in these industries have little choice but to learn to be a part of this global environment.

Information technology can facilitate a global strategy. I/T can be a key facilitator of day-to-day global operations. Many semiconductor manufacturers coordinate and control globally dispersed operations for maximum economic value, known as a "value chain." Wafer fabrication processes are capital-intensive and are performed in countries with high technology centers. Packaging, by contrast, is labor-intensive and is placed where labor costs are low. This requires moving work-in-progress and finished goods from country to country between such stages as fabrication, packaging, assembly, testing, and customer delivery. In an interview with the authors, one executive commented, "This is a business where a device that costs less than one dollar might travel 20,000 miles before it is at its final destination." A dispersed value chain requires tightly-knit information linkages. For example, Texas Instruments Incorporated facilitates its global business strategy with a single-image worldwide telecommunications network connecting several dozen plants in nearly 20 countries. The firm's multivendor fiber-optic computer network allows subsecond response time throughout the world. Common worldwide strategic systems have been implemented for procurement, logistics, manufacturing, financial planning, demand forecast, order fulfillment, and inventory management. These systems are run from the main data center computers in the firm's headquarters.[5]

Information technology also may present a barrier to globalization. Few multinational firms can boast of the globally integrated information processing environment that Texas Instruments' semiconductor business has engineered to support its global strategy.[6] For many firms not committed to global coordination, parochial management of information technology has become a major liability. After identifying areas where global coordination can provide competitive advantage, executives often become discouraged to find country-specific applications of information technology emerging as barriers to implementation. Past investments in information systems, usually reflecting a history of local autonomy, can institutionalize country-specific business practices. Such investments make it costly and difficult, if not impossible, to share large amounts of product-, market-, operations-, and financial-related information across country boundaries.

This paper examines how information technology can facilitate the global strategies that firms are pursuing. The concept of global business drivers is described, followed by a suggested method to provide direction in the determination and prioritization of common, globally integrated I/T solutions. We then explore the "networked organization," an emerging structure that can provide the organizational infrastructure necessary for managing global drivers. Finally, we examine barriers and risks in implementing and managing a global information technology.

AN EXAMPLE OF THE I/T QUANDARY

The story of Worldwide Oil Field Manufacturers (WOFM), a real oil field service firm whose identity is disguised in this paper, provides an example of the information technology quandary facing many firms.

WOFM, a supplier of equipment and materials for oil field production operators, had major production facilities in the United States and eight other countries, with sales offices in another 16. Historically, WOFM products had been developed for the home country market. Products were then adopted, where appropriate, for markets outside the United States by the eight relatively autonomous national business units. Prior to the arrival of the current chief executive officer (CEO), information systems, like most other support functions, had been the responsibility of local country management. In those years, the financial results of the country units were sent via telex each month to the company headquarters where the data were re-entered into a corporate financial reporting database system.

In 1983, a new CEO ordered the development of a worldwide financial reporting system, an inventory management system, and a new customer profitability analysis system. These were to be installed in the various country offices and run on identical mainframe computers. The CEO sought tighter financial control of this diverse empire and saw an opportunity to spread the development costs of the expensive inventory and profitability analysis systems across the organization. It was also hoped that a common inventory system might eventually lead to regional rather than country-by-country inventories of the high-cost replacement equipment the firm was compelled to carry in inventory for its large customers.

Four years and several million dollars later, these initiatives were seen as having been a failure. The financial reporting system provided timely and accurate data, but it had strained the relationship between the CEO and the general managers of the country units. Exchange rates, local tax laws, and country-specific accounting practices all presented stumbling blocks to successful implementation. So too did the lack of vendor support, the unavailable local software, and the widespread apathy of the managers of the various country information systems groups. The use of the inventory management and customer profitability analysis systems had met stiff resistance. In countries where the inventory system had been installed, massive changes were required to meet local requirements. Some changes reflected anticipated language and currency requirements, but the biggest problems centered around the unanticipated differences in operating environments. For instance, variations in distribution channels and methods from country to country required varying approaches to customer profitability analysis. The high costs of telecommunications in many countries required distributed applications that were contrary to the mainframe computer-based solution in the United States. In some countries, telecommunications were so rudimentary that a stand-alone computer workstation solution was the only viable alternative.

Despite the previous setbacks, the CEO in 1991 was more convinced than ever of the necessity for integrating information systems on a worldwide basis. The oil field services industry, always active internationally, had now become a global industry. Quality management initiatives and stiff competition were driving the large oil companies WOFM served to demand consistent standards of performance and service on a worldwide basis. At the same time, the efficiency of foreign competitors increasingly forced the firm to seek out the best suppliers leading to an increased reliance on offshore suppliers. High labor costs and a shortage of qualified engineers in the United States, coupled with available and inexpensive engineering talent in other country units, made offshore product development look preferable. The CEO was convinced that WOFM required a tightly-knit worldwide operation to compete effectively in this new marketplace. But such worldwide coordination and control required the firm to revisit a previous failure—the development of common global systems. This time, the CEO knew, the firm must carefully target the business opportunities that would best benefit from global systems.

GLOBAL BUSINESS DRIVERS

As illustrated in the case of WOFM, without a shared business vision, developing a common global I/T is costly and may be strongly resisted by country managers. However, failure to unearth integration opportunities can result in losses in efficiency, lost market share to local competitors, or dissatisfied global customers.

The investment required for global systems may be substantial. Even executives committed to globalization may be reluctant to approve such an investment without a compelling understanding of how it will contribute to achieving global objectives. As recently discussed by Daniels and Keen, information technology managers must be proactive to identify information solutions that the firm needs to be competitive worldwide and tie them to strategic business imperatives.[7]

The global business driver approach provides a tool for envisioning the business entities that will benefit most from an integrated global I/T management. The approach provides a rich language for communicating information technology requirements of a firm's global vision and strategy within the frame of reference of nontechnical executive-level managers. The objective is a close alignment between the firm's global vision and the firm's I.T. strategy and architecture (see Figure 1). Our studies of over one hundred multinational firms[8] strongly suggest that if information technology is to add value to international business operations, it must be applied through the firm's global business drivers. Global business drivers (GBDs) are those entities that benefit from global economies of scale and scope, and thus contribute to the global business strategy. Managing or partially managing these entities on a global basis, rather than on a domestic or multinational scale, allows a firm to obtain desired incremental benefits.

GBDs are a means for assessing high-level global information requirements. They focus on broad business entities (e.g., customers, suppliers, orders, projects, storage facilities),

FIGURE 1   Alignment of global vision with information technology

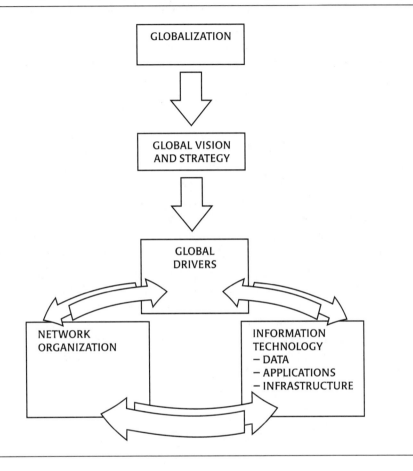

and capture current and future information requirements that are shared across dispersed operating units within a firm's business. GBDs focus on shared entities where the meaning, or the semantics, of the data must be consistent throughout the world.

GBDs can be contrasted with critical success factors[9] (CSFs) that are those few things that must go well to ensure success for a manager. CSFs focus on business processes and functions, and address an individual manager's information requirements. They address functions, or views of the data, and tend to be locally driven. However, CSFs can be helpful in identifying global business drivers when they are collected across country units, functional areas, and levels of management.[10]

The global business driver analysis assumes that the most important prescription for successful global implementation of business application is a shared common data model. Commonality in the hardware, systems software, and organizational structures are secondary concerns. Both the technology architecture and the organization's structure can accommodate some amount of international variability as long as: 1) data can be successfully passed from node to node in a communication network, 2) there is shared meaning of data, and 3) an organization-wide agreement exists regarding how work is to be allocated among country units.[11-12] Of course, there may be opportunities to achieve economies of scale within the systems function by instituting a more standardized approach to managing hardware, software, and telecommunications. As we discuss later in the paper, systems economies are not, by themselves, usually compelling enough to justify a worldwide approach toward managing information technology.

Once GBDs are agreed upon, they form the basis for the I/T strategy and an applications portfolio. For instance, the growing commonality among the world's automobile markets, where much of the market is driven by the shared culture of entertainment technologies, makes a common global product, or "world car," a viable option. Such a product could permit significant savings by elimination of redundant product development operations. A former chief executive officer of Ford Motor Co.[13] asked management to strive for "world car engineering." This vision entailed eliminating redundant engineering activities and dramatically reducing the time required to bring new products to markets. The global business drivers of the vision were a global product, rationalized operations, and human resources. An information technology strategy and applications were needed to facilitate the shared management of these entities. At Ford, this required coordinated engineering-release databases, common computer-aided design tools, and a common repository of national environmental and safety laws. Together, these facilitate the manufacturing and marketing of any part or a whole vehicle in any region served by Ford regardless of where the product is designed or engineered.

EXAMPLES OF GLOBAL BUSINESS DRIVERS

Next we describe typical examples of global business drivers and then use the earlier described example of an oil field services firm, WOFM, to illustrate their applicability. We first discuss global business drivers that are somewhat internally controllable and then turn our attention to marketplace drivers. The list, though reasonably comprehensive, is not complete; firms may have GBDs that are not included among these categories. Table 1 illustrates some questions that are used in the analysis, and also identifies some examples for each of the drivers discussed.

Joint resources. Human resources will increasingly become a key global business driver for many firms. Historically, organizational design focused on efficiently allocating people to work tasks. Throughout the industrial revolution, assembly lines, corporate hierarchies, departmental structures, and the scientific management movement all sought to physically align people so as to most efficiently attack the work. In an information- and knowledge-based economy, the rules are reversed. Information-based tasks can be moved

TABLE 1   Analysis of some global business drivers

Global Business Drivers	Analysis Questions	Example Entities
Joint resources	Can you electronically move work to countries with a highly skilled work force and favorable wage levels? Can you compose and manage work teams with globally dispersed members? Do you manage human resources skills on a global level?	Employee location, employee skill, employee position, work assignments, employee compensation, standard work tools, relationship history between customers and employees
Rationalized and flexible operations	Can you move production around the world? Can you rapidly move knowledge work around the world? Can you share production resources across country boundaries? Are you optimizing plant locations and production planning on a global scale?	Production plan, production schedule, product demand, plant capacity, vehicles, storage facilities
Risk reduction	Do you manage your monetary flows and the associated risks on a daily and hourly basis at the global level? Are you vulnerable to political and economic conditions in particular countries?	Investments, pending investments, foreign exchange, assets, safety of assets
Global products	Are there opportunities for global products and brands? Do you need to launch synchronized product introductions on a global basis?	Product standards, process standards, legal requirements, repair records, marketing plans
Quality	Can you identify the source of a defective component on a global basis? Are you conducting competitive benchmarking on a worldwide basis?	Competitive benchmarks, internal performance standards
Suppliers	Can volume discounts be negotiated on a global scale? Do you know your global position with a major supplier?	Supplier information, parts and material, procurement standards, innovations
Corporate customers	Are your leading-edge customers becoming global? Can you ensure consistent product and service regardless of the location? Can you provide seamless worldwide ordering, order tracking, and billing? Do the needs of global customers provide new business opportunities?	Customer information, customer quality standards, customer product specification, local preferences, preorder history, order status

to the worker. Only about 3 percent of the cost of a typical semiconductor, for example, is sand and other raw materials. Much of the remainder of the costs are attributed to workers such as design engineers, research scientists, computer programmers, investment bankers, and lawyers who provide problem-solving, problem-identifying, and strategic-brokering activities. Information-based work of these people, whom Reich[14] calls "symbolic analysts," can be transported, at high speed and low cost, to the lowest cost source of qualified labor.

As knowledge flows replace the material flow in production of goods, firms will learn to electronically share valued human resources on a global scale. Investment bankers, chemical engineers, product designers, accountants, management consultants, and strategic planners possess considerable knowledge of value to customers. The relationships those professionals have established with existing or potential customers are invaluable strategic assets. Carefully chosen investments in employee skills databases, teleconferencing facilities, and electronic-mail and voice-mail can provide the mechanisms to locate and leverage those human resources through a far-flung multinational corporation. In such an environment, team members working on the same product can be scattered throughout the world. Texas Instruments, for example, designs management systems in Japan, Europe, and the Far East as well as in their Dallas, Texas, headquarters using electronically coordinated teams. In addition to the global communications network, a common computer-aided software engineering tool enables the coordinated effort.

At another firm, managers are beginning to use an experimental system to assemble work teams from around the world. A manager inputs the skills required for a particular team and profiles of the likely candidates. A color picture and description of a prospective team member who might be located (from anywhere in the world) then appears on the manager's computer display. The system can also be used to interview the candidate.[15]

One systems integration company has developed a common set of computer-based training programs that are used in major training facilities in Europe and the Far East. Programs such as those on operating systems and computer languages ensure consistency in systems engineers' skill levels and common terminology. This facilitates the smooth transfer of personnel from one customer account to another regardless of location. The highly interactive educational programs run on a computer mainframe in a regional data center with local interface support from the computer workstation.

Rationalized and flexible operations. Global interdependencies found in operations can be a global business driver requiring integrated I/T solutions. Operational interdependencies might arise from the need for rationalized or flexible production or manufacturing. In *rationalized* operations, different country units build different parts of the same product based on availability of skills, raw materials, or favorable business climate. In *flexible* operations, operations are moved from one country to another, such as in response to labor strife, or raw material or skill shortages. The interdependency among country units is a fairly recent phenomenon in the history of American and European multinational firms that have tended to allow their foreign subsidiaries to operate rather autonomously.[16]

In rationalized operations where the production function is dispersed throughout the world, airlines might move planes, people, and crews from one country to another. This requires careful international coordination of requirements for passenger reservations, fuel, scheduled and unscheduled maintenance, spare parts, and for the planes themselves. International freight carriers face similar requirements for globally dispersed production functions. In addition, they must interface with shippers and their agents, freight forwarders, recipients, domestic carriers, insurance companies, banks, and government customs departments. The vice president of distribution for a large United States retailer once reported that he maintained "a binder an inch thick full of required documentation for every major import from Asia."

MSAS, a large international airfreight firm, is currently replacing its many incompatible, country-specific information technology solutions, customer files, and order information systems with one integrated worldwide information system to support its agent network of 291 offices in 29 countries. Running on multiple IBM Application System/400* processors, the system supports a distributed database design. Sixty percent of the data (for example, route pricing) is stored concurrently in computers in each regional center. The remaining 40 percent of the data at each site are data unique to that site. If necessary, however, local data in a country such as Malaysia can be accessed and updated by MSAS computers throughout the world. The system will provide real-time information on the status of any international shipment that the firm has been contracted to handle. If a delay or an exception occurs at any of the predetermined 16 control points, the customer will be notified by MSAS personnel and the exception is explained.[17] The chairman of the company firmly believes that once the system is fully implemented, "half of our business can be processed without manual intervention." According to the director of logistics, "The system will make it possible for us to accept initial bookings automatically, schedule the transportation automatically, and obtain customs' preclearance on the documents before the merchandise arrives at its destination."

Flexible operations can also provide new economies of scale. The ability to shift production schedules from one country to another helps to optimally manage manufacturing capacity. Firms also may attempt to share logistics resources as they ship work-in-progress around the world. Others share plants or storage facilities across country units. In 1986 Air Products and Chemicals, Inc., implemented a mainframe computer-based maintenance management system for the United States to manage the inventory of expensive spare parts used to repair plants. Six months later the same system was installed on a mainframe computer in the United Kingdom to provide European-wide coordination of spare parts. Requests for spares from anywhere in the world can now be quickly processed. Even after six years, the two versions of the system remained 99 percent common.[18]

Firms pursuing strategies that entail globally dispersed production functions and rationalized and flexible operations find it necessary to share manufacturing planning systems, process control systems, and work-in-process inventory systems across country boundaries. A large industrial equipment supplier installed a worldwide manufacturing planning and scheduling system to support plants in the United States and Europe. The integrated manufacturing system (e.g., forecasting, master scheduling, order entry, materials requirements planning, inventory control, and factory planning and control) runs on mainframe computers in five different data center locations supporting 20 plants. The operational databases of the systems are separate and reside in each plant; however, the data structure in each database is the same, which facilitates shared meaning of data, and allows rapid access and aggregation of data via a network.

Risk reduction. Another business driver relates to managing the firm's cash flows and assets that are affected by real shifts in currency values. This means diversifying the value of the firm's assets. In the aftermath of the developing nations' bad debt crisis, it became apparent that many international banks did not recognize the vulnerability of their portfolios to investments in similar loans. Part of the problem was traced to the lack of coordination across portfolio managers located around the world. Similar problems occur for multinational firms in managing cash flow, overnight investment of cash, purchases of commodities, or oil drilling leases. In this latter case there is a risk that sister divisions of the same firm might be bidding against each other on the same lease. Currency and security traders face a similar need to centrally coordinate risk, as do treasury managers seeking short-term investments for cash. Central databases, risk management systems, and international communications networks provide solutions to these problems. Portions of a portfolio can be assigned to particular managers or even handed off from manager to manager via an electronic trading system through a 24-hour trading cycle. In either case, the firm's total risk position can be readily assessed and properly managed. For example, one financial services firm's worldwide risk management system for capital market trading is updated throughout the day, so as to provide "near" real-time information on the instruments being traded by the firm's traders around the world. Instantaneous or nearly instantaneous information lowers the risk associated with foreign instruments due to exchange rate shifts or other economic uncertainties. Instantaneous access to information will also effectively prohibit the firm's traders from bidding against each other. According to a senior executive in the firm, the system is not only helping "the left hand know what the right hand is doing . . . in some ways the system is leading our business. Because of the system, new financial instruments are being developed."

Global products. This business driver is related to products being introduced that are identical or nearly identical across national boundaries. The reasons are varied. First, global products are emerging because of the increasing influence of multinational corporate customers who seek consistency across their dispersed operations. Second, globe-traveling consumers demand products and services regardless of location. Third, global products can provide the basis for economies of scale. Levitt[19] has proposed a fourth explanation for global products; consumer needs and wants are becoming more homogenized around the world because of both communication technologies and travel. Competitive pressures provide a fifth argument for product consistency. The more rapidly and more widespread a firm can introduce a new product, the greater the potential benefits derivable from both market saturation and subsequent low-cost positioning.

Whatever the reason, world products are becoming more common. Rapid development of products that can be easily modified to different national or regional markets requires considerable coordination and control. Tight international coupling will be necessary during the initial stages of product design and concept testing. For example, an automobile designed to be sold in multiple countries must conform, or be subsequently modified, to meet the safety and environmental standards of each selling country. To ensure conformance, Ford, for example, provides designers in its design centers with a global database of vehicle safety regulations. Similarly, in a large engineering firm, a database of previous designs, accessible from throughout the firm, permits engineers in one country to benefit or embellish work performed elsewhere. Recently, this engineering firm merged its European and United States data centers, thereby partially eliminating some barriers to further I/T compatibility. The technology facilitates the firm's vision of being able to engineer and manufacture equipment in any part of the world, regardless of where the deal is signed.

Designing a world product can be difficult. Timely introduction of that product throughout the world can be even more challenging. For example, preparing the necessary marketing literature, training programs, documentation, advertising copy, product warranties, commission plans, and labeling for 30 countries in 10 languages is a daunting proposition. The task is made no simpler by the varying requirements of such items as copyright laws and product labeling. After-sale service, product recalls, and similar activities lead to further complications. In the pharmaceuticals industry, country-by-country testing and approval can consume a large percentage of a product's patentable life. Advances in information technology can help meet requirements of timeliness, consistency, and low cost. One firm, General Electric Co. Plastics, believes that their worldwide communications network is essential for keeping employees up-to-date with the latest products, while ensuring equivalent offerings regardless of location.[20]

Quality. Total quality management is emerging as another key global business driver. As firms benchmark their operations against "world class" standards and as interdependence increases between their domestic and international operations, a requirement for a cross-border approach to quality improvement is gaining force. In many industries, advances in information technology already permit a defective product to be traced back to a particular worker, machine, or supplier. For instance, an apparel manufacturer uses its sophisticated information system and work-in-progress bar code labels as the basis of its employee incentive system. If a customer receives a size or color that was not ordered, the system can be used to identify the worker who packed the container and instantly adjusts the incentive component of that person's pay. But many companies have yet to fully take advantage of the quality improvement opportunities presented by integrated databases. For instance, an automobile manufacturer was recently required to call back 55,000 vehicles because it was unable to pinpoint the specific cars in which airbags containing one of 135 defective subcomponents had been installed. In a globally interdependent organization, component- or subcomponent-level tracking will become a necessity, with obvious implications for both the development of common systems and corporate-wide standards.

Human resources, quality, operations, and product design are global business drivers for managing the firm's own internal value chain more efficiently and effectively on a global scale. But there are even more compelling global business drivers that manage the relationship of the firm with its business partners, customers, and other external stakeholders. These interorganizational interdependencies are driving firms toward major internal transformations. Information technology is a key enabler of these transformations.

Suppliers. The opportunity to deal with a supplier as one global entity is an exciting potential driver for worldwide integration and coordination. Worldwide procurement offers opportunities for competitive advantage through economies of scale, enhanced buyer power, increased reliability, and the opportunity to redirect shipments among production facilities. For example, volume discounts, once negotiated, can motivate otherwise autonomous plants to rely on preferred suppliers, thus further increasing both the discount and the firm's power over the supplier. Such a shift in supplier power may provide the firm with an opportunity to influence the supplier's subsequent research and development investments, to mandate investments in quality programs, to guarantee the availability of critical inputs in times of shortage, or to be invited to join strategic alliances for the testing and introduction of new innovations. In an industry in which technological innovation is rapid, the advantage will often go to the firm that can most quickly diffuse breakthroughs in materials, components, or tools emerging from their supplier's research and development facilities.

Although such coordination in procurement seems obvious, there continues to be resistance. The following anecdote describes the rocky road that one multinational firm traveled before it finally recognized suppliers as a global business driver and developed a database to support integrated global procurement.

Fifteen years ago a corporate systems director envisioned an integrated procurement system and supplier database. The director felt this could provide value to the firm's many relatively autonomous business units and production facilities. When this vision was shared with the divisional purchasing agents, none were impressed and some were threatened. After several years and a number of division failures attributed to global competition, a corporate head of procurement was appointed. This corporate head also recognized the benefits that could be harvested by a more coordinated approach and once again the business units were invited to participate. Again, there was no interest. After further plant closings and losses due to global competition, the purchasing agents of the larger units formed their own consortium. To the current information systems executive's delight, the consortium asked for assistance in establishing a common supplier database.

Corporate customers. Perhaps the most common drivers of global integration today are customers who are themselves seeking globalization. Such customers will increasingly seek out suppliers who can treat them, to a greater or lesser extent, as a single entity and provide them with consistent service that spans national borders. Providing worldwide support requires rapid and accurate communication and information processing across the firm's country units. For example, Polaroid Corp. is integrating its order management systems in Europe so that a customer can order goods in one country to be shipped to another.[21] This initiative is partially in response to firm remarketers who have purchased Polaroid film in one market and resold it to others, thus gaining a profit from disparities in Polaroid's pricing policy or its slowness to respond to currency fluctuations.

Many firms still find it difficult to provide global customer service. For example, an international oil company sought a computer vendor to help it establish an office automation network that would interconnect the 60 countries in which the firm does business. The hardware consisted of personal computers on the desktops of professionals and secretaries (over 20,000 estimated users), mini- or mainframe computers as office processors, and a global network that would connect all office processors. The hardware and software was to be installed and maintained by the computer vendor's various country offices. But the customer wanted to do the planning for the system out of its offices in the United States. The bill for the system was to be divided up among the customer's several regional offices. The master plan called for identical computer terminals, but with the capability to handle the local language for screens and printed reports. All user documentation was required to be in the local language.

Such requirements are a nightmare for a vendor organized as a collection of autonomous national units. Each of the vendor's country units may still have its own billing procedures and local commission and installation plans. The ramifications are particularly far-reaching for accounting systems that have to handle payments stretched out through time and originated from many sources. The freight forwarder, MSAS, for instance, frequently established separate accounts in several regional offices for the same customer.[17] MSAS recognized that a supplier who could successfully coordinate its international services via globally integrated databases and common systems would have a decisive advantage in serving a multinational customer as a unified worldwide entity. Firms that cannot meet their global customers' requirements will lose in competition to suppliers who can. In the past, this might have meant a small lost exporting opportunity. Now the threat is the potential loss of all or a sizable share of the entire worldwide account. For example, one corporate customer we recently interviewed compared the responses of two value-added telecommunications suppliers when asked to put together a global electronic mail network: "Our regular supplier gave us a list of office phone numbers for their foreign subsidiaries and wished us luck. The other [supplier] told us they would handle the complete job, from specification to training and installation in all of our remote locations. They got the job, and are now getting a big share of our domestic business."

Providing for the unique needs of global customers can also be the source of new business opportunities. QAD, a software company with headquarters in the United States, designed their manufacturing, financial, and distribution management software to focus on integrated global companies whose requirements were not satisfied by regionally focused software vendors. The manufacturing and distribution management software system runs on a wide range of platforms from personal computers to networks, in mini- and main-frame environments, under a variety of operating systems. The product also provides multiple currency transactions in all modules, support for local tax structures, and concurrent multiple language capability. Ten languages are supported.

Applying the global business drivers. In summary, global drivers can address both the firm's internal value chain and its external partners and constituents. As shown earlier in Figure 1, GBDs serve to catalyze the common global vision and business strategy of a firm. Table 1 illustrates questions that may help to uncover GBDs and also identifies some examples of business entities that might be globally shared in an I/T solution supporting a particular GBD.

In Table 2 we illustrate some GBDs by industry. The data represents averaged survey responses from 105 multinational organizations with headquarters in the United States. The respondents were asked to indicate the importance of particular global business drivers in a business unit that was the most globally integrated.[22] For example, the transportation companies such as shipping lines and freight forwarders rated global corporate customers as the most strategic GBD. Table 2 must be viewed cautiously because the GBDs of individual firms are likely to differ widely in any industry; GBDs are closely tied to the particular global strategy a firm or a business unit is pursuing at a given time.

An analysis of global business drivers could have helped WOFM (the disguised oil field service firm previously described) better prioritize their global systems requirements. They were being pushed by their corporate customers toward consistent standards of performance and service on a worldwide basis. Global customers, world products, and worldwide quality standards are emerging in this industry as global drivers. Foreign competition forces a firm to look for major cost-saving opportunities. WOFM frequently looks outside of the United States for suppliers—another necessity that is a potential global driver, though probably only for a relatively small number of items. In the future, the high cost and shortage of qualified engineers within the United States may force WOFM to move product development to locations outside of the United States or to share it across globally dispersed locations. That requirement, and the need to promote personnel from throughout the company, may turn human resources into a global driver as well.

WOFM's management has chosen a growth strategy focused on providing consistent and integrated customer service to worldwide customers. The requirements of local customers will essentially remain in the hands of country management. However, a set of global products and a single customer database will be required to serve worldwide customers. The satisfaction of the requirements of global customers appears to be the best starting point. Here the benefits of successful integration are shared throughout the firm and the risk of failure to meet key customer requirements will be obvious to all.

Caveats of the analysis. While the benefits of GBD analysis can be great, there are a few dangers. First, the analysis can be performed at too high a level. "Global competition," "unified Europe," "joint venturing," "the opening up of Eastern Europe," "global markets," and "Pacific rim" are phrases that can quickly capture management's attention and may

TABLE 2   Importance of some global business drivers by industry

Industry	Number of Responses	Global Business Driver						
		Joint Resources	Flexible Operations	Rationalized Operations	Risk Reduction	Global Products	Scarce Supplies	Corporate Customers
Transportation	5	○	○	○	○	○		○
Financial Services (noninsurance)	12		○		○	○		○
Petroleum	14	○			○	○		
Petroleum-Related Manufacturing and Services	5	○	○	○	○			○
Mining	4	○			○		○	
Computers and Communication	8		○	○		○		○
Semiconductors	2	○	○	○		○		○
Aerospace Manufacturing	9			○				○
Motor Vehicles	10			○	○	○		
Other Manufacturing (i.e., supplies to global firms)	11		○	○		○		○
Foods and Consumer Goods	8			○		○		
Chemicals	12			○	○			○
Pharmaceuticals	3	○	○	○		○		
Medical Equipment	2		○	○		○	○	

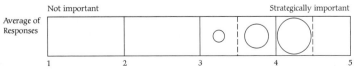

Average of Responses

Not important ... Strategically important

1   2   3   4   5

be life-and-death concerns for many firms. But such generalities are far removed from the day-to-day realities of running a business. The analysis using GBDs must emphasize the specifics of the business, their suppliers, distributors, products, and customers.

Another danger in the analysis comes from failing to recognize differences within the firm. Global business drivers are seldom exactly the same across business units. Although there may be opportunities to build synergy across businesses, the richest opportunities are at the business unit level. For example at Air Products and Chemicals, Inc., global corporate customers are a much more important driver for the Chemicals and Process Systems groups than for the Industrial Gases division.[23] Similarly, in the downstream petroleum industry, global corporate customers are rarely a driving force, but the airlines and shipping firms that are customers of the petroleum company's aviation and marine fuel businesses have for many years required integrated global support.

The third danger is related to cultural differences across country units that may make it difficult to reach consensus initially on the GBDs. For example, Kanter in her recent article demonstrates that there are sharp differences across countries in the factors thought to contribute to a firm's success. While United States managers rated customer service as the most important element, West German and Japanese managers, respectively, thought that work force skills and product development were most significant.[24]

The fourth danger comes from the lack of senior business management involvement in the GBD analysis. Senior management must be willing to sponsor and participate in the GBD analysis and play a leadership role in the move to an integrated global information technology.

ALIGNMENT IN THE NETWORKED ORGANIZATION

Global business drivers are tools to envision and communicate the global requirements of information technology. The prescribed systems and databases, however, will provide few benefits without an organizational infrastructure that is capable of delivering and using them. A new type of organizational form, the electronically-wired network organization, can help satisfy the global consistency and efficiency requirements, while simultaneously maintaining local responsiveness, flexibility, and accountability. We next discuss this new organization form required to harness global business drivers.

We generally think about organizations as hierarchies because, as business historian Chandler has shown,[25] that type of structure has typified successful firms. A hierarchical structure often proved to be the most effective as firms expanded internationally and encompassed multidivisional, multifunctional organizations. Firms like E.I. Du Pont de Nemours & Co., General Motors Corp., Siemens A.G., and Matsushita Electric Industrial Co., Ltd., exploited this type of structure during the first half of the twentieth century. Dubbed the "M-form" organization by economist Williamson,[26] this approach to organization helps generate economies of scale and creates cost advantages through centralized global-scale operations. In the M-form organization, information flows up to the center of the organization and instructions flow down to the local units.

Not all global businesses, however, work best using this structure. Some, for example, require a strong local presence in various countries in order to achieve the sensitivity and responsiveness necessary to satisfy national differences. Unilever N.V., though recently restructured,[27] operated very successfully for many years using this strong local-presence model. In this type of company, information is, for the most part, developed and retained for use at each local site.

Both of these approaches have deficiencies for competing in today's global environment. The M-form lacks the speed and agility necessary to respond effectively to dynamic global markets. It was designed to manage high volumes of consistent, stable activities. The decentralized, local dominance form misses the global view by focusing on the local view. It forsakes opportunities for the firm to deploy its resources, and to disperse its value-chain activities dynamically to the location that can provide the most competitive advantage.

The networked organization was conceived to deal with these deficiencies. In order to create a network, a business clusters its assets and competencies in units (nodes) spread throughout the world so that they are dispersed, interdependent, and specialized. That is, functions are performed at a node where they are best done. Furthermore, not all of these nodes must be owned or managed by the firm. They can result from a strategic alliance.

Reich, providing a rich image of the networked organization, describes it as the "new web of enterprise,"[28] one that resembles a spider's web. Strategic brokers—that is, executives who manage ideas rather than material things and coordinate the activities of others—are at the center. However, there are all sorts of other connections and activities being conducted that do not involve these executives directly. In addition, new connections are being spun (created) or undone all of the time.

According to Miles and Snow, this "dynamic network" organization has four major features:

1. *Vertical disaggregation.* The firm's value chain is dispersed globally and its business functions, such as product design, development, manufacturing, marketing, and distribution, are performed by independent organizations within a network.

2. *Brokers.* Since each function is not necessarily part of a single organization, business groups are identified, assembled, placed in a location, and coordinated by means of brokers.

3. *Market mechanisms.* The major functions are held together primarily by mechanisms such as transfer prices between business units rather than by the plans and controls typical in a hierarchical organization. Contracts and direct payment for results are used as tools of management control more frequently than are progress reports and personal, hierarchically-based supervision.

4. *Full disclosure information systems.* Widely accessible computer-based information systems are used as substitutes for authority relationships and lengthy trust-building experiences. (Trust, however, is still very important to ensure the proper sharing of accurate and formerly proprietary information.) The participants in the network agree on a general structure of payment based on the value they add. They then hook themselves together in a continuously updated information system so that each contribution can be mutually and instantaneously verified.[29]

A prototype illustration of alignment among business strategy, network organization, and I/T in operation can be found at Rosenbluth Travel Agency Inc.[30] Rosenbluth, whose home office is in Philadelphia, Pennsylvania, is one of the five largest travel agencies in the United States. Since 1980 it has grown from a regional agency with annual sales of $40 million into what Miller, the firm's chief information officer, calls a "global virtual corporation." Annual sales now exceed $1.3 billion. Responding to an opportunity to satisfy the needs of global customers who travel between countries, the company formed Rosenbluth International Alliance (RIA) and entered into partnerships with some 34 local travel agents spanning some 37 countries. The alliance's niche strategy is to provide high quality local service for a globe-traveling corporate customer regardless of where the customer might travel. Information technology is the loom that weaves the alliance together and provides RIA's global presence. According to Miller, "Information technology enables the company to coordinate travel services throughout the world. Using relational database technology, specific information concerning clients and travelers is available anywhere in the world to provide superior service to the global traveler. And, through I/T, information can be consolidated across the world to coordinate decision making, and to leverage global purchasing power."[31] A global information system is also used to keep track of the payments and commissions system that binds RIA together. The alliance also spreads the costs of the global I/T infrastructure across the member firms.

A global alliance requires that we decide on the best organizational relationships to establish. Reich identifies five basic forms of relationships that can be instituted between an organization and its nodes in order to create a global network:

1. *Independent profit center,* where authority for product development and sales is pushed down to each node. In this case the node is owned but is rather autonomous.

2. *Spin-off partnerships,* where independent businesses are spawned from the main organization using former employees and assets. The node then contributes to the organization on a contractual basis.

3. *Spin-in partnerships,* where ideas and unique assets from external groups are acquired or set up as separate units and become nodes in the organization itself.

4. *Licensing,* where the headquarters contracts with independent businesses to use its brand name, sell its special formulas, or market its technologies.

5. *Pure brokering,* where the headquarters contracts with independent businesses to solve problems, perform knowledge-based activities, or to undertake direct production or service activities.

Using these categories, RIA is best described as a spin-in partnership. Each partner has an equal vote and an equal say in decisions facing the alliance. In addition, RIA relies on the services of Apollo, an airline reservations system. All members of the alliance access the various functions through Apollo. Apollo provides the normal reservations services as well as a conduit to a customer's profile and itinerary information. Forthcoming front-end interfaces will provide alliance members with easy-to-use access to the functions of the system. An electronic mail system provides direct connections between alliance members.

Global cooperative information processing relationships have also become common among airline reservations systems providers and among global transportation firms. Industry convergence on electronic data interchange (EDI) standards allows a reservation clerk in Europe to access a reservation stored on AMR Corp.'s SABRE** system. The long-term goal of the industry alliances is that a reservation taken anywhere in the firm is nearly instantaneously updated in different reservations systems in the alliance. Similarly, GLS Worldwide, an alliance between Lufthansa, Air France, Cathay Pacific, and Japan Airlines Co. Ltd., was created to develop an automated cargo information system. The system will connect the regional distribution systems of different firms at a global level and provide shippers and forwarders with direct access to the in-house computer systems of the airlines to enable them to make cargo reservations and track shipments.[4]

Information technology makes these new organizational relationships possible on a worldwide scale. Ownership and traditional hierarchical structures are no longer required to provide effective and coordinated worldwide operations.

KEYS TO SUCCESSFUL IMPLEMENTATION

We have proposed that global business drivers can serve as the basis for focusing global information technology investments toward areas with immediate and substantial worldwide payoffs. Yet, moving toward globally-integrated systems is a journey with many pitfalls. Not the least of these is an over-reliance on systems savings as a justification for global sharing. Too often the push for global systems comes with the intention of avoiding investments in apparently redundant systems. Systems already in use or under development at a central headquarters are used as a readily available, "quick and dirty" solution to an apparent lack of technology base in foreign operations. Unfortunately, as we saw illustrated at WOFM, these solutions tend to fail more often than they succeed. Attempting to save systems investments without simultaneously applying global business driver approaches is a recipe for failure. Subsidiaries see little or no gains from adapting to headquarters' solutions; instead, they are likely to anticipate a loss in their own autonomy.

But ensuring appropriate alignment with global business drivers is still no guarantee of success. Next, we discuss a variety of approaches for overcoming barriers to global systems. Among these are managing project risk, utilizing partnerships, and building global infrastructure.

Project risk. Global systems tend to be high risk projects. McFarlan divides risk into three categories: size, structure, and technology.[32] As we describe below, global projects typically score high in all three dimensions.

Global projects tend to be large. An executive in charge of international financial systems commented, "We seldom work on a system with less than three quarters of a million lines of code and that doesn't require an IBM 3090* processor to run." Such projects can span multiple years, even if developed in phases. For example, Ford's Worldwide Engineering Release system, which provides a standardized, computer-based format for all engineering release documents, took more than five years to develop. We previously described a risk management system developed by a financial services company; that project began in early 1984 and was finally operational in all major trading offices in 1990. MSAS, the global freight management company, initiated its global operations support system in 1986; by May of 1992, after a specification freeze, major delays, cost overruns, a change in systems architecture, and the involvement of over 100 development personnel, the system was nearing firm-wide implementation.[17]

Long development cycles introduce problems related to diverted resources, inflated user expectations, and lost project champions. There is also the risk that a gap will emerge between the business strategy the system was designed to support and the strategy the company has evolved toward while the system was under development. For example, one information systems manager we interviewed observed, "We have been working on this system for five years and we have never once operated from a level table; our company has undergone dramatic changes via functional reorganizations, new acquisitions, joint ventures, etc. Since the project started, both the president of the company and the project's original sponsor have left. After every management shake-up we've had to resell the project."

As this example illustrates, structure, or the lack of it, is another contributor to project risk. The requirements for global systems are frequently difficult to specify with sufficient accuracy in advance. Undiscovered differences in the way the business is conducted in different countries, local customer requirements, government regulations, or the evolving needs of a global customer can all introduce uncertainty. In a firm operating in multiple countries, no single individual at the beginning of a project is likely to be familiar enough with operations to have a good understanding of the degree of commonality or local requirements that exist across worldwide operations. The differences that emerge can often be dramatic. An engineering firm working out of the United States, for instance, typically interfaces only with its contractors; its European division, however, orders materials for the contractor, negotiates directly with subcontractors, and provides considerably more detailed instructions about work to be performed. Obviously, this has important implications for a system designed to aid in construction project management.

The final element of project risk, unfamiliar technology, is also common with global systems. Even if the technology is mundane to headquarters' personnel, it is likely to be a large leap forward (or backward) for other parts of the organization. Technological solutions that have worked well at the headquarters might not be available elsewhere in the world. Even if they are, the level of support may be far less than headquarters' personnel are accustomed to. Vendors, particularly software vendors, frequently rely on agents to distribute and support products in some parts of the world. Some vendors will refuse to market software products in certain countries due to weak or nonexistent intellectual property rights legislation. Even if vendors have worldwide operations, local representatives will tend to provide service commensurate with local commissions and standards of performance. Communications vendors, often arms of local governments, may be unresponsive or present major obstacles to progress. Moreover, local country unit systems personnel may have vested interests and significant investments in existing local systems solutions.

The risks of global projects can be reduced. Large projects can be broken into phased deliverables, vendors offering worldwide support can be relied on, and country units converted one at a time. Initial resistance can be overcome by demonstrating feasibility in a country that has the most to gain and the least to lose from joining in a global solution.

Partnerships. Partnerships are one of the most important risk management approaches. Both the lack of structure and the various contributors to technological risk inherent in global projects suggest that both external and internal project integration techniques will be required to reduce project risk. External integration teams can link the systems developers to business representatives to help overcome the lack of structure. Internal integration mechanisms, such as technical design review committees, help to mitigate the risks associated with unfamiliar technology.

Partnerships between headquarters and subsidiary I/T organizations and user areas are critical; no single group or individual is likely to have a complete picture of where similarities and differences lie. A global project manager noted, "The two biggest challenges in getting worldwide requirements are understanding the local customs and distinguishing between what is done because of real local requirements and that which is done because it has always been done that way." Steering committees drawn from systems and business areas and across geographical boundaries can provide an executive level review board. At this level cross-border re-engineering opportunities can be explored, priorities established for particular systems development projects, development responsibilities assigned, and agreements negotiated as to how systems costs will be allocated.

Successful global projects often employ an international design team. The international composition means that the team lives in a multicultural environment on a day-to-day basis, and reflects the environment that the resulting system must accommodate. For example, the design team for a worldwide logistics system included eight people located in two locations in the United States, six located in the Far East, and five others in France. The project manager worked in a location in France. The team met quarterly with their international executive steering committee. Between meetings the design team made heavy use of information technology infrastructure to coordinate their activities. They used the same systems development methodology, computer-aided software engineering tools, and worldwide corporate data standards. Modules to be developed were assigned depending on the expertise within each country unit's systems development staff. Electronic mail was used extensively for daily communication among the team members. Electronic mail bridged the time zone differences and helped to maintain (but not necessarily create) personal relationships between the business and systems personnel.

Infrastructure. The lack or incompatibility of standards in communications and computer infrastructure is a major problem in developing global systems. In the area of communications, these inconsistencies are caused by monopolistic firms that control what communications equipment can be sold and used in a country. In the mid-1980s, for example, a firm that wished to establish an offshore software development operation built a satellite transmission facility for the country. They then were forced to turn the facility over to the government communications agency that leased time back to the firm.

Hardware inconsistencies can also result from governmental policy. To protect their domestic computer industry, several countries have placed limits on importation of computing equipment and services. For example, one executive told us that in Indonesia all equipment must be purchased by a local distributor; if the local distributor does not sell a particular product, it cannot be used in the country.

Human resources can be another infrastructure-related barrier. There will be significant levels of difference across countries in terms of computer expertise and acceptance. In some environments, systems personnel will be few in number and poorly trained. Consulting expertise may also be difficult to obtain. In such environments, firms might choose to provide support from facilities located elsewhere.

But great inconsistencies in infrastructure have usually been brought on by the firm's own management. The comment of one information system executive is typical of many we interviewed: "Our worldwide standards are a joke—we are unified only by a common logo." Often there has been no concerted effort to settle on a consistent worldwide information technology infrastructure. As one executive noted, "If you examined our worldwide hardware portfolio you might imagine that we had gone to a vendor convention with the sole intention of satisfying everyone by acquiring some of their equipment." Even organizations that sought consistency were often driven by economic disparities to incompatible solutions. For example, the high costs of telecommunications in Europe throughout the 1980s drove many systems groups to distributed processing solutions. Meanwhile their sister organizations in the United States were settling on centralized processing approaches. The relative costs of hardware and labor have forced similar choices of incompatible architectures in business units throughout the world.

Some firms have tried to enforce connectivity across platforms by centralizing all hardware and software acquisitions. For example, in one upstream petroleum company, the approval of the director of the global information system has been required prior to the purchase of any piece of hardware (except stand-alone personal computers). Other systems executives have negotiated worldwide contracts for software applications, thus providing an incentive for widespread adoption of consistent solutions. Still other firms provide compatibility through the consolidation of data centers; large semiconductor manufacturers, among the most globally integrated of industries, are consolidating their worldwide operations into two or three data centers.

Other barriers. A variety of other hurdles awaits the developer of global applications. Profit and loss responsibility often lies at the country level, complicating project prioritization and allocation decisions. Local country units may expect global systems to provide the same functions as their current systems and may be reluctant to convert from those current systems. Cultures also differ in the use of and importance placed on information in decision-making and control activities. Language presents predictable problems though the firm may have settled on a single official language. Even then, however, there will be major failures in interpersonal communication. Shop floor or customer interface systems probably will need to be in the local language. The common modules of systems are usually developed in English, but exit points for (or branches to) modules accommodating local requirements and language must be provided. Often, these modules are themselves written in the local language. Currency translation is another obvious requirement; it, like many other barriers, is one that European and Asian systems developers are often far more familiar with than their counterparts in the United States. Transborder data flow restrictions, predicted during the 1980s to be a major concern, apparently have had little impact outside of the area of human resources.

CONCLUSION

Information technology simultaneously drives and facilitates global business. Worldwide networks of computers are inexorably transforming the nature of business even as firms seek to harness this technology to the task of managing that transformation. The winners in this global environment will be the firms that can align worldwide information systems with integrated global business strategies. The synergy that develops from a close strategic linkage between I/T and business strategies will be central to success in highly competitive global markets.

Global business driver analysis helps to identify the business entities where global coordination can provide a competitive advantage and where an integrated global I/T portfolio and infrastructure can realize that advantage. But dangers lie in wait for even the best aligned project. The size of the global I/T projects, the complexity of the environments, the geographical distance, the disparity of available I/T solutions across countries, and the strong likelihood of resistance from subsidiaries all combine to significantly increase the risk and potential magnitude of failure. Cultural and language differences further raise the risk. Managing that risk requires that we focus investments in global systems on those applications where the payoffs will be high. Global business drivers provide the criteria for such a prioritization scheme. Once identified, such drivers can be nourished by, or help define, a network organization. Global applications and databases must be readily accessible throughout the network, whereas local I/T solutions ensure the flexibility required in dealing with problems and opportunities unique to local environments.

We believe that for most industries, the trend toward globalization will only be avoided by focusing on narrow niche markets. As global markets evolve, many previously successful firms will immerse themselves in the unsuccessful concentration on worldwide approaches. Entire industries, such as customs brokerage or freight forwarding, may disappear as integrated information systems transform traditional industry boundaries. Other industries and businesses will evolve that uniquely serve these new global markets. We believe the winners in this chaotic environment will be those firms that understand how information technology is transforming business and then can harness that technology to integrated global business strategies.

ACKNOWLEDGMENT

Our thanks to John Zachman who helped us clarify our definition of global business drivers.

CITED REFERENCES AND NOTES

1. The quotation is by John Welch, Jr., CEO of General Electric, and appeared in the Comments Section, *Kiplinger's*, p. 22 (August 1991).
2. K. Ohmae, *The Borderless World*, Harper Press, New York (1990), p. 162.
3. A. Hamilton, *The Financial Revolution*, The Free Press, New York (1986), p. 33.
4. M.J. Browne, "Prospective Freight Mega-Carriers: The Role of Information Technology in Their Global Ambitions," *Proceedings of the Hawaii International Conference on Systems Sciences*, IEEE Computer Society (1991), pp. 192–201.
5. For firms that are committed to becoming globally integrated, the terms "headquarters" and "subsidiary" are sometimes officially struck from the corporate lexicon. We continue to use the term "headquarters" here, however, because we are focusing on a transition to global business and systems rather than the final goal.
6. The Texas Instruments success story was obtained by the author during personal communications with TI executives.
7. S. Flax, "Global IT Without Tears," *Beyond Computing* 1, No. 4, 18–26 (August/September 1992).
8. These investigations have involved surveys of over 100 organizations, and in-person and phone interviews with over 50 executives. In most interviews, participants were assured that their remarks would be confidential. Therefore, most individuals quoted within this paper are not identified.
9. J. Rockart, "Chief Executives Define Their Own Data Needs," *Harvard Business Review* 57, No. 2, 81–93 (March–April 1979).
10. A.C. Boynton and R.W. Zmud, "An Assessment of Critical Success Factors," *Sloan Management Review* 25, No. 4, 17–27 (Summer 1984).

11. An exception lies in the case of electronic mail where all that is being passed around is unformatted text.
12. P.G.W. Keen, G.S. Brosema, and S. Zuboff, "Implementing Common Systems: One Organization's Experience," *Systems Objectives and Solutions* 2, 125–142 (1982).
13. Donald E. Petersen, former president and chairman of Ford Motor Co.
14. R.B. Reich, *The Work of Nations: Preparing Ourselves for 21st Century of Capitalism,* Alfred A. Knopf, Inc., New York (1991).
15. B. Dumaine, "The Bureaucracy Buster," *Fortune* 123, 36–50 (June 17, 1991).
16. C.A. Bartlett and S. Ghoshal, *Managing across Borders: The Transnational Solution,* Harvard Business School Press, Boston, MA (1989).
17. B. Ives and S.L. Jarvenpaa, "MSAS Cargo International: Global Freight Management," *Strategic Information Systems: A European Perspective,* T. Jelassi and C. Ciborra, Editors (1993).
18. B. Ives and S.L. Jarvenpaa, "Air Products and Chemicals, Inc.: Planning for Global Information Technology," *International Information Systems* 1, No. 2, 77–99 (April 1992).
19. T. Levitt, "The Globalization of Markets," *Harvard Business Review* 61, No. 3, 92–102 (May-June 1983).
20. H.G. Rammrath, "Globalization Isn't for Whiners," *Wall Street Journal,* Vol. XC (April 6, 1992).
21. J. Linder, *Polaroid Corporation: Leading from the Back Office,* Case Study No. 9-191-003, Harvard Business School, Boston, MA (1990).
22. For other results of the survey of multinationals, see B. Ives and S.L. Jarvenpaa, "Wiring the Stateless Corporation: Empowering the Drivers and Overcoming the Barriers," *SIM Network* 6, No. 4 (September/October, 1991).
23. B. Ives and S.L. Jarvenpaa, "Global Information Technology: Some Lessons from Practice," *International Information Systems* 1, No. 3, 1–15 (July 1992).
24. R.M. Kanter, "Transcending Business Boundaries: 12,000 World Managers View Change," *Harvard Business Review* 69, No. 3, 151–164 (May-June 1991).
25. A.D. Chandler, Jr., *Scale and Scope: The Dynamics of Industrial Capitalism,* Harvard University Press, Cambridge, MA (1990).
26. O.E. Williamson, *Markets and Hierarchies,* The Free Press, New York (1975).
27. "Unilever Adopts Clean Sheet Approach," *Financial Times* (October 21, 1991).
28. See Reference 14.
29. R.E. Miles and C.C. Snow, "Network Organizations," *California Management Review,* No. 3, 62–73 (Spring 1986).
30. E.K. Clemons and M.C. Row, "Information Technology at Rosenbluth Travel: Competitive Advantage in a Rapidly Growing Global Service Corporation," *Journal of Management Information Systems* 8, No. 2, 53–79 (Fall 1991).
31. A personal interview with David Miller on January 9, 1992.
32. F.W. McFarlan, "Portfolio Approach to Information Systems," *Harvard Business Review* 59, No. 5, 142–150 (September-October 1981).

* Trademark or registered trademark of International Business Machines Corporation.
** Trademark or registered trademark of American Airlines, Inc., a subsidiary of AMR Corp.

Globalization and Information Management Strategies

JAHANGIR KARIMI & BENN R. KONSYNSKI

1. INTRODUCTION

Recently, the globalization of competition has become the rule rather than the exception for a number of industries (39). To compete effectively, at home or globally, firms often must coordinate their activities on a worldwide basis. Although many global firms have an explicit global business strategy, few have global information technology architectures. A global information management strategy is needed as a result of (1) *industry globalization:* the growing globalization trend in many industries and the associated reliance on information technologies for coordination and operation, and (2) *national competitive posture:* the aggregation of separate domestic strategies in individual countries that may contend with coordination. While Procter and Gamble contends with the need to address more effectively its global market in the branded packaged goods industry, Singapore requires improved coordination and control of trade documentation in order to compete more effectively in the cross-industry trade environment that is vital to the economic health of that nation. Each approach recognizes the growing information intensity in their expanding markets. Each in turn must meet the challenges brought about by the need for cross-cultural and cross-industry cooperation.

Globalization trends demand an evaluation of the skills portfolio that organizations require in order to participate effectively in their changing markets. Porter (41) suggests that coordination among increasingly complex networks of activities dispersed worldwide is becoming a prime source of competitive advantage: global strategies frequently involve coordination with coalition partners as well as among a firm's own subsidiaries. The benefits associated with globalization of industries are not tied to countries' policies and practice. Rather, they are associated with how the activities in the industry value chain are performed by the firms' worldwide systems. These systems involve partnerships (31) with

Journal of Management Information Systems, vol. 7, no. 4 (Spring 1991), 7–26.

independent entities that involve information and management process interchange across legal organization boundaries, as well as across national boundaries.

For a global firm, the coordination concerns involve an analysis of how similar or linked activities are performed in different countries. Coordination (31) involves the management of the exchange of information, goods, expertise, technology, and finances. Many business functions play a role in such coordination—logistics, order fulfillment, financial, etc. Coordination involves sharing and use, by different facilities, of information about the activities within the firm's value chain (30). In global industries, these skills permit a firm to (1) be flexible in responding to competitors in different countries and markets, (2) respond in one country (or region) to a change in another, (3) scan markets around the world, (4) transfer knowledge between units in different countries, (5) reduce costs, (6) enhance effectiveness, and (7) preserve diversity in final products and in production location. The innovations in information technology (IT) in the past two decades have greatly reduced coordination costs by reducing both the time and cost of communicating information. Market and product innovation often involves coordination and partnership across a diverse set of organizational and geographically dispersed entities. Several studies (26,27,38,42) suggest ways in which companies/nations achieve competitive advantage through innovation.

Organizations must begin to manage the evolution of a global IT architecture that forms an infrastructure for the coordination needs of a global management team. The country-centered, multinational firm will give way to truly global organizations that will carry little national identity (49,50). It is a major challenge to general management to build and manage the technical infrastructure that supports a unique global enterprise culture. This paper deals with issues that arise in the evolution of a global business strategy and its alignment with the evolving global IT strategy.

Below we present issues related to the radical changes taking place in both the global business environment and the IT environment, with changes in one area driving changes in the other. Section 2 describes changes taking place in the global business environment as a result of globalization. It highlights elements from previous research findings on the effects of globalization on the organizational strategies/structures and coordination/control strategies. Section 3 deals with the information technology dimension and addresses the issue of development of a global information systems (GIS) management strategy. The section emphasizes the need for "alignment" of business and technological evolution as a result of the radical changes in the global business environment and technology. Section 4 summarizes and presents other challenges to senior managers that are emerging in the global business environment.

2. GLOBALIZATION AND CHANGES IN THE BUSINESS ENVIRONMENT

Since World War II, a number of factors have changed the manner of competition in the global business community. The particular catalyst for globalization and for evolving patterns of international competition varies among industries. Among the causative factors are increased similarity in available infrastructure, distribution channels, and marketing approaches among countries, as well as a fluid global capital market that allows large flows of funds between countries. Additional causes include falling political and tariff barriers, a growing number of regional economic pacts to facilitate trade relations, and the increasing impact of the technological revolution in restructuring and integrating industries. Manufacturing issues associated with flexibility, labor cost differentials, and other factors also play a role in these market trends.

Widespread globalization is also evident in a number of industries that were once largely separate domestic industries, such as software, telecommunications, and services (9,32,40). Recently, the political changes in the Soviet Union and the eastern European countries, plus the evolution of the European Common Market toward a single European market without national borders or barriers by 1992 (13), also have led to growing international competition. Other factors are changing the economic dynamics in the Pacific Rim area, with changes in Hong Kong, Japan, China and Taiwan, Korea, Singapore, and the reentry of certain nations to the global economic community (e.g., Vietnam).

Previous research indicates that significant changes have taken place in organizational strategies/structures during the 1980s because of ever-increasing global competition and growth in the communications and information-processing industry. Researchers in international business have pointed out that the structure of a global firm's value chain is the key to its strategy: its fit with the environmental requirements that determine economic performance (3, 15, 37, 40). Another study found that, in successful global firms, organization structure and strategy are matched by selecting the most efficient or lowest cost structure that satisfies the information-processing requirements inherent in the strategy (12). That is, the firm's strategy and its information-processing requirements must be in alignment with the firm's organizational structure and information-processing capabilities. To understand changes in organizational designs for global forms, these changes are highlighted in relation to the changes in strategies.

2.1. Evolution of the Global Firm's Strategy/Structure

Global strategy is defined by Porter (40) as strategy from which "a firm seeks to gain competitive advantage from its international presence through either a concentrated configuration of activities, or coordinating among dispersed activities, or both. Configuration involves the location(s) in the world where each activity in the value chain is performed; it characterizes the organizational structure of a global firm. A global firm faces a number of options in both configuration and coordination for each activity in the value chain. As implied by these definitions, there is no one pattern of international competition, neither is there one type of global strategy.

Bartlett (3, 4) suggests that for a global firm value-chain activities are pulled together by two environmental forces: (1) national differentiation, i.e., diversity in individual country-markets, and (2) global integration, i.e., coordination among activities in various

TABLE 1   Global Business Environment—Strategy/Structure and Coordination/Control

business strategy/structure	strategic management processes	tactical business processes	coordination and control processes
multinational/ decentralized- federation	informal HQ- subsidiary relation- ships; strategic decisions are decentralized	mainly financial flows; capital out and dividends back	socialization; careful recruitment develop- ment, and accultura- tion of key decision makers
global/ centralized- federation	tight central control decisions, resources, and information	one-way flows of goods, resources, and information	centralization; substantive decision making by senior management
international/ coordinated- federation	formal management planning and control systems allow tighter HQ-subsidiary linkages	assets, resources, responsibilities decentralized but controlled from HQ	formalization; formal systems, policies, and standards to guide choice
interorganizational/ coordinated federation of business groups	share activities and gain competitive advantage by lower- ing costs and raising differentiation	vertical disaggregation of functions	formalization; multiple and flexible coordination and control functions

countries. For global firms, forces for integration and national differentiation can vary depending on their global strategies. Table 1 shows the evolution of the global firms' strategy/
structure and their coordination/control strategies as a result of globalization of competition.
The vocabulary of Bartlett (4) and Porter (40) will be further used in our framework.

Under a *multinational* strategy, a firm might differentiate its products to meet local
needs and to respond to diverse national interests. In such an approach, the firm might
delegate considerable operating independence and strategic freedom to its foreign subsidiaries. Under this *decentralized* organizational structure, highly autonomous national companies are often managed as a portfolio of offshore investments rather than as a single
international business. A subsidiary is focused on its local market. Coordination and control
are achieved primarily through personal relationships between top corporate management
and subsidiary managers rather than by written rules, procedures, or a formal organizational structure. Strategic decisions are decentralized and top management is involved
mainly in monitoring the results of foreign operations. Figure 1 presents the organizational strategy/structure.

FIGURE 1

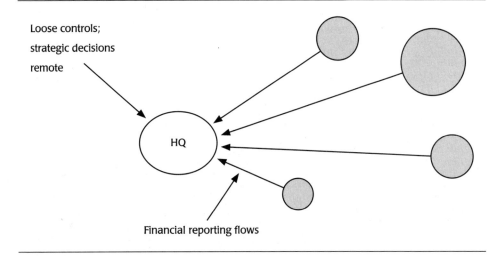

This model was the classic strategy/structure adopted by most European-based companies expanding before World War II. Examples include Unilever in branded packaged products, Philips in consumer electronics, and ITT in telecommunications switching. However, much changed for European companies in the 1970s with the reduction of certain tariff barriers by the EEC and with the entrance of both American and Japanese firms into local markets.

In the machine lubricant industry, automotive motor oil tends toward a multinational competitive environment. Countries have different driving standards and regulations and regional weather conditions. Domestic firms tend to emerge as leaders (for example, Quaker State and Pennzoil in the United States). At the same time, multinationals with country subsidies (such as Castrol, UK) become leaders in regional markets. In the lodging industry, many segments are multinational as a result of the fact that a majority of activities in the value chain are strongly tied to buyer location. Further, differences associated with national and regional preferences and lifestyle lead to few benefits from global coordination.

Under a pure *global* strategy, a firm may seek competitive advantage by capitalizing on the economies associated with standardized product design, global-scale manufacturing, and a centralized control of worldwide operation. The key parts of a firm's value-chain activities (typically product design or manufacturing) are geographically concentrated. They are either retained at the center, or they are centrally controlled. Under this *centralized* organizational structure, there are primarily one-way flows of goods, information, and resources from headquarters to subsidiaries; key strategic decisions for worldwide operations

FIGURE 2

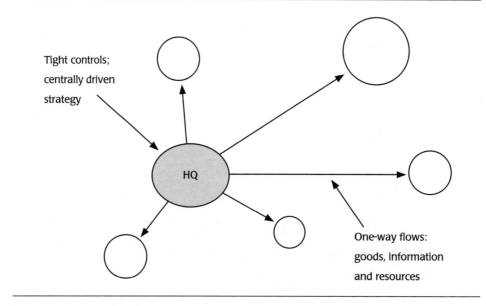

Tight controls; centrally driven strategy

HQ

One-way flows: goods, information and resources

are made centrally by senior management. Figure 2 depicts this organizational strategy/ structure.

This export-based strategy was/is typical in Japanese-based companies in the postwar years. They typically require highly coordinated activities among subsidiaries. Examples include KAO in branded packaged products, Matsushita in consumer electronics, NEC in telecommunications switching, and Toyota in the automobile industry. Toyota started by capitalizing on a tightly controlled operation that emphasized worldwide export of fairly standardized automobile models from global-scale plants in Toyota City, Japan. Lately, because of growing protectionist sentiments and lower factory costs in less-developed countries, Toyota (among others) has found it necessary to establish production sites in less-developed countries in order to sustain its competitive edge. The marine engine lubricant industry is a global industry that requires a global strategy. Ships move freely around the world and require that brand oil be available whenever they put into port. Brand reputations thus become global issues. Successful marine engine lubricant competitors (such as Shell, Exxon, and British Petroleum) are good examples of global enterprises.

In the area of business-oriented luxury hotels, competitors differ from the majority of hotel accommodations and the competition is more global. Global competitors such as Hilton, Marriott, and Sheraton have a wide range of dispersed properties that employ common brand names, common format, common service standards, and worldwide reservation systems to gain marketing advantage in serving the highly mobile travelers. Expectations of global standards for service and quality are high.

FIGURE 3

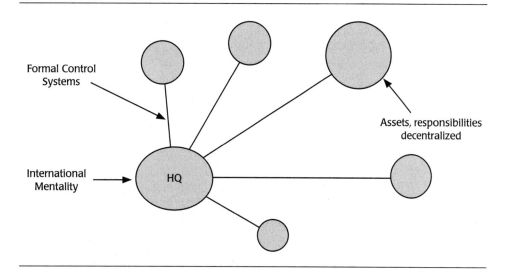

Under an *international* strategy, a firm transfers knowledge and expertise to overseas environments that are less advanced in technology and market development. Local subsidiaries are often free to adapt new strategies, products, processes, and/or ideas. Under this *coordinated federation* organizational structure, the subsidiaries' dependence on the parent company for new processes and ideas requires a great deal more coordination and control by headquarters than under a classic multinational strategy. Figure 3 depicts this organizational strategy/structure.

This strategy/structure defines the managerial culture of many U.S.-based companies. Examples include Procter and Gamble in branded packaged products, General Electric in consumer electronics, and Ericsson in telecommunications switching. These companies have a reputation for professional management that implies a willingness to delegate responsibility while retaining overall control through sophisticated systems and specialist corporate staffs. But, under this structure, international subsidiaries are more dependent on the transfer of knowledge and information than are subsidiaries under a multinational strategy; the parent company makes a greater use of formal systems and controls in its relations with subsidiaries.

Under a *transnational* strategy, a firm coordinates a number of national operations while retaining the ability to respond to national interests and preferences. National subsidiaries are no longer viewed as the implementors of centrally-developed strategies. Each, however, is viewed as a source of ideas, skills, capabilities and knowledge that can be beneficial to the company as a whole. It is not unusual for companies to coordinate product development, marketing approaches, and overall competitive strategy across interdependent national units. Under this *integrated network* organizational structure, top

FIGURE 4

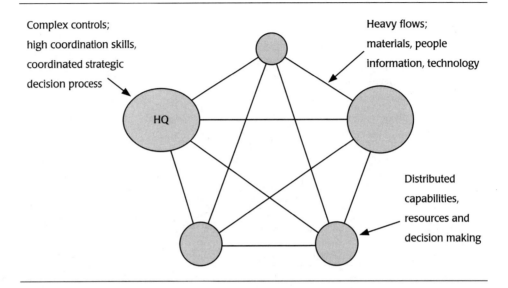

managers are responsible for: (1) coordinating the development of strategic objectives and operating policies, (2) coordinating logistics among operating divisions, and (3) coordinating the flow of information among divisions (3). Figure 4 presents this organizational strategy/structure.

During the 1980s, forces of global competition required global firms to be more responsive nationally. As a result, the transnational strategies are being adopted by increasing numbers of global firms (3). This adoption is becoming necessary because of the need for worldwide coordination and integration of activities upstream in the value chain (e.g., inbound logistics, operations) and because of the need for a greater degree of national differentiation and responsiveness at the downstream end (e.g., marketing, sales, and services). For example, adoption of a transnational mode allowed companies such as Procter and Gamble, NEC, and Unilever to respond effectively to the new and complex demands of their international business environments. They were able to replace exports with local manufacture and to develop more locally differentiated products (3,9). In contrast, the inability to develop a similar organizational capability is seen by some to be a factor contributing to the strategic and competitive difficulties faced by companies such as ITT, GE, and KAO.

Special situations relate to another form of the *coordinated federation* organizational structure, *interorganizational* design, which is a particular form of the organizational framework represented in Figure 4. An interorganizational design consists of two or more organizations that have chosen to cooperate by combining their strengths to overcome individual weaknesses (51). There are two modes of interorganizational design: equity and non-equity collaboration. *Equity collaborations* are seen in joint ventures, minority equity investments, and franchises. *Non-equity collaborations* are seen in forms of licensing arrangements, marketing and distribution agreements, and interorganizational systems (2, 21, 30, 31). For example, in the airline industry, achieving the economies of scale in developing and managing a large-scale reservation system are now beyond the capacities of the medium-sized airlines. In Europe, two major coalitions have been created, the Amadeus Coalition and the Galileo Coalition. Software for Amadeus is built around System One, the computer reservation system for Continental and Eastern. Galileo makes use of United's software. Even the largest carriers have acknowledged their inability to manage a large-scale reservation system by themselves; they have joined coalitions (31).

Another highly visible example that demonstrates the notion of regional or national coordination in order to compete in a global market is the paper industry of Finland. The 19 Finnish paper companies comprise a $3 billion industry that is heavily dependent on exports. Recently they determined that, to compete effectively in that service-oriented business, they must provide online electronic data interchange (EDI) interfaces with key customers and their sales offices. The Finnpap organization combined the efforts of the mill owners to develop an information system that reaches around the globe. The initial budget estimate of $40 million for five years has grown to an annual commitment of $10 million for the foreseeable future. None of the individual companies in the Finnish paper industry had the size, skills, and/or financial strength to create and deliver the world-class services necessary to compete against the large American, Canadian, and other global competitors. A regional cooperation was needed among the competitors in order to compete in the global market.

There has been a virtual explosion in the use of interorganizational designs for both global and domestic firms as a result of increased global competition during the 1980s. In 1983 alone, the number of domestic joint ventures announced in communications and information systems products and services industries exceeded the sum of all previously announced joint ventures in those sectors (17). Research suggests that interorganizational designs can lead to (1) "vertical disaggregation" of functions (e.g. marketing, distribution) typically conducted within the boundaries of a single organization performed independently by the organizations within the network, (2) the use of "brokers," or structure-independent organizations, to link together the different organizational units into "business groups" for performance of specific tasks, and (3) the substitution of "full disclosure information systems" in traditional organizations for lengthy trust-building processes based on experience (36).

2.2. Evolution of the Global Firm's Coordination/Control Strategies

Strategic control is considered to be the key element for the "integration" of a firm's value-chain activities; it is defined as "the extent of influence that a head office has over a subsidiary concerning decisions that affect subsidiary strategy" (10). Previous research found that, as resources such as capital, technology, and management become vested in the subsidiaries, head offices cannot continue to rely on control over these resources as means of influencing subsidiary strategy (1, 10, 44). The nature of strategic control by the head office over its subsidiaries shifts with time; there is a need for new forms of administrative control mechanisms such as those offered through improved information management strategies.

In a study of nine large worldwide companies and by interviewing 236 managers both in corporate headquarters and in a number of different national subsidiaries, Bartlett and Ghoshal (4) found that many companies had reached a coordination crisis by 1980. New competitive pressures were requiring the global firms to develop multiple strategic capabilities, even as other environmental forces led them to reconfigure their historical organization structures. Many familiar means of coordination (e.g., socialization, centralization, and formalization—shown in Table 1) characteristically proved inadequate to this new challenge.

The study further reports that European companies began to see the power and simplicity of more centralized coordination of subsidiaries. The Japanese increasingly adopted more formal systems, routines and policies to supplement their traditional time-consuming, case-by-case negotiations. American managers took new interest in shaping and managing the previously ignored informal processes and value systems in their firms. The study also found that the challenge for many global firms was not to find the organizational structure that provided the best fit with their global strategies, but to build and manage the appropriate decision-making processes that can respond to multiple changing environmental demands. Furthermore, because of evolving global strategies from multinational to transnational, decision making is no longer concentrated at corporate headquarters. Today's global firm must be able to carry a great deal of complex information to diverse locations in its integrated network of operations.

As we have seen, research on international business suggests that globalization has caused a change in the coordination/control needs of global firms. As a result, new organizational designs are created to meet new organizational coordination needs and to deal with increased organizational complexity and size. The traditional organizational designs (18, 29) such as functional, multidivisional, and matrix forms, are largely inappropriate for today's global firms.

Research further suggests that different organizational strategies/structures are necessary across products or businesses with diverse (global) environmental demands. In response, there have been two relatively new trends in organizational strategies: (1) a shift from a multinational strategy with decentralized organizational structures to a transnational strategy and globally integrated networks of operations, and (2) a rapid proliferation of interorganizational designs and structurally independent organizational units and business groups.

In short, the success in global competition depends largely on (1) a proper fit between an organization's business strategy and its structure, (2) an organization's ability to adapt its structure in order to balance the environmental forces of national differentiation and global integration for its value-chain activities, and (3) the manner of coordination/control of the organization's value-chain activities. As presented above, the globalization of competition and the evolving business environment suggest that the success of today's global firms' business and its coordination/control strategies may be linked to a global information management strategy. In the following section, the roles and characteristics of global information systems (GIS) and their differences with traditional distributed data-processing systems are discussed. A global information system management strategy is proposed. The need for "alignment" of the organization's business strategy/structure with its information system management strategy is emphasized as part of this strategy.

3. GLOBAL INFORMATION SYSTEMS

Due to the dramatic changes in it, and the increased skills in organizations to deploy and exploit those advances, there are an increasing number of applications of IT by global firms in both the service and manufacturing industries. The earliest were in international banking, airline, and credit authorization. However, during the 1980s, due to rapid improvements in communications and IT, more and more activities of global firms were coordinated using information systems. At the same time, patterns in the economies of IT development are changing (19, 22, 38). The existence or near completion of public national data networks and of public or quasi-public regional and international networks in virtually all developed (and a few developing) countries has resulted in rapid growth in data-service industries, e.g., data processing, software, information storage and retrieval, and telecommunications services (26,46).

Today global firms not only rely on data-service industries and IT to speed up message transmission (e.g., for ordering, marketing, distribution, and invoicing), but also to improve the management of corporate systems by: (1) improving corporate functions such as financial control, strategic planning, and inventory control, and (2) changing the manner in which global firms actually engage in production (e.g., in manufacturing, R&D, design and engineering, CAD,CAM/CAE) (46). Therefore, more and more of global firms' mechanisms for planning, control and coordination, and reporting depend on information technology. According to the head of information systems at the $35 billion chemical giant, information systems will either be a facilitator or an inhibitor of globalization during the 1990s (35).

A *global information system* (GIS) is a distributed data-processing system that crosses national boundaries (7). There are a number of differences between domestic distributed systems (25) and GISs. Because GISs cross national boundaries, unlike domestic distributed systems, they are exposed to wide variations in business environments, availability of resources, and technological and regulatory environments. These are explained briefly below.

Business Environment. From the perspective of the home-base country, there are differences in language, culture, nationality, and professional management disciplines among subsidiary organizations. Due to differences in local management philosophy, business/

technology planning responsibilities are often fragmented rather than focused in one budgetary area. Business/technology planning, monitoring, and control and coordination functions are often difficult and require unique management skills (24).

Infrastructure. The predictability and stability of available infrastructure in a given country is a major issue when making the country a hub for a global firm. "It is a fact of life that some countries are tougher to do business in than others" (8). Regional economic dependence on particular industry and cross-industry infrastructure may be informative. Singapore (26) has provided, through TradeNet, a platform for fast, efficient trade document processing. Hong Kong (27), on the other hand, is still dealing with its unique position as the gateway to the People's Republic of China, and its historic "free port" policies in developing its TradeLink platform. Lufthansa, Japan Airlines, Cathay Pacific, and other airlines are trying to pool their global IT infrastructure in order to deliver a global logistics system. At the same time, global banks are exploring the influence their IT architectures have on the portfolio of instruments they can offer on a global basis (37).

Resource availability can vary due to import restrictions or to lack of local vendor support. Since few vendors provide worldwide service, many firms are limited in choice of vendors in a single project, because of operational risk. Finally, availability of tele-communications equipment/technology (e.g., LAN, private microwave, fiber optic, satellite earth stations, switching devices, and other technologies) varies among countries and geographic regions.

Regulatory Environments. Changes in government, economy, and social policy can lead to critical changes in the telecommunications regulations that pose serious constraints on the operation of GISs. The price and availability of service, and cross-border data-flow restrictions vary widely from one country to another.

The PTT (post, telephone, and telegraph) in most countries sets limits based on volume of traffic rather than based on fixed-cost leased facilities. By doing so, the PTT increases its own revenues and, at the same time, prevents global firms from exploiting economies of scale. The nature of the internal infrastructure systems may also influence the interest and ability to leverage regulation (38,49,50).

There are regulations restricting usage of leased lines or import of hardware/software for GLSs. These affect the GIS options possible in different countries: restrictions on connections between leased lines and public telephone networks, the use of dial-up data transmission, and the use of electronic mail systems for communications. It is not unusual for some companies to build their own "phone company" in order to reduce dependence on government-run organizations (8). Hardware/software import policies also make local information processing uneconomical in some countries. For example, both Canada and Brazil have high duties on imported hardware, and there are software import valuation policies in France, Saudi Arabia, and Israel (6).

Transborder dataflow (TBDF) regulations, in part, govern the content of international data flows (5). Examples are requirements to process certain kinds of data and to maintain certain business records locally, and the fact that some countries don't mind data being "transmitted in" but oppose interactive applications in which data are "transmitted out." Although the major reasons for regulating the content of TBDF are privacy protection and economic and national security concerns, these regulations can adversely affect the economies of GISs by forcing global firms to decentralize their operations, increase operating costs, and/or prohibit certain applications.

Standards. International, national, and industry standards play a key role in permitting global firms to "leverage" their systems development investment as much as possible. Telecommunications standards vary widely from one country to another concerning the technical details of connecting equipment and agreements on formats and procedures. However, the conversion of the world's telecommunications facilities into an integrated digital network (IDN) is well underway, and most observers agree that a worldwide integrated digital network and the integrated services digital network (ISDN) will soon become a reality (34,48). The challenge is not a problem of technology—the necessary technology already exists. Integration depends on creating the necessary standards and getting all countries to agree.

Telecommunications standards are set by various domestic governments or international agencies, and by major equipment vendors (e.g., IBM's Systems Network Architecture (SNA), Wang's Wangnet, Digital Equipment's DecNet, etc.). There are also standards set by groups of firms within the same industry, such as SWIFT (Society for Worldwide International Funds Transfers) for international funds transfers and cash management, EDI (Electronic Data Interchange) for formatted business transactions such as purchase orders between companies (ANSI, EDIPACT, etc.) (16), and SQL (Structured Query Language) as a common form of interface for coordinating data across many databases.

3.1. Global Information Management Strategy

Table 2 shows the alternative information systems management strategy/structure as a result of the evolution in global business environment and technology. New information technologies are allowing closer integration of adjacent steps on the value added chain through the development of electronic markets and electronic hierarchies (33). As that study reports, the overall effect of technology is the change in coordination mechanisms. This will result in an increase in the proportion of economic activities coordinated by markets rather than by hierarchies. This also supports and explains change in the global firm's strategies from multinational, global strategies to international (interorganizational), transnational strategies.

The task of managing across corporate boundaries has much in common with that of managing across national borders. Managing strategic partnerships, coalitions, and alliances

TABLE 2   Alignment of Global and Information Management Strategies

business strategy/structure	coordination/ control strategy	coordination/control mechanisms	IS strategy structure
multinational/ decentralized-federation	socialization	*hierarchies*; managerial decisions determine the flow of materials and services	decentralization/ standalone databases and processes
global/centralized-federation	centralization		centralization/ centralized databases and processes
international and interorganizational/ coordinated federation	formalization	*markets*; market forces determine the flow of materials and services	IOS/linked databases and processes
transnational/ integrated network	co-opting		integrated architecture/ shared databases and processes

has forced managers to shift their thinking from the traditional task of controlling a hierarchy to managing a network (11,31,43). As discussed earlier, managers in transnational organizations must gather, exchange, and process larger volumes of information; formal strategies/structure cannot support such huge information-processing needs. Because of the widespread distribution of organizational units and the relative infrequency of direct contacts among those in disparate units in a transnational firm, top management has a better opportunity to shape relationships among managers simply by being able to influence the nature and frequency of contacts by using a proper information system management strategy.

The strategy should contain the senior management policy on corporate information systems architecture (ISA). Corporate ISA (1) provides a guide for systems development, (2) facilitates the integration and data sharing among applications, and (3) supports development of integrated, corporate systems that are based on a data resource with corporate-wide accessibility (19). Corporate ISA for a global firm is a high-level map of the information and technology requirements of a firm as a whole; it is composed of network, data, and application and technology architectures. In the international environment, the network and data architectures are generally considered to be the key enabling technologies because they are the highway systems for a wide range of traffic (24).

A new GIS management strategy needs to address organizational structural issues related to coordination and configuration of value-chain activities, by proper ISA design. The key components of a GIS management strategy are (1) a centralized and/or coordinated business/technology strategy on establishing data communications architecture and standards, (2) a centralized and/or coordinated data management strategy for creation of corporate databases, and (3) alignment of global business and GIS management strategy. These are explained below.

3.1.1. Network Management Strategy and Architecture

Network architecture describes where applications are executed, where databases are located, and what communications links are needed among locations. It also sets standards ensuring that all other ISA components are interrelated and working together. The architecture is important in providing standards for interconnecting very different systems instead of requiring commonality of systems. At present, the potential for network architecture is determined more often by vendors than by general industry or organizational standards (24).

Architecture. Research on international business points out that the structure of a global firm's value chain is the key to its strategy; its fit with environmental requirements derives economic performance. However, the environments of GISs are external to their global firms and thus cannot be controlled. Services provided by GISs must be globally coordinated, integrated, standardized, and tailored to accommodate national differences and individual national markets.

Deciding on appropriate network architecture is a leading management and technology issue. Research in the global banking industry found that an international bank providing a wide range of global electronic wholesale banking services has some automated systems that need to be globally standardized (e.g., global balance reporting system), while others (e.g., global letter of credit system) need to be tailored to individual countries' markets (37). The research also suggests that appropriate structure for GISs may vary for different product and service portfolios: uniform centralization/decentralization of strategy/structure may not be appropriate for all GIS applications. Further, the research found that international banks cannot expect to optimize the structure of environmentally diverse information systems with a symmetrical approach to GIS architecture, since any such approach may set limits on the product and service portfolios called for by the bank's global business strategy. An asymmetrical approach, structuring each system to suit the environmental needs of the service delivered, although more complex, can significantly improve international banks' operational performance. Such an approach may, however, significantly increase coordination costs.

Standards. Use of standards is an important strategic move for most companies, since many of today's companies limit the number of intercompany formats they support. With the success in the development and adoption of global standards, in particular in narrow areas (e.g., EDIFACT), it is much harder to make standards mistakes than was possible several years ago. By using standards, companies can broaden their choice of trading partners in the future. Absence of uniform data and communications standards in international, national, and industry environments means that no single product can address more than a fraction of the hardware and communications protocols scattered throughout a firm.

Standards are often set by government rules and regulations, major computers and communications vendors, and/or cooperative arrangements within an industry. Regardless of how the standards are set, they are critical to the operations of GISs. Because standards are the key to connectivity of a set of heterogeneous systems, explicit senior management policy on standards is important to promote adoption and compliance. There should be one central policy regarding key technologies/standards (e.g., EDI, SQL). This policy should include a management agenda for understanding both standards and the standard-setting process within industry, national, and international environments (23). Such a central policy accomplishes several objectives, reducing cost, avoiding vendor viability, achieving economies of scale, reducing potential interface problems, and facilitating transborder data flow. Therefore, decisions about the components of network architectures and standards require a move toward centralized corporate management coordination and control. However, decisions regarding adding traffic need decentralized planning; they require conformity by IS managers to data communications standards.

3.1.2. Data Management Strategy and Architecture

Data architecture concerns the arrangement of databases within an organization. Although every organization that keeps data has a data architecture, in most organizations it is the result of evolution of application in its various departments and not the result of a well-planned data management strategy (14, 45). Data management problems are amplified for large global firms with diverse product families. For a global firm with congested data highways, the problems of getting the right data in the right amount to the right people at the right time multiply as global markets emerge (8).

Lack of a centralized information management strategy often causes corporate entities (e.g., customers and products) to have multiple attributes, coding schemes, and values across databases (14). This makes linkages or data sharing among value activities difficult at best; establishing linkages requires excessive time and human resources; costs and performance of other data-related activities within the value chain are affected. These factors make important performance and correction data unavailable to top management for decision making, thereby creating important obstacles to the firm's competitive position and its future competitive advantage.

Strategy/Architecture. To increase coordination among a global firm's value-chain activities, its data architecture should be designed based on an integrated data management strategy. This strategy should mandate creation of a set of *corporate databases* derived from the firm's value-chain activities. A recent study has pointed out the significance of a firm's value-chain activities in deploying IT strategically (20); however, no specific information management strategy is proposed.

Corporate data is used by more than one functional area within the value-chain activities. In contrast, departmental data is often used mainly by departments within the functional area that comprises a value-chain activity. Corporate data is used by departments across functions.

Corporate databases should be based on business entities involved in value-chain activities rather than around individual applications. A firm must define (1) appropriate measures of performance for each value activity (e.g., sales volume by market by period), (2) corporate entities by which the performance is measured (e.g., product, package type), (3) relationships among the entities defined, (4) entities' value sets, coding schemes, and attributes, (5) corporate databases derived from the entities, and (6) relationships among the corporate databases. For example, for a direct value-adding activity such as marketing and sales within a firm's value chain, the corporate databases may include: advertisement, brand, market, promotion, sales.

Given this data management strategy, corporate databases are defined independent of applications; they are accessible by all potential users. This data management strategy allows a firm's senior management to (1) integrate and coordinate information with the value-adding and support activities within the value chain, (2) identify significant trends in performance data, and (3) compare local activities to activities in other comparable locations.

This data management strategy creates an important advantage for a global firm, because activities used for the firm's strategic business planning are used to define the corporate databases. The critical establishment of linkage between strategic business planning and strategic information systems planning is possible when this strategy is used, because the activities that create value for the firm customers also create data the firm needs to operate. However, the strategy does not imply that all application databases should be replaced by corporate databases. Application databases should remain (directly or indirectly) as long as the applications exist; but there should be a disciplined flow of data among corporate, functional, and application databases.

3.1.3. Alignment of Global Business and GIS Management Strategy: A Plan for Action

One challenge facing management today is the necessity for the organization to align its business strategy/structure to its information systems management/development strategy. A proper design of critical linkages among a firm's value-chain activities results in an effective business design involving information technology and an improved coordination with coalition partners, as well as among a firm's own subsidiaries. Previous research has emphasized the benefits of establishing proper linkages between business-strategic planning and technology-strategic planning for an organization (22, 28). Among these are proper strategic positioning of an organization, improvements in organizational effectiveness, efficiency and performance, and full exploitation of information technology investment.

Establishing the necessary alignment requires the involvement of and cooperation with both the senior business planner and the senior IS technology manager. This results in a new set of responsibilities and skills for both. For the senior business planner, new sets of responsibilities include (1) formal integration of the strategic business plan with the strategic IS plan, (2) examination of the business needs associated with a centralized and/or coordinated network, technology, and data management strategy, (3) review of the network architecture as a key enabling technology for the firm's competitive strategy and assessment of the impact of network alternatives on business strategy, (4) awareness of key technologies/standards and standard-setting processes at the industry, national, and international levels, (5) championing the rapidly expanding use of industry, national, and international standards.

For the senior information technology manager, new and critical responsibilities include (1) awareness of the firm's business challenges in the changing global environment and involvement in shaping the firm's leverage of information technology in its global business strategy, (2) preparing a systems development environment that recognizes the long-term company-wide perspective in a multi-regional and multi-cultural environment, (3) planning the development of the application portfolio on the basis of the firm's current business and its global strategic posture in the future, (4) making the "business purpose" of the strategic systems development projects clear in a global business context, (5) selecting and recommending key technologies/standards for linking systems across geographic and cultural boundaries, (6) setting automation of linkages among internal/external activities within the firm's value chain as goals and selling them to others, (7) designing corporate databases derived from the firm's value-chain activities, accounting for business cultural differences, and (8) facilitating corporate restructuring through the provision of flexibility in business services.

4. SUMMARY AND CONCLUSIONS

Changes in technologies and market structures have shifted competition from a national to a global scope. This has resulted in the need for new organizational strategies/structures. Traditional organizational designs are not appropriate for the new strategies, because they evolved in response to different competitive pressures. New organizational structures need to achieve both flexibility and coordination among the firm's diverse activities in the new international markets.

Globalization trends have resulted in a variety of organizational designs that have created both business and information management challenges. A global information systems (GIS) management strategy is required.

The key components of a GIS management strategy should include: (1) a centralized and/or coordinated business/technology strategy on establishing data communications infrastructure, architecture, and standards, (2) a centralized and/or coordinated data management strategy for design of corporate databases, and (3) alignment of global and business and GIS management strategy. Such a GIS management strategy is appropriate today because it facilitates coordination among a firm's value-chain activities and among business units, and because it provides the firm with the flexibility and coordination necessary to deal effectively with changes in technologies and market structures. It also aligns information systems management strategy with corporate business strategy as it provides a foundation for designing information systems architecture (ISA).

In addition to the global enterprise's competitive posture, globalization also refers to the competitive posture of nations and city-states (26, 27). The issues related to coordination and control in the global enterprise also invest the nation/state to review the alignment of its cross-industry competitive posture (31, 42). It is incumbent on governments to seek appropriate levels of intervention in the business practices of the state that influence the state's competitive position in the global business community.

The challenges to general managers in the emerging global economic environment extend far beyond the IT infrastructure. At the same time, with the information intensity in the markets (products, services, and channel systems) and the information intensity associated with coordination across geographic, cultural, and organizational barriers, global general managers will rely increasingly on information technologies to support their management processes. The proper alignment of the evolving global information management strategy and the global organizational strategy will be important to the positioning of the global firm in the global economic community.

REFERENCES

1. Baliga, B.R., and Jaeger, A.M. Multinational corporations, control systems and delegation issues. *Journal of International Business Studies*, 15, 2 (Fall 1984), 25–40.
2. Barrett, S., and Konsynski, B. Interorganizational information sharing systems. *MIS Quarterly*, special issue (1982), 93–105.
3. Bartlett, C.A., and Ghoshal, S. Organizing for worldwide effectiveness: the transnational solution. *California Management Review*, 31, 1 (1988), 1–21.
4. Bartlett C.A., and Ghoshal, S. *Managing Across Borders: The Transnational Solution*. Boston: Harvard Business School Press, 1989.
5. Basche, J. Regulating international data transmission: the impact on managing international business. Research report no. 852 from the Conference Board. New York, 1983.
6. *Business Week*. Special report on telecommunications: the global battle (October 1983).
7. Buss, M. Managing international information systems. *Harvard Business Review*, special series (1980).
8. Carlyle, R.E. Managing IS at multinationals. *Datamation* (March 1. 1988), 54–66.
9. Chandler, A.D. The evolution of modern global competition. In (39), 405–44.
10. Doz, Y.L., and Prahalad, C.K. Headquarters influence and strategic control in MNCs. *Sloan Management Review* (Fall 1981), 15–29.
11. Eccles, R.G., and Crane, D.B. Managing through networks in investment banking. *California Management Review*, 30 (Fall 1987), 176–195.
12. Egelhoff, W. Strategy and structure in multinational corporations: an information processing approach. *Administrative Science Quarterly*, 27, 3 (1982), 435–458.
13. Frenke, K.A. The European community and information technology. *Communications of the ACM* (special section the EC '92, 33, 4 (1990), 404–412.
14. Goodhue, D.L.; Quillard, J.A.; and Rockart, J.F. Managing the data resource: a contingency perspective. *MIS Quarterly*, 12, 3 (September 1988), 372–391.

15. Ghoshal, S., and Noria, N. International differentiation within multinational corporations. *Strategic Management Journal*, 10, 4 (July/August 1989), 323–337.

16. Hansen, J.V., and Hill, N.C. Control and audit of electronic data interchange, *MIS Quarterly*, 13, 4 (December 1989), 403–413.

17. Harrigan, K.R. *Strategies for Joint Ventures.* Lexington, MA: 1985.

18. Huber, G.P. The nature and design of post industrial organizations. *Management Science*, 30 (1984), 928–951.

19. Inmon, W.H. *Information Systems Architecture.* Englewood Cliffs, NJ: Prentice-Hall, 1986.

20. Johnston, H.R., and Carrico, S.R. Developing capabilities to use information strategically. *MIS Quarterly*, 12, 1 (March 1988), 36–48.

21. Johnston, H.R., and Vitale, M. Creating competitive advantage with interorganizational information systems. *MIS Quarterly*, 12, 2 (June 1988), 152–165.

22. Karimi, J. Strategic planning for information systems: requirements and information engineering methods. *Journal of Management Information Systems*, 4, 4 (Spring 1988), 5–24.

23. Keen, P.G. An international perspective on managing information technologies. ICIT Briefing Paper no. 4101, 1987.

24. Keen, P.G. *Competing in Time: Using Telecommunications for Competitive Advantage.* Cambridge, MA: Ballinger Publishing Co., 1988.

25. King, J. Centralized vs. decentralized options. *Computing Surveys* (December 1983).

26. King, J., and Konsynski, B. Singapore TradeNet: a tale of one city. N1—191—009, Harvard Business School, 1990.

27. King. J., and Konsynski, B. Hong Kong TradeLink: news from the second city. N1—191—026, Harvard Business School, 1990.

28. King, W.R. Strategic planning for IS: the state of practice and research. *MIS Quarterly*, 9, 2 (June 1985), Editor's comment, vi–vii.

29. Knight, K. Matrix organization: a review. *Journal of Management Studies.* 13 (1976), 111–130.

30. Konsynski, B., and Warbelow, A. Cooperating to compete: modeling interorganizational interchange, Harvard Business School working paper 90–002, 1989.

31. Konsynski, B., and McFarlan, W. Information partnerships—shared data, shared scale. *Harvard Business Review* (September/October 1990), 114–120.

32. Lu, M., and Farrell, C. Software development: an international perspective. *The Journal of Systems and Software*, 9 (1989), 305–309.

33. Malone, T.W.; Yates, J.; and Benjamin, R.I. Electronic markets and electronic hierarchies. *Communications of the ACM*, 30, 6 (June 1987),484–497.

34. Martin J., and Leben, J. *Principles of Data Communications.* Englewood Cliffs, NJ: Prentice-Hall, 1988.

35. Mead, T. The IS innovator at DuPont. *Datamation* (April, 15, 1990), 61–68.

36. Miles, R.E., and Snow, C.C. Organizations: new concepts for new forms. *California Management Review*, 28 (1986), 62–73.

37. Mookerjee, A.S. Global Electronic Wholesale Banking Delivery System Structure. PhD thesis, Harvard University, 1988.

38. O'Callaghan R., and Konsynski, B. Banco Santander: el banco en casa, 9—189—185, Harvard Business School, 1989.

39. Porter, M.E. *Competition in Global Industries.* Cambridge, MA: Harvard Business School Press, 1986.

40. Porter, M.E. Competition in global industries: a conceptual framework. In (39), 15–59.

41. Porter, M.E. From competitive advantage to corporate strategy. *Harvard Business Review* (May/June 1987), 43–59.

42. Porter, M.E. The competitive advantage of nations. *Harvard Business Review* (March/April 1990), 73–92.

43. Powell, W. Hybrid organizational arrangements. *California Management Review*, 30 (Fall 1987), 67–87.

44. Prahalad, C.K and Doz, Y.L. An approach to strategic control in MNCs. *Sloan Management Review* (Summer 1981), 5–13.

45. Romero, V. *Data Architecture: The Newsletter for Corporate Data Planners and Designers* 1, 1 (September/October 1988).

46. Sauvant, K. International transactions in services: the politics of transborder data flows. *The Atwater Series on World Information Economy*, 1. Boulder: Westview Press, 1986.

47. Selig, G.J. A framework for multinational information systems planning. *Information and Management*, 5 (June 1982), 95–115.

48. Stallings, W. *ISDN: An Introduction*. New York: Macmillan, 1989.

49. Warbelow, A.; Kokuryo, J.; and Konsynski, B. Aucnet: TV auction network system. 9—190—001, Harvard Business School, 1989, p. 19.

50. Warbelow, A.; Fjeldstad, O.; and Konsynski, B. Bankenes Betalings Sentral A/S: the Norwegian bank giro. N9—191—037, Harvard Business SchooL 1990, p. 17.

51. Zammuto. R. *Organization Design: Structure, Strategy, and Environment*. The Dryden Press.

SECTION IV
Global Connectivity and Telecommunications

Modern global business enterprises depend almost totally on tele-communications networks to support their business operations. The development and management of international networks present enormous opportunities and challenges to information systems (IS) managers. The articles in this chapter examine the challenges of managing global telecommunications and offer practical guidelines for dealing with these challenges.

In the first article, Kamman explains why worldwide connectivity is necessary for gaining a competitive advantage and describes how networks are evolving from single enterprise systems to extended enterprise networks. He further emphasizes the importance of the quality of the network's services as a key distinguishing factor. Those aspects of the global network that yield the highest level of customer service satisfaction provide the key to achieving a competitive advantage.

In the second article, Liebhaber describes the revolutionary changes taking place in the telecommunications industry and the resulting implications for businesses, governments, and societies. Telecom-munications and information technologies have become key strategic weapons for corporations competing in today's global marketplace. The challenge corporations face is how best to balance competition and cooperation in an effort to achieve worldwide communications networks that meet the needs of tomorrow's information age.

Corr and Hunter next provide the reader with an overview of the various technologies now available and with examples of their applications. Based on the evolution of these technologies and recent developments, the authors make predictions about future tele-communications capabilities and their potential impact on global business organizations.

Gilbert and Hunter's article identifies five new areas in which IS managers must be skilled in order to meet the networking challenges of corporations today: technical knowledge, network design and planning, country-by-country service requirements, network management operations, and network management interoperability. Network managers need to be concerned with the configuration of the corporation's total network environment.

The final article provides specific advice for establishing and managing global telecommunication networks. Wiggins offers practical guidance on how to deal with various government-controlled PTTs (Poste Télégraphique et Téléphonique) and how to avoid costly mistakes in building a global telecommunication infrastructure. International networking is becoming the core component of doing business. Understanding some basic rules pertaining to globalization can likely avoid some very expensive network failures.

Global connectivity and telecommunications have become essential to operating in an international business environment. The tele-communications infrastructure provides the foundation support base for a company's operations. The following section focuses on the ability of global networks to support information flows and the effective management of information.

Global Networks

ALAN B. KAMMAN

SHORT OF CAPITAL ITSELF, the most powerful catalyst in the history of modern business is the communications network. Starting with the telegraph and moving through the microchip, the technologies that link individuals and ideas have done more to shape the world as we know it than any other single force. Soon, the network that links individuals and ideas may represent an even greater asset to the organization than the capital upon which the organization is built—indeed, for the organization of the future, the information in that network may *be* the assets upon which the organization is built.

Evolving the ability to gather, share, manipulate, and manage information will be the key to profitability for the organization of the future. As such, it will be among the high priorities of both the business and I/T managers in every organization. It will also be one of the most challenging endeavors either manager has ever undertaken, alone or in concert with others. Bringing about this evolution requires activity on a number of simultaneously engaged campaigns:

- The business organization must be strategically redesigned. The hierarchical organizations that dominated the organizations of the 60s must evolve into the networked organizations of the 90s. Business processes will be cross-functional and linked with down-stream external business partners. The design of the organization will be built upon the added value of knowledge of workers and the leverage inherent in networking groups of knowledge workers. [See figure on following page.]

- The information infrastructure of the organization must be redesigned in conjunction with the business redesign. The processing of information will move out of the centralized paradigms associated with the hierarchical organizations of the past and into the distributed paradigms of the information era. Workstations and other distributed work platforms will dominate this environment: each workstation will facilitate the added value of the knowledge worker, and all the work platforms will be linked by a network that promotes the dissemination of information throughout the organization.

Kamman, Alan B. "Global Networks." *Stage by Stage*, by Nolan, Norton, and Co., vol. 9, no. 6 (1990), 1–6.

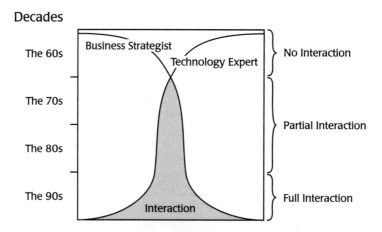

"For companies on the 'fast track,' business strategists and technology experts
must combine forces to drive the organization forward."

- The individuals in the organization must develop the skills required to participate in this information infrastructure. On the managerial level, this means development of the skills for motivating change among knowledge workers; on the knowledge worker level, this means the development of the skills that will bring their value added into the information infrastructure.

Why must all three campaigns be undertaken simultaneously? For several reasons: first, if not undertaken simultaneously, the end result of the endeavors will not be as tightly integrated as the organization of the 90s requires: second, attempting these endeavors in a serial fashion will take too long. The fact of the matter is that companies all over the globe are already deeply invested in the evolution of the information organization of the 90s. Survival in the 90s depends upon the speed of implementation.

TODAY'S EVOLVING ORGANIZATIONS

In his recently published work *Microcosm,*[1] George Gilder points out that today's global telecommunications network carries more valuable goods than all the world's supertankers. The evolutionary implications of this shift are monumental: until this time, the production of wealth has been tied to the movement and manipulation of massive objects against friction and gravity. Wealth and power came mainly to the possessor of material things or to the ruler of military forces capable of conquering the physical means of production: land, labor, and capital. Today, wealth comes not to the rulers of slave labor but to the liberators of human creativity, not to the conquerors of land but to the emancipators of mind.

The new technologies of the information age—artificial intelligence, silicon compilation, and parallel processing, to name but a few—allow entrepreneurs to use the power of knowledge to economize on capital and enhance its efficiency. Connectivity is increasingly being used to gain a competitive edge:

- Digital Equipment Corporation is operating one of the largest private global networks in the world. It has over 41,000 nodes in 26 countries. Sixty percent of Digital's 120,000 employees have access to it. For telecom, network, and MIS managers, Digital's network is critical. It enables the company to use networking for a host of strategic and competitive advantages. Furthermore, it allows Digital to maintain an elaborately decentralized matrix organization while still maintaining the bureaucratic procedures necessary to run a $13 billion giant. Digital's commitment to this network in 1989 reached $40 million in annual operating costs.

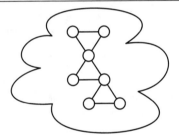

Single Enterprise Network

While Digital's network reflects the basic paradigm of a private network, the *single enterprise network*, the fastest growing networks involve inter-organizational information systems. An example of such an *industry-specific value-added network* is found in the U.S. apparel industry, which has been hard-hit by foreign imports:

- J.C. Penney, the largest U.S. retail department store chain, has developed an information network in a novel way. It not only linked its own employees, but it also tied in a number of apparel and fabric manufacturers, including J.P. Stevens, Milliken Company, and DuPont—all giants in their own right. J.C. Penney automatically transmits orders to the fabric and fiber manufacturers, which then deliver the needed materials to the apparel manufacturers, through a just-in-time delivery system. While each participant in the value-added information network benefits, the bulk of the benefits have accrued to J.C. Penney, whose profits have reflected the wisdom of the investment.

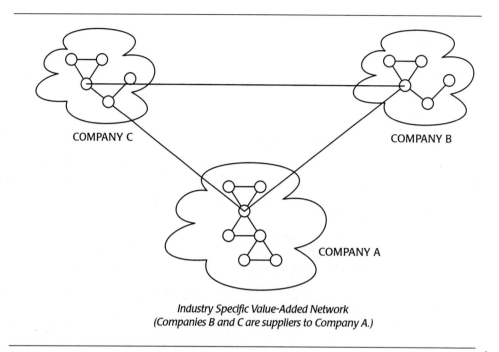

Industry Specific Value-Added Network
(Companies B and C are suppliers to Company A.)

While industry-specific value-added vertical networks represented the mainstream of information network expansion in the 80s, another form of this network had an even greater impact on the information transaction marketplaces. The *extended enterprise network* enables, in simple terms, many corporations to extend their *single enterprise networks* so as to share many kinds of information with other participants. The industry-specific lines that bound the value-added vertical networks are abandoned in the extended enterprise network, and the result is an information consortium of unprecedented potential.

Some compelling examples of the *extended enterprise networks* can be found among major organizations the world over:

- The Mitsubishi Group, an affiliate of 28 "immediate family" members, includes an oil company, a chemical firm, a steel manufacturer, and a bank—to describe just a few of the diverse family members. This group of 28 members has been joined by more than 100 other corporations with financial linkages of some type that tie them to the 28. The extended list includes Nikon Camera, Kirin Beer, and many others. The Mitsubishi Group calls the project "MIND"—Mitsubishi Internal Data Network—and says that it has two major goals: one is to link the 28 family members; the other is to provide communications channels to any enterprise engaged in transactions with members of the Mitsubishi system. It represents a $20 billion investment to link thousands of enterprises over a global network.

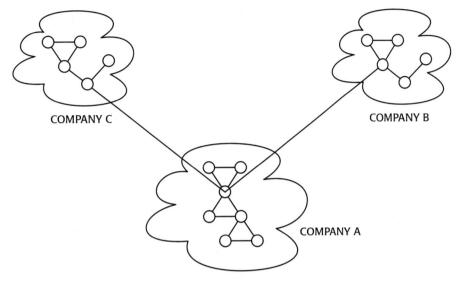

Extended Enterprise Network
(Companies share data with other participants. No firm need be dominant.)

- In the United States, General Motors has invested more than $3 billion since 1987 for the development of a private information network that will provide electronic linkages with its suppliers and dealers. The objective is to have customers walk into any showroom and select an automobile based on the floor models and test driving. Once selected, the customer would go to a terminal and configure the choice of car to his or her precise specifications. The dealer would then transmit the configuration. That order would be integrated directly into the various project schedules, thus triggering the purchase of necessary material and components from suppliers.

WHEN THE WORLD DOES IT RIGHT

These networks have something in common above and beyond simple connectivity: each one is constructed to enhance quality of service. The organizations building these global networks are realizing that the quality of the network's services are what will distinguish them in the marketplace. While many customers base an initial purchase decision on a combination of price and features, they purchase the *second* time on the basis of service. The key to competitive advantage, therefore, is focused attention on those aspects of the global network that yield the highest levels of customer service satisfaction.

The public networks, upon which most of the private corporate networks are built, have evolved to reflect this service orientation. For most of the years that the old Bell

System was in existence, it set the requirements for its products and services with the customer in mind; it defined how clear the connection must be; it defined how quickly a customer got the dial tone after picking up the receiver; and it defined how many calls must be completed successfully.

However, the house that Bell built was founded upon untested assumptions. Bell built what they *thought* would satisfy the customers: the customers had no say in the matter. Only after deregulation in 1984 did the *customer* begin to set the requirements for telecommunications products and services. Because they had freedom of choice and a field of competitors offering low prices and a wide range of services, the state of the public network became a source of competitive advantage. The Regional Bell Operating Companies (RBOCs), which inherited Bell's gold-plated, embedded network, could not afford to wait for equipment to depreciate before upgrading to the new technologies. The survival of the RBOCs in this new, competitive world depended upon their ability to offer the levels of service and responsiveness that their new challengers were able to provide from day one.

Within many telecommunications administrations, criteria called "key service indicators" (KSIs) measure the customer's reactions to the company's ability to provide service information, reliable dial tone, clear transmission, prompt installation and maintenance, and operator services. The basic characteristics of internal measurement are:

- *Sensitivity*—detecting changes before a customer is adversely affected.

- *Timeliness*—providing information soon enough to make corrections before the customer experiences a problem.

- *Relevance*—meeting the key requirements of the customer for a particular product or service.

In the case of the old Bell System, many of the domestic KSIs reflected internal perceptions of service (such as the duration of customer contacts, hours to install or repair, and missed appointments) rather than *customer* perceptions of service. Today's RBOCs turned this around: they use mailed questionnaires, returned to a central audit bureau to understand how the customer really feels about service rendered. Furthermore, the RBOCs have set customer service thresholds at very high levels as part of its financial incentive plan for management. Compensation depends on the percentage of "minimum performance levels" (MPLs) met or exceeded in a particular period.

The KSI measurement and MPL concepts have given the stewards of the old Bell network a new set of metrics by which to judge their success or failure in the delivery of their service. That they have taken these approaches is an indicator of the degree to which they recognize the importance of a service oriented infrastructure supporting global networks. Their business, they realize, is the delivery of services that support the gathering, sharing, manipulation, and management of information, and their continuing commitment to improvement is yet another indicator that the global network will only grow more important over time.

BACK TO THE FUTURE

Nicholas Negroponte, director of MIT's Media Lab, once predicted that in the not too distant future only face-to-face conversations and artistic performances would exist in analog format. All else will be digitized and transported over a global network. "In 20 years," he said, "each TV set will have a ready access memory of close to 50 megabytes. It will have computing power of 40-50 MIPS. That means the TV set you will have in your home will never again receive a picture. It will receive data and *construct* a picture."[2]

The infrastructure required to support the future Negroponte describes is already being constructed in the public and private global networks of the world. The "technology creep" that Negroponte also talks about is inextricably upon us: the technology of the global networks is surging ahead uncontrollably, past all attempts to predict or legislate it.

"Broadly considered," notes Gilder in *Microcosm*, "the computer is the most important product of the quantum era. By exploring this central machine of the age, however, we discover not the centrality of machines and things but the primacy of human thought and creativity." Global networking technology has clearly emerged as crucial to the organization that intends to innovate and profit in the next decade. Connectivity brings together the essential creative forces of business—people and knowledge—and therein lies its fundamental importance to the organizations of the future.

REFERENCES

1. George Gilder, *Microcosm, the Quantum Revolution in Economics and Technology*, (New York, Simon and Schuster, 1989).
2. Stuart Brand, *The Media Lab Inventing the Future at MIT*, (New York, Penguin Books, 1987).

Competition, Cooperation, and Change

RICHARD T. LIEBHABER

IN EVERY DISCUSSION of the international telecommunications services market, the use of certain descriptive terms seems all but obligatory. Privatization, globalization, competition, and change are a few of the most frequently employed words. But the key term that describes what will happen in the worldwide telecommunications business in the coming years is more far-reaching. That word is *revolution*.

The enormous changes of the past decade, while historic and significant in their own right, will be dwarfed by the degree of change now unfolding in the 1990s. The forces driving this revolution are many and complex, but they can be boiled down to three: technology, customer demand, and marketplace competition or liberalization. Together, these forces have altered the shape and scope of the global telecommunications industry, posing new challenges and creating unprecedented opportunities for public network carriers. This dynamic environment is forcing both cooperation and competition among carriers as they seek to serve customers in newly opened markets around the world.

Competition sets the wheel in motion, empowering and propelling customers at every turn. As customers embrace enhanced services, they begin almost immediately to demand improvements. Service enhancements thus plant the seeds of their own obsolescence as subsequent improvements come on-line. It's a never-ending cycle of progress.

Experience shows that newly-opened markets serve as a kind of magnet for investment capital because they present once-excluded companies with attractive business opportunities. The availability of capital, in turn, spurs technological innovation as competing companies vie for customers by offering services that meet changing customer needs.

Competition for customers also has a direct impact on pricing. Lower prices, combined with the improved quality and convenience of services, stimulate customer usage across the board. Greater usage drives revenue growth, which in time attracts additional companies and investors into the industry.

This proliferation of new technologies, services, and suppliers has created the reality of information technologies as a valuable business tool—computers and electronic databases linked together by advanced telecommunications networks. In technology, we are approaching the virtualization of both switched voice services and data on a global basis. Our networks are huge computers, action processors that collect and manage information as they transmit, at very high speeds, voice, data, and image traffic. We have brought technology to the point that our networks are a software-defined platform of capabilities that can respond to the needs of individual customers.

Information technologies also create a new world of opportunities by contributing to the globalization of business and the erosion of geography, time-zones, and national boundaries as barrier to commerce. Use of information technologies is helping to streamline business organizations into leaner, more flexible, more competitive entities, making a substantial contribution to the strategic success of companies across the board and around the world.

GLOBALIZATION OF BUSINESS

In the 1980s, the globalization of business became a reality. So-called "stateless" or "transnational" corporations emerged, connecting and managing far-flung operations via globe-spanning communications technologies. For the first time in human history, business could be conducted around the world regardless of time and distance. The realities of the global marketplace demand that transnational companies have access to an increasingly sophisticated, seamless communications network, enabling them to conduct business around the clock and around the world.

This globalization has occurred in virtually every industry—retailing, manufacturing, construction, distribution, agriculture, insurance, and financial services. The rules of the game have changed dramatically. Telecommunications and other information technologies have become strategic weapons in the battle for growth and success in today's global marketplace. They help companies enter new markets, create new products and services, improve the speed and quality of decision making, create lean and efficient organizations, and improve customer service.

Given the increasing sophistication of what the world demands, a state-of-the-art public telecommunications network should be included—along with a quality education system, health care, housing, and transportation—among the basic infrastructural pillars upon which any viable and prosperous society rests. Individuals, companies, communities, countries, institutions of all kinds—even entire geographic regions—all share a common interest in and need for a modern, flexible, high capacity public telecommunications network.

This ideal presents public network providers with both a golden opportunity and a severe challenge. Competition promises the opportunity for major growth and the chance to play a key role in the advancement of society. However, unless we move rapidly to facilitate this seamless global network, our largest users will become increasingly skeptical of our ability to meet their needs on a global scale, possibly resulting in two-tiered societies of information haves and have-nots. Thus, the challenge we face is how to balance competition and cooperation to achieve a worldwide public communications network designed and constructed for the post-Information Age of tomorrow.

ADAPTATION IS KEY

Adaptation will be the name of the game throughout the 1990s. It has become a cliché, but it is nonetheless true that change will be the only constant. Everyone in the telecommunications industry will have to learn to adapt if they want to compete in the world's network economy.

The competitive battle will most likely be centered around network and network intelligence, rather than through the control of basic transport and switching facilities. In addition, the networks of the future will be controlled as much by customers as by operators. These transnational players in the global marketplace—the financial systems, the trading houses, the manufacturing combines, the agricultural production industries—each will have the ability to participate in the management of the intelligent network applications critical to their competitive success or failure.

With customers in the driver's seat, the whole structure of the industry is turned upside down. All of a sudden, telecommunications services providers have to learn an unfamiliar and important skill: customer responsiveness.

There truly is no limit to the sophisticated services customers will demand. Transnationals in particular are not willing to wait around for new technologies and capabilities to come on-line. That's why public networks need to move aggressively to offer advanced global services or risk losing the biggest customers in favor of private networks. Customers seem to be saying: "I'm willing to wait a little while for the impossible, but I want the difficult right away."

This urgency raises a host of public policy issues. Clearly, all public network providers should support a worldwide regulatory regime that not only allows but actually facilitates the construction of advanced global public networks that bring the benefits of the Information Age to a broad cross-section of society.

No society can hope to prosper without a modern, reliable telecommunications network at its disposal. Regulatory regimes need to keep pace with technology and customer demand because, if we've learned one thing in the United States, it's that customers will demand the technology they need to do the job. If they can't get the services they need from the public network providers, they'll find some alternative. That's why it's absolutely crucial for public network providers everywhere to stay on the cutting edge of technological development. Public networks need to continually invest in network enhancements—and they need to be customer driven.

All international operators—MCI included—will rely on global partnerships and alliances to serve this changed marketplace. We will have to make room at the alliance table for others with the skills to integrate all the systems necessary. Such partnerships will be as important to success in the U.S. market as elsewhere in the world. Specific local knowledge and understanding of the customer's needs and practices are critical to any alliance's ability to perform effectively in the world's major commercial centers.

THE POWER OF INFORMATION

If we embrace change and see competition as an opportunity to bring the benefits of information technologies to an ever-widening circle of customers, then the interesting times we face will turn out to be promising and prosperous.

The more competition is seen as a blessing and not a curse, the faster information will emerge as one of the world's greatest nondepletable resources. With the ongoing merging of global networks, people everywhere soon will be able to tap into electronic information sources, use what they need, and leave the total supply of information undiminished. In fact, unlike so many depletable natural resources, the supply of information actually increases with use. Only by using information can more information be added to the world's storehouse of knowledge. That growth of knowledge is called research, and information technologies help to spread the benefits of that research and knowledge to more and more people around the world.

Just think for a moment about the effect instant information has on the entire world. Timely access to information can help build affordable housing, supply nutritious foods, encourage precautions against natural disasters such as drought, floods, or hurricanes. Information readily available can save lives through preventive medical care, treatment, or surgery. The list of potential benefits is endless.

This year, we celebrate the 500th anniversary of Columbus' arrival in the New World—an historic voyage that launched an age of discovery. New navigational instruments and transportation modes propelled explorers and facilitated the large-scale movement of labor, raw materials, and agricultural and finished goods to the four corners of the globe.

Today, we are embarking on a new age of discovery. The instruments are powerful information handling and storage devices. Digital networks provide the transport systems needed to carry the precious cargo of information around the world. Our ability to predict the eventual effects of all this information transfer is about as precise as the ability of those early explorers to envision the full effect their discoveries would have on human history.

If used properly, the power of instant information could be the greatest boon to humankind ever imagined. It is certainly the greatest threat to tyranny ever devised. They say the pen is mightier than the sword, but just think of the power contained in an average personal computer—and the exponentially increased power of a truly seamless global network that links together the world's PCs and other information technologies.

Two things appear certain: The impact of the Information Age on business and society is and will continue to be profound. The potential benefits of information technologies are limited only by the bounds of the human imagination.

Worldwide Communications and Information Systems

FRANK CORR & JOHN HUNTER

GLOBAL USAGE of electromagnetic telecommunications was marked for a century by conspicuous milestones such as the first transoceanic telegram, the first overseas telephone call, and, more recently, the first intercontinental direct-dial call. On the contrary, the first trans-Atlantic electronic mail communications between personal computers and the first North American home computer to access a data base in Japan have not found their way into newspapers, much less history texts. Often taken for granted, expansion and diffusion of worldwide information systems, particularly in the last decade, have brought palpable change to commerce and daily life in a remarkably short time.

With an upsurge in demand due to trade and tourism, international telephone service revenue grew sixfold from 1975 to 1989. More impressive are forecasts for the 1990s. Increases in carrier revenues from digital private lines to each of 15 United States communicating partners will range between 17 percent and 100 percent in 1992 alone (1). International virtual private networks for voice, nonexistent before 1989, are now offered in 13 countries. By 1994, 40 IVPN service offerings are expected in over two dozen countries. A fast-growing news and financial network reaches 200,000 computer screens in 130 countries (2). Another of the many worldwide data networks provides electronic mail and data services to 37,000 organizations and 1.4 million people across six continents; a third now has three million users (3,4).

Are information systems using worldwide communications straightforward extensions of localized systems? Do global information systems have objectives and technical requirements substantially different from those encountered within national or local confines? What applications drive the extraordinary growth in global communications usage? What further technological changes will occur?

This paper addresses these questions, beginning with contrasts between global and more-confined systems. Then, we illustrate unique facets of global systems with IBM's worldwide information system, an example of an integrated enterprise network. Progress is sketched in other uses including travel reservation, banking and financial, military, research and education. Future trends follow, which concludes that (despite their special character) global systems' evolution can be predicted, in large measure, from prior progress in shorter-reach applications.

WORLDWIDE INFORMATION SYSTEMS

Globe-girdling systems bear many similarities to those confined geographically. Any design is affected by new digital technology, whatever its network span. Requirements for reliability, transmission-cost savings, and responsive network management are stringent for data networks of long and short range. Multiple protocols, multimedia applications, peer-to-peer operations among powerful workstations, and interconnection of local area networks (LANS) appear in both global and confined systems. Yet, likeness in technology, design requirements, and use notwithstanding, global systems are affected by elements absent or less consequential in confined systems.

When a data system provides services in many countries, its design, implementation, and operation involve coordination of numerous carriers, customers, and software and hardware vendors. This multiparty teamwork across great distances may be the most obvious trait of international networking.

Also notable is the number of interconnections; a single system may access thousands of networks. Gateways can facilitate interconnection without imposing complicated procedures on users. Electronic data interchange (EDI) is almost a sine qua non, especially for data flows to customers and business partners on other networks across the globe.

Intra-enterprise electronic mail is a business asset which, together with facsimile transmission, can compensate for work-schedule differentials across time zones and improve comprehension across language barriers. In global systems, electronic mail is generally the most-used feature. Electronic fora and bulletin boards also are effective in international collaboration, as noted by later example.

Prior to 1989, intra-enterprise vocal communications rarely were implemented internationally on private networks. Instead, direct distance dialing public facilities were used and private voice networks relegated to national systems. Now, global networks are following in the footsteps of confined networks, an example of technology eventually migrating to global networks. International virtual private voice networks will emerge in the next few years through joint efforts of customers, telecommunications administrations, and PBX and other suppliers.

Mixed software, hardware, and telecommunications implementations are commonplace. International systems can employ satellite transmission, underseas fiber, leased and circuit-switched services, video circuits, private and public packet switching, X.25 value-added network services, high quality digital circuits and noisy analog circuits; sometimes all in the same system, choices determined by conditions in each part of the world. Of course, hybrid usage of public and private services also is encountered in confined systems, but heterogeneous telecommunications are a global-system hallmark.

Among constraints on global systems are high transmission costs, limited bandwidth, questionable reliability on some links, and spotty development of up-to-date digital infrastructures.

Not only is a private line crossing a border more expensive than a similar one confined to a single nation, but the price of a leased circuit within a country varies widely around the world. The cost of a 100 to 200 kilometer leased 64 Kb/s line varies over a range of 8 to 1 in Europe alone. Sixty-four Kb/s between two European countries can cost over half the price of a circuit crossing the Atlantic. Trans-Atlantic T1 with a monthly bill, including tail circuits, costing between $70,000 and 100,000, further demonstrates that circuit-utilization efficiency and careful network management can have a big payoff in systems using global communications (5-8).

In view of high costs, techniques for efficiency enhancement are popular. Global networks provide a cost-reduction motivation for image, voice, and data compression, packing more information through expensive circuits. International ISDN in Japan is used mainly for high-speed facsimile, videophone, and video conferences, where circuit-switched digital services offer economies (9). Sharing of high-speed intercontinental links by voice and data often is justified by economic tradeoffs. Adept use of distributed processing can reduce international traffic flows and communications costs. Cost-reducing hub-and-spoke and hub-as-gateway configurations in Europe (7) and on the Pacific rim have been adopted by some systems.

Transmission rates on cross-border links and within less-developed nations may be limited with consequent reduction in throughput or increased response time. Moreover, granulation of bit rates, in the range between 9.6 Kb/s and 1.5 or 2.0 Mb/s, may be inadequate to address requirements cost-effectively. Fractional speeds are occasionally provided (5); otherwise, the using architecture must support multiple 9.6 or 64 Kb/s channels on the same link.

Weak reliability can be a consideration for some international circuits and their local tails. When provided, digital links bring inter-country connections up to a reliability level more-or-less consistent with national circuits. Where reliability of a national infrastructure is questionable, satellite communications, with small-aperture terminals, are sometimes used to reach the distant premises of the international user directly. A new cellular system can temporarily compensate for an outmoded local wired plant. Another technique for tenuous links is the interconnection of hubs for backup and rerouting, for which an example appears later. In addition, user nodes can be connected by spoke lines to more than one hub.

With its constraints, a global system represents a network-management challenge. Techniques must allow autonomy for monitoring and reaction at distant control points, while insuring centralized oversight for overall resource allocation. In addition, global networks need to adjust resources during the working day as traffic patterns follow the sun. The foregoing discussion of general practice is supplemented, in the next two sections, by descriptions of several system types, starting with an integrated enterprise example.

IBM'S WORLDWIDE INFORMATION SYSTEM

IBM's system supports its integrated research, development, manufacturing, sales, and administration wherever performed. Incorporating many of the practices in the preceding section, the IBM information system reaches more than 90 countries, has 800,000 user identification codes, and provides access to 4000 other networks. Communications beyond the system's boundaries include: X.25 for access to packet carrier networks, X.400 using the ever-growing number of electronic mail services, and EDI for electronic data interchange with customers and suppliers.

Systems network architecture (SNA) is used to form and manage IBM data networks in the United States, Canada, Europe, Latin America, Africa, Australia, and Asia. Individual SNA networks operate smoothly together using SNA network interconnection (SNI). SNI allows an individual networkwide latitude in managing its resources, but simultaneously provides seamless integration of electronic mail development and manufacturing systems, and other uniformly accessed applications across the global network. A principal thrust in IBM's Networking Blueprint, Advanced Peer-to-Peer Networking, is now used by over 2000 attached devices, providing powerful support for cooperative processing.

Links at 1.5 Mb/s span the Atlantic and Pacific on submarine optical-fiber cables. Other 1.5 and 2Mb/s links form backbones within the United States, Canada, Japan, and Europe. International requirements often fall between 9600 b/s and 1.5 or 2 Mb/s, with implementation of multiple 64 Kb/s circuits where intermediate services are unavailable.

About 100 bandwidth-management devices are used to configure backbones and individual access circuits. Digital links are used when possible, but analog circuits with modems still are needed to reach many locations. Satellites are valuable in regions where terrestrial facilities do not fully meet needs. A few intercontinental links terminate at small-aperture earth stations on IBM premises.

Outside North America, the IBM network has hubs in the United Kingdom, the Netherlands, Tokyo, Singapore, and Sydney. Hubs are connected to the nodes they serve by "spoke" circuits, frequently at 64 Kb/s. Each hub connects to other hubs in triangular or ringlike arrangements for backup in event of failure. As another precaution, nodes often are connected to two hubs. More hubs may be added in the future, but their number probably will not increase in any major way.

From multiple Netview management locations around the globe, the system is supervised in distributed fashion. For comprehensive control, these centers communicate status and other information on a timely basis with one another.

Across some links, voice circuits are carried on digital backbone and tributary routes of the IBM information system; in other cases, public-switched telephone networks are used for voice. Relative costs govern the extent of backbone voice/data integration in different regions of the world.

Private voice networks, internal to an enterprise, usually are confined to individual countries, with international direct distance dialing (IDDD) via public services used for calls between countries. IBM now has limited overseas private network calling. Planned for the near future, a worldwide virtual private network, with a simple uniform numbering plan and call-up procedure, will set up desk-to-desk conversations, or facsimile transmissions, between any IBM facilities, without recourse to IDDD.

The network integrates applications across the corporation. Administration, sales, customer service, manufacturing, development, and office support systems operate in a uniform, easy-to-use way around the globe. Distributed processing of applications often is used, eliminating unnecessary data transmission and improving user service. Voluminous information, such as long reports, is handled by the 280 nodes of the bulk data network.

An excellent means for interaction among people with varied work schedules across time zones, electronic mail encompasses 60 countries and 4400 store-and-forward nodes; full extension to every employee is planned. Alphanumeric, graphical, and image interchanges between employees are fast and essentially error-free. Multiple-address messages facilitate interaction within geographically scattered groups.

All applications operate without perceptible effects from the gamut of communications means forming the underlying network. As a rule, response times observed by a user of long international links approach what he or she experiences where communication is confined to shorter distances. Where exceptions exist, they often are due to slow-speed tail circuits (e.g., from employees' home terminals).

Full-motion video conferences gradually are replacing a more primitive still-frame approach which has already effected significant travel reductions. International full-motion video conferences now are carried between North America and the United Kingdom, with links planned to Japan. Compression algorithms, from 128 to 768 Kb/s are used within several countries. Public-switched ISDN services carry full-motion video within Europe and Japan. Use of public video transmission services on a broad scale is planned.

Among other benefits derived from the worldwide system are elimination of paper telephone directories, use of secure electronic signatures, rapid expert assessments via computer fora, continuously updated technical data bases, and wireless access. Electronic identification is used for expense accounting, time management, and other functions for which secure verification is important. Computer fora allow anybody on the network to call upon technologists and other specialists on a worldwide, almost instantaneous, basis to answer questions and exchange ideas. An IBM'er with a PC radio, in a United States hotel room, can access fora and other data capabilities of the global system, without a wired connection.

GLOBAL SYSTEM EXAMPLES

A fully integrated enterprise network, like IBM's, is only one among many varieties of global systems. Another prototypal international network is the airline reservation, or, more generally, computer reservation system (10). With Sabre's design origins in 1959 and the rapid spread across national boundaries of airlines systems in the 1960s, reservations networks can be considered the first large-scale commercial interactive global systems (11,12).

Besides a primality claim, reservations systems are distinctive in the rate people query them for travel information. The larger airline networks deal with peak loads of 2000 or 3000 transactions per second at central data-base sites, and that traffic is increasing. Each transaction usually is complex enough to require 10 or 20 disk accesses. Powerful computing and storage resources, with specialized software, ensure a two- or three-second response time for most transactions.

While requirements continually mount for fast and comprehensive centralized operations, the airlines also have been among early implementers of advanced work stations, LANS, and client-server concepts (13). There is strong interest in LAN interconnection for some information flows.

Like many global networks, reservations systems meet demands for continuous availability across 24 time zones. Among techniques to insure reliability are multiply-connected hubs, load-balancing across a spread-out network, alternate routing, dial backup, and rapid fault-recovery (14). Reservation systems have numerous gateways to other networks, such as travel-agent, aircraft communication, hotel, credit, weather, and airport services. Also oft-seen is an array of public and private communications means such as multipoint lines, X.25 packet switching, megabits per second via submarine cable, and small satellite terminals for hard-to-reach locations. Illustrating yet another worldwide-network trait, travel reservation systems often evince cooperation and resource-sharing among competitive enterprises to achieve efficient global operations.

In the future, evolution will continue from industry-peculiar protocols to de facto and de jure standards for easier interconnection and use of software developed outside the airline industry (15,16). Gradual introduction of OSI-based protocols is a principal objective (17). X.400 gateways for electronic mail are being introduced. Like others, travel reservations networks look to frame relay for improved reliability and performance, compared to multipoint lines and X.25 networks. Voice response units are being introduced for customer service, and, once the technology is ready, voice recognition can assume its place. Home-access reservations systems (such as those in Prodigy) are powerful, but still have limited ability to deliver tickets electronically; these too may see expansion with advancing technology. Air-ground communications (e.g., accessed through the ARINC network) (12), could bring the full resources of the terrestrial systems to in-flight aircraft.

International banking and financial networks have many properties like those of other businesses. Rapid traffic growth, hybrid public-private telecommunications, packet switching, satellites to remote regions, voice compression on private international circuits, rapid re-routing upon circuit failure, and hub-spoke structures are among the similarities. Also, banking and financial networks are further examples of competing organizations cooperating to ensure the integrity of a vital international system.

What sets international financial flows apart from other information is message value; one clearing house network carries a trillion dollars in money transfers daily (18). A proprietary electronic network for spot foreign currency exchange handles close to $300 billion of transactions per day (19). Yet, networks carrying international financial transactions are designed to hold down communications cost to maintain competitiveness of the financial services performed.

In the biggest proprietary international United States-bank network, about 100,000 messages per day handle corporate fund transfers between the United States and Europe (20). SWIFT, in use since 1977, provides international transfers for its 3000 member banks at a pace of about 1.5 million messages a day (21). The World Bank delivers most messages in less than three seconds (22). These throughput and transit-time figures are solid achievements, but not disproportionate to those of contemporary networks. The distinctiveness of banking and finance networks lies elsewhere: in the reliability and security provided for high-value transmissions. Reactions by the financial community in the wake of New York's 1990 power outage are indicative of the need for prompt, reliable delivery of their electronic messages.

For security and reliability, specialized formats and protocols have been developed for interbank transfers. Adopting EDI for data exchanges has not proven quick and easy for banks. However, the need to connect to many other entities is spurring EDI usage (23-26). Commonly used communications protocols, architecturally below the layer where EDI and other applications are positioned, find continued acceptance in accordance with international standards like X.25 and de facto industry protocols like SNA's LU6.2 (20, 22). Application trials, built around ISDN standards, are occurring.

Volume and value of international flows among banks and financial institutions probably will see continued expansion. Image applications in financial documents, including electronic signature, are likely to expand and generate more traffic. Another source of increased traffic will be easy-to-use, powerful multimedia workstations facilitating distributed processing via interconnected LANS. ISDN and frame relay will add to the panoply of communications techniques in financial networks after a period of testing. Voice response and, later, voice recognition systems may be employed broadly through future networks, providing financial services to remotely located users.

Military networks were pioneers in use of global telecommunications. AUTODIN, AUTOVON, and other defense networks provided automatic message switching, full dial-up voice connectivity, and interactive applications around the globe. Like their commercial counterparts, worldwide military information systems employ both private and public facilities, use intercontinental satellite and cable links, combine integrated and distributed management, and have thousands of interconnections to other networks. Two features traditionally emphasizing local military networks are security and survivability. In 1990 and 1991, their flexibility and mobility also were demonstrated during the Desert Shield and Desert Storm operations in the Middle East.

A feat of communications engineering created, in a few months, a versatile set of networks, with worldwide connectivity, functioning in unitary fashion while carrying 700,000 telephone calls and 128,000 record messages daily. This was accomplished 7000 miles from home bases, in a theater whose indigenous communications could not help much. Transmission encompassed many radio and fiber technologies, but satellites were most important in bringing the networks into operation quickly (27). On-the-spot traffic and system management eliminated anomalies like low call-completion rates (28).

An aspect of possible pertinence to commercial enterprises is the success of the Defense Data Network (DDN), in the first use of a shared packet network for such an operation. Packet data grew steadily from September 1990, until March 1991, when throughput approached 2,000,000 packets per day. Fifteen hundred electronic mail systems were supported by DDN (29).

The deployed forces depended on their information systems and access to them via reliable communications. Much of the hardware, software, and specialist support was left in the United States and other base areas; the rapidly set-up network substituted for overseas deployment (30). Remote access to computer resources, including data bases halfway around the earth, proved effective. A widespread distributed-processing system was put into operation in a few months with thousands of personal computers and larger processors throughout the theater, communicating among themselves and with main frames back in the United States and Europe.

Research and educational networks have grown at a striking rate. With a 10 percent rise in traffic each month, or a doubling every seven months, the global Internet now has over 2000 separate networks and 3 million users. The United States Internet backbone rate will increase from 45 Mb/s to a rate nearly 100 times faster as part of the National Research and Education Network (NREN) (41). Similar fiber-based enhancements are being discussed in other countries (31,32).

The Internet is distinctive among networks in its open access, early usage of electronic mail, and development of de facto networking standards. Easy use, coupled with extraordinarily fast growth reaching one million attached computers, can sometimes engender security problems; these continue to be addressed (33).

University systems are not alone in supporting education; other emerging networks are dedicated to improving primary and secondary schooling. Like their higher level counterparts, these networks began as confined systems and later developed international extensions to Canada, Latin America, Europe, Asia, and Australia. Modest in performance, relatively inexpensive, and easily joined, systems connecting primary and secondary schools have brought shared research projects, group interaction across distances, and electronic access to curricular resources to the classroom. With their practical approaches to educational challenges, these efforts hold promise for the future (34,35).

An example of still smaller, but vital, information systems is the linkage between a medical center in Manila and a renowned medical center in Stanford, California. Medical images are sent on dial-up circuits to California at 19.2 Kb/s for consultation and remote diagnosis (36).

This sampling of global systems surely is not exhaustive. International facsimile, space-flight support systems, and library hookups, for example, also perform valued functions. Despite perils of generalization from a few cases, predictions can be attempted based on the kinship between global and confined systems.

FUTURE USES

A 1961 lecture series at MIT brought together experts who had contributed to two decades of rapid and extraordinary growth in computers (37). Among prescient ideas exchanged were parallel computation, distributed processing, and routing-by-network-choice when data bases are divided among sites around the country. That the global information systems of 1991 were not foreseen is evidence that 30-year foresight is fallible where a multiplicity of technical disciplines and nontechnical forces affect the outcome.

Nevertheless, assuming trade and other stimuli continue to accelerate demand for international information flow, technical advances in confined systems can be forecast, with time lags of one to 10 years, to find their way into global use. In turn, international networks will stimulate trade with new exports like software and information services made profitable through globalization of communications (38). International information systems dedicated to direct support of trading activities will be enhanced (39). Design and operation of a system operating across 50 or 100 countries will still call for many administrations and other participants to work in concert.

Despite new communications services such as ISDN and broadband ISDN, frame relay, and multi-mb/s links becoming available, there will still exist many obsolescent infrastructures with data transmission limited to 2400b/s on fragile channels. Architectures with edge-to-edge error control for high speeds at low error rates will still have to be integrated with error control via link-by-link protocols. In other words, the heterogeneity of global architectures will increase as new services bring further contrast to the range of public and private telecommunications around the world. The need for hub-based structures and autonomy in managing distant parts of heterogeneous networks will not diminish in the next decade.

Progress in workstation processing capability in the 1990s is predicted, based on current experimental technologies, to move past 100 million instructions per second to 10 times that power by the year 2000 (40,41). Continued exponential increase in fiber transmission speed, particularly for undersea cable, is foreseen with new technologies such as erbium-doped photonic amplifiers (42,43). Image, graphics, video, visualization, and speech input will benefit from technology advances in confined systems (44). With a delay of a few years, confined advances should take hold in parts of international networks, especially in integrated enterprise systems with their drive toward worldwide unitary service. Internetworking between LANs already has appeared across global networks; continuation of this trend is expected. Ease-of-use features will migrate to global networks, with consequent increases in communications traffic. Maturation of packet radio will bring the mobile work force broader access to global data resources via their small portable computers.

Certain technical advances could have particular pertinence for worldwide systems. New cooperative processing and compression techniques will strike a changing balance in processing versus communication-bandwidth tradeoffs for global systems with their more costly links. Video conferences, medical-image transmission, and automatic language translation can improve communications across linguistic barriers. Similarly new constructs building on the success of expert fora, computer-assisted conferences, and other creativity-enhancing techniques, might stimulate innovation on an international scale by taking advantage of varied perspectives and knowledge.

New services, including international virtual private networks for voice and facsimile communications, will spread in the 1990s. Services based on the synchronous digital hierarchy and the asynchronous transfer mode can extend the reach of advanced work stations and their multimedia capability. Global access via low-earth-orbit satellites in the late 1990s could overcome the lack of reliable data transmission in many parts of the world (45).

SUMMARY

A global electronic information system is a modern phenomenon achieved through synergistic efforts of many people. It has its own characteristics: manifold interconnections among networks, heterogeneity, a melange of public and private services, widely distributed network management, and architectural structures to achieve a sensitive balance among cost, reliability, and performance. Systems vary: some are huge, others tiny, some distributed, others more centralized. They can enable otherwise unattainable commercial economies of scale or support medical, educational, and research work of international scope. Further growth in number and capability of information systems using worldwide communications will occur by applying technology from networks of more modest dimensions.

ACKNOWLEDGMENT

In addition to perspectives obtained from published sources, many ideas in this paper are derived from discussions and network-based exchange with colleagues around the world. Their help is acknowledged and appreciated.

REFERENCES

1. "International Private Line Growth," *Network World*, p. 27, Jan. 13, 1992.
2. Annual Report for 1991, Reuters.
3. L. Sproull and S. Keisler, "Computers, Networks, and Work," *Scientific American*, Sept. 1991.
4. A. Gore, "Infrastucture for the Global Village," *Scientific American*, pp. 150–153, Sept. 1991.
5. "VW Views Nets as Key to Business Mission," *Network World*, p. 27, Dec. 2, 1991.
6. "Telecommunications Survey," *The Economist*, p. 7, Oct. 5, 1991.
7. D. Rappaport, "Selecting a European Network Hub Location," *Bus. Commun. Rev.*, April 1991.
8. "The Coming Transatlantic Price Wars," *Data Commun.*, p. 101, Jan. 1991.
9. S. Champeny, "Major Applications of International ISDN in Japan," *Network World*, Feb. 3, 1992.
10. M. Hopper, "Rattling Sabre New Ways to Compete on Information," *Harv. Bus. Rev.*, May/June 1990.
11. B. Bochenski, "The OLTP Bandwagon Traces Back to Sabre," *Software Mag.*, Feb. 1989.
12. M. Robinson, "In the Transportation Industry I/S Offers New Advantages," *IBM Directions*, Fall 1989.
13. J. Desmond, "Max Hopper Knows Sabre's 'Software Guts,' " *Software Mag.*, Feb. 1989.
14. "American Airlines Keeps T1 Network at 99.8% Availability," *Commun. News*, Oct. 1991.
15. B. Francis, "Two Views of Open Systems," *Datamation*, June 1990.
16. B. Crockett, "Airline Reservation Nets Finally See Fit to Dump Out-dated Protocols," *Network World*, Sept. 24, 1990.
17. P. Desmond, "American Airlines Plots OSI Migration," *Network World*, March 18, 1991.
18. S. O'Heney, "Keeping CHIPS Safe and Private," *ABA Bank. J.*, May 1991.
19. M. Maremont, "Reuters Unveils Supertrading," *Bus.Week.*, Feb. 1992.
20. P. Glaser, "Telecommunications in Banking," presented at 1988 *IEEE Conference on Communications, Conf. Rec.*, pp. 1567–1571.
21. B. Crockett, "SWIFT2 Completion Adds Needed Capacity," *Network World*, Sept. 17, 1990.
22. H. Stryer, "The World Bank's Open Network," *Datamation*, Feb. 15, 1990.
23. R. Jimison and L. Feder, "Why Banks Use EDI to Send Dollars and Data Together," *Infor. Strat.: The Exec. J.*, Spring 1990.
24. M. Violano, "Why Do Stubborn Bankers Pooh Pooh EDI?" *Bankers Monthly*, Nov. 1989.
25. A. Smith, "EDI: Will Banks Be Odd Man Out?" *ABA Bank J.*, Nov. 1988.
26. D. Jones, "Electronic Messages: New Role for the Carriers," *Banking World*, Feb. 1989.
27. J. Toma, "Desert Storm Communications," *IEEE Commun. Mag.*, Vol. 30, No. 1, pp. 19–21, Jan. 1992.
28. D. McKenzie, "U.S. Air Force Communications in Desert Storm," *IEEE Commun. Mag.*, Vol. 30, No. 1, pp. 42–47, Jan. 1992.
29. J. Stupik, "DISA Comes Through," *IEEE Commun. Mag.*, Vol. 30, No. 1, pp. 22–25, Jan. 1992.
30. W. Donohue, "Operation Desert Storm Communication Challenges Faced by the Multinational Forces," a luncheon address at the NCF91 Conference, Chicago, Ill., Oct. 1991.
31. G. Anthes, "Challengers Rise to Internet," *Computer World*, Sept. 23, 1991.
32. J. Prevost, "The French National Research and Technology Network," *Comput. Net. and ISDN Sys.*, June 1991.
33. E. Kozel, "Commercializing Internet: Impact on Corporate Users," *Telecommun.*, Jan. 1992.
34. M. Riel, "Four Models of Educational Telecommunications: Connections to the Future," *Education and Computing*, pp.261–274 (Elsevier Science Publishers, 1989).
35. D. Harkins, "FrEdMail: An Inexpensive Network for Teachers," *Education and Computing*, pp. 161–164 (Elsevier Science Publishers. 1989).

36. A. Buelva, "Hospital Relies on International Net to Feed Images to Doctors," *Network World*, Feb. 3, 1992.
37. M. Greenberger (Ed.), "Computers and the World of the Future," (MIT Press, March 1962).
38. G. Anthes, "Offshore Software Crews Save Labor Costs," *Computerworld*, Oct. 28, 1991.
39. E. King, "World Trade Goes on Line," *Global Trade*, Feb. 1990.
40. M. Alexander, "Looking Ahead to the Next Century," *Computerworld*, March 4, 1991.
41. J. McGroddy, "2021 A.D.," presented at the March 1991 ComForum Plenary Session at the Nat'l. Engin. Consort., Phoenix.
42. R. Lucky, "2021 A.D.," Presented at the March 1991 ComForum Plenary Session at the Nat'l. Engin. Consort., Phoenix.
43. A. Fraser, "Designing a Public Data Network," *IEEE Commun. Mag.*, Oct 1991.
44. M. Southworth, "The Power of Visualization," *Think*, No. 2, pp. 26–28, 1992.
45. J. Grubb, "The Traveller's Dream Come True, *IEEE Commun. Mag.*, Vol. 29, No. 10, Oct. 1991.

The Five Challenges of
Managing Global Networks

WILLIAM E. GILBERT

WHEN J.P. MORGAN sought industry help in establishing and managing a global data network earlier this year, the company's needs were leading edge. Yet Morgan's needs are still representative of those of many corporations today.

Morgan, a New York-based financial firm, serves corporations, governments, institutions, and individuals worldwide. The company needed a network that could deliver instantaneously—and simultaneously—financial data to operating offices in 13 countries. Such high-speed data networking would allow Morgan to integrate operations in its global marketplace.

Morgan's proposed data network had to cross networks operated by 13 different foreign telecommunications companies (Fig. 1) and connect a multitude of local area network (LAN) environments—including Apple, Ethernet, DEC, and others (Fig. 2). In addition, the PTT (Postal Telegraph & Telephone) networks featured a wide variety of communications systems and equipment operated to varying standards and legal requirements. The PTT companies charged widely varying rates, operated in a variety of time zones and languages, and provided unique billing services using local currencies. The same diversity applied to the support for equipment and network components such as routers. Also, the PTTs' and equipment vendors' network support services—from response times to recovery procedures and network reliability—were inconsistent at best, and incomplete at worst.

The answer for Morgan was a combination of expanding its own internal network management expertise and purchasing certain multinational services. With AT&T's assistance, Morgan now has a managed data network that uses multiprotocol routers to provide high-speed data connections between the company's existing LANs worldwide. The network is designed to promote LAN-based data sharing among the company's international business units. It supports a variety of client/server, electronic mail, and file-transfer applications.

The kind of network-management facilities needed by Morgan are fast becoming the norm. Corporations attempting to reach rapidly expanding global markets face similar networking challenges. To meet those challenges, corporations must address five major areas of networking: technical knowledge, network design and planning, "country-by-country" service requirements, network management operations, and network management interoperability.

CHALLENGE I: TECHNICAL KNOWLEDGE

The cultivation and maintenance of a technical knowledge base in LAN/WAN design, deployment, and maintenance is critical to the success of managing state-of-the-art global networks. For example, router-based networks are quite complex, relative to PBX networks or even T1 multiplexer-based networks. Multiprotocol routers have not been on the market long compared to other technologies and relatively few technicians and engineers worldwide understand their intricacies.

In addition, because of the nature of router-based networks, interfaces are not "clean." Changes in the configuration of a corporation's LAN environment can adversely affect the performance and functionality of a global network. Fault management also is complicated by this condition. Thus, a network manager must be concerned not only with WAN configuration management, but with the configuration of a corporation's total network environment. Such a thorough understanding of wide area networking on a global scale is a rare commodity these days.

CHALLENGE II: NETWORK DESIGN AND PLANNING

A corporation's network planners must be able to work closely with carriers and equipment vendors to create or adapt each country's network services to meet business needs—with appropriate consideration for emerging technologies. The goal of this process is to develop long-term strategies, phased evolution plans, and detailed, short-term implementation plans that meet a corporation's individual global networking needs.

The design and planning process must include:

- Access to advanced network design tools, tariff data, and world-class, internationally experienced network designers.

- A clear understanding of network optimization criteria, such as targeted service levels, grades of service, throughput requirements, resource utilization, costs, and security.

- Broad technical-assurance capabilities to reduce implementation problems and delays.

The last point is a more critical function than is readily apparent. Corporations looking to establish global networks must be sure either they or their vendors have long-established

FIGURE 1   The configuration of a typical wide area network across a single international boundary. Networking segments often cross several PTT networks before reaching their end point.

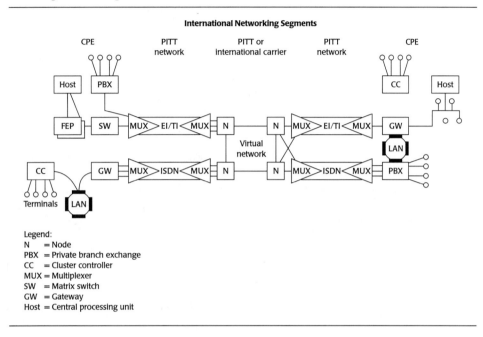

relationships with foreign service and equipment providers. Only through such relationships can a corporation guarantee proper selection and testing of all major hardware and software required for private services—especially owned or leased terminal equipment on a corporation's premises. The equipment must be pretested for proven hardware/software interoperability.

A whole host of unforeseen problems can be estimated through this pretesting process. In one recent case, for example, AT&T Bell Laboratories conducted tests with a German PBX vendor, Telenorma, and found an unexpected networking "glitch." Touch-tones, or dual multifrequency tones, could not be sent in-band from Telenorma's digital telephones once a call had been set up over either analog or digital central-office trunks in Germany, preventing users from accessing remote voice-mail systems. With the cooperation of Telenorma, adaptations were developed and verified in further testing.

This is only one small example of the differences that can arise between a corporation's expectations and a product's ability to operate across international boundaries. The unmodified Telenorma PBX met all specifications for acceptance in the German network, but the German specifications did not require interoperability.

FIGURE 2   The complexity of end-to-end connections within the J.P. Morgan global wide area network developed with AT&T.

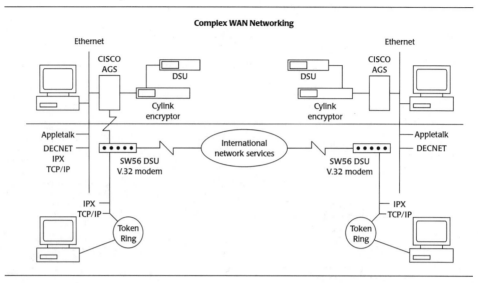

CHALLENGE III: "COUNTRY-BY-COUNTRY" SERVICE REQUIREMENTS

Because service offerings and regulatory procedures vary widely from country to country, corporations must actively deal with both inter- and intra-country ordering of private-line services and equipment, on a locale-specific basis. Corporations must be able to coordinate all network services required and monitor the implementation process to ensure on-time delivery. They must also coordinate circuit design with service providers, obtain circuit routing (including local loops), coordinate circuit and equipment installation, and monitor status updates. Besides these inherent complexities, the rapid pace of change in many countries enhances the attractiveness for many corporations of purchasing network services.

In addition, it is desirable, if not necessary, for each country's services to include proactive network monitoring, fault management, and performance analysis 24 hours a day, seven days a week. This is the essence of protecting a corporation's investment in its global network. Only through such proactive services can potential problems be identified and corrected before information flow is disrupted.

To have the absolute best in international network management today, a corporation should also be able to isolate problems and reconfigure a network to restore service via alternate paths. Top network managers must also provide for centralized trouble reporting and testing and must track troubles in real time.

Most of these tasks are very difficult to do, but they are evolving—albeit slowly—as service providers and equipment vendors add increasingly sophisticated network management features and functionality.

CHALLENGE IV: NETWORK MANAGEMENT OPERATIONS

Most network managers today also want regular reports on network and vendor performance, repair times, problem areas, costs, usage and other corporate operational data. That kind of information may not be considered absolutely critical by some corporations, but such reports often improve overall operations and maximize network management resources and strategic planning. Network operations data also helps network managers validate the financial and operational resources needed to maintain global networks, including a full understanding of the cost of managing networks and the value of developing or expanding networks to support business requirements.

Only through such planned and progressive assessment processes can corporations fully understand the information and data needed to maximize their current resources and determine if additional investment in information networks is warranted.

CHALLENGE V: NETWORK MANAGEMENT INTEROPERABILITY

Connectivity and interoperability of network services and equipment are difficult but critical to the marketplace performance of multinational corporations. These capabilities, however, are only part of the larger network management puzzle. Indeed, network management interoperability—between vendors, carriers, and countries—is becoming essential to effective equipment and service networking in global environments.

Despite the availability in some global markets of interconnection technologies—such as X.25 and ISDN—network management remains a difficult proposition in most international arenas. It is still largely a labor-intensive process. Relatively little automation exists, and resources are often managed in bits and pieces on a vendor-by-vendor basis. This situation adds unnecessary costs and is more reactive to problem solving than proactive. Moreover, the challenges are growing in scope. Initially, corporations wanted to manage different devices in a network. Later, integration of management systems became the focus. Now the objective is complete end-to-end management of all components in modern computer and communications networks.

It's a tall order, to say the least. But it is one that the Network Management Forum, for one, has taken on with total commitment for corporations and carriers worldwide. The Forum is an international consortium of 100 major computer vendors and service providers that are working to accelerate the availability of standards and technology to manage complex global networks. The Forum has joined forces with key consortia worldwide and with government and commercial users to move the industry forward.

FIGURE 3   Open Roadmap partners

CCTA	Central Computer and Telecommunications Agency
COS	Corporation for Open Systems
CTS3/NM	CTS3/Network Management
INTAP	Interoperability Technology Association for Information Processing
NIST	National Institute of Standards and Technology
OMG	Object Management Group
OSF	Open Software Foundation
OSTC	Open Systems Testing Consortium
SPAG	Standards Promotion and Application Group
UAC	User Advisory Council
UI	UNIX International
X/OPEN	X/Open

The main result of the Forum's efforts to date is a series of Open Management Interoperability Points, or OMNIPoints. Each OMNIPoint is a stable set of implementation specifications, including a selection of formal standards and industry agreements that satisfy the full range of requirements for managing today's most complex networked information systems. The OMNIPoints are defined as part of a process called the Open Management Roadmap. Roadmap partners include virtually every consortia currently involved in open systems management (Fig. 3), as well as representatives of major public procurement agencies and commercial user groups. Each OMNIPoint satisfies a user-defined set of needs and provides meaningful support to vendors in implementing the specifications.

Progress is being made. It is sometimes slow and sometimes painful, but it is progress. In the meantime, many equipment and management system vendors have adopted one or both of two common management protocols: SNMP (Simple Network Management Protocol) and OSI (Open Systems Interconnection). Each is evolutionary, and each represents an additional step toward the more robust management systems of the future.

For instance, the OSI model provides an international framework for defining data communications standards, as well as physical and electrical interface characteristics of network equipment and services. The network management model consists of a manager and agent that use the object-oriented CMIP, or Common Management Information Protocol (Fig. 4). The adoption of this model, which is the basis for CCITT TMN standards (x.700), makes possible robust management, through the sharing of network management information between management systems. The OSI management model allows users to specify which system is the manager and which the agent for any specific instance. In this way, information can be selected (using OSI scoping and filtering) for transmission to an "integrating" application acting in the manager role.

FIGURE 4   Standard manager/agent relationships within an ISO (International Standards Organization) model of interactions

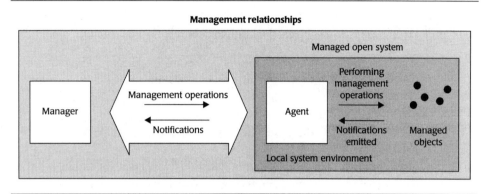

The SNMP management model is based on a manager/agent relationship in which the agent is simple and the manager is intelligent. Information stored in the SNMP's information base is minimal. SNMP management is easy to implement in simple devices but is less robust and modular than OSI management.

Also needed for interoperability among management systems is a common information model. The abstraction of a real network or computing device, referred to as a "managed object," must conform to particular Structure of Management Information (SMI), the rules used in determining the information about the managed object that can be monitored and manipulated through the management protocol.

The NMF's goal is to coordinate these various "interoperable interfaces" to permit the global exchange of management information. This includes provisions for SNMP and CMIP, common information models, managed-object definitions, and even underlying technologies (such as application programming interfaces).

MAKING DO TODAY

Global corporations must draw on their own resources and facilities, as well as those of international telecommunications providers and equipment vendors, to create and operate end-to-end network service capabilities for their employees, customers, and suppliers. Higher-level services to many countries and regions today are often limited. While fiber optic infrastructure and other leading-edge equipment is being deployed rapidly in many parts of the world, advanced services are still unavailable in many industrialized and non industrialized nations. It almost goes without saying that network management systems and services, therefore, are incomplete and fragmented.

Despite the lack of technical sophistication in networks worldwide, most users today—whether through switched or private services—can achieve a certain level of network management support as a basic element of their long-distance service. For instance, many dedicated international circuits are now serviced through international transmission maintenance centers. Moreover, many carriers hold in reserve special international digital circuits for quick trouble restoration. For example, Kokusai Denshin Denwa (KDD, the Japanese telecommunications company), AT&T, and British Telecom International have jointly established a messaging system that allows technicians to exchange information about mutual circuits. As a result, time is saved when comparing test results and the system provides for automatic fault reporting, streamlined response procedures, and real-time reporting and analysis.

Such systems and services offer base-level management of simple voice and lower-speed data communications circuits. But the watch-words in industry today are "high-speed" and "instantaneous." These requirements, coupled with the critical nature of today's global communications, mean that companies can ill afford downtime or inaccurate transmissions. And, when problems do occur, corporations want immediate resolution—from a central point. They also want network management that is efficient and cost effective. For this advanced level of service and protection, a partnership with suppliers is the only reasonable solution.

Corporations have a wide selection of services and capabilities to choose from on the open market. They can:

- Build extensive network management expertise themselves from the inside out and procure from industry vendors the necessary equipment, training, and technical assistance.

- Deal with evolving consortiums of PTTS, equipment vendors, and service providers for more specific elements and aspects of network management.

- Work with a single vendor that can provide all or part of its needs for end-to-end coordination, provision, management, reporting, and analysis.

No matter how a corporation decides to go, network management in today's global environment is still far too limited. Emerging standards—especially the OSI-based standards referred to as CMIP and X.700—offer the primary path for making complex networks more manageable. Fortunately, there is a growing industry consensus that the Network Management Forum's OMNIPoints effort will work to make these standards available sooner rather than later.

For OMNIPoints to work, however, corporations and suppliers dealing with global networks must become more knowledgeable about how to use them. Only through widespread industry focus and cooperation will the many challenges facing today's global network managers be fully met and solved. Yes, the needed investment in time and technology is substantial, but the commitment to networking has never been more critical to a company's competitiveness—at home and abroad.

The Golden Rules of
Global Networking

GEOFF WIGGIN

THE GROWTH IN GLOBAL INDUSTRIES, particularly in finance, transportation, and manufacturing, has presented corporations with great challenges in setting up successful communications links. Those challenges must be met if companies are to improve the management of their international operations and provide enhanced services. Setting up an international network, however, is not easy. It is essential that corporations understand the golden rules of global networking, since international business is fast becoming a networking game.

The network budget for multinationals represents a major investment of strategic importance. The decision to set up a global network must rest on solid business reasons; otherwise, there is no point to the strategy. Those business reasons can be identified by working out what the network will be used for, how the applications can benefit the corporation, and where the company is headed. The installation of each new access node must be based on an analysis of cost versus anticipated traffic.

In most firms, initially, the net will connect international sites and offices. Ultimately, it may link these sites to the firm's trading partners—agents, suppliers, and customers. That means it has to be a true multiuser network supporting different computing hardware and carrying a wide range of information, with a great diversity of transmission sizes, transmission frequency, and "value" or "importance" of content.

The underlying applications will be equally diverse, but fall into three main categories:

- *Batch transfers between major sites.* This usually includes financial reports, orders from distribution sites to factories or central warehouses, CAD and similar design information from design offices to factories, and feedback on sales, product quality, and customer and supplier performance. In each case, the source and destination of the material are fixed. Volumes tend to be high and transfers are regular, often scheduled.

- *Interactive consultation with central databases or application programs.* This includes user requests for information, perhaps on prices or stock quantities or shipping schedules, updating central files to record new sales and orders, the completion of safety checks, and so on.

- *Messaging systems.* This includes electronic mail for direct communication between people at different sites, often in different countries. This type of application will also cover electronic data interchange (EDI), which links the company and its trading partners.

Batch transfers and, to a lesser extent, inquiry systems are the more traditional communications activities. The third type, messaging, is relatively new and it is growing rapidly. The network must be able to handle the random volumes and routing of traffic that messaging applications require. With batch transfers and interactive database access, either one or both ends of the communication is known. With messaging systems, the sender usually has no idea of the location of the recipient and network managers are unable to predict anything much more than a tendency for traffic to grow . . . and grow.

The following rules cover only the basic concerns of setting up a global network. If a corporation doesn't abide by these rules, then its networking effort at best will be only partially successful; at worst, it will be a very expensive disaster.

Reach Out to the Users. The network must clearly reach out to every user. For the multinational corporation, this means most countries in the developed world and a growing number of nations.

Networks are expensive to deploy, so there will be an element of compromise between internal and external network links. Users have demands and network managers must arrange links with public data networks and perhaps the international telex network to provide service in areas they are unable to link up quickly or directly.

As more devices are connected, and more users join in electronic mail and EDI communities, the network must expand its capacity in two ways. There must be an adequate number of access ports, so users can get into the network when they need to, and there must be enough capacity to handle increasing volumes.

Thousands of electronic mail users will require their incoming mail at 9 a.m. on workday mornings, and will then make but sporadic use of the network for the remainder of the day. The interactive users will be busy during much of the working day, while the batch users possibly will be more active before and after normal office hours. Their port requirements are different, and network managers must understand this and provide equally good service for everyone. Fortunately, e-mail and interactive users tend to be clustered into office buildings, so that by extending the network to a multiplexor in the building and hardwiring the terminals to the multiplexor, the need for huge numbers of dial-in ports can be controlled.

The second aspect of capacity covers the volume of material to be moved from node to node. The very existence of the network will enable corporate communications to flow sideways through the organization rather than predominantly up and down. The network suddenly has to cope with unplanned and sometimes unforeseen information flows that may dwarf the volumes of conventional information traffic.

Establish a People Network. Global network users speak different languages, their working hours are different, and they probably know nothing about computers. A fairly typical new user works in a small office and is introduced to the network by a memo or telex from his corporate hierarchy that says, "Here's your user ID and password. Have fun."

They won't. Users need advice on the choice of terminal or on the communications hardware and software required for their existing device. They need to be shown, or at least told, how to access the network, how to drive whatever application they are expected to use, and what to do when things go wrong. From time to time they will hit snags and will require advice and reassurance. This user support is needed locally and preferably should be through face-to-face contact.

It is not practical for the corporate network team to offer this level of support. They do not know the local regulatory environment—for example, some telephone authorities have monopolies on the supply of modems. The corporate team does not know what equipment will work in each country, which is the best value for the money, or how it will connect to the local access node. They do not speak the language and will often be asleep when the user gets to the office.

Thus, support must be local and can only be supplied by a people network that understands the problems. In many cases, unless this type of support is made available right from the start, a new application is likely to be a complete failure. For many networked applications, the installation process—getting terminals to work and familiarizing the staff with its new duties—is more onerous than designing and writing the underlying software. A smooth installation is also more important to the success of the project as a whole and is utterly reliant on local network support staff.

Find Friends in the PTTs. The people network, in fact, has two tasks. The second is the support of the network itself.

When a new node is planned in a foreign country, the local team must ensure that those plans conform to local regulations. They have to negotiate for operating licenses and circuits with the local PTT, working in the language and according to the customs of the country concerned. Such negotiations often have an educational aspect, because PTT officials and engineers may be involved in an international network for the first time and they may not be able to answer apparently simple questions. Negotiators who are aware of the rules in comparable countries may be able to help shape the telecommunications policy of the new host country. This implies staff of a very special nature; there are few of them around.

PTT regulations don't cover only the physical network, but also the applications running on it. Once again, the network support staff is in the best position to become acquainted with new or modified regulations, and to ensure that everyone is informed.

Once the network is set up and running . . . it will break down. The local support staff then has to pinpoint the fault and persuade the PTT engineers to repair anything under their jurisdiction.

In all these areas, it is a clear advantage if the network staff can establish good working relations with the local PTT management and engineers.

Success Is the Ability to Cope with Failure. When a network is set up, users expect to be able to press a button and connect to wherever or whatever they want. The network must be ready and waiting.

Network managers need to satisfy this expectation and make every effort to ensure that the network will be available 24 hours of every day. That's almost impossible, but it is a worthwhile goal and often involves a large "invisible" investment. For a reliable network this means duplicating or, even triplicating every communications link, ensuring that the secondary links are routed over completely different paths. The aim is to protect the user from dredging operations near underwater cables, broken land lines, malfunctions in satellites, and every other possible disruption. The pairs of communications links should arrive in the country at separate communications computers. These must be interconnected to ensure that there is always at least one clear path from the user to his desired destination.

All of these communications devices and links have to be managed. The network must detect broken elements, reconfigure itself to bypass them, reconstruct or retransmit data that was in transit at the time, and inform the operators of the nature and location of the problem. This must be done in real time, automatically, and without affecting the users who are on-line at the time. As the components are returned to service, the reconfiguration must be reversed; again, it must be transparent to the users.

Security Is a Dual Responsibility. Modern global communications networks are used for a wide variety of applications, some containing information of great commercial value. That means it must be secure.

The network has to keep unauthorized users out and prevent third parties from reading, copying, repeating, or changing transactions either while en route or while stored in central computers. Data can often be encrypted and access controlled by tamper-resistant authorization codes. Network managers must realize, however, that this imposes greater processing loads on the network.

Almost every link in the network will be carrying traffic belonging to a number of users. Therefore, each packet must be labeled and great care taken to ensure that it cannot be misrouted. This is especially important when third parties such as dealers or suppliers are using the net. The virtual circuits between sender and recipient must always be completely isolated, even though they share physical circuits, computers, or disk space.

Also, user data must never be garbled, truncated, duplicated, or missequenced. Every packet, over every link in the end-to-end communications packets must be checked to ensure that what went up came down. In cases of error or doubt, the suspect packets must be retransmitted, with the entire message being correctly and completely recreated before the receiver gets it.

Since whatever can go wrong usually does, the integrity aspect of data communications must be complemented by comprehensive rollback and recovery procedures. Like the network management and reconfiguration facilities, these procedures must, as far as possible, be transparent to the user. When data loss is unavoidable, the loss, and as much descriptive information as possible, must be provided to the user so that he or she can bring personal recovery procedures into action.

The majority of applications that run over international networks involve programs running in the computers that form the hub of the network itself. Most security and integrity procedures therefore can be duplicated, with the network procedures backed up by others within the application. These will be under the control of local managers, and this underlines the fact that, in the final analysis, security is in the hands of the users.

Know the Costs and All the Options.   The costs of setting up a network are split three ways.

There is an up-front design and construction cost necessary to provide a network covering users' needs over the medium term. The equipment costs are high, and the controlling software is not necessarily available off the shelf, which can mean considerable additional investment. A hidden factor is the need for people who are able to design such systems—and people who can negotiate with the PTTs. These people are difficult to recruit and difficult to retain—and they expect to be paid accordingly.

Ongoing costs include leases on premises and circuits; keeping a close eye on changes in line tariffs around the world is therefore important. These costs also cover the detection and correction of faults in both hardware and software, often involving expensive and sophisticated test and diagnostic equipment. There must also be well-trained and experienced operational staff both to maintain the network service and to support the users.

Finally, there are the less easily quantifiable costs to the company: maintaining flexibility and independence. Most multinationals regularly sell off operations or acquire new ones. The architecture and scope of the network should not be a limiting factor in these decisions. There is also a built-in risk with a network that any new applications or extensions won't work out well.

One option is to restrict internal developments to those areas that are regarded as safe and easy. This can be done using the local public data network and leased intersite links connecting major in-house computer centers. There are also applications where external network services are inappropriate. These cover high-security applications where cost is a secondary concern, such as military and diplomatic systems, and networks where very fast response times are needed. The airline reservations systems and interbank message systems are good examples.

THIRD-PARTY BENEFITS IN GENERAL

For more general use, third-party network suppliers may offer a better deal, since they already will have amortized the up-front cost, spread the operational costs over a large number of users, and invested in new technologies in order to stay competitive. The costs associated with the use of a third-party supplier are not negligible, but they are controllable. They are, in general, volume dependent, and users are provided with detailed breakdowns of the traffic for which they are charged.

Invest in the Future. The network has to serve many types of users, and must be able to handle a wide range of terminal equipment. The magnitude of this task grows over time as new technologies, higher transmission speeds, and new techniques are introduced. The network must grow to accommodate all of these technologies without affecting the existing user base.

At any given time, some users will be pondering their next generation of equipment, and some will choose the most modern, most cost-effective machines. These may well be the first commercial offerings of equipment using some new protocol. The user will expect the network to handle it.

The effect is to force network managers to stay one step ahead and attempt to figure out what users will need next year—to make the needed investment that allows the network to cope.

New types of applications will also make demands. The network will probably offer a native electronic mail system, which will be fine for itinerant users and for connecting small sites equipped with dumb terminals or microcomputers. The big sites may well have large communities using the proprietary e-mail systems provided by their hardware manufacturers. It is incumbent upon the network manager to provide the interfaces between the on-site and the international systems.

The need for these application-level interfaces will grow as networks carry more material between sites, and, particularly, between companies. The increase in electronic data interchange systems is, to a certain extent, dependent on the ability of the network to convert business documents into different formats. More specialized applications include the conversion of revisable-form word processor documents so that, for example, contracts may be reviewed and revised by people in sites with incompatible equipment. What's more, there is a growing demand for the exchange of CAD/CAM files between sites with incompatible machines.

In this changing world of global networking, managers must make continuing and forward-looking investments to cope with what the users, and the corporation, need to do.

SECTION V
Management of Global Information Flows

Although information networks provide the necessary infrastructure for transmitting business information, they alone do not guarantee business success. The success of a global business organization depends on how these networks are used to deliver the right information to the right place at the right time. This chapter is concerned with global information flows and the issues and challenges of managing them.

The first two articles explore the information needs of international business organizations. In the first article, Czinkota presents the results of a survey of the information needs of international business and government trade executives. The results of the study provide some valuable insights for the management of international business information.

Iyer and Schkade in their paper describe the characteristics and fundamental requirements of management support systems for developing global strategies and managing worldwide operations. The article first identifies the information needs for decision making at strategic, managerial, and operational levels. It then describes the three types of management support systems for multinational business organizations: data support, decision support, and executive information systems.

As businesses become more global, the ability to move material and products throughout the world is becoming extremely important. Managing logistics on a global scale is a major challenge for management in global firms. Bagchi presents a case for globalization of logistics information. He describes the essential features of an international logistics information system and provides guidance for designing and managing such a system.

In the next paper, Rosenberg and Valiant show how the flow of trading transactions with customers, suppliers, and business partners can be handled electronically with electronic data interchange (EDI). The article describes the characteristics, advantages, limitations, and potential of EDI in the international business arena.

While the rapid growth of international networks has vastly contributed to global trade, it has also raised concerns for many governmental organizations and consumer interest groups. Many governments see the growth of transborder data flows (TDF) as a threat to their sovereignty and the privacy of their citizens. As a result, they seek to impose controls and restrictions through various regulations and laws. In the final article of this chapter, Saraswat and Gorgone identify various types of laws and regulations that govern transborder data flows and describe the challenges that multinational corporations face in complying with these laws.

The transnational firm of the future will accept the telecommunications network as an essential component of its operations. The competitive focus will shift to managing the vast array of information resources and identifying strategic means for managing information assets. The following section shows that the challenges of managing various technology platforms and integrating systems across the globe provide some interesting insights as corporations continue to identify effective means for competing through technology and information.

International Information Needs for U.S. Competitiveness

MICHAEL R. CZINKOTA

INFORMATION IS A CRUCIAL STRATEGIC RESOURCE for those who use it. In business, "management has come to realize that managing a business well is managing its future and managing its future is managing information" (Daser 1984). For researchers, information is critical in theory formulation and hypothesis testing and for gaining insights into phenomena. In governmental organizations, voluminous briefing books and jealously guarded access to them amply demonstrate the value policymakers place on information.

Information is even more important in the international setting, where entirely new parameters and environments are encountered. Business executives, policymakers, and researchers alike need to know about the economic environment, the technological level, and the cultural and social dimensions of foreign countries. It is also important to understand foreign political systems, determine their stability, comprehend pertinent legal issues, and identify differences in societal structures. International information is extremely important for policymakers to set good policy and negotiation goals, for business executives to be successful in the global market, and for researchers to obtain in-depth insights.

The international business literature provides frequent examples of the linkage between the importance of international information and international competitiveness. Johanson and Vahlne (1978) suggest that a lack of foreign environmental knowledge about such issues as language and culture is an important obstacle to the internationalization of the firm. Kedia and Chahokar (1986) believe that lack of needed information is the major deterrent for the entry of small and medium-sized firms into the export market. Research analyzing international market failures ex post facto found that most errors could have been avoided if the firm and its managers had obtained adequate information about the business environment (Ricks 1983).

Czinkota, Michael R. "International Information Needs for U.S. Competitiveness," *Business Horizons*, Nov.–Dec. 1991, 86–91.

Research also shows that exporters conduct a more intensive search for information than non-exporters, attach more importance to market knowledge, and are more likely to conduct their own market research (Burton and Schlegelmilch 1987). Czinkota and Ricks (1981) report that exporters believe increased market information gathering and information on business practices are key variables in improving their foreign trade performance. Czinkota and Ronkainen (1990), in turn, state that exclusive information can be a key motivation in providing the firm with strategic competitive advantage and international marketing success. The overall point and urgency is perhaps summarized best by Farmer (1987, p. 113), who states that "to be world class one needs world class information."

TYPE OF INFORMATION

Given the importance of information stressed by so many authors, the question then becomes what type of information is needed for international business competitiveness. The literature provides a number of suggestions about such information requirements. Davidson (1983) postulates that macrodata need to allow firms to focus on the general relationship among market characteristics, marketing mix strategies, and consumer response. In their seminal book on international marketing research, Douglas and Craig (1983) suggest that macrodata help companies select countries or markets that merit in-depth investigation, make an initial estimate of demand potential in a given country, or monitor environmental change. Davusgil (1984) proposes the usefulness of macro-level information on industry in foreign markets, broad economic and demographic variables, political indicators, and cultural indicators. He also suggests that the information requirements of firms vary based on different stages of market research. In the preliminary screening stage, information about the physical, political, economic, and cultural environment is most important. When analyzing industry market potential, market access information, such as limitations on trade, tariff levels and quotas, legal restrictions, local production, imports, consumption, and conditions for local manufacture, is necessary. For the analysis of company sales potential, he recommends that information about size and concentration of customer segments, projected consumption statistics, competitive pressures, and costing methods be available (Cavusgil 1985).

Walters (1983) finds that useful background knowledge is provided by information on export and import shipments, trade barriers, and data on overseas markets. A detailed analysis by Wood and Goolsby (1987) reports that key information should consist of knowledge about market potential, trade restrictions (tariff and non-tariff barriers and transportation barriers), politics and their effects on trade, and economic and legal factors.

All the literature points toward two different types of data needs: macro information, providing mostly knowledge about different environments, and micro information, providing details about markets, activities within those markets, and the changes taking place in them. The unifying conclusion, however, remains, data and the knowledge derived from them are crucial for success in the international environment.

GOVERNMENT AND INTERNATIONAL INFORMATION

Governments have learned about and shared this concern over international information needs. The U.S. government realized the importance of international information early on, when William H. Seward recommended that payment be made to Aaron Haight Palmer "for services for collecting information of statistics, resources, trade and commerce of the independent Oriental nations" (Seward 1867). Comprehensive studies of export promotion programs around the world find that virtually all industrialized countries collect many forms of trade information and disseminate it. A report by the U.S. Foreign Commercial Service indicates that government expenditures on advisory and research activities in the export field ranged from $23.6 million in West Germany to $206 million in the United Kingdom in 1985 (Director General 1988).

In spite of the common acceptance of the need for accumulated and disseminated trade information, little knowledge exists about what types of international data are most crucial. Neither the research literature nor the government have presented a hierarchical rank order of data importance, which would help identify the relevance of international information.

In times of budget deficits and competing priorities, it seems an important task to develop such an international information hierarchy. By knowing which data are most crucial, government can selectively focus its efforts and at least ensure that the most important information needs are served best, thus enhancing the international competitiveness of firms. It is the purpose of this article to report such a rank-ordering effort. In addition, the work differentiates among three types of potential users of trade information: policymakers, business executives, and researchers. This differentiation is introduced to trace possible differences among these three groups based on differing activities for which information is used. Finally, data were gathered on the form of data presentation.

METHOD

Even though international trade research can be exciting to those involved in it, it is not a subject of broad appeal. Because people often judge the quality of research by its data quantity, it is tempting to send questionnaires to many policy participants, researchers and business executives. However, as stated by Czinkota (1986), "It is better to obtain selected in-depth responses of a few experts who know and do, rather than to seek the average responses of many with limited knowledge." Therefore, it was decided to seek information from those who deal with trade data on a daily basis: government executives in the international trade area, researchers in the international business and marketing field, and executives active in international business. A questionnaire was designed that differentiated data needs into international economic (macro) data and international business (micro) data.

The questionnaire was pretested by four policymakers, three researchers, and four business executives, who clarified terms of ambiguity. Subsequently, key policymakers in the U.S. government were identified who would need to use trade data in fulfilling their policy objectives. To reflect the diversity of government responsibility in the trade field, the policymakers were stratified to reflect regional concerns, international negotiations, multilateral views, and industry-specific concerns. Altogether, individuals in ten government organizations received questionnaires. The individuals ranged in title from Deputy Assistant Secretary to Division Director, and represented Japan, Europe, the Western Hemisphere, Africa, the Near East, South Asia, East Asia, and the Pacific. Industry was represented by capital goods, international construction, services, aerospace, automotive affairs, and consumer goods. In addition, input was obtained from trade negotiators. The total number of individuals queried was 25.

To obtain corporate input, members of the Industry Sector Advisory Committees (ISACS) were chosen. These advisory committees provide private sector advice in the international trade field to both the U.S. Department of Commerce and the U.S. Trade Representative Office. Membership on these committees is by joint appointment of the Secretary of Commerce and the U.S. Trade Representative. Members are chosen based on their representativeness of U.S. industries and their involvement in international business. Thirty-four industry representatives provided filled-out questionnaires for this study.

Researchers' priorities were assessed by identifying leading members of the academic community who use trade data in their research and teaching activities. They were selected based on past publication activities that demonstrated their use of trade data. Only researchers in the U.S. were queried. All researchers selected for the study were approached personally and asked to fill out the trade data questionnaire. Out of 26 selected individuals, several were unavailable due to travel or other commitments. A total of 21 persons agreed to participate in this research.

First, the grand means were determined for each information issue. Subsequently, a comparison of means was carried out with occupation as the dependent variable. Respondents fell into the following groups: government, industry, and academic. Group mean differences were then tested using analysis of variance. The tests compared the occupational group means with total sample means. The SAS package used automatically compensated for unbalanced group size. A 90 percent confidence level was chosen for statistical significance purposes.

FINDINGS AND DISCUSSION

The respondents answered questions about two different data issues: the importance of specific trade data to their work and the form in which the data were used. The summary responses are depicted in Tables 1 and 2.

Table 1 first shows the type of data and their overall importance rankings. Because the data are from a small group of respondents, not too much stock should be placed in the individual ranking of the data type. However, three major clusters of importance emerged. For international economic data, Cluster 1 contains the most critical information: data on

TABLE 1   Importance Rankings of International Information

	Grand Means	Academics	Industry	Government
International Economic Data				
Cluster 1				
U.S. Import/Export Data	2.8	2.9	2.8	2.6
Tariffs	2.8	2.8	2.9	2.6
Non-Tariff Measures	2.8	2.8	2.8	2.8
Foreign Import/Export Data	2.7	2.8	2.8	2.6
Government Trade Policy	2.6	2.8	2.6	2.6
Cluster 2				
Foreign Production Data	2.4	2.4	2.5	2.3
U.S. Production Data	2.4	2.4	2.5	2.1
Exchange Rates	2.3	2.4	2.3	1.9
FDI in U.S.*	2.2	2.6	1.9	2.2
International Service Transactions	2.1	2.6	2.2	1.7
International Interest Rates	2.1	2.0	1.9	1.5
Wage Rates Abroad*	2.1	2.2	2.2	1.7
Cluster 3				
Labor Productivity*	2.0	2.3	1.9	1.8
Unemployment Rates	1.8	1.8	1.8	1.8
State Trade Data*	1.8	2.1	1.6	1.6
International Business Data				
Cluster 1				
Local Laws and Regulations	2.7	2.7	2.7	2.7
Size of Market	2.6	2.7	2.6	2.8
Local Standards and Specs	2.5	2.5	2.6	2.3
Distribution System	2.5	2.6	2.4	2.3
Competition Abroad	2.5	2.6	2.5	2.5
Cluster 2				
Specific Business Operations	2.4	2.5	2.2	2.6
Common Business Practices*	2.4	2.2	2.4	2.8
Licensing	2.4	2.3	2.5	2.3
Export Financing*	2.4	2.7	2.3	2.3
General Economic Conditions	2.2	2.4	2.1	2.3
Trade Officials	2.1	2.1	2.1	2.2
Barter & Countertrade*	2.1	2.4	1.9	2.1
Cluster 3				
Government Officials	1.9	1.8	1.9	2.0

3 = Critical; 2 = Useful; 1 = Of Little Value

* Significant differences among groups at .10 level.

TABLE 2   Form of Data: Automated or Printed

	Grand Means	Academics	Industry	Government
International Economic Data				
U.S. Import/Export Data	1.9	1.8	1.9	1.9
International Interest Rates	1.7	1.6	1.5	1.9
Exchange Rates	1.7	1.5	1.9	1.7
Foreign Import/Export Data	1.6	1.9	1.5	1.6
U.S. Production Data	1.5	1.5	1.5	1.6
International Service Transactions	1.5	1.7	1.5	1.3
State Trade Data	1.4	1.6	1.2	1.0
Tariffs	1.4	1.5	1.5	1.3
Non-Tariff Measures	1.3	1.3	1.1	1.4
Labor Productivity	1.3	1.3	1.0	1.6
Government Trade Policy	1.2	1.3	1.0	1.1
Unemployment Rates	1.2	1.0	1.0	1.5
FDI in U.S.	1.2	1.4	1.0	1.0
Foreign Production Data	1.2	1.4	1.1	1.2
Wage Rates Abroad	1.1	1.0	1.1	1.2
International Business Data				
Specific Business Operations	1.4	1.6	1.3	1.3
General Economic Conditions	1.4	1.5	1.5	1.2
Size of Market	1.2	1.3	1.0	1.0
Distribution System	1.2	1.4	1.0	1.0
Export Financing	1.2	1.3	1.0	1.0
Competition Abroad	1.1	1.1	1.0	1.0
Local Laws and Regulations	1.1	1.2	1.0	1.0
Local Standards and Specs	1.1	1.1	1.0	1.0
Government Officials	1.1	1.1	1.0	1.0
Trade Officials	1.1	1.1	1.2	1.0
Common Business Practices	1.1	1.1	1.0	1.0
Licensing	1.1	1.2	1.0	1.0
Barter & Countertrade	1.1	1.1	1.0	1.0

3 = Automated; 1 = Printed; 2 = Both

tariff and non-tariff measures, U.S. and foreign export-import data, and data on government trade policy. Cluster 2, ranging between critical and useful, consists of data on foreign production, U.S. production, exchange rates, foreign wage rates, services, interest rates, and foreign direct investment. Cluster 3 consists of data of little value and contains state trade data and data on unemployment rates.

For international business data, the spread of importance ratings was not as wide as was the case for economic data, but similar clusters emerged. Information about local laws and regulations, market size, local standards and specifications, competition in the market, and the distribution system was deemed most critical. A second cluster then consists of data on specific business opportunities, common business practices, licensing regulations, export financing, general economic conditions, trade officials, and barter and countertrade. The third cluster consists of information on government officials. The business information evaluated as the most critical was, overall, given a lower rating than was the case for economic data. However, the business data in the last cluster were rated as somewhat more important than were the economic data.

In comparing the evaluations of data importance by the different groups, some major differences emerged. For example, researchers considered information on international service transactions important, but government policymakers gave it little value. Similarly, researchers believed foreign direct investment data to be quite critical, whereas this was much less the case for business executives and policymakers. The same held true for state trade data, information on labor productivity rates, and wage rates abroad. Researchers also believed information on export financing and barter and countertrade to be more important than did the two other groups. By contrast, policymakers and business executives believed information on common business practices to be more critical than did researchers.

Form of Data

Respondents were also asked whether data were used in automated or printed form. Clearly, current usage patterns will have a major influence on how data should be distributed. For economic data, evidence indicates that some automated data are being used. This was particularly the case for U.S. and foreign export-import data, interest rates, and exchange rate information. In most instances, however, the vast majority of respondents indicated they were using data primarily in printed form. This also was the case for international business data, but to an even greater degree. No major difference among the groups emerged (see Table 2).

CONCLUSIONS

The research findings lead to several conclusions. First, it becomes clear that not all data are created equal. Respondents indicated major priorities among data sets. Simply put, some data are more important than others, and respondents seem to be clearly able to rank them. If one intends to provide international information to enhance competitiveness under conditions of scarce resources, it appears useful to focus on the most important data priority first to satisfy data users' needs best. Second, in spite of much discussion surrounding the gradual conversion of the U.S. into an electronic information society, major demand continues to exist for printed information.

It is also clear that different data users have different needs. Depending on whether government, industry, or the research community is to be the user of trade information, different priorities emerged. Several surprises were visible here. For example, the low ranking of services data for policy purposes was unexpected in light of the U.S.'s conversion to a service-based economy. This could be attributable either to a lack of respondents' information, or possibly to in-depth knowledge about the lack of reliability of current data on international services transactions. It also appears that academics are in a cutting edge position in their demands for attributing more importance to services data. The same is also true in the area of foreign direct investments.

The data priorities that were found also reflect the changes of the global environment. For example, the high ranking of non-tariff measures shows the importance of these issues, reaffirmed by the clear outdistancing of other areas such as foreign production data. Similarly, the major emphasis on local laws and regulations highlights how important this dimension has become to the international business community. In addition, this high ranking underscores the need to continue the emphasis on these issues in international negotiations. The same applies to information about local standards and specifications where international variations are significant.

Overall, respondents appear to find macro trade data mostly useful in conducting a broad scan of international business opportunities and obstacles. In-depth information such as knowledge about distribution systems or specific business opportunities are ranked significantly lower. Perhaps this indicates that businesses believe the specifics of transactions are mainly the situation-specific responsibility of the firm. Perhaps one could even say that in spite of the public availability of such data, the private sector would still be highly likely to conduct its own research and investigation into these crucial business specifics.

Surprising was the discovery that the desire for knowledge about government and trade officials abroad was rated rather low. Considering the major lobbying activities of foreign countries and companies in the U.S., perhaps this low ranking reflects the fact that many U.S. firms are far less successful in their interaction with governments abroad and far less intensive in their attempts to influence these governments than are foreign entities in the United States.

Finally, in spite of major advances in communication technology in recent years, most respondents still appear to mainly use hard copies of data rather than information in electronic form. While the electronic age probably will gradually precipitate electronic data usage, clearly, this time has not yet arrived. Any group interested in data dissemination must therefore search for ways of making data available in printed form.

There are several important implications of the findings reported here. Firms have a clear idea about their international data needs. The clusters identified can assist newcomers to the international market in identifying the types of information they should scrutinize. Only if they continue to be aware of crucial macro and micro information can companies expect to remain competitive in the global marketplace.

The ratings of data importance gathered here indicate that government should perhaps concentrate its international information gathering and dissemination in those areas that are most important, given the increasingly tightening resource constraints of government budgets and the priority and usage articulations found here. This may mean dropping data dissemination efforts in the areas of exchange, wage, and unemployment rates. However, the data that are collected and disseminated should be as detailed and disaggregated as possible to increase their benefits. In other words, it may be better for government to do fewer things, but do them well, rather than try to cover every potential need in sight.

Academics must be aware that their data needs often vary significantly from those of the business and policy communities. This indicates that academics need to make themselves heard when it comes to data collection and dissemination decisions. Waiting passively for the policy sector to make these choices may leave researchers out in the cold. However, at the same time, it is important to consider the extent to which one can afford specific data collections that are mainly of use to academics. This trade-off will require academics to demonstrate more clearly how the fulfillment of their data needs is likely to benefit the business and policy communities.

In future research, it would seem worthwhile to place more emphasis on data usage. The availability and flow of information is too crucial to international business, policy, and research success to be neglected. It is important to remain aware that the types of data needed for policy-making are clearly different from those needed to encourage international business transactions or enhance research activities. It also would seem worthwhile to further explore linkages between data and specific business decisions, both on the policy and business sides; if one were to identify the degree to which data can or cannot improve the quality of decisions, major assistance could be provided to decision makers. It would also be useful to explore data flow within both policy and business operations, to assess ways in which such flows could be structured best and thus lead to better communications within the unit.

Finally, research should evaluate the success of existing or incipient trade data bases, be they sponsored by governments or the private sector. Such research would aid others to structure their information dissemination efforts better. To do so has become imperative in an age of information need, the criticality of which is matched only by the danger of information overload.

REFERENCES

F.N. Burton and B.B. Schlegelmilch, "Profile Analyses of Nonexporters vs. Exporters Grouped by Export Involvement," *Management International Review*, 27 (1987): 38–49.

Tamer S. Cavusgil, "International Marketing Research: Insights into Company Practices," *Research in Marketing*, 7 (1984): 261–288.

Tamer S. Cavusgil, "Guidelines for Export Market Research," *Business Horizons*, November-December 1985, pp. 27–33.

Tamer S. Cavusgil and Michael R. Czinkota (eds.), *International Perspectives on Trade Promotion and Assistance* (New York: Quorum Books. 1990).

Michael R. Czinkota, "International Trade and Business in the Late 1980's: An Integrated U.S. Perspective," *Journal of International Business Studies*, Spring 1986, pp. 127–134.

Michael R. Czinkota and David Ricks, "Export Assistance: Are We Supporting the Best Programs?" *Columbia Journal of World Business*, Summer 1981, pp. 73–78.

Michael R. Czinkota and Ilkka Ronkainen, *International Marketing*, 2nd ed. (Hinsdale, Ill.: The Dryden Press, 1990).

Sayeste Daser, "International Marketing Information Systems: A Neglected Prerequisite for Foreign Market Planning," in E. Kaynak (ed.), *International Marketing Management* (New York: Praeger Publishers, 1984).

William H. Davidson, "Market Similarities and Market Selection: Implications for International Marketing Strategy," *Journal of Business Research*, 11 (1983): 439–456.

Director General, Report by Alexander Good, Export Promotion Activities, U.S. Department of Commerce, International Trade Administration, Washington, D.C., 1988.

Susan P. Douglas and Samuel C. Craig, *International Marketing Research* (Englewood Cliffs, N.J.: Prentice-Hall, 1983).

Richard N. Farmer, "Would You Want Your Granddaughter to Marry a Taiwanese Marketing Man?" *Journal of Marketing*, 51 (1987): 111–116.

J. Johanson and J.E. Vahlne, "The Internationalization Process of the Firm—A Model of Knowledge Development and Increasing Commitments," *Journal of International Business Studies*, Spring-Summer 1978, pp. 23–32.

Ben L. Kedia and Jagdeep S. Chahokar, "An Empirical Investigation of Export Promotion Programs," *Columbia Journal of World Business*, Winter 1986, pp. 13–20.

National Industrial Board, *Export Promotion by Governments in Nine Countries*, Stockholm, Sweden, 1985. p. 165.

David A. Ricks, *Big Business Blunders: Mistakes in Multinational Marketing* (Homewood, Ill.: Dow Jones-Irwin, 1983).

William H. Seward, "Report Presented to the Senate of the United States," *Congressional Globe*, February 13, 1867, p. 662.

Peter G. Walters, "Export Information Sources—A Study of Their Usage and Utility," *International Marketing Review*, Winter 1983, pp. 34–43.

Van R. Wood and Jerry R. Goolsby, "Foreign Market Information Preferences of Established U.S. Exporters," *International Marketing Review*, Winter 1987, pp. 43–52.

Management Support Systems for Multinational Business

RAJA K. IYER & LAWRENCE L. SCHKADE

1. INTRODUCTION

The expansion of many businesses into multinational operations and markets has created added dimensions of information requirements, as their management must now function in a global environment. It appears that many firms can no longer maximize performance by limiting their strategy to increasing market share within a single national boundary. The failure to adopt a global market strategy will not only lead to competitive deficiency abroad, but also to the threat of erosion in domestic competitive position, as evidenced in the case of the consumer electronics industry. Faced with the necessity to respond effectively to increasing multinational competitive forces, businesses are using information technology (IT) and resources to provide vital support to global strategic management.

Such applications are rapidly increasing in both domestic and foreign firms. In addition to the traditional transactions oriented applications, IT has been utilized to achieve several strategic advantages (12,19,20) and its potential has been tapped by many multinational firms to gain competitive advantage (19). For example, Texas Instruments (TI) has established an elaborate communications network (7) that links geographically dispersed organizational entities. One aspect of this global communications network is the ability to bring the organizational units together, essentially leading to the much desired phenomena of reduction in time and distance and improved coordination among the geographically dispersed business units. In addition, this global communications network provides major competitive advantages by enabling inter-organizational information sharing (2) and vertical integration of IT (19) to deliver appropriate information intelligence to suppliers and customers. In this regard, TI is opening up its IT resources to its customers to confirm product orders rapidly, communicate product design changes, and monitor product quality constantly (7,13). These customer-oriented applications of information and communications technology provide valuable competitive advantages such as built-in switching

Iyer, Raja J., and Schkade, Lawrence L. "Management Support Systems for Multinational Business." *Information and Management*, vol. 12, no. 2 (1987), 59–64.

costs and barriers against new entrants or new products into the industry (21). These types of developments, reported in academic as well as commercial literature, provide ample evidence that there has been a fundamental and significant restructuring of the manner in which IT is viewed and utilized by corporations.

Foreign firms are also adept in utilizing information technology for competitive advantages. For instance, British Telecom is offering customers a fully switched integrated services digital network (ISDN) that combines voice, data, text, and video services into a single transmission line, and Danish telecommunications authorities are developing a common national videotex system (15). Europe's major food retailer, Sainsbury's, is in the process of integrating scanning systems into its stores (9). The competitive application of information technology has also had an impact on the international apparel industry. Three dimensional CAD is now being used for apparel styling. The system has the capability of quickly visualizing subtle changes in a photographed garment's color, pattern, proportions, and fabric texture and deriving basic parameters for patterning, grading, and marketing (5).

It is clear that firms everywhere are finding that information technology can be used as an effective competitive and strategic weapon in the international market place. This includes the awareness that it is imperative to use information technology and resources which can transcend organizational and national boundaries. Effective use of the technologies and resources requires that business information needs be addressed from a holistically systemic view. In this manner, management support for international business strategies and operations can be developed and implemented successfully.

2. MANAGEMENT SUPPORT SYSTEMS

Management support systems use information technologies to enhance management decision-making (18). This broad definition includes not only traditional data processing systems, but several other forms of information technology such as decision support systems (DSS), teleconferencing, electronic data bases, graphics, workstations, and methodological tools from the decision and management sciences (23). The classic information technologies utilized by management support systems include hardware, software, communications, and methodological tools.

Management support systems that are information technology-based include data support, DSS and executive support systems (ESS) (18). DSS support systems include database management systems (DBMS) and provide information regardless of use of user. Examples of data and information stored in or provided by data support systems include organizational performance, extra-organizational and competitive/industry, government, regulatory, economic, and other types of data. DSS can provide computer-based interactive problem solving support for a specific type of decision or a class of decisions. Examples of DSSs include brand management for marketing (17), portfolio management and capacity information (14), financial planning and budgeting (16), and capital investment decision support system (3). An ESS focused on a manager's or a group of managers' information and decision support needs across a range of managerial decision processes. A main distinction between DSSs and ESSs is that most of the latter are data retrieval-oriented whereas DSSs are model-oriented (23).

3. THE NEED FOR MSS IN MULTINATIONAL BUSINESS

International businesses need all three types of management support systems to ensure effective global strategy formulation and implementation. International business environments are characterized by complexity and uncertainty because of the diverse political, social, technological, economic, financial, market and competitive, and cultural features of the various countries in which a multinational firm conducts business. Consequently, data support systems must not only be developed to capture all feasible sources of information but also to provide the capability for quick and user friendly retrieval of information. Complexity and uncertainty are common features of the task environments that managers face in making international decisions. DSSs can provide computer-based interactive support that is essential for reducing complexities by providing data and model oriented systems, extend a manager's information processing and problem solving capabilities, and examine and plan for uncertainty through sensitivity analyses and 'what if' cases (1). ESSs are necessary in international businesses to support managers in making decisions that involve the implementation of globally oriented strategies and policies, as well as the integration of geographically dispersed organizational units to achieve organizational goals and objectives. The global strategic management process is well documented (4,6).

Data support systems, DSSs, and ESSs are especially crucial to the international managers for several reasons, such as:

1. Geographical dispersion of activities requires a high level of coordination and integration and modern communication technology provides a feasible means for meeting this need.

2. The difficulties in determining a viable organizational structure can be more easily met by use of management support systems that aid in the design of an organizational structure based on information processing (10). With the aid of management support systems, organizational structures can evolve and change in response to the needs of the organization.

3. Determining appropriate levels of differentiation (division of skills) and integration (synthesis of skills) for a global level organization can be enhanced by use of management support systems that provide guidance for selecting from alternate approaches in geographically dispersed organizational units and for determining the optimal or satisficing global organizational structures as integrating mechanisms.

4. Cultural, legal, economic, and political diversities dictate that consideration be given to the special conditions for information acquisition, processing, and dissemination.

5. High degrees of uncertainty in factors that are beyond a manager's control require sophisticated tools for impact evaluation, sensitivity and 'what if' analyses, and contingency planning. In these areas, DSSs and ESSs can make significant contributions to international managers as they are called on to make decisions in complex and uncertain environments.

4. MULTINATIONAL DATA SUPPORT SYSTEMS

To provide comprehensive management support for international business strategies and operations, data support systems must include DBMSs and capabilities to manipulate and retrieve information from the data bases. DBMSs must include online capabilities to retrieve a single item of information, to provide means for *ad hoc* analysis, and to provide prespecified aggregation of data in the form of reports. These capabilities must be easily accessible and readily available for use at all organizational levels and all geographic locations of the international corporation.

For international management, data support systems must contain or have access to internal, organizational data bases, as well as external, environmental data bases. Internal data bases must include data on all aspects of strategy and operations of the organization, including accounting information under different national accounting standards, market information, customer and supplier information, and production and component sourcing information with regard to all countries in which the firm operates or plans to operate. External, environmental data bases may either be contained within the corporate data bases if affordable, or be made available through contracted services. It may be economical to obtain publicly available information and have it entered into corporate data bases. It may, however, be better to contract for access to commercially maintained international data bases from firms specializing in such services. These firms provide not only the data bases, but also mechanisms for *ad hoc* data analysis and modelling. Table 1 summarizes the aspects of data support systems which are required for effective management support in international business strategies and operations.

5. MULTINATIONAL DECISION SUPPORT SYSTEMS

A DSS is an interactive, computer based system which utilizes decision rules and models, coupled with a comprehensive data base. It aids a decision maker in solving unstructured or semistructured problems, possesses interactive query facility, and utilizes user-friendly, man–machine interface and dialog languages. Furthermore, a DSS is designed for knowledge workers in an organization, providing the necessary support for individual, group, and organizational decisions which require strategic, operational, and intelligence information. With the data support systems providing the foundation, a DSS should include

TABLE 1   Data Support Systems for Multinational Business

Decision Components	Data Support Systems Applications
Strategic	
Export versus offshore investment	Economic, political, financial, cultural, operational factors
What form of investment, licensing, joint venture, wholly-owned subsidiary	Local and regional market sizes and growth opportunities
	Competition: local/global
What products are to be manufactured offshore	Production possibility and differentiation parameters
Managerial	
Organizing for operating overseas: integrated structure versus national responsiveness	Economies of scale due to integration across national boundaries
Financial policies and treasury operations	National policies for production content and ownership requirements
	National policies relative to financial parameters such as: —Price controls —Profit repatriation controls —Foreign exchange limitations
	Transfer pricing parameters for effective integration policies
Operational	
Marketing/sales	Market and sales forecasts
Production planning	Entity role and impact with respect to component sourcing
Component sourcing	

the capabilities to estimate the consequences of proposed decisions and to suggest one or more decisions required in a managerial decision making situation.

In international management, the capabilities of a DSS are certainly welcome, if not absolutely needed. Most international decision making situations are unstructured due to operation complexities, political, economic, and cultural differences among countries, and uncertain and unsettled market environments. A DSS based on a complete and comprehensive data support system is necessary to assess opportunities and threats in the international market place and to evaluate corresponding strategy and resource requirements.

TABLE 2   Decision Support Systems for Multinational Business

Decision Components	Data Support Systems Applications
Strategic	
What products are to be manufactured offshore	Offshore investment planning as part of the long range strategic planning or as required
When and where to make foreign investments	Modeling strategic options for international market entry or exit
What form of investment: licensing, joint venture, wholly-owned subsidiary	Sensitivity analysis to assess impact of environmental factors in the global markets
Managerial	
Organizing for operations overseas: integrated structure versus national responsiveness	Assessment of impacts of various organizational structures on overall profitability
Financial policies and treasury operations	A priori modeling of effects of national policies for proactive, and not reactive, strategy development
Operational	
Marketing/sales management	Modeling for marketing, production planning, and servicing strategies
Production planning/control	
Component sourcing	

For instance, a DSS can be extremely valuable in a comprehensive and structured evaluation for international investment planning decision (11). Similarly, a DSS can aid managers in dealing with uncertainty with respect to environmental factors, such as unsettling foreign exchange rates, different inflation rates in various countries, existing or anticipated price controls in different countries, profit repatriation controls, and threats of expropriation or expulsion by national governments. Table 2 summarizes the major aspects of DSSs which are necessary for effective management support in international business strategies and operations.

6. MULTINATIONAL EXECUTIVE SUPPORT SYSTEMS

ESSs typically focus on a manager's or a group of managers' information and decision support needs across a range of managerial decision processes. ESSs are more data-oriented than model-oriented. ESSs are concerned with broad organizational goals which may be conflicting. Since executives spend most of their time in communication and assimilation of information, an ESS should provide the capabilities for storing and scanning of written or orally-communicated information. In executive decision making, four types of scanning are utilized (8). *Passive scanning* occurs when the executives receive unsolicited information. *Reactive scanning* involves active search for solutions to specific problems. There are two types of *proactive scanning* modes: coincidental surveillance and routine monitoring. *Coincidental surveillance* involves the serendipitous surveillance of non-habitual information sources. *Routine monitoring* involves the systemic surveillance of habitual information sources. An ESS must provide for and support all modes of scanning. The environmental scanning information and organizational planning and operational data must be maintained and be easily accessible to managers to ensure proper data support and decision support in managerial decision making.

Managers concerned with global strategies and operations will particularly appreciate ESSs which enhance information scanning and *ad hoc* analysis to evaluate decision tasks. In multinational settings, managers are inundated with unsolicited information from many sources. While such information may certainly be important, an ESS can aid in retaining and organizing them for later access and use, thereby eliminating the need for immediate assimilation by managers. With the data support systems and the DSS as foundations, an ESS can provide the necessary problem-directed reactive scanning. International cash management, sourcing strategies, and country risk evaluations are illustrative of specific problems in international business strategies and operations which require reactive scanning by executives to search and seek specific solutions. The very nature of the international environment, characterized by complexities and uncertainties, requires that executives constantly monitor both the internal and the external environments. The internal environment of an organization must be monitored to continually assess the organizational strengths and weaknesses for serving worldwide markets. External environments, beyond the executives' control, must be monitored to evaluate opportunities and threats in the international markets. An ESS should provide the necessary proactive scanning capabilities such that executives can be armed with timely and effective strategic responses to gain from strengths, eliminate weaknesses, harvest opportunities, and alleviate ill effects from threats. Table 3 summarizes some of the aspects of executive support which are essential for comprehensive management support in international business strategies and operations.

7. CONCLUSION

It is imperative that multinational businesses integrate management support systems into their decision and control process to retain and enhance global competitive advantages. One of the many examples of this vital need is cited by the ". . .increasingly important role of technology as banks and investment houses seek global opportunities for competitive advantage. Using satellites and computers, a small group of them are wiring the world, linking once-isolated markets and changing those markets fundamentally in the scramble for an edge" (22). Current information technology enables an organization to develop data support systems, DSSs, and ESSs, and it also makes it possible to share these resources, when appropriate, for global competitive advantage, as illustrated by the TI case. Most of

TABLE 3   Executive Support Systems for Multinational Business

Decision Components	Executive Support Systems Applications
Strategic	
What products are to be manufactured offshore	Analysis of a specific country of interest
When and where to make foreign direct investments	Exception of information
	Comparative competitive data
What form of investment: licensing, joint venture, wholly-owned subsidiary	Comparative product market data
Managerial	
Organizing for operations overseas: integrated structure versus national responsiveness	Organizational performance by country/regions/global
	Competitive performance by product/geography
Financial policies and treasury operations	Customer profiles and detailed information on exceptions
	Supplier profiles and reports on exceptional suppliers
	Information on competition from potential new entrants and substitute products
Operational	
Marketing/sales management	Country information and company performance as needed for:
Production planning/control	Passive scanning
	Reactive scanning
Component sourcing	Proactive scanning
	Coincidental surveillance
	Routine monitoring

the required technological resources: DBMS, user-oriented modelling, office automation and work stations, networking, electronic mail, personal computers and end-user computing, teleconferencing and telecommunications, etc. are now available. The challenge for information systems professionals and managers alike is clear—develop and utilize management support systems for decision making and control of domestic and international marketing and operations. Businesses that have taken the lead in the use of information technologies in managing multinational business are already reaping strategic and competitive advantages. These are the firms that are most likely to be the hardy survivors in a global environment that is becoming increasingly competitive.

REFERENCES

1. Alter, S.L., *Decision Support Systems: Current Practice and Continuing Challenges*, Addison-Wesley, Reading, MA, 1980.

2. Barrett, S. and Konsynski, B. "Interorganizational Information Sharing Systems", *MIS Quarterly*, Special Issue, December 1982.

3. Cooper, D.O., Davidson, L.B. and Denison, W.K., "Tool for More Effective Financial Analysis", *Interface*, February 1975.

4. Davidson, W.H., *Global Strategic Management*, Ronal Press Publication, John Wiley, New York, 1982.

5. DiMaria, E., "High-Tech's 3D to Throw High-Fashion Curves", *MIS Week*, July, 1985.

6. Doz, Y., *Strategic Management in Multinational Companies*, Pergamon Press, New York, 1986.

7. Edelman, L., "ATT, British Telecom in Net Pack", *MIS Week*, July 31, 1985.

8. El Sawy, O.A., "Personal Information Systems for Strategic Scanning in Turbulent Environments: Can the CEO Go On-Line?", *MIS Quarterly*, Vol. 9, No. 1, March 1985.

9. Fallon, J., "ICL Beats IBM, Winning 28M POS System Pact", *MIS Week*, July, 1985.

10. Galbraith, J., *Organizational Design*, Addison-Wesley, Reading, MA, 1978.

11. Iyer, R., "An IFPS-Based Decision Support Process for International Investment Planning", *Proceedings of the 1985 National Conference of the IFPS Users Association*, 1985.

12. Ives, B. and Learmonth, G., "The Information System as a Competitive Weapon", *Communications of the ACM*, Vol. 27, No. 2, December 1984.

13. Jacobson, G., "Texas Instruments Unleashes System's Potential for Speed", *Dallas Morning News*, March 29, 1986.

14. Keen, P.G.W. and Scott-Morton, M.S., *Decision Support Systems: An Organizational Perspective*, Addison-Wesley, Reading, MA, 1978.

15. Kerrigan, M., "British Begin ISDN in 20-Firm Project", *MIS Week*, July, 1985.

16. Klaas, R.L., "A DSS for Airline Management", *Data Base*, Winter, 1971.

17. Little, J.D.C., "Models and Managers: The Concept of a Decision Calculus", *Management Science*, Vol 16. No. 8, April, 1970.

18. McFarlan, F.W. (Editor), *The Information Systems Research Challenges*, Harvard Business School Press, Boston, MA, 1985.

19. Notowidigdo, M.H., "Information Systems: Weapons to Gain the Competitive Edge", *Financial Executive*, Vol. 52, No. 2, February 1984.

20. Parsons, G.L., "Information Technology: A New Competitive Weapon", *Sloan Management Review*, Fall, 1983.

21. Porter, M.E., *Competitive Strategy*, The Free Press, New York, 1980.

22. Schmitt, R., "The Technology Gamble" in *A Special Report on Global Finance and Investing*, The Wall Street Journal, September 29, 1986.

23. Scott-Morton, M.S., "The State of the Art of Research", in McFarlan, F.W. (Ed.), *The Information Systems Research Challenges*, Harvard Business School Press, Boston, MA, 1985.

International Logistics Information Systems

PRABIR K. BAGCHI

WORLD TRADE has reached an all-time high. Experts worldwide believe companies, if they are to prosper, have to treat the whole world as their stage. In the 1980s, the world's financial systems became more open. Easier location of cheaper capital and supplies anywhere in the world helped spur the growth of global trade. The planned integration of Europe in 1992, the dismantling of the iron curtain, continued growth in the Far East, and the US-Canada free trade agreement pave the way for renewed vigor in international trade. In the recent past, worldwide exports and imports grew 8.0 per cent and GNP grew 3.2 percent(1). The spectacular growth of international trade is taking place both in international sourcing of raw materials, components and semi-finished assemblies, and in distribution of finished goods. In a recent survey of Fortune 500 multinational companies, 64 per cent reported that they source raw materials and 72 per cent said they source finished products from foreign sources(2). Domestic markets in developed countries no longer mean domestic competitors. Thus, in the coming decade, the continued existence of a company may depend on how successfully it can tap the global marketplace. Even today, there are leading edge companies who are sourcing their raw materials and components in one country, fabricating in a second country and assembling in another part of the world for global consumption. For example, Sony sources materials from various countries in the Far East, assembles finished products in Mexico, and sells these products in North America, Europe and other places.

OBJECTIVES

This study aims to achieve the following objectives:

1. Understand and analyze the logistics needs in the emerging global marketplace.

Bagchi, Prahir K. "International Logistics Information Systems." *International Journal of Physical Distribution and Logistics*, vol. 22, no. 9 (1992), 11–19.

2. Study with the aid of examples how leading edge global firms have been using information systems in logistics.

3. Uncover issues in international logistics information systems (ILIS) design and implementation.

4. Present a generic framework for an ILIS for a global company.

In order to understand the global marketplace, and the related logistical challenges, in the following section we examine its characteristics in general and the international logistics environment in particular.

INTERNATIONAL BUSINESS ENVIRONMENT

In the current marketplace, characterized by faster declining product life cycles, the winning strategy is to be quick to market. To succeed in this marketplace, successful companies will have to reduce significantly the time to market and they will have to emphasize efficient co-ordination of all business functions. This will require a congruence of manufacturing, marketing and logistics strategies and effective co-ordination between various units located in different countries. Product or process innovation cannot be a monopoly of the home country only. Global companies tap excellence in product and process innovation in any part of the world. These companies set up R&D centers in different parts of the world to benefit from the local talent. For example, Ford pioneered the concept of "world car" with the introduction of the Escort model. Each component for the model was produced at one location, utilizing the local expertise, and then distributed around the world to the assembly lines. At each market, the car was assembled considering the local tastes. Organizing integration of manufacturing and logistics in this manner helps companies drastically reduce product introduction cycle time. Success in this environment, however, involves efficiently managing international logistics.

International Logistics

International logistics is the process involved in managing uninterrupted flow of materials (e.g. raw materials, components and finished goods) for a firm from the source to the final destination independent of national boundaries.

Often this process includes materials movement across continents and thus has to face myriad rules and regulations of various governments, and the needs and constraints of various handling agencies involved. A number of authors have studied the global marketplace and have noted the following characteristics of international logistics(3,4).

International transport and distribution can be very different from domestic transportation and distribution. The host government policies, the modal rules and regulations in the host country, customs/trade policies equipment and, above all, the business practices may be radically different. For example, Coca Cola has 70 per cent of the Japanese market share for soft drinks. This has been possible because the company took time to understand the Japanese distribution practices and build up a fully dedicated route sales force. The company also used private trucking instead of depending on trucks of independent truckers and wholesalers, the usual practice in the home country(5). Furthermore, the operating procedure as to the following major areas in the international arena can be markedly different. First, documentation needed to process a transaction may be more complicated, may involve many more parties, may require much more data, and thus often requires an expert to complete the documentation formalities. Next, different currencies in various countries have to be taken into account. In addition, the hardware, e.g. rolling stock, railroad track, type and capacity of trucks, may be totally different. Partial or total monopoly of international freight forwarders in some markets adds another level of complexity and makes it imperative to have a good information system to aid in the co-ordination process(6).

Co-ordination

All the complications that we see in global logistics lead to the need for proactive co-ordination between different functions within and outside the firm for success in the marketplace. The conventional wisdom of concentration and export, as practiced by many multinational companies, is gradually giving way to geographically dispersed activities linked with each other in a very significant way. The linkages involve co-ordinating R&D activities, engaging in product design across continents, networking plants in different parts of the world, worldwide sourcing of raw materials, components and finished parts, distributing finished product all over the world and, above all, maintaining effective communication among employees of totally different cultures. Co-ordination of these interlinked complex activities is an essential ingredient for success in global business. Michael Porter, a noted authority on strategic management, has summarized the situation: "Today's game of global strategy seems increasingly to be a game of co-ordination—getting dispersed production facilities, R&D laboratories, and marketing activities to truly work together"(7,8).

Information Management

It has been shown by companies in global business that judicious use of information technology is essential for achieving close co-ordination between different functions located in widely dispersed geographies. Digital Equipment Corporation's "Notesfile" concept has helped employees in different parts of the world disseminate job-related experience and knowledge, for the benefit of fellow employees in other units and as a forum for solving job related problems by making expertise available within the company to all locations. Baxter Travenol's worldwide distribution centres are linked by an automated inventory control and purchasing system. Baxter can assure quick and reliable deliveries of pharmaceutical products, both those manufactured by Baxter and those from outside suppliers, to its hospital customers worldwide(1). The Limited, Inc., a leader in the time-sensitive fashion industry, uses an innovative information system which links its stores in various locations with the distribution centres and vendors to automatically arrange replenishment. This has helped the company achieve higher customer service levels and thus larger market share. Meanwhile, some global companies who had inefficient order-processing systems have realized the need for on-line order processing to achieve higher levels of customer service to gain and retain market share in today's global business. For example, Digital Equipment Corporation is developing an integrated on-line order-processing system to handle all incoming orders from any part of the world. This system is planned to have on-line link to the manufacturing resources planning system (MRP II) so as to enable the order processing clerk to make delivery commitments to the customer at the time of taking orders. Digital expects this system will drastically reduce the delivery time. As a result, the company will be able to commit more accurately the delivery date and track undelivered order status in spite of the fact that supplies will come from various units in various countries. Johnson and Johnson has spent eight years developing a similar order-processing system to handle all export order processing and documentation(1). Boeing is employing computer-aided design technology to jointly design components on-line with foreign suppliers(9). Successful companies in international business will be those who can identify tools like information systems, and exploit these in overcoming the structural barriers to gain competitive advantage.

Managing Interdependence

In today's complex global business environment with longer logistics channel, managers spend the greatest amount of time managing interdependence. Success or failure of one function casts a huge shadow on others. This interdependence is more critical in the international business. Purchasing managers in one country are dependent on the manufacturing engineers and logistics managers in another country for the receipt of right quality components at the right time. Also, there is significant interdependence between manufacturing, distribution and marketing functions. Standard manufacturing and distribution systems, like MRP II and DRP, do not sufficiently meet the interdependence needs in all manufacturing and logistics set-ups. To address the functional and locational interdependence issues in a business, authors have emphasized the need for integrated logistics strategy or enterprise logistics, the centerpiece of which is a management information system. An excellent discussion of "Enterprise Logistics" and the role played by an information system is provided by Wolfe(10).

Better Communication

Another formidable challenge in international business comes from distance and time differences. Effective coordination across continents demands efficient means of communication. Computer information systems networks help make physical distances less of a barrier. A major part of the negotiations among channel members can be done on-line if they can be connected in a computer network.

INTERNATIONAL LOGISTICS INFORMATION SYSTEM

The dramatic reduction in the cost of obtaining, processing, storing and transmitting information is changing the way we do business. More managers believe information technology, used judiciously, can enhance a firm's ability to be more competitive and profitable. In a global or a transnational economy, as defined by Bartlett and Ghosal(3,4), manufacturing and distribution are no longer carried out in a single location. This situation may become even more dominant after the planned integration of Europe in 1992. Companies desiring to do business in integrated Europe may have to undertake a sizeable portion of manufacturing in Europe. The so-called "screwdriver plants," engaged in assembling finished products from complete kits of parts and components imported from abroad, may no longer be considered European manufacturing organizations and may, in all probability, be subject to tariff and non-tariff barriers. For global firms, this may mean establishment of a much wider manufacturing and R&D base in the host country. A wider manufacturing and R&D base offers several rewards. It helps a firm achieve host-country-specific specialization. Also, this structure may provide the means to enjoy the fruits of creativity of the host country R&D all across the global firm by easier technology transfer. Moreover, global firms are better geared to face country-specific downturns in business. In a recent paper, Cohen and Lee(11) have shown that the development of global manufacturing and distribution sources has provided an American PC manufacturing firm with more flexibility and resilience. As a result, the firm has responded better in different business environments by adjusting sourcing, production and distribution plans. However, as discussed in the previous section, a much higher level of coordination is needed in the off-shore manufacturing and distribution facilities and their parent organizations in the home country as well as among the facilities in various countries. This is where an information system helps by providing an essential ingredient for close co-ordination.

Need for Systems Integration

In many firms, information systems development has been applications-driven. As a result, it is not unusual to find many applications-oriented software which do not share information with each other. For example, one American automobile manufacturer, which has a number of very useful applications software for various aspects of the logistics function, has instituted a program team for developing an integrated logistics information system. In many firms, much precious time is often spent in reconciling results obtained from different applications databases. Integrated systems based on a common database help alleviate these problems and are essential for managing international logistics among diverse people in far-flung areas. While it is conceded that such reconciliation poses as

FIGURE 1   Linkages in International Logistics Information Systems

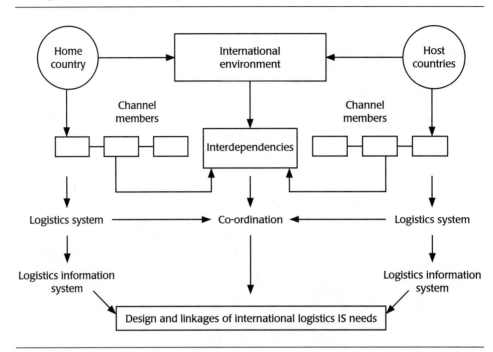

much of a problem in the domestic environment, in global logistics such reconciliation may be impossible to manage and should not be attempted. Information systems meant to handle the international logistics functions will clearly be more complicated as shown in the generic design in Figure 1.

From Figure 1, it is evident that an information system connects organizations with interdependent facilities in diverse locations and multiple channel members. These channel members in different countries will depend on the information systems to compete effectively in a global economy. It is expected that such an information system will provide necessary information to all channel partners in the home country and the host countries from a common database, thus eliminating the need for unproductive reconciliation of results. Unisys Corporation's "data transaction highway" concept attempts to accomplish many of the above-mentioned objectives. The goal of the "data transaction highway" at Unisys is to achieve worldwide integrated logistics management. The system connects all distribution channel partners which include: order and supply management specialists; manufacturing on-dock distribution points; integrated logistics centre operations both in the USA and Europe; and a worldwide trading company operation (12). The complexities involved in connecting diverse channel members across the globe point to the need for building an ILIS.

Globalization of Logistics Information

Designing an international logistics information system will also involve, at a minimum, the provision of a common database linked with all the country-specific information systems. This will enable users to obtain necessary information from the same source. The most crucial task in designing an international logistics information system to fit the present needs of global logistics is to overcome the country-specific dominant culture, while still respecting individual and national pride. The key to success in implementing an ILIS is in its ability to be flexible to the needs of the evolving marketplace, as has been demonstrated by the successful implementation of the "data transaction gateway" system at Unisys(12). The data transaction highway concept is similar to the common database concept described above. Individual applications access the data transaction highway to retrieve and store required data.

Managing Human Resources

Another important problem in developing an ILIS consists of understanding the similarities and dissimilarities in business modes and norms, and yet respecting each other's views in finding a common ground. The human aspects of the problem are as important as the technological aspects. Thus the common modules of the global logistics information systems must be designed to accommodate local add-ons to provide local responsiveness. The add-ons might reflect the differences in marketing and distribution strategies, local rules and regulations, local currency, or variations in local hardware and software features.

Planning an ILIS

Logistics is a transaction-intensive set of functions. Keeping records of the physical activities of logistics, e.g. units received, stored, shipped, source, destination, etc., requires extensive computer data-processing capability. How can we best capture and utilize this transaction-based information? The answer largely depends on how we plan the logistics structure and design the information system. This in turn will depend on what its business objectives and strategies are. Any activity that touches multiple functions will have to draw its relevance from the business objectives and be supported by top management in order to be useful. An international logistics information system (ILIS) falls in that category. If a firm's global strategy is to manufacture in one location and market in multiple countries, then clearly it can manage with a simpler ILIS with most of the applications and the central database located in the home country, with modest links to the host countries. On the other hand, if the firm's strategy is to adopt a totally decentralized manufacturing and logistics strategy, a more distributed ILIS architecture with a common database will be necessary. Additionally, with a decentralized logistics strategy, if the firm decides to manage the channel function with its wholly-owned subsidiary, the complexity of the ILIS may be significantly less. Use of same software standards, common data definitions, identical applications and hardware will make the design of an ILIS architecture a lot easier.

Before Union Pacific could design their logistics information control system (LINCS), it had to specify a standard set of codes for identifying shipments on any of its trains. It had to have a shipping network in place, with formal rules for initiating, transporting and delivering shipments(13). The point to remember here is that an ILIS will not by itself correct problems or lead to the solutions, rather it can be useful only when a proper structure is in place. The design of an ILIS should, therefore, be based on global logistics strategy. For a firm following a multinational strategy operating its foreign subsidiaries nearly autonomously or in a loose federation so as to respond quickly to local needs, the ILIS may not need a very high level of integration. On the other hand, for a global firm which closely co-ordinates its worldwide activities through central control from headquarters, the ILIS will require a very high degree of integration. The firm following a transnational strategy(3,4) seeking to retain local flexibility, while at the same time trying to achieve global integration will require a core database and a core system common to all its subsidiaries. Yet such a firm will allow add-ons to its ILIS to reflect local needs.

Complexities of an ILIS

Figure 2 demonstrates the nature and complexity of an ILIS of a truly global company. It shows the relation between the level of integration of an ILIS and the stages of global business. The level of integration and complexity of an ILIS can vary based on the nature of the company. In the early stages when a company's global business strategy is to produce in the home country and export, level of integration of an ILIS may be less than for a truly global company. As global business progresses to a joint venture and finally to truly global manufacturing, the level of integration of the ILIS increases as would be evident in Figure 2. An excellent description of the prevalent conditions at Unisys, a global company, leading to the development and implementation of the "data transaction gateway" system bears testimony to the relation between the degree of interdependence of the channel members and thus the complexity and level of integration of the ILIS(12).

CONCEPTUAL MODEL OF AN ILIS

The design of an ILIS should be preceded by a well developed statement of business, technology and organization strategies. It must be understood that an ILIS can be effective only when it is derived from the business strategy and has active participation from the top management. The strategic alignment, as it is often called, keeps the focus on track. The strategic triangle shown in Figure 3 demonstrates a sample alignment between business, organization and information systems.

ILIS Modules

The starting point of an ILIS (International Logistics Information System) can be traced to a generic information system. It must satisfy the requisites of an efficient information

FIGURE 2   Integration of ILIS in Global Business

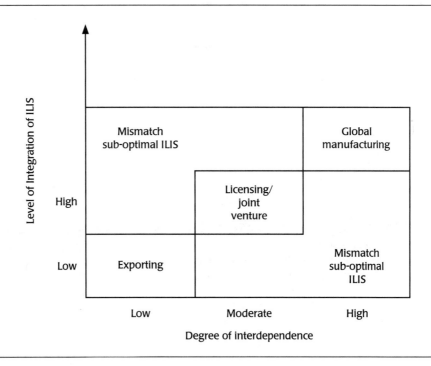

system. Turban(14) defines a management information system as "a formal, computer-based system to provide timely information necessary for managerial decision making." Based on this definition, an ILIS will have to provide timely information for the following broad areas:

1. *The order processing module.* This module is the organization's interface with the customer. The order processing module, along with the forecasting submodule, drives the downstream modules, e.g. MRP II, DRP. Direct customer interface with this module is a desirable attribute.

2. *The production and inventory control module.* This module takes care of production planning, inventory control, scheduling and controlling of the shop floor. Typically, plants running on MRP II system will have many of these functions included in MRP II. Forecasting would be a part of this module. Forecasts and orders from the order processing module will provide the basis for the production plan.

3. *The physical supply or procurement module.* This module will be concerned with material procurement from domestic and foreign sources. The physical supply system will be closely tied to the MRP II (Manufacturing Resources Planning) system or any

FIGURE 3   The Strategic Alignment

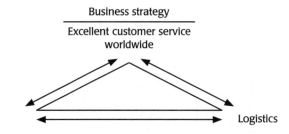

Business strategy

Excellent customer service
worldwide

Logistics

IS strategy

— New technology
— Education and training for all channel
  members
— Emphasize value added vendors across the
  logistics channels
— Higher non-traditional skills requirement
— User involvement in ILIS development
— Respect local practices/tastes in system
  design development, and testing
— Common data definition

Organizational strategy

— Participation and involvement
— Win-win co-operation among channel
  members
— Long term vendor relation
— Total quality management
— Channel member involvement in
  product/service design
— Decentralized control
— Considerate management
— Think globally, act locally

Adapted from Bagchi, Prabir K. "International Logistics Information Systems," *International Journal of Physical Distribution and Logistics.*

other similar system used to drive the manufacturing activities in both the home country and the host countries. Vendor and carrier selection and performance monitoring will be included in this module.

4. *Distribution requirement planning (DRP) module.* The function of this module is to schedule and keep track of deliveries to customers and control inventories at the warehouses. Each host country will have separate DRP system module with appropriate data sharing taking place through the common database. The concept of using a common database through which all logistics operations are processed has been amply demonstrated in the Unisys "data transaction highway" system reported in the literature(12).

It is interesting to note (in Figure 4) that all four modules share the same database and thus the data definitions are standardized. Although processing frequency and data detailing may be different for the above planning and operating systems, at an aggregate level these systems share the same data sources. In other words, all these modules speak the same language. By appropriate selection and with proper security clearance (to maintain

FIGURE 4   International Logistics IS Structure

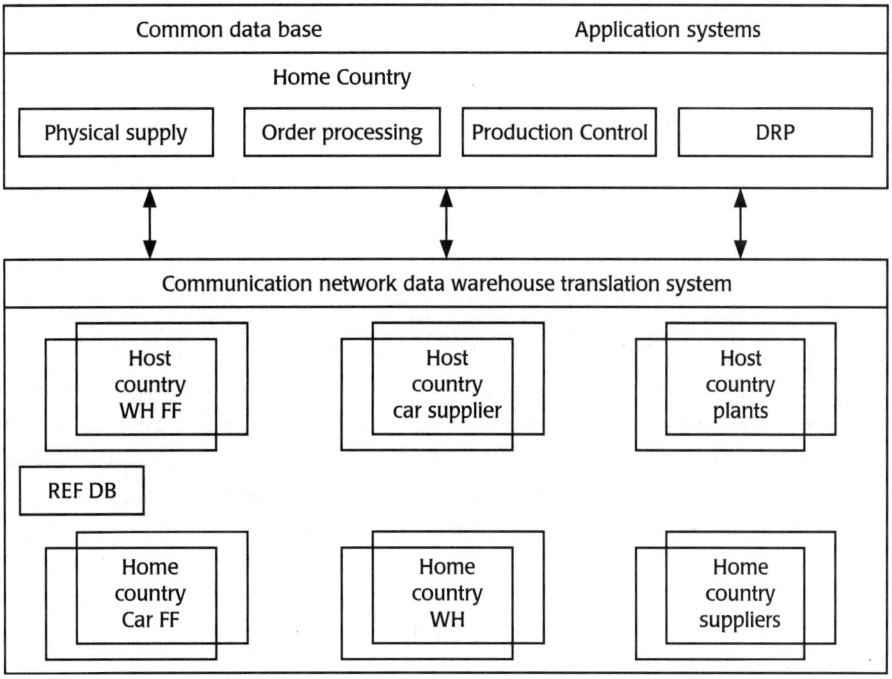

```
┌─────────────────────────────────────────────────────────────────────┐
│        Common data base                    Application systems        │
│ ┌───────────────────────────────────────────────────────────────────┐ │
│ │                        Home Country                                 │ │
│ │ ┌──────────────┐ ┌────────────────┐ ┌──────────────────┐ ┌───────┐ │ │
│ │ │Physical supply│ │Order processing│ │Production Control│ │  DRP  │ │ │
│ │ └──────────────┘ └────────────────┘ └──────────────────┘ └───────┘ │ │
│ └───────────────────────────────────────────────────────────────────┘ │
└─────────────────────────────────────────────────────────────────────┘
        ↕                       ↑                        ↕
┌─────────────────────────────────────────────────────────────────────┐
│      Communication network data warehouse translation system         │
│  ┌──────────┐       ┌──────────┐        ┌──────────┐                  │
│  │   Host   │       │   Host   │        │   Host   │                  │
│  │  country │       │  country │        │  country │                  │
│  │  WH FF   │       │car supplier│      │  plants  │                  │
│  └──────────┘       └──────────┘        └──────────┘                  │
│ ┌────────┐                                                            │
│ │ REF DB │                                                            │
│ └────────┘                                                            │
│  ┌──────────┐       ┌──────────┐        ┌──────────┐                  │
│  │   Home   │       │   Home   │        │   Home   │                  │
│  │  country │       │  country │        │  country │                  │
│  │  Car FF  │       │    WH    │        │ suppliers│                  │
│  └──────────┘       └──────────┘        └──────────┘                  │
└─────────────────────────────────────────────────────────────────────┘
```

data integrity, one should be able to access and retrieve data pertaining to any host country for any business needs.

Logistics Data Warehouse

The cluster of the above four modules are connected by means of a communication system with a data warehouse. The data warehouse can be thought of as a storage of data originating with vendors, carriers, freight forwarders and other channel members. An organization doing business in many countries may have country-specific data warehouses. Similarly, there will be a home country data warehouse which will capture all pertinent data from the home country carriers, freight forwarders, warehouses, etc. These data warehouses will have links with each other. It would be worthwhile to point out that a data warehouse is designed to be a repository of up-to-date data pertaining to certain parts of the business. A data warehouse, by design, is not meant to contain live transaction-specific data. Thus it serves as a data resource library for a decision support system. Apart from the above modules, the following stand-alone systems (external to the ILIS) from home and the host countries may feed data to the data warehouse:

- warehouse information system;
- carrier information system;
- freight forwarder information system;
- supplier information system;
- offshore plant or subsidiary information system.

The data warehouse would also contain a reference database which will be, among many other useful applications, a resource for locating future vendors and carriers, both domestic and foreign, and other channel members in the selection process. The reference database will contain all pertinent information about the raw material and other parts and components sources and other logistics channel members, their expertise, a history of past experiences with these channel members, the country of operation and other relevant information relating to price, delivery terms, etc. This read-only resource will be available to the people concerned throughout the company in all countries for future reference. This makes the future source development process easier. For example if a part number has once been procured from a country, next time this information is available to all future buyers across the organization in all countries. Thus, the buyers do not have to start from the very beginning. All existing and/or past part numbers will be included in the reference database. For obsolete parts, there will be a periodic audit to decide about future retention of these parts in the database.

Integrating Channel Partners

The systems external to the home country information systems may use different data definitions and thus data available in the data warehouse may have to be translated or normalized to some standard data definitions before they can be used by the application systems in the domestic environment. It is very likely that some partners in the logistics channel may not be as computerized as others. In such circumstances, some manual intervention may be required to capture the information generated at source and input into the data warehouse either through local presence or through the help of the foreign agent/ freight forwarder. It is easier to link channel partners using common standard. This is one more reason why selection of the channel partners is important. This is not to suggest that the use of common information technology standards will be the dominant factor in logistics channel member selection process, but considerable time and effort should be given to this. The success of a firm in the global business hinges very much on the fit between the firm and its channel partners. According to Porter's (7) value chain theory, suppliers and other channel partners provide an essential linkage in the value chain. A company can create a competitive advantage in global logistics by optimizing or co-ordinating these links. An ILIS can tie the channel members closely because of the substantial investment in systems development and the associated training needs. Such a close and costly linkage often provides a disincentive to leave the channel. This is true of all the channel partners. Switching partners in an integrated logistics channel can be very expensive due to disruption in work in the interim and the cost of retraining. Compatible information systems or, at the very least, the desire of the vendor to co-operate with the global firm, may be considered an asset in the selection process.

Essentials of an ILIS

In order to be effective, an ILIS should have a few essential features. The following list provides some of these features:

1. *Order processing system* capable of providing price, delivery terms and delivery lead time during order taking through on-line retrieval process. This will require this system being tied to the production and inventory module and that delivery lead times for all products are known to the system. As an order is committed, the quantity so allocated is deducted from the balance and thus is not available for future orders.

2. *Reference database* which lists details of sources of raw materials, components, and sub-assemblies or finished items procured in all countries and the associated terms. It would also provide similar pertinent information about other channel members, e.g. carriers, freight forwarders, etc. In essence, accessing the reference database would be the first step for buyers and traffic managers in vendor and carrier selection process.

3. *Tracing system* which will be capable of tracing materials on-line anywhere in the supply chain. Such systems are already available in some countries. In the USA, for example, Federal Express, Roadway Express, PIE Nationwide, and a few other companies in the transportation industry, already offer such services either through enquiries on computer terminals or voice activated shipment tracing service throughout the continental USA. One such tracking system uses a two-way satellite communications link between senders and receivers(15).

4. *Interfaces with manufacturing and marketing* to provide accurate delivery outlook to customers. Such interfaces may be provided via an on-line interface to the firm's manufacturing and marketing information systems or by virtue of application-to-application interface using electronic data interchange (AD). For example, if a supplier in the Far East makes a delivery for a plant in the USA the information may be instantly fed to the manufacturing system in the plant, and necessary arrangements for customs clearance at the port and subsequent shipment to the plant may be organized efficiently.

5. *Decision support systems* (DSS) to select the lowest cost procurement and distribution channel or to implement other operations research applications. Some of the other capabilities of DSS may include: distribution modeling, inbound and out-bound freight consolidation modeling, statistical process control, vehicle routing

and scheduling, multicriteria carrier and/or vendor selection modeling, etc. A common database will be essential to have these features available throughout the firm.

6. *Ability to prepare order status reports* or any performance measurement reports on demand. The performance reports will help the firm in channel member selection/audit procedures.

7. *Extension of the system* may be offered to foreign vendors and agents via the network. This will provide a closely knit channel and thus provide an entry/exit barrier.

8. *Standard forms in host country specified format* to help with documentation in each country. This should be constantly updated as and when standards and/or requirements change in a country.

9. *A database containing the current currency exchange rates*. This database has to be always kept up to date. This feature will enable the firm to evaluate the effects of currency fluctuations on sourcing, manufacturing and marketing decisions.

10. The ILIS should incorporate *means to measure efficiency and effectiveness*. Common measures such as inventory turns, return on assets, operating ratio, on-line performance, etc. should be easily obtained from the information system. Other country-specific performance measures or any other specialized measures should be obtainable via end-user computing facilities.

Need for Close Co-operation

As we can see, a successful implementation of an ILIS presupposes close co-ordination between the channel members. This will also mean substantial initial investment by all the channel members. A long-term agreement of co-operation between the channel members and a favorable disposition towards placing long-term orders may be necessary to make this happen. In some cases such close partnership may mean sole source relationship with vendors and carriers. The following areas of close co-operation among the channel members may be needed:

1. The host country supplier and the home country manufacturer may have to enter into a long-term agreement of close working relationship. Such agreements may often culminate in long-term purchase orders. Single sourcing may be desirable to affirm the commitment. Price negotiations have to be based on a clear determination of the cost of production.

2. The channel members may have to agree on the mode, carrier and freight forwarder or agent to be used in the supply channel. With long supply lines and little or no buffers to work with, it is very important to ensure that channel members are able and willing to provide desirable service with high degree of reliability.

3. Similarly, the manufacturer and the distributor have to agree on the mode, carrier and freight forwarder or agent to ensure efficient distribution.

4. It is important for all channel members to have compatible computer systems for easier communication. It is very likely that these systems will not be identical. However, it is absolutely essential that each channel member can communicate with the other members electronically. Translation systems may be necessary to provide the interface needed between the different systems. Also, it is essential to have these systems up and working around the clock.

ISSUES IN ILIS DEVELOPMENT

Keen(16) contends that ". . . the telecommunication architecture is generally the strategic driver for evolving a truly international capability." He recommends that management should fund the backbone global communications network as a "corporate business asset, rather than allowing local case-by-case, cost-based decisions about communications facilities." However, he warns that information systems developers must be careful about seeking international standards because some countries, notably Japan, Germany, Brazil and France, have used information policy to protect their national concerns.

Variations in the available hardware and software features force firms to use different vendor products in different countries. This poses major problems in integrating communication networks, hardware and disparate systems software for global applications. Vendors' protectionist policies for their products are cited as the major barrier for agreement on standards(17). In the area of electronic data interchange (EDI), standards like EDIFACT are being developed under the auspices of the United Nations with co-operation from ANSI.

The international flow of data has received attention in the literature and much of this has been focused on the issues of data privacy and transborder data flows (TDF). TDFs have been defined as "movements of machine-readable data for processing, storage, or retrieval across national boundaries." TDF laws limit transfer of personal data that pertain to credit records, travel reservations or employment records, although some countries also restrict transfer of technical and scientific data.

An ILIS must be developed for and operate in a multicultural heterogeneous environment. Business practices, rules and regulations are different in various countries. Cross-cultural information systems research has found major disparities that call for attention in developing global information systems applications(18). Research on decision support systems has shown sensitivity of information systems features to cultural norms in a country(19).

IMPLEMENTATION AND SUMMARY

In this article, some insights to the needs and related issues of an ILIS have been provided. Based on the global business environment and the strategic justification of an ILIS, this

TABLE I Phased Implementation Process of ILIS

Key ingredients	Phase I Generate the context for ILIS	Phase II Designing an ILIS	Phase III ILIS implementation and support
Alignment	Strategic alignment of business, organization channel members and technology objectives	System design aligned with strategy and vision	Operation aligned with strategic vision; plan for revision aligned with changes in strategy
Commitment	Top management participation and commitment; channel member/ stakeholder ownership of ILIS development process; user participation in ILIS development	System designed to encourage user involvement and channel member ownership	System design involving users and channel members in planning and assessment; draw up action plan for support with input from users
Competence/ Mastery	Promote competence in ILIS by encouraging and institutionalizing learning among users and channel members	System designed to promote learning; involve users and channel members in experimentation with beta version	Manage implementation of ILIS by promoting user/channel member involvement and assumption of leadership in the introduction process; maintain system with a high level of up-time

article has sought to offer a generic structure for designing an ILIS and to present a number of issues related to ILIS development. Given this background and a firm's strengths and weaknesses in the marketplace, special features can be incorporated in the ILIS to give the firm a competitive weapon for success in the global business. The type of communication desirable in an ILIS may be obtained using electronic data interchange (EDI) technique. An excellent example of an ILIS is the "data transaction highway" system recently developed and implemented at Unisys(12).

The successful implementation of an ILIS depends largely on: (1) a focused direction including a strategic alignment of business, information technology and organizational objectives; (2) top management participation and commitment; (3) stakeholder support and ownership; (4) willing user participation; and (5) strong technical competence and leadership(20). These key ingredients play a major role in a phased implementation method shown in Table I.

It is not clear, however, how easy it would be to develop such massive systems which will tie all the channel members in multiple countries and thus necessitate common data definitions and/or some kind of translation software. For a firm adopting a global strategy where rapid deployment of operating strategy across the organization is the prime mover, or a transnational firm which seeks to retain local flexibility while simultaneously achieving global integration, EDI offers the promise to provide the means to share data across borders on-line. It is unclear as to how funding to develop such global systems can be justified given the short-term fiscal emphasis of our corporations. Justifying such large systems, the benefits of which will be realized in future in multiple countries—and that too may not always be tangible in dollar terms—would be a real challenge to the logistics managers. They will have to quantify some very qualitative factors and project various scenarios clarifying how an organization or its competitors will behave whether or not the required investment in ILIS is made. User involvement across borders will become the most important element in obtaining support for such systems. The logistics managers will have to drive home the point that "soft" considerations merit as much attention as the hard ones in dollar terms. It is to be brought home to top management that global information systems like ILIS deserve to be treated as a corporate business asset rather than merely a logistics tool.

REFERENCES

1. Kearney, A.T., *International Logistics: Battleground of the 1990s*, Chicago, 1987.
2. Temple, Barker & Sloane, Inc., *International Logistics—Meeting the Challenges of Global Distribution Channels*, April 1987, Lexington, MA.
3. Bartlett, C.A. and Ghoshal, S., "Managing across Borders: New Strategic Requirements," *Sloan Management Review*, Fall 1987, pp. 7–17.
4. Bartlett, C.A. and Ghoshal, S., "Managing across Borders: New Organizational Responses," *Sloan Management Review*, Fall 1987, pp. 43–53.
5. Ohmae, K., "Managing in a Borderless World," *Harvard Business Review*, May-June 1989, pp. 152–7.
6. Davies, G.J., "The International Logistics Concept," *International Journal of Physical Distribution and Materials Management*, Vol. 17 No. 2, 1987, pp. 20–27.
7. Porter, M.E., *Competition in Global Business*, Harvard University Press, Boston, MA, 1986.
8. Porter, M.E. and Millar, V., "How Information Gives You Competitive Advantage," *Harvard Business Review*, July-August, 1985, pp. 149–60.
9. Rockart, J.F. and Short, J.E., "IT in the 1990s: Managing Organizational Interdependence," *Sloan Management Review*, Winter 1989, pp. 7–17.
10. Wolfe, J.R., "Enterprise Logistics: The Right Tool for the Job," *International Journal of Logistics Management*, Vol. 1 No. 2, 1990, pp. 41–6.
11. Cohen, M.A. and Lee, H.L., "Resource Deployment Analysis of Global Manufacturing and Distribution Networks," *Journal of Manufacturing and Operations Management*, Vol. 2 No. 2, 1989, pp. 81–104.
12. Clayton, B.R., Hart, T.R. and Fairclough, A.W., "Global Logistics Management: A Data Transaction Highway," *Annual Conference Proceedings, Council of Logistics Management*, Vol. 1, 1989, pp. 357–73.
13. Laudon, K.C. and Laudon, J.P., *Management Information Systems—A Contemporary Perspective*, 2nd ed., Macmillan, New York, 1991, pp. 33–5.
14. Turban, E., *Decision Support and Expert Systems*, Macmillan, New York, 1988.
15. MacDonald, M.E., "Satellite Tracking Has Trucking Industry Beaming," *Traffic Management*, July 1989, pp. 38–43.

16. Keen, P.G.W., "An International Perspective on Managing Information Technologies," *An ICIT Briefing Paper, International Center for Information Technologies*, Washington, DC, 1987.

17. Cash, J.I., McFarlan, F.W. and McKenney, J.L., *Corporate Information Systems Management: The Issues Facing Senior Executives*, Irwin, Homewood, IL, 1988.

18. Dagwell, R. and Weber, R., "System Designers' User Models: A Comparative Study and Methodological Critique," *Communications of the ACM*, Vol. 26 No. ll, November 1983, pp. 987–97.

19. Ho, T.H., Raman, K.S. and Watson, R.T., "Group Decision Support Systems: The Cultural Factor," *Proceedings of Tenth International Conference on Information Systems*, Boston, MA, December 1989, pp. 119–29.

20. Walton, R.E., *Up and Running*, Harvard Business School Press, Boston, MA, 1989.

FURTHER READING

Galbraith, J., *Organization Design*, Addison-Wesley, Reading, MA, 1977.

Mintzberg, H., *The Structuring of Organizations*, Prentice-Hall, Englewood Cliffs, NJ, 1979.

Electronic Data Interchange—
A Global Perspective

ROBERT ROSENBERG & STEVE VALIANT

THE MERGER OF TELECOMMUNICATION and computer technologies and the globalization of competition have created a favorable climate for the utilization of enhanced network services. The stakeholders have recognized the advantage of one enhanced service, Electronic Data Interchange (EDI), as both a revenue opportunity and a valuable service. EDI solves business problems while delivering a competitive advantage in the marketplace.

Global business competition has created the need to coordinate standards efforts in the US and with its trading partners abroad. The format standard used in international EDI is EDIFACT (EDI for administration, commerce, and transport). According to the EDIFACT Board, "Electronic Data Interchange (EDI) is the electronic transmission from computer to computer of commercial or administrative transactions, using an agreed standard to structure the transaction of message data."

In less stilted prose, EDI is a means for one corporation to send business data from its computer to another corporation's computer, from buyer to seller, ensuring the exchange of business data without computer system modifications. The data are transmitted over voice or data lines in a standard, public format. A value added network (VAN), EDI permits the transmission of specially formatted documents (i.e., purchase orders, price quotes, invoices, and shipping advice) more accurately and at less cost than traditional methods of business communications, such as mail, telephone, or telex. It translates data from format to format and provides message storage and retrieval functions. EDI has been positioned to become the standard for exchanging business documents because it improves the cost structure of three business basics: order entry, transaction and payment.

EDI, however, is doing more than just business-to-business communications; it is, above all, situated to change the way businesses operate. A recent study conducted by EDI Research Inc. found that 79 percent of document exchange between businesses in the US was in the form of paper transmission; 15 percent of the communications were exchanged

Rosenberg, Robert, and Valiant, Steve. "Electronic Data Interchange—A Global Perspective." *Telecommunications* (July 1992), 50–53.

verbally, while 4 percent were exchanged through either facsimile transmission or through E-mail networks. The remaining 2 percent of business documentation were EDI transmissions. Despite the small percentage of business documents currently exchanged through EDI, however, its use is expected to grow rapidly.

The EDI market in the Eurodata Foundation countries (the 18 Western European PTTs) will grow from $160 million per year in 1991 to nearly $2010 million by 2000—a compounded annual growth rate of 37 percent per year. The reason for this rapid growth is simple: EDI is a rarity in information technology, offering both cost savings and strategic benefits to its users. Payback on an initial investment of two to four years is typical—through reduced labor costs, stock levels, cash requirements, and telephone and postage bills. At the same time, EDI's speed of response offers a competitive advantage by enabling a company to respond more quickly to market trends, by shortening delivery times, and by offering a wider range of goods for the same stockholding cost.

LIMITING FACTORS

At the same time, however, EDI will not replace hardcopy documents entirely. Many firms are just too small to justify an initial EDI investment. Also, a small company faces special problems when implementing EDI. Often it is forced to implement EDI by a large customer that refuses to trade except via EDI. The small company must then buy a PC (frequently for the first time) and use it for order entry to respond to purchase orders, and as a display for incoming EDI messages, which it can then incorporate into its manual procedures. For such a company, EDI increases the number of manual processes rather than reducing them. As would be expected, our research suggests that there is resistance to EDI from such companies. If use of EDI is to continue growing at its current rate of 40 to 70 percent per year through the mid-1990s, this resistance must be overcome.

Possible measures that EDI-community builders can take to overcome the resistance include: offering free or low-price software to small companies; stressing the benefits that EDI brings to small suppliers through faster payment for provided goods and services; and developing (with relevant suppliers) integrated accounts packages and EDI software for PCs, which small companies can use to realize the real benefits of EDI.

Generally speaking, EDI is often viewed as simply a way of replacing paper documents with electronic documents—replacing traditional methods of transmission. This is only half the story; above all, EDI is a way to replace manual data entry with electronic data entry. The purpose of EDI is not only to eliminate paper, but also to eliminate processing delays and data re-entry.

Major service providers in the EDI market are the clearing houses. They all offer a store-and-retrieve (and sometimes a store-and-forward) file or message transfer service that the subscriber can access using a range of communications protocols (i.e., X.25, SDLC, BSC) and networks (i.e., public data networks, leased lines, the PSTN). The typical service also offers document validation, document conversion between message standards and

FIGURE 1   The EDI process

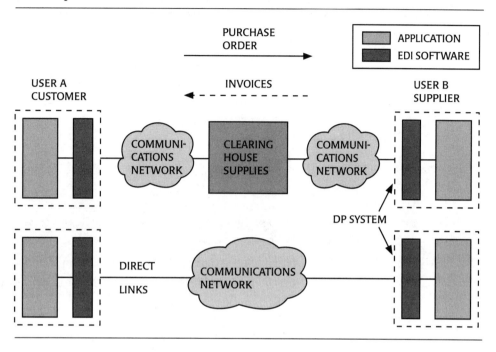

client reports. Also tendered are various security functions and data management facilities to manipulate messages, address lists, and passwords stored at the clearing house.

Typical fees charged by clearing houses are a joining fee, a monthly charge, and a usage charge. Joining fees vary from $40 for simple registration (GEIS) to $6000 for registration, training, software installation, and some consultancy. Monthly charges range from $25 per month (Transpac) to $120 (INS). Some companies charge subscription fees; others have minimum monthly usage charges. Usage charges also vary considerably. Some companies charge a fixed fee ($200 to $400 per month); others charge $0.30 to $0.50 per message; and some charge $0.20 to $0.30 per message, plus $0.10 to $0.20 per thousand characters. Several service providers offer significant volume discounts up to 70 percent.

Figure 1 illustrates how EDI works in practice. The local computer-accounts system of Company A, the customer, generates a purchase order. Instead of printing out the purchase order and mailing it to the supplier (Company B), Company A processes the output from the accounts system through EDI software. This translates the purchase order into a standard message format and syntax agreed upon by the trading partners. If a direct link has been established, the message is then delivered—as a file transfer—to Company B's data processing (DP) system.

The more usual procedure would be for Company A to use an EDI clearing-house service. Here, Company A sends its message to the clearing house, where it will wait for retrieval by Company B. On arrival at Company B, the standard message containing the purchase order information is translated into Company B's internal format for processing by its DP system.

To summarize, data are moved electronically, without additional human interpretation, or rekeying, between the sender's application program and the receiver's application program. With EDI fully integrated with application programs, not only does data flow electronically between trading partners without the need for rekeying, the data also flow electronically between internal applications of each trading partner.

As Figure 1 illustrates, a company needs four components in order for EDI to work:

- A local application that generates and receives data. Companies that do not use computers locally for administration and commercial transactions cannot really benefit from EDI.

- EDI software to translate messages from local application formats into standard EDI message formats, to manage the EDI messages and the addresses to which they are sent, and to provide the communications protocols with which to access the network.

- A hardware platform on which to run the EDI software. Often the software runs on the same mainframe or mini as the local DP application generating the data. But more frequently, companies use PCs to run the EDI software, especially in the pilot phase of an EDI implementation. The PC is located between the network and the main DP system.

- Access, via a communications network, to an EDI clearing-house service. The clearing house will typically support a variety of network access protocols (e.g., X.25, SDLC) and EDI message standards (e.g., EDIFACT, ANSI X.12, Tradacoms) and provide central data management and security facilities. Most companies now use such services. There are, however, still some companies, notably in Germany, that use direct communications links to their trading partners for transferal of the transaction message.

APPLICATION TYPES

The bulk of EDI involves exchange of trade data. Two main types of application: direct trading and trading support can be distinguished.

- Direct trading applications are used in the basic commercial relationship of buying and selling. The bulk of current EDI falls into this category. Ordering is the major trading application, followed by invoicing. The message exchanges involved in these two trading applications are illustrated in Figure 2.

- Trading support expands the benefits of EDI to other parts of the trading process, such as payment for goods or services, delivery of goods, or customs clearance of goods. These applications typically involve intermediaries, such as banks, transport companies, or government departments, as well as the trading partners themselves. This involvement increases the complexity of the EDI community and brings increased pressure for international standards. Also, these trading-support applications are usually

FIGURE 2   Direct trading applications

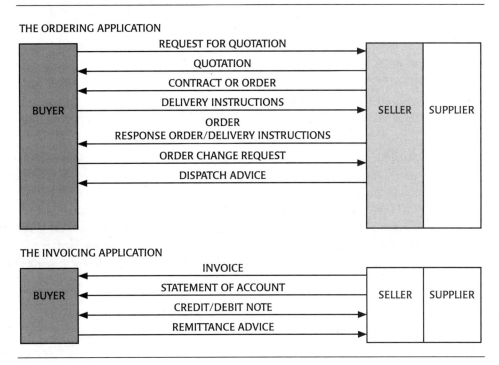

THE ORDERING APPLICATION

BUYER

REQUEST FOR QUOTATION
QUOTATION
CONTRACT OR ORDER
DELIVERY INSTRUCTIONS
ORDER
RESPONSE ORDER/DELIVERY INSTRUCTIONS
ORDER CHANGE REQUEST
DISPATCH ADVICE

SELLER   SUPPLIER

THE INVOICING APPLICATION

BUYER

INVOICE
STATEMENT OF ACCOUNT
CREDIT/DEBIT NOTE
REMITTANCE ADVICE

SELLER   SUPPLIER

implemented after the direct trading applications. In general, companies start with direct trading, appreciate the benefits these applications bring, and then look for further applications of EDI. In consequence, only a small proportion of today's EDI traffic (mainly involved in delivery of goods) can be classified as solely direct trading.

Given the cost, complexity, and processing delay of the hardcopy transaction process, EDI benefits to corporate users can be substantial; the larger the enterprise, the greater the potential benefits. A recent study of 1094 respondents from private sector US firms confirms that cost savings and delay reductions are the primary reasons for EDI implementation. A recent survey of UK-based companies shows that 50 percent have implemented EDI because they expect to gain operational benefits (i.e., cost reductions); 30 percent, in response to pressure from trading partners; and 20 percent implement EDI for strategic reasons—expecting to maintain or improve their competitive positions and market shares.

THE PROBLEMS OF EDI

As well as revealing significant benefits from EDI, our case studies of users also highlight a number of problems:

- Reluctance. Trading partners are reluctant or refuse to participate in an EDI community. Senior management in these companies may lack commitment to the idea; or, the company may have difficulty in fitting EDI software into an already substantial applications backlog. The EDI-community builder must be prepared to involve its own senior management in the program and offer cheap EDI software, if it is to overcome these problems.

- Quality. The service quality from clearing-house suppliers is often poor. In the UK, large EDI users have formed pressure groups and insisted on service agreements with their clearing-house suppliers.

- Standards limitations. Everyone recognizes the need for a single set of EDI standards to cover all EDI message types. That set of standards is now emerging from the EDIFACT board. There is virtually universal long-term commitment to EDIFACT from users and suppliers alike. But there are also problems. Current users of generic and industry-specific standards, such as Odette (for the pan-European motor industry), Tradacoms (for the UK retail and related industries), and ANSI X.12 (used by many industries in the US), have major problems in migrating to EDIFACT. So the generic standards are expected to be used in parallel with EDIFACT for a number of years. At the same time, development of EDIFACT standards is too slow for many users. There are gaps in the EDIFACT standards that will delay migration from the generic to industry-specific standards.

- Legal constraints. EDI trading will undoubtedly lead to disputes that will need resolution within some legal framework. Yet most legal systems are not designed to deal with EDI. Interchange agreements, which stipulate rules for trading within a community, help to overcome these problems. For Europe at least, the growth of more complex EDI communities that cross national boundaries means that there is an urgent requirement to establish a pan-European model interchange agreement. In the long term, there is also a need to clearly establish the legal status of electronic trading documentation and to harmonize this status globally.

- Security issues. Most companies believe that interchange agreements and clearing-house services currently offer adequate security against fraud or errors in EDI transactions. But they also see the need for increasing security and the number of standardization processes as the complexity of EDI communities grows.

FUTURE TRENDS

Clearing-house services are becoming high-volume commodities. The overall North American EDI market, including software, amounted to about $200 million in 1989. By the mid-1990s, the market is expected to grow past the $2 billion mark. The corresponding figures for Europe are $20 million in 1989 and $1.25 billion in 1995, with a corresponding growth in the number of EDI user companies from 550 in 1990 to the nearly 40,000

WHAT ABOUT SOFTWARE?

The typical EDI software package consists of:

- an applications interface through which local user-defined applications pass or receive messages to or from the document database;

- the document database, where messages are stored in local-application formats;

- the preparation module, which translates outgoing messages into standard EDI syntax and structure, and batches them for transmission;

- the processing module, which processes incoming messages, translating them back into local formats and storing them in the document database.

- the communications interface, which sends and receives network commands and EDI messages to and from the EDI clearing house.

- Software-package sources include the clearing houses, systems houses, DP suppliers, standards organizations, and small independent software houses. Package prices depend on the hardware platform used. A package for a PC might cost from $2000 (unbundled) to $4500 (with training and installation included). A package for a midrange mini might cost three to four times this amount; for a mainframe, six to eight times the PC prices.

---

predicted for the end of 1994. The increase in EDI users will be accompanied, of course, by a corresponding rise in traffic volumes.

As the number of user firms increases, so will the proportion of small companies. With this changing mix of users will come a drop in total EDI expenditure per user company—from $16,000 per year in 1990 to a projected $10,000 in 1994. But sustaining the growth in EDI will depend upon making it attractive to smaller users. If the projections are to be realized and sustained into the second half of the 1990s, substantial numbers of companies with less than 200 staff will have to realize the benefits from EDI. Many of them are not doing so at present.

Based on these trends, a fall in the price of EDI services has already started. For example, the usage charges of Transpac (a new entrant) are 75 percent cheaper than the usage charges of some of the established EDI clearing-house service providers.

In Europe, there is a move toward a small number of national service providers. This is already the model in the UK, where INS and AT&T/Istel dominate. With the move to commodity pricing and the economies of scale possible in offering EDI services, one or two suppliers are expected to dominate in each European country by the mid-1990s.

There is a similar move toward two to three dominant suppliers of pan-European services. The arguments for a shake-out in this market are similar to those for the national markets, but the process will take longer. The main competitors here are IBM, GEIS,

AT&T/Istel, Infonet, BT Tymnet, and services based on telco cooperation. It is still unclear which suppliers will succeed. Through research by Insight Research Corp., three main trends in the software marketplace have been identified:

- As the EDI communities grow more complex, so the users need their software to supply more standards and access more networks. At the same time, the move to X.400-based file-transfer services—with relatively limited functionality in the network when compared with some of the early proprietary EDI clearing-house services—will also stimulate demand for high-functionality software for the customer premises.

- There is a growing need for the development of EDI software that can plug into accounts packages. Integration of accounts software and EDI software could help ease the problems of small companies in interfacing local applications to EDI software.

- The number of small independent software companies will decrease as EDI software—such as EDI services—become commodity products.

Our analysis indicates that the market for EDI services will be slow in developing momentum: Not until 1993 can a growth trajectory that will produce a CAGR of 45 percent for the period under consideration be expected. Specifically, our estimates suggest that the EDI market will produce revenues of $1.9 billion by 1995, up from $200 million in 1989.

In the USA, the EDI market will be largely the domain of the IXCs, VANs, and data processing service organizations of the ADP type. Potential significant competition for EDI business will also come from computer and office systems vendors such as IBM, DEC, Xerox, Boeing, EDS, ADP, Wang, and Westinghouse. The impact of the latter group will probably be substantial because of their own procurement and billing experience; their customer and supplier relations will be of particular value.

In Europe, we see the telcos focusing on national clearing-house services where their competitive strengths are greatest. Their main competitors in this field are:

- IBM—With a good understanding of big companies and their business operations, IBM has a reputation for locking companies into proprietary systems. It has a strong presence in all Eurotel countries and is an established EDI provider, but has a small market share.

- GEIS—Focusing on the multinational and international markets, GEIS is reluctant to enter the commodity business end of EDI.

- AT&T/Istel—A leading EDI service provider in the UK, AT&T/Istel has announced aggressive marketing plans toward the rest of Europe.

- INS—The number one EDI service provider in the UK, INS is limited by its agreement with GEIS in its ability to expand into the rest of Europe.

The Issues and Policy Implications of Transborder Data Flow on Multinational Corporations

SATYA PRAKASH SARASWAT & JOHN T. GORGONE

THE ENORMOUS APPETITE of the growing service industry for information technology is transforming the world economy into a global village and increasing the demand for information exchange across national boundaries. Most of this information is now exchanged with the help of advanced computer technology. Called transborder data flow, this automated exchange of information has acquired international importance with far-reaching implications for multinational insurance, financial services, banking, airline, hotel, and media services corporations.

These corporations exchange enormous amounts of essential information between their headquarters and subsidiaries in different locations. Their information exchange patterns continue to be radically transformed by the cost-effectiveness and universal availability of advanced data communications technologies. The problems they encounter can be as complex as the regulation of geostationary orbits for satellites, which requires the intensive involvement of governments and international organizations, and as simple as the pricing of data communications channels in the domestic markets of individual countries. Managers wishing to take advantage of the emerging global economic opportunities should have a thorough understanding of these issues.

The rapid growth in transborder data flow has evolved from two advances in data communications technology: the digitization of voice with pulse-code modulation techniques and the evolution of sophisticated computer information processing approaches. The application of these technologies to solve business problems created by the demands of global competitiveness has resulted in the development of communications-intensive information systems and the subsequent globalization of the world economy during the 1980s.

Reprint from *Information Strategy: The Executive's Journal*, (New York: Auerbach Publications). © 1993, Warren Gorham & Lamont. Used with permission.

Pulse-code modulation allows the conversion of the human voice, graphic images, and many inherently analog scientific measurements to digital bit streams that can be transmitted on relatively error-free channels. The declining cost and increasing power of computers as well as the evolution of processing approaches from centralized batch to distributed multimedia in the relatively short span of 30 years have also contributed to the growth of transborder data flow.

Telecommunications networks were traditionally used by corporations for increasing the efficiency of operations; scant attention was paid to the strategic implications of networking. However, large corporations are now exploiting networking technology to create competitive advantage in the global marketplace. Transborder data flow has become an essential element in meeting the strategic information requirements of multinational corporations.

Political transformations in Europe and the former Soviet Union (despite the lack in the various republics of a solid banking or legal system for business) are creating vast trade and investment opportunities for multinational corporations based in the US, Europe, and Japan. The economic integration of Europe has created a flurry of activity in which major multinational corporations are positioning themselves to take advantage of expanding trade and investment opportunities. The coordination of global economic activity among multinational corporations, their subsidiaries in foreign countries, and the governments of the various host countries has also contributed to the substantial growth of electronic data transfer and other data transaction services that cross national boundaries.

The challenges multinational corporations face with transborder data flow arise from two general difficulties associated with the trading in electronic data. First, because of its abstract nature, information as a commodity is difficult to define under the rules of the General Agreement on Trade and Tariffs (GATT). Second, technical intricacies make measuring the value of information for regulatory purposes a difficult task. Concerns about transborder data flow under these circumstances relate to:

- *The implementation of restrictive regulations by many countries.* For example, Xerox Corp. was forced to open a data processing center in Sweden; even though its London center has sufficient capacity to handle all European data, the Swedish Privacy Law of 1973 requires that the processing of all personnel- and bank-related records of Swedish nationals take place in Sweden.

- *The monopolistic and exorbitant pricing of communications services by many countries.* For example, a US chemical company in Italy was forced to spend millions of dollars to purchase expensive communications equipment in Italy because the Italian government requires that all modems on public networks be rented from Societa Italiana per l'Esercizio Telefonico.

- *The trade barriers imposed on information exchange.* For example, the government of India accused Time, Inc., of reaping profits from stories transmitted as electronic data by its New Delhi bureau. A payment of $100,000 in special trade and exchange taxes was required.

- *The connectivity problems associated with incompatible technical standards in different regions.* For example, a European subsidiary of a US corporation obtained insurance on its data communications equipment from Lloyds of London. Because of sudden changes in the European Community's data communications standards, the equipment was rendered obsolete. Consequently, the insurance premiums for the corporation's data communications equipment for transborder data flow were sharply increased.

- *The security of transborder data networks.* For example, a renegade virus program devised by a student at Cornell University invaded Internet, a networking service linking ARPANET, MILNET, NSFNET, and other networks. More than 6,000 computers were infected by the virus, creating a global data communications problem, before the attack was detected and subsequently neutralized at MIT.

The problems associated with transborder data flow are currently addressed by professionals from a narrow perspective restricted to their own disciplines. For example, lawyers have concentrated on the legal and regulatory concerns, engineers have been preoccupied with the technical issues, and accountants and economists have been concerned primarily with costs. Although network security has become a universal concern, the challenge of transborder data flow can be successfully met only by developing an integrated perspective on and understanding of all of these issues and adopting a strategy for initiating appropriate policies regarding them at all levels of organizational decision making. The following sections address these concerns and explain the problems and issues in more detail.

RESTRICTIVE REGULATIONS

Laws for controlling transborder data flow have become increasingly restrictive. Many countries are taking a rather inflexible approach to this regulation by including economic and social dimensions in laws that were originally designed for the protection of individual privacy. Although some US-based multinational corporations do not consider the current regulatory environment a matter of great concern, the potential difficulties restrictive regulation can cause are numerous.

By 1985, at least 60 countries had already passed laws that have an impact on transborder data flow. The Organization for Economic Cooperation and Development (OECD) raised the issue as early as 1974, and a formal treaty was signed in 1983 for the regulation of transborder data flow among member countries. As a reaction against the restrictive regulations, the United Kingdom, Canada, and the US signed a convention known as the Glenerin Declaration in 1987 for the free flow of information. Many Third World countries are passing restrictive regulations to preserve their national sovereignty, safeguard their national security, and conserve their cultural heritage.

Many foreign transborder data flow laws regulate private recordkeeping operations and impose an additional burden on multinational corporations to protect the privacy of individuals. A corporation with branches in several countries can be adversely affected by the lack of uniformity in legislation across countries and the ambiguous scope of different laws. Some countries have extended the scope of restriction to manual recordkeeping systems along with the electronic systems. In addition, in other countries, proposals have been made to treat data gathered by multinational corporations as a commodity for tax purposes. Increasing international regulation of satellite orbits and radio frequency spectrums often results in artificially high costs of satellite services.

PRICING OF SERVICES

The lack of availability of leased lines in competitive markets has become, in some cases, an economic barrier to transborder data flow. Networking equipment and software have traditionally been available in most countries in competitive markets; however, with the exception of Japan and the UK, communications channels are a regulated monopoly of national post and telegraph departments.

In the pricing of data communications channels, the two major principles followed by most countries are value of service pricing and cross-subsidization. Under the value of service consideration, businesses are typically charged higher rates than individuals for telephone service because they derive a greater economic value from this service. In cross-subsidization, revenues from telephone services are used to subsidize the costs of specialized data communications services.

Decreasing the reliance on public channels can ameliorate this situation. For example, Citicorp implemented a private data network—spanning 75 countries at a cost of approximately $15 million in 1983—that, despite restrictions on the personnel and customer information the bank can exchange between its branches, has resulted in a savings of 30% in the cost of transborder data flow across the network. Multinational corporations may want to strike a deal with developing countries that own satellite slots but do not have the technological capability to use them to implement semiprivate telecommunications channels.

TRADE BARRIERS

Excessive tariffs, restrictive quotas, high excise taxes, and questions about the quality of computer and telecommunications products from a foreign country are some common trade barriers affecting transborder data flow. Increased costs resulting from discriminatory pricing and other trade barriers in such countries as Brazil and Japan have been the subject of various trade negotiations in recent years. Many corporations have been hindered in acquiring computer equipment for networking because of these barriers.

STANDARDS AND CONNECTIVITY

A paramount need for standards to connect networking equipment from multiple vendors is widely recognized in the communications industry. Multinational corporations face major problems associated with the incompatibility of standards: a lack of system integration because of incompatible hardware, equipment obsolescence because of changing standards, the need for complex software to make the hardware compatible, and increasing network complexity and management problems.

Efforts are now under way at the international level to develop universally acceptable connectivity standards. European and Japanese companies have indicated a greater willingness to accept these standards than many US corporations. Because US companies in the computer and communications industry play a dominant role in establishing de facto standards that may not be compatible with international standards, they often resist new standards.

However, many countries have adopted the network architecture recommended by the International Standards Organization (ISO). Standards for the Integrated Services Digital Network (ISDN) have also been widely accepted in the US, Europe, and Japan. But even within ISDN, incompatible techniques (e.g., Mode Two, a proprietary method of AT&T, T-Link from Northern Telecom, and V. 110 and V. 120 from CCITT) have emerged. ISDN terminal adapters designed for one technique cannot communicate with the equipment designed for the other techniques.

In 1990, USA Committee T-1 on telecommunications standards initiated and hosted (in Fredericksburg VA) an important conference in which several agreements were reached between European, US, and Japanese telecommunications agencies to resolve the standards issues associated with transborder data flow. Various countries agreed that:

- International standards should be managed in accordance with the requirements of the market.

- Standardization must have a precise scope.

- Regional and national standardization bodies should cooperate to create international standards.

- Ad hoc and plenary sessions of the international regulatory bodies should be held more frequently.

- An electronic document exchange facility using worldwide ISDN should be implemented as soon as possible.

A second Interregional Telecommunications Standards Conference held in 1991, under the auspices of the international Telecommunications Union (ITU), the European Telecommunications Standards Institute (ETSI), and the International Standards Organization, addressed these issues in greater detail. An awareness of these developments is essential for proper policymaking regarding transborder data flow.

SECURITY

The increasing complexity of network technology, the sophistication of attackers, and the presence of a large number of vulnerable points in an international network have made the issue of transborder data flow security more acute for many corporations. Such standard techniques for network security as the data encryption standard (DES) have been found inadequate for international networks and many companies are using proprietary techniques for network security.

For example, security has become a major concern in the commercial global telecommunications network operated by General Electric Information Services. This network spans 75 cities in 30 countries; its security is based on a layered scheme that combines the DES and ANS encryption standards with proprietary message and user authentication techniques. With such a system, the sophisticated key management, advanced cryptographic techniques, and high degree of vigilance required by personnel at all levels of management can add greatly to the cost of transborder data flow operations.

ADDRESSING THESE CONCERNS

Managers of multinational corporations should adopt strategies and policies that address these concerns and that recognize the unique requirements of the various geographical regions in which a corporation operates. A structured set of approaches can transform the challenges of transborder data flow into opportunities in rapidly expanding global markets.

Although US government agencies are restricted from direct participation in the policy formulation process of such regional organizations as the European Commission and the Organization for Economic Cooperation and Development (OECD), multinational corporations, as influential private users, can make these organizations aware of their important business concerns about regulation by direct representation. Multinational corporations should also closely follow the policy developments taking place in such emerging telecommunications markets as Europe and Japan.

Japan, a major competitor of the US in the telecommunications industry, has been deregulating the Nippon Telegraph and Telephone Corp. since 1985 and is now permitting providers of data communications networking services from other countries to compete with Japanese companies in domestic markets. A unified Europe is now an equally important variable in such policymaking with the emergence of a continental information and telecommunications infrastructure.

At the national level, multinational corporations can urge the US government to support the criteria proposed for worldwide data flow regulation by OECD. The criteria include these premises:

- Legislation should be in the public benefit.

- Legislation should impose minimum restrictions on transborder data flow.

- Laws should be enforceable by regulatory and monitoring agencies.

- Only those areas in which networks are likely to have negative external effects on users and other third parties should be regulated.

A vigorous advocacy of these positions by the US government is essential for multi-national corporations. An awareness of the existence of restrictive transborder data flow regulation in various countries on the part of executives can minimize the problems arising from the violation of existing regulations.

The use of regional public data networks (e.g., Datapack in Canada) for local use in the host countries and the implementation of private backbone networks (e.g., Globalnet by Citibank) can help alleviate the problem of exorbitant pricing communications channels in different countries. Caution when adopting emerging data communications technologies can also minimize the costs of networking. The creation of transborder data flow con-sciousness among senior executives and a commitment to let important transborder data flow decisions be made by local executives can be recommended as a strategy at the organizational level. The policy of finding an appropriate balance between decentralization and centralization of data on the one hand and the distribution of procurement and decision-making policies in telecommunications areas on the other should be encouraged.

Increasing the use of networking equipment available in the host countries at the international level, supporting a uniform global trade policy at the national level, and establishing subsidiaries in countries with liberal telecommunications policies can be recommended as a broad policy to meet the challenge of tariff and nontariff barriers imposed on transborder data flow.

The economic importance of the harmonization of data communications standards for Europe as a whole has become a focus of telecommunications policy in the European Community. This fact underscores the importance of standardization as a policy issue in transborder data flow for multinational corporations. These companies should encourage the adoption of internationally accepted networking standards, avoid proprietary architectures, and implement uniform networking procedures in the entire organization to minimize the impact of diverse and incompatible standards.

Electronic Data Interchange (EDI) is emerging as an international standard with Europe's adoption of its own version called Trade Data Interchange (TDI). Development of such standard methods and procedures for transmitting electronic data as EDI is being pioneered by many user groups in the US. At the national level of policy formulation, executives in US multinational corporations should encourage an active participation by their executives in these groups.

In a diversified global telecommunications environment, threats to network security can arise from multiple sources, and it is virtually impossible for a corporation to take sufficient precautions against all possible threats. Therefore, a constant network security consciousness among managers at all organizational levels is equally as important as implementing sound security mechanisms for encrypting data, managing key distribution, and protecting the network resources.

At the international level, transborder data flow security threats can be minimized by bilateral agreements between multinational corporations and their host governments for protecting sensitive data. At the national level, multinational corporations are meeting the threats to transborder data flow security by supporting uniform computer security legislation and its vigorous enforcement by the US government.

EXPLOITING DATA COMMUNICATIONS TECHNOLOGY

A recognition of the transborder data flow issues and associated problems is essential for IS managers and executives at all levels of organizational decision making. In a constantly changing global economic and technological environment, successful integration of information technology within the organizational infrastructure of a multinational corporation is an important challenge. With a proper understanding of the transborder data flow issues, managers can successfully meet this challenge by implementing communications-intensive information systems and exploiting them for global competitive advantage.

RECOMMENDED READING

ACM, "EC Commission Communication on Establishing an Information Service Market," *Communications of the ACM 4*, no. 33 (1990), pp. 426–432.

Budwey, J.N., "Interregional Summit on Telecommunications Standards," *Telecommunications* (April 1990), pp. 25–26.

Mier, E., "Top ISDN Switches Lack Mutual Compatibility," *Network World 7*, no. 23, p. 1.

Wright, K., "The Road to the Global Village," *Scientific American* (March 1990), pp. 83–95.

SECTION VI

Integrating Technology, Systems, and People across the Globe

This final section addresses one of the most difficult challenges facing IS managers in global firms—the challenge of integrating various technology platforms, business processes, and subsidiaries into a well-performing transnational business organization. The scope of issues is immense, and this section concentrates on some of the more significant of the aspects that affect the overall integration of a firm's global information infrastructure.

In the first article, Guez underscores the importance of worldwide integration through standard solutions to hardware and software development. He also suggests that integration of technologies is not enough; integration must extend to business processes and people in different countries if it is to be successful.

The next two articles address the issues of developing software that can be used by business units worldwide. Gagliardi describes the main concerns in designing international software products. He identifies four major problems: (a) multiple languages, (b) multiple currencies, (c) varying methods of taxation, and (d) differing government reporting requirements. He concludes that global software must be "modifiable-by-design," meaning that it must look and behave differently in each country while maintaining absolute consistency of data and source code.

Ambrosio discusses the difficulties of implementing global software in business units of different national, cultural, and social makeup. She describes various barriers to adopting global software and offers guidance for successful implementation.

The question of where to develop software or provide information processing services is examined by Apte. He discusses the advantages and disadvantages of outsourcing information systems functions to countries that provide the best competitive edge. He describes how to identify candidate activities, how to choose a vendor, and what types of contractual arrangements are appropriate for global outsourcing.

One of the most serious impediments to achieving global integration of information systems is not technical, but cultural. A successful implementation process must take into consideration the national and cultural settings of the various host countries in which the company operates. Technologies and systems developed in one country are not necessarily easily transferable to other countries. In their article, Robey and Rodriguez–Diaz examine subsidiaries in two South American countries that experienced different degrees of success in implementing an IS project.

People are becoming increasingly more aware of the importance of quality as a key factor in business success. It is therefore appropriate that, just as the first chapter began with an article on quality, this last chapter closes with a paper related to quality. In his article, Dover addresses the role of ISO 9000, the new European quality standard that is gaining international momentum. Dover describes the overall objectives of the standard, its qualification process, and its potential impact on global information systems managers.

Systems Integration for the International Company

JEAN-CLAUDE GUEZ

GLOBALIZATION is no longer just a trend to develop markets all over the world, it is a significant means for obtaining competitive advantage. The fact that the leaders in business—companies such as IBM, Northern Telecom, Coca-Cola, Volvo, Amadeus, Sabre, and McDonald's—have embraced the borderless concept signifies globalization's future importance. Some corporations conduct more than 60 percent of their business outside their "home country"; Nestle does 90 to 95 percent of its business outside of Switzerland, and more than 90 percent of Philips' business is outside the Netherlands.

With the elimination of national borders, international corporations can reduce trade problems, avoid political problems and sidestep regulatory hurdles, achieve labor gains, balance costs, and even take greater advantage of technological breakthroughs. But with such significant benefits also come external pressures and internal risks. A successful international corporation must know how to deal with the external pressures and, more important, conquer the internal battles—not the least of which is integration of systems on a global scale.

One of the greatest external challenges, for example, is the move to a Single Market in Europe. It opens the way for more pan-European projects and joint ventures, which, while positive for international corporations, also makes business problems more complex. Even more challenging is Eastern Europe's longing to catch up to Western Europe's models and technologies, which may prolong the uniting of European business.

These external pressures compound the internal challenges an international company faces. The immediate concern when moving to an international level is to develop a global vision of the business at the transnational level to guide the company's international goals. Once its goals are defined, the company must begin planning strategies and integrating the business, which includes harmonizing the information systems. Information systems must be compatible between heterogeneous components and organizations. And information technology networks must be interconnected.

Reprinted with permission by Faulkner & Gray, Inc., 11 Penn Plaza, New York, NY 10001, 800-535-8403.

Integrating systems on an international basis is an awesome task—there are no clear-cut solutions and the needs of each organization vary. In general, however, successful companies have examined three key components of systems integration: technology platforms and networks, business processes, and people. Looking at these three areas, which are approached differently around the world, can help outline the risks and opportunities an international company realizes.

TECHNOLOGY PLATFORMS AND NETWORKS

Within the technology platforms and networks component, the main areas to consider are telecommunications, computer platforms, and software engineering. Because technological methods vary greatly across the world, making them compatible can be challenging.

Telecommunications. Telecommunications is the most obvious technology area for international ventures, probably because of the vital need to establish successful communication of information throughout the corporation. Before integrating communications worldwide, a corporation should examine the dramatic changes affecting telecommunications today:

- Changes are occurring rapidly throughout the industry. Technologies are benefiting from digitization and the advent of powerful microchips; many governments, vendors, and users are promoting "open architectures"; and in the era of globalization, regulators are trying to develop new solutions for controlling the flow of information, but it is more and more difficult as the number and types of services increase.

- Usage is increasing while unit costs are decreasing. This translates into increased telecommunications budgets in corporations—in some cases, where information is the lifeblood of an organization, telecom budgets are as much as 3 to 4 percent of total revenues.

- Communication is becoming a central force for the future. Because international companies require more cohesion and integration in their telecommunications, the communication function that used to be last and least important is becoming first and foremost for effectiveness and efficiency.

The last point magnifies the communication needs for an international corporation. Fortunately, some technology has evolved to address those needs. The development of digital technology is particularly important for the international network customer because it permits the full integration of networks as well as the emergence of many new services. Additionally, other emerging technologies include increases in network bandwidth, which are the result of the new telecommunications technologies, and global standardization of hardware and software platforms.

Yet, despite the progress, challenges remain for international networking customers. Around the world, services and regulations are heterogeneous and lead times for circuit delivery vary. Technology still has not completely answered the situation of weak links in company networks—while the link may be strong from the U.S. to Paris, the link on to Africa, or even neighboring countries, may be very weak, affecting the quality of the entire system. Costs also differ by country. A telecommunications line from Paris to the Swiss border costs the same as a line from Geneva to the same border, even though Geneva is virtually on the French border.

Even before the company deals with linkage and costs issues, it must obtain certification to establish a network in every country it wants to link. Until Europe changes to a Single Market, companies will continue to face difficulties getting different authorizations from every country.

Not helping matters for the international company, many vendors offer segmented responsibility zones only, so they are unable to help an international customer effectively. This adds to the frustration a company has in international network management. For example, a link between a European country and the U.S. may use several national telecommunications infrastructures in which each operator controls his or her own country's infrastructure. This makes it very difficult for the user to control the link. The hurdles are truly global.

To jump over those barriers and take advantage of the technologies, experience has shown that several strategies are helpful. A company should:

- Allow a long lead-time. Develop international networks well in advance, taking into account business goals. The business strategy should be defined early in the process.

- Use local skills and staff to understand the local environment.

- Seek expertise and assistance from those who have faced similar problems.

- Use a proven international network planning methodology.

- Reassess needs and technical strategies on a regular basis.

These strategies have helped others develop their international networks; they are proven to work. Take a major multinational pharmaceutical company conducting business all over the world. To integrate the entire business, the company built a corporate network for voice, data, and image traffic concerning 72 subsidiaries and 110 locations across 54 countries. In another case, a U.S. manufacturing company set up plants, warehouses, and commercial offices in Europe, using electronic data interchange (EDI) to communicate with clients. But U.S. and European standards for EDI vary, so the company used a Value Added Network (VAN, a third party that provides network services, such as EDI) to help translate and convert information.

Computer Platforms and Software Engineering. Although less striking, the problems in unifying computing platforms and software engineering across borders are similar to those in telecommunications. And for an international organization they are just as important.

Across borders there are a lot of similarities in platforms and engineering: For example, the same relational database management systems, system development tools, and methodologies do exist in the U.S. and Europe. The problem arises when, for a variety of reasons including performance, regions prefer to use their home brands, instead of an international brand that may be as powerful. Take a computer-aided software engineering (CASE) example with the IBM AS/400: SYNON CASE from the U. S. SYNON Cy is well known and respected in Europe. But local European products may crowd the shelves and be more common, such as ADELIA in France.

European-based companies frequently choose to use their national software development methodologies (Merise in France, SSDM in the U.K.), causing differences in software. Adding to the confusion, development standards and time can vary greatly on opposite sides of the Atlantic: In Europe software development may take six to eight days per program, while in the U.S. it often takes 12 to 15. The variance results from a difference in the way a programming effort is perceived—in Europe developers may spend more time up front in the design phase, while in the U.S. they may move faster into the programming phase. U.S. information executives should be prepared to deal with these differences.

When trying to integrate systems in Europe, the U.S. executives must consider each country's use of national hardware and system software vendors, which is leading to proprietary architectures. Fortunately, in this area there has been some progress for the international customer. The recent thrust toward open systems concepts and products in Europe, testified by the various national administrations and the European Commission procurement handbooks, has widened access. As they continue to develop, open systems should reduce the differences across the Atlantic and make it easier for international companies to find compatible solutions.

Combating the preference for national or regional development tools and methodologies, executives of international companies increasingly wish to standardize the use of packaged software solutions across countries and subsidiaries. While this will ease the problems of incompatible systems, it presents several thorny issues:

- Even standardized packages must be localized. They must be adapted to local languages, habits, and regulations, such as accounting procedures and tax calculations.

- There are at least two ways to standardize packages among many locations. First, the same full package may be used in each location. In this case, the integration is completed at the expense of the local functionalities. Or, the same core package may be used with local versions installed, leaving the local level with the responsibility of developing local functions and extensions.

- Integrating packaged applications across countries or geographical areas requires massive support activities, including software distribution and release management. Increasingly, this area is critical enough to justify contracting with a systems management firm, which takes over the burden of international support and provides a guaranteed service level agreement.

- Package costs may differ from country to country. In the U.S., the cost of the package is expressed in dollars, while in other countries another currency may change the price. It is possible that the same package may double in price from one country to the next.

Software developers need to face the challenge of standardizing software solutions. While developing answers to the technological difficulties of integration, they must also address external pressures, such as the major regulatory changes that will accompany Europe's transformation to a single market in January 1993. To keep in time with big international clients, developers must meet these challenges.

As in the telecommunications field, emerging technologies should help the developers improve software engineering on an international level. In one case, software reverse engineering tools exist to extract business functions from old and non-documented assemblers or COBOL applications. This technology should assist firms that wish to integrate pre-existing systems.

REFORMING BUSINESS PROCESSES

While technologies and networks are the most obvious areas of concern when integrating a business internationally, business processes and people issues are just as important and are probably less understood, recognized, or developed.

Business processes may differ greatly across borders. As competitive markets change and widen, companies must take into account the new environment and quickly revisit their strategies. In Europe, for example, the privatization of major public companies has brought on many business reengineering activities. Increasingly, to stay on top of the international pile, organizations must look at their business processes as intently as their technologies and networks.

INTEGRATING PEOPLE

The same challenges politicians and diplomats encounter also face international companies with employees all over the world, or even in two or three countries. A company must recognize the cultural, linguistic, and national differences among its people and must adapt to them. It is crucial that the company try to adapt to the people; the people cannot completely change to adapt to the company.

In Europe, political changes compound the people issues. There are still a myriad of political challenges that inhibit the unification of the business world and make it difficult to establish a strong business culture.

The major differences among people in different countries make it impossible to take a solution that worked in one place and transplant it to another. While in technologies we can learn from the experiences of other countries, in people issues we must examine and understand each country in its own right. As U.S. executives introduce new technologies in different countries, they must address the training needs of local personnel in a manner appropriate with the culture and the people, not just the technology.

Companies that have been successful worldwide are leading the way with competitive and productive international work forces. More and more international companies are building true multinational management and professional teams to capitalize on their cultural differences.

MOVING FORWARD

The concerns and issues experienced by companies that have integrated internationally are great; yet the thrust toward globalization pushes development of new, more efficient technologies, as well as better understanding of the business processes and people issues that vary country to country. And the success of companies like Nestle and Coca-Cola adds promise to the many issues of integrating a company internationally.

Global Software:
The Issues in Selecting
International Software

GARY GAGLIARDI

AT ONE TIME, a "multi-national" company was always a large corporation. But the world is changing, becoming smaller. Improved communication and transportation systems are making it possible for even the small and medium sized manufacturer to realize a significant part of its income from the global market.

International trade has become an issue for almost every business in America. Even small businesses are, today, finding that development of international markets is critical for success. For large corporations, this has been true for decades and is becoming more-so with every passing month.

If any software package is truly to become an "open standard" within today's multi-national organizations, it must be designed for use internationally. Software and shared data have created a new basis for communication. If each national office has its own software package or if the various elements of international transactions cannot be addressed in the software at the home office, one more barrier to smooth international operations is presented.

People often think that the main issue in creating international software products is one of simple translation, but the problem is much more complicated than that. Even for relatively simple word-processing and spreadsheet packages, the issues of dealing with different character sets and monetary systems are more complicated than they seem at first. However, the real software need is not for word-processing and spreadsheets, but for packages that process company transactions. In those kinds of packages, a number of other more serious difficulties arise in implementing international standards.

Gagliardi, Gary. "Global Software: The Issues in Selecting International Software." *Open Software Journal*, vol. 5, no. 3, 6–10.

In this article, we are going to address the main issues of global standard transaction-processing software. These are the software packages a company might use in order to conduct international business from a single location or from different locations around the world. As we shall see, the problems with creating and maintaining packages center around four issues: 1) multiple languages, 2) multiple currencies, 3) variety of taxing methods (such as value-added tax (VAT) and general state tax (GST)) and, 4) satisfying local government reporting requirements.

Is there a need for an international standard? Can't each office simply purchase a local product that addresses their local needs for transaction processing? Certainly, this is one alternative and perhaps the more common choice made today. However, companies are finding a number of problems with this alternative. Among these problems are: 1) the cost of searching for and selecting systems for each nation, 2) the cost of integrating information flow between different units with different packages and, 3) the on-going cost of supporting different products from different vendors.

Aside from these problems there is a larger problem with integrating information from various international operations. At least one package in the corporation has to be "international" at least in the sense that it can consolidate the transactions recorded by all of the other packages. Some piece of software within the organization must know about monetary exchanges and how to convert and report on those exchanges.

The historical solution has been to graft these functions onto the headquarters package, but more and more, this solution is proving unsatisfactory. The major problem is that each of the local units are, themselves, conducting international business. The problem is not just converting the accounting information from the unit in Frankfurt into the currency of the corporate headquarters. How does the unit in Frankfurt deal with the customer in France who wants to be billed in Francs? How does the unit in Belgium deal with stock transfers to Italy? Does all of this information have to be sent back to the headquarters to be processed? This solution is less and less tenable.

It is not just the organization that is becoming international, it is the character of its business that is becoming international as well. This means a global need exists for each unit to be capable of dealing with a number of international issues.

Once more, you could try and address this general problem by finding a different internationally enabled package in each country, but that also seems less and less realistic. How is each local organization going to deal with setting up and maintaining its own systems of currency conversions?

It seems like the only reasonable solution is for the organization to find a single package that in some way reduces this burden. If a single product could be found, it would speed the organization's ability to set up international offices, speed the communication among different international operations, reduce the number of errors in such communication, cost much less to support, and allow the organization to establish and maintain consistent and efficient rules for international transactions and currency exchange.

THE LANGUAGE BARRIER

The first barrier that must be overcome is that of language. This problem is much more complex than it appears on the surface. Different nations not only have different words, but different writing systems. There are subtle differences among the alphabets of western Europe, but those differences become more extreme as you move eastward across Eurasia. Greece and Russia have their own alphabets with many regional variations. Arabic has its own alphabet. India has several.

When you get to the Asian countries, much of the alphabet vanishes entirely. In Japan, you have not one, but actually three character systems. One for writing words of foreign origin, a phonetic system, and a system of pictograms borrowed from the Chinese. In China, you have not one, but two pictogram systems, the "reformed" system used in the People's Republic and Hong Kong and the "classical" system used in Taiwan.

The job of dealing with these different systems of writing has fallen, in most cases, to those developing operating systems and programming languages. Most of these characters are accessed through the keyboard by typing a series of keystrokes instead of one. Most are what we call "two-byte" character sets because that is how many digital bits it takes to encode them. However, some countries have even more complex systems, such as Thailand's requirement for a "three-byte" character set.

Once the language is enabled on the computer and operating system, it falls into the hands of application developers to implement that language into their programs. With traditional programming methods, (encoding the "strings" of characters that create the user interface directly into the application's "code") real problems arise. If the actual way the program works is tied to the language, creating a version for another language is extremely difficult and time consuming.

For example, what if your program says something like "Press E to Exit." Changing the line that displays the message may be a relatively trivial problem, but you do have to change the program language. At some point the program is expecting an "E" to be pressed on the keyboard. The program logic must be changed so that users can press the key appropriate in their language or, in the case of oriental languages, perhaps the series of keys required.

These kinds of changes can mean programming changes to thousands and perhaps even tens of thousands of program lines. Each change is a potential problem or "bug" if not handled correctly. And once these changes are accomplished, a bigger job awaits. Once a separate language version of the software has been created, it must be maintained separately from "original" source code. As bugs are identified and fixed in one version, they must also be located and fixed in every different language version.

The only way out of this trap is to redesign the software. It must be rewritten so that the language the user sees on the screen, and the input the program expects to receive, are not driven by the programs themselves, but by database files. This means that at every interface point, the program looks up a table to see what language is being run and finds the appropriate set of bytes to display on the screen for that language.

In FourGen Accounting, for example, program screens are put in "template" files. Each different program has its own set of templates filed by language. When a user logs in, the system identifies the language of that user and creates the appropriate environment for them. If the user is French, it uses French screen forms. If the user is Spanish, it uses the Spanish version. Forms for any language can be created assuming that the language is supported by INFORMIX-4GL (the programming language in which FourGen applications are written).

The screen forms only solve one part of the problem however. There are messages that appear on the screen from time to time, and menus from which the user can select various options by typing the character beginning the option. These various character strings are actually stored in the relational database in tables set up specifically to hold screen messages, menus, and keystroke translations. Maintaining the files that contain these translations is much easier and safer than changing lines of programming, especially since most of these messages and menus are reused many times at different places within the programs. Since they are all stored in the database, each term only needs to be changed once to affect all of the different places in the application where it might be used.

Creating applications in this way doesn't create different versions of the software. Instead, it creates a language-independent version. The application is maintained completely separate from the languages that drive it.

One benefit of this approach is that different users who speak different languages can use the same system at the same time. Their system's "personality" is determined by the language they choose. Since the interface is separate from the application, their use of different languages cannot conflict with one another. This is especially important in nations such as Canada and Switzerland when more than one language is commonly used in a single office since the nation itself promotes a multi-lingual environment.

Multiple languages must be supported in such a way that the program does not have to be changed in any way to support a new language. The language which appears for the user should be independent of the program. The commands, menus, boxes, screens, and so on, must appear in the language specified without having to create a set of "source code" to drive the program. New translations should be made simply by entering the new language equivalents of existing commands and text. The user should be able to specify the language he or she wants to use when running the system. Simultaneous use of a single application in different languages should be allowed. Some issues, such as the support of the Japanese double-byte kanji character sets must be resolved in the initial design of the product since they can't be easily added later.

MULTIPLE CURRENCIES

Any global product must support transactions and reporting in multiple currencies. It must keep the books and data in the corporate office's home currency while allowing transactions to be entered in the local currency or other foreign currency. Customer files, vendor files and other records must allow you to define the currency to use.

Differences in value with respect to your home currency caused by changes in exchange rates over the payment cycle must be tracked automatically and posted to an account for tracking those differences. Currency translations should be done automatically.

Once more, within a program, the problems of implementing this can be difficult. Programs must be designed from the ground-up to deal with the different types and styles of currencies. Some currencies, such as the Japanese Yen and Italian Lira, are always shown as whole numbers and can get quite large. Other currencies can break their monetary units down into three decimal places instead of the two we commonly see in U.S. Dollars. Different nations also have different styles of punctuation. For example, we separate dollars from cents with a decimal point and indicate thousands with a comma. There are currencies which divide one type from another with a comma and indicate thousands with periods.

In building FourGen products, we didn't have to deal with many of these formatting issues because Informix handles them very capably. But we did have to design our programs so that they could utilize Informix's multi-currency systems and we had to write those programs so that they made no assumption about the nature of the currency.

In the same way that programs can be language independent, they can be written to be currency independent. Rules about how currencies are used have to be handled independently from the main processing of the system.

This means having database tables that allow you to enter conversion rates on a daily basis and record the financial transactions related with the conversion from one currency to another. Some of these problems are very difficult to solve, especially as you start building systems that have to deal with different currencies used within a single business. Some sites might bill this customer in Yen and this customer in Hong Kong Dollars, but do their own accounting in Singapore Dollars. And even this is not the most difficult case. In some cases, customers might want a single invoice to contain line items in different currencies to reflect the currencies in which they are being purchased from the manufacturers.

These problems are difficult and can become complicated, but it is the job of a truly international piece of software to hide this complexity from the user and simply allow them to record and process the transactions as they need to be made. The system should not stand as a barrier to doing business as the customer desires.

DIFFERENT METHODS OF TAXATION

The tax picture in the United States seems to be getting more complicated all the time as states, counties, and cities not only utilize, but continuously change their taxation methods. As you go into the international arena, the situation becomes even more complex and fluid. You not only have our governmental divisions, but completely different sets of divisions and different kinds of taxing authority.

The need is for a system that is also "tax structure independent." A parameter-driven method of specifying a large variety of taxation methods that are being adopted today by different countries, states, provinces, counties and localities must be built into the package. The system should support a number of different levels, each with their own rules, each of which can be selected for a particular document.

Multi-level taxation today must support different forms of taxation such as value-added tax (VAT) which taxes the difference between what you buy a product at and what you sell it at. Though not yet in use in the United States, this system and derivatives of it are becoming increasingly popular worldwide. The design of the system also must allow you to define other special taxation methods as they are developed on a country by country basis. In other words, it must be designed so that new rules can be added as they are invented. They must be added in a way that requires no change to the program and allows the users to operate in different tax environments on a single system.

At FourGen, we have handled these capabilities by building a multiple level tax definition system. This system allows you to define various taxation rules in the database and then assign code to the various levels of taxation. As transactions are entered, users can select from the various types of taxes the system understands which are appropriate for a given transaction. The system can also be set up so that given transactions automatically default to certain methods of tax calculation unless overridden by the user.

DIFFERENT GOVERNMENT REQUIREMENTS

Generally accepted accounting principles vary from country to country. Each government or taxing authority may require a different set of financial reports. Screens may need to use different languages, sometimes in the same country. Even accounting terminology is different. For example, in the United Kingdom an Accounts Receivable ledger is called a Sales Ledger.

The financial reports must easily be adapted to each country. By defining different report lines that do include a different set of ledger accounts in each roll-up, you should be able to easily create different sets of financial reports for different countries.

At FourGen, these differences are handled in a variety of different ways. For reporting, we offer both financial and general purpose report-writers that allow the creation of any kind of report from the information in the database.

However, in most cases, users shouldn't be expected to make these kinds of local modifications. The product should be supported locally in countries that are using it. Ideally, installation, training, and customization should be available in those countries from companies that speak the language and understand the local laws. This is no easy task, and building such a support network takes time. The technologies we are discussing make the creation of a truly international product possible, but creating a support network means technological transfer on a grand scale. FourGen's leading position in the open systems accounting market and our reliance on partnerships has allowed us to build the start of the support network that is required.

MODIFIABILITY-BY-DESIGN

Global software must look and behave very differently on the surface while maintaining complete consistency, in data and in source code. In order to implement these systems, we have developed a technology we call "Modifiability-By-Design."

Our technology allows our international partners to make additions to our software that allow local processing without changing the basic underlying product. This means when we release a new version of the software, they are able to simply "plug-in" their alterations to the new version to allow it to address these issues as well.

In this environment, most of the critical variables, such as language, currency, and taxation rules, are table driven so that they can be more easily maintained and expanded. Other changes, such as those to financial logic, are plugged in as they are needed.

What this technology means to a company is that a single product can be used and supported world-wide. That product cannot only address the immediate issues of managing international transaction processing, but can also be run in any corporate office anywhere in the world.

Modifiability-By-Design also means that the corporation, business unit, or even the location can add their own additions to the program that make the generic version more amenable to their needs, and that those additions can be moved to a new version of the software as it becomes available. This means that as the transaction processing functions are altered to directly address company needs, the company is not "orphaning" itself in terms of support and eliminating itself from accessing future improved versions.

This type of technology is what turns global software, and in some cases, global business, from a possibility into a reality.

Global Softwhere?

JOHANNA AMBROSIO

PETE BATES, VICE PRESIDENT of systems at clothing manufacturer Esprit de Corp. in San Francisco, found out the hard way that sharing software on a global basis does not always work according to plan.

About a year ago, Esprit's U.S. subsidiary adopted a production management system developed at the company's Far East affiliate. The software tracks where an item is manufactured, sewn, pressed and so on. But the software was only a "moderate" success here, Bates says, because "the ways of doing business are quite different in the two hemispheres."

Bates' company ran into a wall shared by virtually all major corporations that do business overseas: Despite good intentions and the business benefits, sharing software does not always work because of differences in how people work around the world.

Although many companies are going global and information systems groups are under increasing pressure to maximize technology investments, seasoned IS hands say not all software can or should be common everywhere.

In the Far East, for example, it is standard for the shop sewing the garment to handle the other steps of finishing and washing. In the U.S., however, convention dictates that the individual steps be contracted out to different parties.

The end result, Bates says, was that "the system that Hong Kong put together did not have the features for us to manage effectively the transition from factory to factory." Consequently, Esprit's U.S. group is converting to another package.

Deciding on the basic infrastructure of what will be shared is just the beginning, according to IS executives and consultants. The biggest management hurdles by far involve cultural issues: convincing overseas management that the systems people at headquarters are there to help and involving the overseas managers in the whole process.

Other "gotchas" include the following:

- Arranging for service and support in remote locations.

- Making sure the package as well as the documentation support all the major national languages.

- Dealing with import restrictions and other legalities in foreign countries.
- Tracking vendors' different prices and business requirements worldwide.

With all these different balls in the air, managing global software is akin to "playing a chess tournament at 15 different tables while spinning plates," says one former chief information officer who attempted it, with mixed success.

MANAGING CHAOS

The most critical factor—which can make or break a global software situation—is getting buy-in from the managers overseas. This requires the tact of a diplomat and the selling skills of a superstar salesperson, as well as an honest attempt to include the foreign managers in as many steps of the process as possible.

Otherwise, managers will never truly implement the software the way it was intended and will likely erect all kinds of barriers to prevent the project from being done.

Experts say it's also helpful to remember two prime rules that apply to many IS endeavors. Rule No. 1: It always takes longer than you think, so patience is definitely a virtue. Rule No. 2: See rule No. 1.

Not even megacompanies with many subsidiaries and expertise in overseas dealings are immune to pitfalls. Nearly everyone has problems, as did a huge energy concern that recently tried to introduce into two Canadian groups software that had been running in certain U.S. operations.

Complicating matters was the fact that the two Canadian facilities had at one point been competitors: an acquisition had forced them to rethink their formation technology infrastructure.

"So we go into the Canadian guys and ask them what they think about using X or Y," the clearly exasperated CIO says. "And once one found out that the other was going to use it too, well then he didn't want it."

What was originally scheduled to take three or four months wound up requiring the better part of a year, the CIO says. "We resolved it by basically working with them, building them up so they could get to a point where they could share things."

While that may be an extreme example, CIOs say it is common for people in far-flung operations to partially mistrust the IS group that is sent by headquarters to "help." One counter tactic: Get overseas management involved as early as possible and position the new system as something that will help everyone meet the company's goals.

That philosophy worked well at Corning Glass Works' Japanese operation. Corning does not have a mandate to standardize on software worldwide but will share "where it makes sense," says Harvey Shrednick, senior vice president of information services at the Corning, N.Y., headquarters.

In this instance, Corning developed a plant floor reporting system used domestically. The Japanese group needed the same basic functions, customized to their requirements.

"It probably would have been a lot easier to pull something from domestic and say, 'Use it,' but the involvement of the Japanese IS people in the process probably did more to gain acceptance of the system than any other factor," Shrednick says. In the end, "they felt it was their system, not the U.S.,' even though there was a U.S. guy over there facilitating things."

The IS facilitator went to Japan three times during a six-month period, working with the Japanese to help transfer knowledge about the system and what they needed to change— for example, a hot key to switch between English and Kanji characters.

HOW MUCH TO STANDARDIZE?

Some applications are local in nature, so it doesn't make sense to seed them throughout a corporation. Others are appropriate to share throughout a business division or in a specific region—North America, for example. Only a very few applications can truly be standardized for use virtually anywhere.

Sid Diamond, former CIO at Black & Decker Corp. and now an independent consultant in Stevenson, Md., figures that only between 5% and 15% of a company's applications are truly global in nature. These include functions such as financial reporting and electronic mail, he says.

"You must be careful in what you designate as a common system. It must be companywide in terms of business functions, and there must be an overwhelming business case for doing so," Diamond says. "And even then you have to provide some room for local flexibility." For example, a common order-processing system must allow for local differences in billing conventions.

Financial-reporting systems are good candidates for standardization: They enable multinational firms to make sense of the numbers coming in from all over the globe. But even here, local differences in monetary units and reporting practices must be accommodated.

Another good business case can be made for operations that run virtually the same around the globe—Pepsico, Inc.'s Pizza Hut chain, for example. "The Pizza Hut business from country to country is not that different," says Alan Deering, vice president of management information services at Pepsico in Purchase, N.Y. "There's a rather significant cost advantage to using software that is already developed rather than developing it again and again." He says this creates consistency and speeds up implementation of systems that are already proved and bug-free.

But even here, the software is "not a mirror image" from country to country, Deering says. "You're implementing about 80% the same; then there are differences in language and tax code." Most IS shops that have rolled out software among different locales estimate that between 60% and 80% of a given system is truly the same, with regional variations accounting for the rest.

SERVICE IN BORA BORA

IS managers looking for a real kick can try installing a PC local-area network in some remote region of a foreign country. When the LAN goes down, or if there are any other problems or questions, who handles them? Someone in the U.S. headquarters group, an IS staffer in a more local place, a vendor in the U.S. or a vendor representative overseas?

As Deering puts it: "When someone who can speak only Polish calls up a vendor's support line here in the states, it can get very interesting." As such, global software implementation can lend an entirely new meaning to the concept of "help desk." Support and service issues must be thought through at the beginning of the process—whether the company will handle it on its own or if there is an outside vendor to provide the service.

Roger Pierce, manager of international accounting at Russell Reynolds Associates, Inc., an executive search firm in New York, has a war story of his own. Russell Reynolds has offices in 12 foreign locations. It implemented an accounting package in four of those offices from a Big Six accounting firm that Pierce declined to name.

"We thought they would be big enough to support the product, and we bought their story that the support would come through their international network of tax, audit and consulting locations," Pierce says. "But it turned out that the product just wasn't a big enough revenue producer for them to manage on a worldwide basis." The vendor's European offices "just weren't interested" in supporting the product, and the Far East affiliates "just didn't know enough," he explains.

Russell Reynolds has since installed an accounting package from another vendor. But the first time through was definitely a "learning experience," Pierce says, and this time "we really did our homework and talked to references instead of taking it at face value."

SOUND ADVICE

When looking at global support and service, keep in mind the following tips:

- As you would with any other software product, talk to actual customers about their experiences.
- Ask for a list of the vendor's overseas support facilities. Find out which ones are bona fide employees and what their skill levels are vs. which ones may be agents or representatives working on behalf of a larger number of suppliers.

Lori Fena, a principal at Fena & Bates, a software licensing consultancy in San Jose, Calif., suggests paying particular attention to "local-to-local" support. This means users in Australia, for example, get supported by whatever vendor location is closest, preferably in the same country but maybe in Hong Kong, instead of being supported by the Boston office.

Whatever happens, it may be worthwhile to consider some advice from Robert Rubin, vice president of information services at Elf Atochem North America, Inc. in Philadelphia. "It's simply a matter of style. Different cultures may solve the problems very differently, but businesspeople have very common objectives."

Globalization of Information Systems Outsourcing: Opportunities and Managerial Challenges

UDAY M. APTE

INTRODUCTION

The problems of U.S. manufacturing industry, including the loss of blue-collar jobs to the overseas countries in the 1970s and 1980s, are well documented and debated (Hayes and Wheelwright, 1984). Recent evidence suggests that the service sector in the U.S. is beginning to face similar difficulties (Apte and Mason 1993, Wysocki 1991). This growing migration of white-collar jobs to overseas is disquieting indeed.

Interestingly, most of all the out-migrating white-collar jobs are characterized by their intensive use of information technology. These jobs are mainly of two types: information systems-related and information processing-related services. The first category of information systems services encompasses managing of information technology—hardware, software, and telecommunications technology. This includes activities such as development and maintenance of software and operating a computer and communications facility. The second category of information processing services involves using information systems to transform, store, or generate information. Thus, the clerical, back-office jobs, such as data entry, transaction processing, data-base creation or updating, and using information systems to make simple, routine decisions, belong to this category. These information service jobs are generally moving to countries such as Barbados, the Philippines, India, and Ireland, where wages are low, where talented and English-speaking labor is plentiful, and where a telecommunications infrastructure is generally available for linking to a host company's computer in the United States.

Apte, Uday. "Globalization of Information Systems Outsourcing: Opportunities and Managerial Challenges." Edwin L. Cox School of Business, Southern Methodist University, Sept. 1994.

Information, unlike products such as automobiles or bags of grain, can be transported quickly and cheaply. Thus, the tasks that deal with information can be conceivably moved halfway across the world if it makes economic sense and is technologically feasible. The trend toward global outsourcing (i.e., selectively turning over certain functions to a sub-contractor) of information services can be traced primarily to two factors: cost reduction pressure and advances in information technology. Faced with increasing pressure to reduce costs, a growing number of U.S. companies are finding the option of global outsourcing of information services quite attractive since the wage rates in many underdeveloped and newly industrialized countries are significantly lower than those in the United States. For example, wages of data entry clerks in the Philippines can be as low as one-fifth of wages in the United States (Hamilton 1988). The progress of information technology has also been an important factor enabling this trend. Telecommunications advances, for example, have allowed companies to move information processing abroad without causing disruption to end users' work (McMullen 1990).

This discussion simply points to the emerging trend of Americans becoming part of an international labor market. The competitiveness of Americans in this global market is essentially going to depend on the functions they can perform and the value those functions can add to the global economy. The corporate executives of today and tomorrow, therefore, should not only be cognizant of this global outsourcing trend but also be able to face the challenges and take advantage of the opportunities made available by the global outsourcing of information systems and processing services.

In discussing the phenomenon of global outsourcing, we adopt the viewpoint of a U.S. business and focus on presenting guidelines to managers in dealing with this issue. The guidelines we develop, however, are equally useful for managers from other developed countries. Similarly, for brevity, the discussion will focus on the information systems services, although the conclusions drawn will be equally applicable to the information processing services. The types of information services being currently outsourced are reviewed first. Next, we analyze in detail the advantages and disadvantages of the outsourcing option. We then take a closer look at various global outsourcing examples and their general characteristics. Analyzing this important and growing phenomenon, finally we develop guidelines for managers in dealing with global outsourcing of information systems. We conclude by presenting a summary of the paper.

OUTSOURCING OF INFORMATION SYSTEM SERVICES

Tracing its roots to the traditional timesharing and professional services of the 1960s, outsourcing has become a valid option today in all areas of information services (Apte 1991). Outsourcing is an umbrella term which covers many information services:

- Information processing services include data entry, transaction processing, and back-office clerical tasks. These tasks are typically well defined, routine, and require little interaction between outsourcer and vendor.

- Contract programming addresses software development and maintenance activities including systems analysis, design, programming, testing, implementation and subsequent maintenance including porting and conversion of systems.

- Facilities management (FM) agreement places the responsibility of operation and support of a system or data center functions, including hardware, software, networking, and personnel with a subcontractor.

- System integration involves development of a fully integrated system (hardware, software, and/or networking) from design through implementation. Once the system is implemented the vendor typically turns the system over to the customer.

- Support operations for maintenance/service and disaster recovery are sometimes covered under FM agreement, but more frequently these are treated as specialties. Other special services include training and education, telephone "hot-line" support, PC support, and so forth.

As seen from the above list, the term outsourcing covers the entire spectrum of information services. It ranges from leasing a whole IS department, to just having a programmer or two develop a simple application, or having a clerk enter non time-critical data.

The growth of outsourcing as an important strategy can be attributed to a number of factors. Cost reduction pressures often trigger companies to consider outsourcing of information services. Other important reasons include the difficulty of finding suitable information systems professionals, the need for access to a leading-edge information technology, and the increased availability of outsourcing services in the marketplace. Outsourcing also has a number of drawbacks, most particularly the loss of control and the natural resistance of IS executives to the outsourcing option.

OUTSOURCING: ADVANTAGES AND DISADVANTAGES

The factors underlying the attractiveness and growth of outsourcing are as follows:

- *Cost reduction, containment, and predictability.* Double-digit growth in the information system (IS) budget was the norm in 1980s, but given the current recession, the present trend is toward flat or low growth IS budgets (Rifkin 1991). The challenge for IS management today is to accomplish more with fewer resources. This mounting cost pressure is seen as the most significant factor driving today's corporate interest in outsourcing (Wilder 1990). Even if the cost of outsourcing is not significantly less than an in-house effort, it tends to become more predictable, because the responsibility of cost overruns often gets placed on the vendor (Clermont 1991). The vendor may also be contractually obliged to meet deadlines, preventing costly delays. The lessened need for in-house IS staff is a significant benefit of outsourcing, given the growing shortage of skilled IS professionals in the United States.

- *Improved focus on strategic use of IT.* Even the IS departments fortunate enough to have a group of experienced and productive IS professionals find outsourcing an important and useful alternative. Outsourcing allows management to focus the available IS talent on IT activities, promoting competitiveness, rather than spending time on routine activities of systems maintenance or operations.

- *Access to leading-edge technology and know-how.* Outsourcing IS functions to an appropriate vendor provides immediate access to the latest in technology and increases the competitiveness of product offerings through the use of state-of-the-art technology that may not be easily available in-house.

- *Availability of outsourcing services.* Recent years have seen a dramatic increase in the number of outsourcing vendors. Aside from the traditional vendors such as Anderson Consulting, EDS, and the big eight accounting firms, the outsourcing market has attracted the traditional hardware vendors including IBM, Digital, and Unisys. As estimated by The Yankee Group, a consulting firm, the size of the outsourcing market in United States alone was about $26 billion in 1989. The market is expected to grow annually at a rate of about 15% to reach $50 billion by 1994. In the same time frame, the global outsourcing market is expected to grow from $101 billion in 1989 to $240 billion in 1994 (McMullen 1990).

In short, outsourcing offers a variety of ways for a corporation to better leverage its resources, manage its costs, and focus on core applications to increase IT's value to corporate objectives. While many outsourcing vendors exist in the United States, the global outsourcing of selected information system functions, discussed subsequently at length, can potentially offer even greater benefits.

Despite the benefits listed above, IS executives frequently resist outsourcing. They see it as a clear threat to their own and to their subordinates' long-term career prospects (McCusker 1991; Mead 1990). After all, by adopting the outsourcing approach they are disbanding their own organization with the likelihood that many IS professionals will not find suitable jobs, or promising career paths, in other functional areas of the corporation. The personnel displacement caused by outsourcing discourages IS executives from taking an objective approach in evaluating outsourcing decisions. More often than not, therefore, evaluation of outsourcing options is initiated by business executives (Clermont 1991).

The costs of negotiating and monitoring the outsourcing contract with the vendor and the cost of reverting to the insourcing option should outsourcing fail, can be substantial. In practice, a company considering an outsourcing option and deciding to do so often finds its best IS staff being absorbed by the outsourcing vendor or jumping the ship to a competitor. The residual staff that is required to monitor the outsourcing contract or to focus on strategic applications is often woefully inadequate to make insourcing a viable option if the company later finds itself unhappy with the outsourcing vendor. Thus the only option available may be to select another outsourcing vendor. The real or perceived irreversibility of outsourcing decisions is often considered a serious risk of this option.

IS executives also complain that outsourcing reduces their control over the quality of the software and the project's timetable since the work is now being carried out by another organization. The company that chooses to outsource a major portion of its IS function can also lose touch with the advances in information technology, a significant shortcoming if IT is strategically important.

GLOBAL OUTSOURCING

The significant disparity of salary levels of personnel between developed and underdeveloped countries is one of the primary reasons behind interest in foreign outsourcing. As we noted earlier the salary levels of underdeveloped and newly industrialized countries are considerably lower than those in developed countries. Vendors from underdeveloped and newly industrialized countries see outsourcing as a very lucrative target market for their IS services, and their pricing advantage has made global outsourcing a small but rapidly growing segment of the overall outsourcing market.

Not all information systems activities are suitable for global outsourcing. For example, facilities management would suffer from the geographic limitations inherent in a global setting. The telecommunication costs would simply be too high for global outsourcing of facilities management to be cost competitive. On the other hand, the data entry and contract programming, and to some extent the systems integration and support activities, are arenas where vendors from underdeveloped countries can certainly compete. And compete they do with vigor especially in data entry and contract programming services.

Data entry was one of the earliest tasks to be globally outsourced. It requires the lowest level of computer literacy. It also requires very little interaction between the customer and the vendor. The customer can mail data forms to the vendor, and the vendor in turn can send the computerized data back via telecommunication lines or by mailing magnetic tapes. Use of systems for data entry or processing of simple forms can be accomplished without the strict need for a common language requirement. For example, Pacific Data Services had been contracting data entry services from China since 1961 (Noble 1986). Even with the trouble that Chinese have with the English language, Pacific Data Services guarantees a 99% accuracy rate for data entry tasks. Today, vendors from many countries participate in data entry partnerships. For example, Mead Data Central has citizens of South Korea, Jamaica, Haiti, and Barbados entering information for its large data bases, such as Nexis (Noble 1986).

Outsourcing has not been limited to simple data entry. Semiskilled jobs are also being globally outsourced. For example, New York Life Insurance and Cigna Corporation have claims processing operations in Ireland (Lohr 1988; Wysocki 1991). An interesting illustration of a high-skill end of the back office work being performed overseas is the Quarterdeck Office Systems' technical-support staff in Ireland, that handles technical queries from users of the Quarterdeck System from all around the world, including the United States (Wysocki 1991).

A small, yet growing trend is also observed in outsourcing of software development activities. India's distinct advantages in this regard are again the existence of very low salaries and abundant availability of English-speaking, technically trained graduates, numbering about a quarter of a million new technical graduates per year (Senn 1991; Hazarika 1991). Some of the major problems faced by operations in India include an inadequate and unreliable telecommunications infrastructure and the shortage of mainframe computers.

Several well-known American companies, including Hewlett-Packard, Texas Instruments, Digital Equipment Corporation (DEC), and more recently, IBM, have set up operations in cities of Bangalore and Bombay. Digital Equipment Corporation writes diagnostic software used in the entire company. To overcome the telecommunications problems, DEC has acquired a dedicated satellite link. The recent announcements of incentives and liberalization of ownership requirements has led to a joint venture between IBM and Tata Industries, an Indian industrial house, for production of PS/2 computer hardware and other software.

Design work is also being outsourced. Texas Instruments employs Indian engineers to write computer aided design software which can design integrated circuits for the company's semiconductor group (Shereff 1989). Boeing Company, in a joint project with a vendor in the Philippines, is developing an airbase inventory-management system. In this project, Filipinos will train Americans in the system's use after its development and implementation (Hamilton 1988).

Many of the outsourcing vendors already have significant command of the English language. Vendors from the Philippines, Singapore, India, and Ireland, for example, pose no communication problems for companies from English-speaking countries such as the United States, United Kingdom, or Canada. The language barrier for companies from non English-speaking countries such as Germany, France, or Japan, however, may be a stumbling block for the same vendors. As shown by the Quarterdeck example earlier, some of these countries can also provide hot-line telephone support for software products of American companies, assuming of course that suitable arrangements for the high quality, reliable telephone lines are made.

GLOBAL OUTSOURCING: FURTHER ADVANTAGES AND DISADVANTAGES

The advantages listed earlier for IS outsourcing in general are also valid for global outsourcing. But there are additional considerations:

- *Substantial cost reduction.* The pricing structures of global outsourcing vendors tend to be extremely attractive. This can lead to significant additional cost saving for an outsourcer. Another way to think about this is that with the same budget, an outsourcer can clear backlog and broaden the portfolio of projects it can complete by using the services of a global outsourcing vendor.

- *Global outsourcing provides a good option for developing and operating a global information system essential for global operations.* Managing global IS, an essential element of global operations, can be very difficult and expensive. Having a global outsourcing vendor can be beneficial in this case. For example, a U.S.-based software package vendor may sell its products around the world and then contract an outsourcing vendor to provide the after-sales support.

- *Access to a large pool of skilled professionals well versed in the latest technology.* Given the economic conditions of some of the third world countries, this benefit may not seem obvious. However, a typical American IS professional is now burdened with old software development technology and habits—a disadvantage of being a first user of information technology. For example, it is easy to find a COBOL programmer, but it is hard to find, at a reasonable cost, a programmer knowledgeable in networking, object-oriented programming, or UNIX environment. In comparison, India, a more recent arrival to IS technology, has a sizable pool of software developers trained in the latest high-tech knowledge and techniques. An added advantage of the labor market in third world countries is the low turnover rate caused by higher unemployment rates.

- *Faster cycle time for development.* Given the size of the human resource pool that the foreign vendors of contract programming can tap into and deploy, and the advanced software engineering methodologies that at least some of them do utilize, product development can proceed quickly.

- *Access to foreign markets.* Protectionism is still an obstacle that the companies interested in global operations must overcome. Many countries do not allow foreign companies to enter the country and market products without substantial tariffs. Others have strict limits on the ownership of companies. Outsourcing partnerships can provide an appropriate foothold in the growing, sizable, and lucrative marketplace of third world countries.

Thus, there are substantial gains to be made through the selective use of global information outsourcing: significant cost savings and capital market gains, faster cycle time, help in developing or operating global information systems, and the access to foreign markets and a skilled labor pool. These benefits have encouraged many companies to begin use of, or investigation into, the global outsourcing option. However, with advantages come certain disadvantages:

- *Communication and coordination.* Even if we assume that the system requirements are well specified, the specifications often change while the system is being designed or programmed. Hence, constant communication—both interpersonal and data communication—between the user, the designers, and the programmer becomes a key for developing quality software. The poor telecommunications infrastructure, a common problem in the underdeveloped countries, can be a serious drawback in this case. High quality, reliable telephone lines necessary for data communication are still rare although available at a premium on a leased-line basis from telephone companies. In developing a large and complex system, the problem of coordinating activities of multiple teams is always a difficult one. These difficulties are only magnified in a global setting.

- *Potential for violation of intellectual property rights.* Many third world countries have lax regulations and laws regarding the honoring of intellectual property rights. For example, for all practical purposes, Taiwan has no copyright protection law. Under these circumstances, an unscrupulous outsourcing vendor may be tempted to violate the intellectual property rights by sharing the software specification with the outsourcer's competitor. Thus, a global outsourcing arrangement may leave an outsourcer open to the risk of theft of its strategic information systems technology. This risk is considered to be a significant drawback of global outsourcing.

- *Lack of control of software quality and project timetable.* With inadequate or ever-changing system specifications, the outsourcing vendor may not be able to deliver the quality software that the outsourcer desires on time. The physical remoteness also makes it difficult to monitor a project's progress and to take corrective actions. Hence, the worry of possible project delays and a sense of having no control over the quality of software is always on the mind of an outsourcer.

- *Unclear government attitudes toward transborder data flows and IS services.* Underdeveloped countries are becoming aware of the potential for increasing their national income by taxing information systems products and services created within their borders. The United States and Europe are lobbying for reducing these duties, but no clear resolution of the conflict has been accepted.

The outsourcer should, therefore, approach the global outsourcing option with sufficient care. As identified above, there are many problems in managing the global outsourcing relationship which are not found in in-house software development or in dealing with the U.S.-based out sourcing vendor. We now examine the managerial considerations pertaining to the global outsourcing option.

GLOBAL OUTSOURCING: MANAGERIAL GUIDELINES

In globally outsourcing information systems, managers are faced with three main decisions: identifying the activities that may be globally outsourced; choosing the right service providers and countries; and creating appropriate arrangements between the domestic and foreign organizations.

IDENTIFY CANDIDATE ACTIVITIES

Not all information systems and processing services should be outsourced. The decision should be guided by two considerations: strategic importance of a service to the company, and the relative efficiency with which the company can perform that service. Consider a

FIGURE 1   Insourcing versus outsourcing (Adapted from Walker 1988)

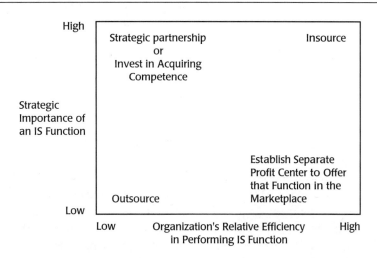

service such as the payroll processing. This service is normally not considered strategically important, since performing it at a level better than the minimum required does not add to the competitiveness of the company. Neither can a small-to-medium company hope to perform payroll processing at a cost lower than an outsourcing vendor, such as ADP, who has specifically set up operations that are fine tuned to carry out payroll service at a large volume and a great efficiency. Thus, it may be appropriate to outsource the payroll processing function.

In general, the higher the strategic importance of a function, and the higher the relative efficiency of performing that function, the less desirable it is as an outsourcing candidate. The actions preferable under different combinations of two underlying factors are given in Figure 1. Thus, a function that scores low (high) on both the dimensions should, in general, be outsourced (insourced). If a function is strategically important and if it cannot be performed with relative efficiency, the company should make the necessary investment so that it can be performed internally with efficiency. Other option is to establish a strategic partnership with another company that can perform it with relative efficiency. In the final case, when a function is not strategically important but can be performed with relative efficiency, the company may want to become an outsourcing vendor for that service. Thus, it may want to establish a separate profit center for offering that service in the marketplace.

Global outsourcing provides information systems managers with new options for meeting their needs. The type of work being outsourced can vary with a company's familiarity with the global environment; with the experience, knowledge, and size of its IS department;

FIGURE 2   System development activities

and with the profile of information system development needs. We have seen in the examples described earlier that a variety of IS activities can be globally outsourced. We believe that the most important requisites of a successful outsourcing relationship are the cost savings potential and the ability to manage the communications process. The simplest way to ensure good communications is to outsource only those activities that are well structured and specified. Thus, global outsourcing of data entry or claims processing activities has a good chance of being successful. The facilities management services such as the data center operation are well structured, but the cost savings potential, due to geographic remoteness, is either very small or nonexistent. Hence, these FM services are normally not globally outsourced. Similarly, the outsourcing of abstract design tasks may meet with greater difficulties because the foreign designer may not have immediate access to the users of the system, and therefore, may not clearly understand the system requirements.

We can view the systems life cycle as a continuum of activities, from the most abstract to the most structured (Figure 2). We propose that in general the structured activities are more amenable to global outsourcing than the abstract activities.

Problem recognition requires an in-depth knowledge of the company to spot the inherent causes, as opposed to the mere symptoms, and to understand which solutions are feasible. While one could imagine asking a consultant to come and study a company, it is doubtful that such consultant could be a foreign one. Cultural and language barriers would make the task that much more difficult for a foreign consultant.

The design phase is also a very abstract process. One must work closely with the users to guarantee the development of a system that meets their needs. Too many systems have failed because of a lack of communication between the designers and the users. This problem would be exacerbated by two teams on opposite sides of the world, or speaking different languages.

Once the specifications have been fully developed, the programming can become a fairly straight-forward process and, therefore, this activity is considered a good candidate for global outsourcing. While the specifications are bound to change over time, these could be managed with well-defined procedures for signing off on the design phase and for approval of changes. These changes should be transmitted from the designer to the programmer. This would improve the communication between individuals and mitigate the possibility of confusion.

Testing and implementation are well-structured activities. These tasks may not require as highly trained individuals, nor is there need for much interaction between the outsourcer and the vendor. Subsequent to system implementation, the training of the outsourcer's employees can be done by those people in the vendor firm most fluent in the language and customs of the outsourcer. The activities such as porting and conversion of systems are highly structured since the task is essentially to move system from one hardware/operating/data-base environment to another. Also given that the current system is usually in operation, the time pressure on system completion is somewhat less. Hence, porting and conversion of systems are considered two of the most ideal activities for global outsourcing.

CHOOSE THE VENDOR

The next important issue that faces an outsourcer is the choice of the global outsourcing vendor. In addition to an obvious factor such as pricing, there are several important characteristics of a vendor that must be analyzed:

- *Track record.* The companies most likely to successfully complete a software project are those with previous experience in outsourcing. Hence, the previous track record of the vendor is a very important factor. In this task one can check the references to determine the quality of outsourcing services previously provided by the vendor.

- *Human and technology resources.* In essence, the basic resource that an outsourcer is purchasing from the vendor is human skills and capacity. Hence, in outsourcing decisions both the project management skills and experience and the specific software engineering skills, such as languages, data-bases, networking skills, and so forth, should be verified. The technology resources should also be checked. For example, if the task involves the use of a particular type of a mainframe, it is imperative that the vendor must either own or have guaranteed access to that mainframe.

- *Staying power of the vendor.* Outsourcing an information system function to a vendor who then goes bankrupt while the work is incomplete is one of the worst scenarios for the outsourcer. Hence, the financial strength and the overall sustaining power of the vendor should be verified. This factor assumes added importance due to the global setting, with its inherent uncertainties regarding the bona fides of the entities.

In addition to the vendor company's qualities, the IS manager must be aware of the political and social environment of the vendor's home-base country. Working with third world countries can create difficulties not typically encountered in dealing with vendors from the developed countries. Some important factors related to the home-base country of the vendor are:

- *Stability of the political and social environment.* This is a very important consideration since a stable environment is the requisite foundation for achieving a beneficial and continued relationship. For example, a change in the style of political governance means a tremendous shock to the operation of the country. Even changes seemingly for the better (such as those found in today's Eastern Europe) do not guarantee increased stability. Countries with sharply divided populations along religious or racial backgrounds are also generally unstable.

- *The attitude of the host country's government toward foreign investment and collaborations in IT.* The attitude of the host country government can make the alliance easy or difficult to manage. Many of the third world countries have been creating incentives to encourage foreign investment. India has created special incentives and relaxed ownership rules for foreign companies (Hazarika 1991). Ireland has financed the upgrading of its telecommunications infrastructure and is offering loan guarantees, interest subsidies, and a maximum corporate tax rate of 10% (Wysocki 1991). The Singaporean government's role in implementing a series of national computer plans designed to make Singapore an economic power in the post-industrial Information Age is particularly noteworthy (Gurbaxani et al. 1990). In specific, the government has emphasized development of necessary IT infrastructure (including advanced telecommunications and human resource development) and maintenance of a favorable investment climate to attract IT producers and sophisticated IT users to the island.

- *Foreign currency restrictions.* An important aspect of the business environment, especially in a case where the outsourcer chooses to establish a wholly owned subsidiary, is the guarantee that the host country's central bank provides access to and allows repatriation of the money earned in the venture. Some governments have dismal histories of nationalization of foreign-owned businesses, while others have stringent restrictions on the foreign exchange. The currency must also be convertible. While many Eastern European countries welcome foreign investment with open arms, the currency earned may be worthless on the world's foreign exchanges.

- *Size of the pool of skilled software professionals.* The low average salary of IS professionals is one of the strongest incentives for global outsourcing. However, in addition to the cost advantage, the host country must have a large population of well-educated, underemployed citizens with a sizable pool of skilled software professionals. Many countries also have large groups of well-educated women of all ages who are traditionally unemployed.

- *Communications.* The necessity of appropriate telecommunication infrastructure has been discussed. Another consideration is the question of command over the common language, as the software projects typically require a substantial amount of verbal communication between the outsourcer and the vendor. Many countries support English as their primary or secondary language, so this is not a great limitation for English-speaking customers. In projects which are quite self-contained, such as data entry, the language of the workers is not as important. However, the vendor management must share the language with the outsourcer to ensure that the work is up to standard.

FIGURE 3   Contractual arrangements

Customer-Vendor Contract	Strategic Partnership	Owned Subsidiary

Increasing Control

- *Time zone difference.* Another consideration is the time zone difference between the customer and vendor if it can be used as an advantage in designing the working arrangements with the global outsourcing vendor. An appropriate time difference and an on-line environment with shared data bases can allow for around-the-clock work, resulting in fast turn-around times. Additionally, if the vendor is using the outsourcer's computers for development, the time difference can allow the vendor employees access to the computer during the outsourcer's off-peak hours, and thereby reduce the ultimate cost to the outsourcer.

Having suggested a number of factors important in analyzing the suitability of the homebase country, we can identify several countries which seem prime candidates for outsourcing relationships. For simple data entry tasks, countries such as the Philippines, Jamaica, Haiti, Barbados, and Ireland have proven records. For more sophisticated design, program testing, and conversion activities, countries such as Ireland, India, Singapore, the Philippines, the Netherlands, and Australia are good choices.

CONTRACTUAL ARRANGEMENTS

The third issue of importance to the outsourcer is the creation of appropriate contractual arrangements with the vendor. Several alternate contractual arrangements are possible. These range from forming a wholly owned foreign subsidiary, to forging a strategic partnership, to developing a standard customer/vendor contract (Figure 3).

The various contractual arrangements identified above provide an outsourcer with different degrees of control. Information processing jobs of data entry or claims processing tend to be well defined, simple, and repetitive. Therefore, the need for control over vendors for these jobs is relatively small. Hence, a simple customer-vendor contract is adequate in this situation. The arrangements required for information system services, however, are different and more complicated. A software development project requires a significant amount of project management and control to ensure success. Conceptually, there are two ways of managing a software project: by controlling outcome or by controlling process.

Outcome standards create clear specifications for what is acceptable work and what is an acceptable schedule. For the customer-vendor relationship this is an obvious choice of control. Development specifications, deliverables, and dates of delivery must be clearly stated. These should include functionality, documentation, and so forth. Appropriate penalties should be outlined for any deviation from the contract.

If the customer has more control over the outsourcing vendor, then the development process itself can be more closely managed and thereby the quality of outcome is assured. This will take more effort on the part of the controlling company than the effort required to control through outcome specification. However, it can help prevent the waste of time and money incurred when a project is belatedly found to be out of specifications and behind schedule. Project management techniques which help control budget and structure tasks can be implemented. Project milestones can be checked regularly to ensure that the project is progressing smoothly. An added advantage of the subsidiary or partnership arrangement is that the risk of intellectual property rights violation is minimized.

It can be seen that the owned subsidiary arrangement gives the maximum amount of control over process. As opposed to this, the standard customer-vendor contract may only allow for control of outcome. Hence, depending on the strategic importance of systems being outsourced and the rules and regulations of the vendor's home-base country, an appropriate contractual arrangement for dealing with the vendor may be chosen.

SUMMARY AND CONCLUSIONS

Although outsourcing of information systems has recently received a considerable press, it has always been used as a solution to the problem of increasing capacity or lowering costs without undertaking an additional fixed cost burden. The information systems executives, faced with significant cost containment pressures, naturally see outsourcing as an important option as it allows them to better leverage their resources, manage their costs, and focus on core applications to increase IT's value to corporate objectives. This has given rise to a large and growing IS outsourcing industry in the United States.

Several countries have large pools of IS professionals who are well trained and whose salary expectations are significantly less than those of their U.S. counterparts. Software vendors from these countries see outsourcing as a lucrative target market for their IS services, and their pricing advantage has made global outsourcing a small but rapidly growing sector of the overall market.

Global outsourcing can lead to substantial benefits: significant cost savings and capital market gains, faster cycle time, help in developing and operating global information systems, and the access to foreign markets and a skilled labor pool. These benefits have encouraged many companies to begin use of, or investigation into, the global outsourcing option. However, with advantages come certain pitfalls which await the unwary. Some of the main drawbacks are problems of communication and coordination, lack of control of quality and timetable, possible violation of intellectual property rights, and rules, regulations, and infrastructure within the vendor's home country.

In exercising the global outsourcing option, a manager is faced with three main decisions: identifying the candidate IS activity for global outsourcing, choosing the right vendor, and finally creating the appropriate contractual arrangements with the vendor. In determining if a given information service activity is suitable for global outsourcing, a manager should consider three characteristics: the strategic importance of the activity, the relative efficiency with which the company can perform that activity, and if the activity is well structured or specified. In choosing the vendor, a manager should consider both the vendor characteristics, such as track record, resource level, and staying power, and the economic-political environment of the home-base country of the vendor. In arriving at the suitable contractual arrangement, a manager should consider the degree of control that is desired for the activity. To ensure better conformity to quality and timetable, and to ensure that intellectual property rights are not violated, the approach of creating an owned subsidiary is preferable.

REFERENCES

Apte, U.M. 1991 "Global Outsourcing of Information Systems and Processing Services," *The Information Society*, Vol. 7 pp. 287–303.

Apte, U.M. and R.O. Mason, "Global Disaggregation of Information-Intensive Services," *Management Science* (forthcoming).

Clermont, P. 1991. "Outsourcing Without Guilt," *Computerworld*, 9 September.

Gurbaxani, V., K.L. Kraemer, J.L. King, S. Jarman, and J. Dedrick. 1990. "Government as the Driving Force Toward the Information Society. National Computer Policy in Singapore," *The Information Society*, 7(2): 155–185.

Hamilton, J.M. 1988. "Jobs at Computer Terminals Link Philippines and US," *Christian Science Monitor*, 8 August.

Hayes, R., and S.C. Wheelwright, 1984. *Restoring Our Competitive Edge: Competing Through Manufacturing*, New York: J. Wiley & Sons.

Hazarika, S. 1991. "In Southern India, a Glimpse of Asia's High-Tech Future," *The New York Times*, 6 October.

Lohr, S. 1988. "The Growth of the Global Office," *The New York Times*, 18 October.

McCusker, T. 1991. "There Is Life After Outsourcing," *Datamation* 1 April.

McMullen, J. 1990. "New Allies: IS and Service Suppliers," *Datamation*, 1 March.

Mead, T. 1990. "Will Your Job Be Outsourced?" *Datamation*, 15 December.

Metzger, R.O., and M.A. von Glinow. 1988. "Off-site Workers: At Home and Abroad," *California Management Review*, Spring: 101–111.

Noble, K. 1986. "America's Service Economy Begins to Blossom—Overseas," *The New York Times*, 14 December.

Rifkin, G. 1991. "Heads That Roll if Computers Fail," *The New York Times*, 14 May.

Senn, J. 1991. "The Emerging Software Passage to India," *SIM Network*. VI(I), Jan/Feb.

Walker, G. 1988. "Strategic Sourcing, Vertical Integration and Transaction Costs," *Interfaces*, 18(3):62–73.

Werner, M. 1986. "Transborder Data Flows: A Cost Benefit Analysis," *Canadian Banker*, 93(5): 36–39.

Wilder, C. 1990. "Outsourcing: Fad or Fantastic," *Computerworld*, 1 January.

Wysocki, B. 1991. "Overseas Calling," *The Wall Street Journal*, 14 August.

The Organizational and Cultural Context of Systems Implementation: Case Experience from Latin America

DANIEL ROBEY & ANDRES RODRIGUEZ-DIAZ

INTRODUCTION

Multinational corporations (MNCs) often experience difficulty in the implementation of new technologies, including computer-based information systems, into subsidiaries in other countries. Some of these difficulties pertain to technical matters, but many can be traced to the social context of implementation. Researchers have recognized the importance of social factors on the implementation process for some time. For example, Vertinsky, Barth, and Mitchell (1975) conclude that technical solutions often mobilize counter forces aimed at reversing significant social changes and that changes in technical systems often generate conflict between management styles. A successful implementation process must carefully consider both the technological readiness of the target organization and the social context of implementation.

The social context of implementation includes the specific organizational setting which is the target of the implementation and the wider cultural and national setting within

Robey, Daniel, and Rodriquez-Diaz, Andres. "The Organizational and Cultural Context of Systems Implementation: Case Experience from Latin America." *Information and Management*, vol. 17, (1989), 229–239.

Earlier versions of this paper were presented at the IFIP conference on The Impact of Information Systems in Developing Countries (November 1988 in New Delhi) and at the Business Association of Latin American Studies conference (February 1989 in Boca Raton, Florida). The authors thank Sushil Gupta, Karen Hambrick, Bonnie Kaplan, and Christine Specter for their contributions to this paper.

which the organization operates. Organizational theorists have recently acknowledged the importance of the cultural properties of organizations by focusing on values, symbols, belief systems, and deep assumptions held by members in an organization (Kennedy and Deal, 1982; Ott, 1989; Peters and Waterman, 1982; Schein, 1985). This organizational culture affects the meanings that members attach to their physical and social surroundings and can potentially affect behavior and performance of an entire organization. The importance of national cultures have been well-documented for a long time (Smircich, 1983). In the case of MNCs, both of these contexts may become influential.

This paper reports the efforts of one MNC in the transportation industry to automate certain accounting functions by implementing a computer-based information system in two of its Latin American subsidiaries. The case illustrates that social factors affect the success of implementation and illustrates how these social factors can be both managed and mismanaged during the implementation process.

CULTURAL CONTEXT AND IMPLEMENTATION

A Conceptual Model

Much has been written about the transfer of technology between cultures, particularly transfer from industrial nations to developing countries. One strand of this literature focuses upon the role of organizations, particularly MNCs, in effecting technology transfer (Kedia and Bhagat, 1988). This view regards technology transfer as the aggregation of transactions between organizations operating in different cultural environments. Rather than focusing on the characteristics of the adopting organization or country alone, this emphasizes the compatibility between the transferring and adopting organizational and national cultures. The successful adoption of new technologies for production and administrative work rests upon a process of implementation that minimizes the differences between two cultures. This conclusion is consistent with the writing on organizational culture (e.g., Schein, 1985; Ott, 1989), where the importance of *shared* meanings is emphasized. Thus, if an MNC were to implement a new technology into its third-world subsidiaries, cultural differences would pose problems, whereas compatible cultures would ease implementation.

Organizational culture, rather than national culture seems most relevant to management issues that focus upon organizational tasks and technologies (Kiggundu, Jogensen, and Hafsi, 1983). Where management issues pertain to an organization's relationship to its environment (for example, strategic or public regulation), broader national cultures become more relevant. Because an information system is essentially an administrative technology, the relevant sources of resistance to an information system would appear to be focused at the organizational level. Of course, there is always some connection between national and organizational cultures.

FIGURE 1   A conceptual model for understanding cultural constraints on technology
transfers. Adapted from Kedia and Bhagat (1988).

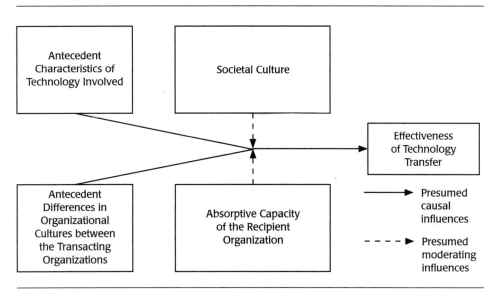

Kedia and Bhagat (1988) developed a model for understanding cultural constraints on technology. Figure 1 is a modified version of their model, which shows technological characteristics and organizational cultural differences as the antecedents of successful technology transfer. National cultural characteristics and local characteristics of adopting organizations are shown to moderate the relationship between the antecedents and effectiveness. The central point of this model is that organizational differences make implementation more difficult. By considering organizational cultural differences to be a primary cause of implementation success, and national culture to be a moderating influence, the model forces an examination of specific issues within the organizations engaged in a transaction (Kedia and Bhagat, 1988:563). In short, compatibility between the cultural assumptions of the implementors and those of the target organization contributes to successful implementation, whereas incompatibility contributes to failure in implementation.

Culture and Meaning

Culture, at either the national or organizational level, provides an interpretive context that enables members of the culture to make sense out of their surroundings. It guides their actions with deeply held collective assumptions about their environment and the appropriate courses of action to take within that environment (Schein, 1985). All types of behavior are guided by culture, from complex business negotiations to simple interpersonal greetings.

Because cultural assumptions are acquired through early socialization, people are usually unaware of their effect on behavior. Only when a person is confronted by different cultural assumptions does he or she become aware of the cultural context. For example, in Japan the basic reference point for behavior is the group, not the individual (Sethi, Namiki, and Swanson, 1984). In Western cultures, the individual tends to be the reference point. Personal ambition, particularly an eagerness to move up the hierarchy of an organization, is inappropriate organizational behavior in Japan whereas it is expected in North American companies. Effective management requires an understanding of such cultural differences and the way they influence behavior.

Any study of system implementation should recognize that technology can carry different social meanings in different cultural settings (Barley, 1986: Robey, 1988). Cultures develop and use technologies, or artifacts, for various purposes, and computer-based information systems are an important group of artifacts. It is often assumed that computer technology plays a strong role in economically developing countries. This is undoubtedly true, but the complexity of the change process cannot be appreciated in a simple "technological imperative" model. More accurately, the same technology may have different meanings within an adopting organization's culture than it has in the developing organization's culture. The process of resolving these incompatible interpretations will undoubtedly affect the degree of implementation success and the resultant consequences of the technology.

Cultural meanings emerge over time as members gain experience with the technology and see its possibilities for supporting certain cultural values and threatening others. As members collectively make sense of the technology, they may view it as an attempt to control their actions or as a liberating tool. They may resent the implementors' cultural assumptions and resist using the system regardless of its technical features, or they may embrace the opportunity to move into the computer age and learn new skills. The information system may come to symbolize undesirable themes within a culture (such as American imperialism) or positive ones (technological progress and economic development). Much of this sense-making process is difficult to predict, but the way in which technology is introduced has a strong influence along with the objective properties of the technology. Any organizational changes that accompany the introduction of information technology, therefore, are the product of an emergent process rather than the result of deterministic external forces (Markus and Robey, 1988).

For any specific case, the consequences of implementing an information system are best explained by tracing the history of system development and implementation. The case study remains a valid research method for tracing these processes (Benbasat, Goldstein, and Mead, 1987). In the following research we are interested in observing how an information system project that was proposed and developed in one culture (that of the parent corporation) encountered resistance in the culture where it was implemented. We are interested in both the immediate organizational cultures as well as the national cultures because both are relevant to implementation. We are also interested in describing the

FIGURE 2   Partial organizational chart of the airline and its Latin American subsidiaries

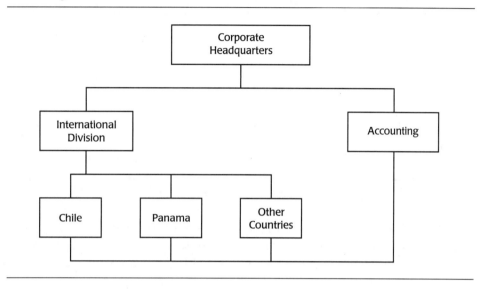

actions that the implementor took in response to resistance and how a revised strategy increased the success of the same system when implemented in a second subsidiary.

CASE STUDY

Corporate Setting

The corporation described in this paper is a major U.S. airline company, operating subsidiary sales offices in various parts of the world. With deregulation of the U.S. airline industry, the company experienced severe financial problems due to competition from newer, low-cost carriers. With a mature work force of older pilots and flight attendants, the company found it difficult to cut its labor costs to remain competitive. The role of computer-based information systems in reducing costs was important in this environment.

The company operates nine subsidiaries in Latin America, each located in a city on the airline's route system. Figure 2 shows the relationships among corporate headquarters, corporate accounting, the international division, and the Latin American subsidiaries. The function of the international division was to exercise financial control over sales offices.

Before automation of the sales offices, passenger flight coupons were collected by each subsidiary and mailed to the corporate accounting office in the U.S. to be entered into a centralized accounting system. Reports on the performance of each office were routed back through the international division and on to the subsidiary's management. Local managers typically enjoyed high status within their countries, which enabled them to interact frequently with financial and governmental figures in those countries. As in many developing countries, these relationships were important in conducting daily business.

Objectives of the Automation Project

Several problems experienced by the airline led to a proposal to automate the processing of sales data in the subsidiaries' accounting offices. First the corporation was attempting to integrate the accounting functions of its newly acquired international operations with the established corporate accounting practices. An automated accounting system would provide consistency in the reporting methods of the South American subsidiaries by imposing common data formats on tapes sent to corporate headquarters.

Second, the cost of data entry would be reduced by redistributing the operation to locations in Latin America with lower labor costs. Data entry in the U.S. was much more costly, especially when the fringe benefits of U.S. workers were taken into account. The individuals in corporate accounting who were currently responsible for processing the data from the South American stations could be either eliminated by attrition or reassigned to perform other tasks.

Third, local management would receive more timely information for making decisions. A computer-based system would also assist them by providing electronic spreadsheets, word processing, and other office automation products.

The project was approved in early 1984 on a one-year payback criterion, which was necessary during this period due to the ongoing financial problems of the airline.[1] The system proposal convinced corporate management that the savings gained from reduction of personnel alone would provide the necessary cost justification. The additional benefits gained from utilizing a common, corporate-wide accounting practice and assisting local management were considered "icing on the cake."

System Design and Development

System development consisted of writing programs to allow the local clerical staff to record sales and make journal entries. Data were to be entered by operators at the terminal, keying in the data as they read the passenger flight coupons. The system prompted input, signaled errors, and prompted corrections that were detected. Data input would be controlled by a system of tables that validated input and controlled important items such as exchange rates, customer account numbers, and so on. History files would be updated each day, and weekly tapes would be generated and sent to corporate headquarters. The new system's outputs would have to match the formats of the host corporate computer.

---

1   The one-year payback was not subject to a post-implementation audit in the company. Once justified, systems were not held to their payback projections nor were projects disbanded because of the payback period if system development time was excessive.

Hardware for the local system consisted of a Motorola 68020-based Unix operating system capable of supporting up to eight CRT terminals and two line printers per device. Storage consisted of 80 megabytes of direct access disk storage and unlimited offline tape capacity. Application programs were written in COBOL and in C. The system contained some dial-up communications, used mainly in supporting trouble-shooting efforts directed from corporate headquarters in the U.S.

The project was initiated in March, 1984 by the corporate accounting department, which had the responsibility for receiving and entering sales data for the South American countries. The historical relationship between corporate accounting and the subsidiaries was abrasive. Corporate accounting thought they had all the information and authority necessary to make any decision that had to do with implementing systems, and local management resented the fact that corporate headquarters imposed certain rulings on them without requesting their input. Corporate management was concerned with the immediate reduction of costs and was not really interested in obtaining input from the South American countries.

The extent of the subsidiaries' involvement in the design stage was headquarters' circulation of a copy of the final design specifications with a request for input from local management. The inputs from local management, if ever provided, never found their way back to corporate management. Further, corporate accounting dealt directly with the local management without involving the assistance of the international division, which was the department formally in charge of South American operations.

Once the project was approved, the location for pilot implementation was considered. Corporate management selected the subsidiary located in Santiago, Chile because it had low enough volume to provide a safe test, but Chile also provided enough data to perform an adequate evaluation. Selection was made at corporate headquarters without soliciting input from the local management of any of the potential sites.

The system was developed by the corporate computer services department. The development schedule experienced minor setbacks due to a transfer and replacement of one member of the computer services staff. Acceptance testing was still underway a week before the scheduled implementation, and the first hands-on user testing in Chile had to occur approximately two weeks before implementation, and that testing could only last two days.

Implementation in Chile

Hardware shipping and installation. The transportation of the system hardware from the test area to the final destination took about 60 days, including the delays due to export requirements and customs clearance in Chile. The implementation schedule slipped by about two weeks due to missing or improper documentation required to remove the equipment from customs in Santiago. Had the paperwork not been readily available in the U.S. the schedule would have been severely delayed because the required paperwork usually took a few weeks to prepare. In order to expedite importation proceedings, the services of a customs broker were used in Santiago.

Once the equipment was cleared through customs and arrived at the office in Santiago, the boxes were stored in a room designated to house the new system. The manager responsible for the local accounting department ordered that the boxes and crates remained sealed and that access to the room was forbidden.

After its arrival, the computer services team set up the system unit, an expansion unit, a printer, and three terminals. While they were setting up the equipment, they overheard comments from some of the clerical workers expressing feelings of fear and concerns about the time required to learn this new machine. Some wondered whether they could avoid having to work on the machine. Since all these comments were spoken in Spanish, only one of the individuals on the implementation team (who was bilingual) understood what was being said.

After discussing the potential problem of operator resistance, the implementation team made a decision to remove the strict security associated with the computer room. The clerical staff was given a hands–on demonstration intended to relieve their anxieties. Some assurances were made regarding job security and the role of the machine in helping them and the company. After this brief introduction the atmosphere in the office seemed less anxious.

Selection and training of system administrators. The computer services team then turned to the selection and training of candidates for the job of system administrator. This supervisory position was required by the local management because this person would train the clerical staff in the operation of the system. Candidates were selected through a joint effort from all the parties involved, including local management, computer services, and corporate accounting. Three candidates were selected, each of whom currently supervised one of the three functional areas in the local accounting department. Each was respected by his or her peers and understood the current accounting procedures well.

The team's corporate accounting representative trained all three of the candidates on the new accounting procedures first, then the two computer services representatives trained them in the operation of the system. Because the new procedures changed the chart of accounts, all users would have to learn new account numbers for making journal and ledger entries. In addition, training was confused by the manager of the accounting department's discovery of several areas where new accounts had to be created in order to handle some intricacies of Chilean business.

The responsibility for these unexpected specifications belonged to both the local and corporate personnel. Local management had received copies of the new chart of accounts in advance but had not responded to corporate headquarters. Headquarters had provided the chart of accounts and the accompanying documentation in English with no real effort to ensure that the local office understood the changes. While all of the candidates knew some English, their proficiency was quite low. The adjustments to the chart of accounts were handled by telephone conversations between the team and headquarters in the weeks that followed.

The system-related training was provided by the only team representative who was fluent in both English and Spanish. He had developed part of the system application in the United States as a member of the corporate computer services department. The system-related functions also lacked Spanish-language manuals. The training progressed well considering that the individuals involved had never worked with a computer. The concepts in the English language manuals were presented in Spanish by the trainer, who covered basic concepts such as temporary work files used during data entry, permanent work files, and history files.

Of the candidates being trained for the role of system administrator, one individual expressed interest far beyond that of the other two candidates. After a few training sessions the interest levels of the other two candidates fell to the point that the implementation team no longer considered them as candidates for the position. They remained in training to provide backup to the primary system administrator. Unfortunately, one of the drop-outs was the choice of the manager of the local accounting department to become the system administrator.

Training of the system administrators continued with a detailed explanation of the data flow from the data entry screen to the point where it became part of the history files. The candidates were also trained on the physical functioning of the system (use of floppy diskettes, cartridge tapes, printers, and terminals) and on the data entry and report producing aspects of the clerical job. They were instructed on how to solve problems dealing with data entry, such as batches out of balance and incorrect entries, and other common data entry errors.

Final selection of the system administrator was the source of some conflict between local management and corporate accounting. In effect, the system administrator would become the data processing and accounting representative in the local country, reporting through a direct line to corporate, by-passing the local country's management structure. The system administrator would become responsible for the day to day operation of the system, supply system knowledge to local management, and serve as the corporate representative for the project. In addition, the system administrator would retain all responsibilities held prior to the conversion and perform all of these tasks for no additional compensation.

Creation of a role this influential was controversial, and the U.S. team and Chilean management disagreed on who was the best candidate. There was only one clearly qualified candidate from the implementation team's viewpoint, but this person was viewed as too independent by the local managers. Local management's favored choice was someone with more loyalty, but corporate viewed this person as too much of a "yes man." The corporate team won this contest and established their choice as system administrator over the opposition of the local managers.

Clerical training and testing. The training of the clerical staff also lacked Spanish-language manuals and was complicated by the new account numbers. Most of the clerical staff did not understand English at all. The terms shown on the data entry screens were in Spanish, but not in the local dialect.

The candidates for system administrator assisted in the training of the clerical staff in their respective areas. This allowed the computer services representatives to train advanced individuals from each group on their specific job functions, i.e., sales and accounts receivables. The sales processing portion was the most important from the corporate standpoint, because it would allow them to off-load the sales processing to the local management. The accounts receivables portion was the most important to the local management, because it would allow them to track their receivables more effectively.

Clerical training was conducted during regular office hours in addition to the normal work load and was not compensated with an increase in pay. The stress generated by such intense training produced exhaustion and lowered employee morale. During the training session many clerks feared losing their jobs if they did not complete their work.

Testing was performed in parallel with the current accounting system to validate the information through two separate systems. Parallel testing proceeded for two months because of system problems and users' misunderstandings of the new accounting procedures. After the second month of parallel testing, the team was satisfied with validity and integrity of the system and authorized the cut-over to the new system.

Evaluation and redesign. Soon after the cut-over, the Chilean managers began to complain to the corporate accounting office about problems with the system. Similar complaints came to corporate accounting laterally through the international division, which had line control over the Latin American subsidiaries (see Figure 1). So far, the international division had not been involved with the project. However, its influence became apparent when a newly appointed director in corporate accounting, whose specific responsibility was to run the South American accounting operation, suggested a new look at the system in Santiago. The vice president of the international division had taken the opportunity to discuss the Chilean problem with the vice president of corporate accounting, exerting pressure on them to "accept help" in getting the system to work better. The essence of the international vice president's message was that accounting lacked the necessary finesse in dealing with local managements in South America.

Based on this advice, corporate accounting took a closer look at the system with thoughts of redesign. Specifically, the system's procedure for making journal entries was much too cumbersome. A streamlined solution was sought that allowed the user to make the same number of entries per screen but to retain the cross-reference necessary to meet both the reporting requirements of corporate headquarters and the Chilean government. The initial design had underestimated the incompatibility between these conflicting reporting requirements.

Redesign efforts lasted from December, 1984 until June, 1985. The international division was given the role to coordinate the relations between corporate accounting and the local management, becoming the primary mediator between them. In an effort to increase the involvement of the Chilean management, the international division proposed that the manager from Chile go the U.S. and become the representative for all the other Latin American countries for the duration of the redesign process. Several conferences were held that allowed teams from specific countries to understand the new system of accounting procedures that they would soon have to use. These managers also visited Santiago for an on-line demonstration of the system. At each demonstration a U.S. computer services representative participated actively.

Once the redesigned system was accepted by all the parties involved, the development effort commenced at an accelerated pace for another six months. When the redesigned system went into final test in Chile, it was a custom-tailored product, complete with full documentation on system and accounting procedures in Spanish which the locals could understand.

Implementation in Panama

The decision to implement the system in a second South American accounting office was a very sensitive issue for corporate headquarters. Corporate accounting wished to continue the project, but the international division insisted that this implementation be free of the problems encountered in Chile. The computer services department in the U.S. agreed to provide the support necessary to bring Panama up on the system, including a pre-delivery site survey and "get acquainted" meeting with the local management and staff.

At this meeting the candidates for system administrator were selected. Selection was made jointly by the data processing department and the local manager. The data processing representatives provided the local manager with a set of qualifications needed for the system administrator position, and the local manager selected three primary candidates. The initial meeting gave local staff the opportunity to meet the implementation team and to receive copies of system documentation printed in both English and Spanish.

Whereas the team in Santiago consisted of one accounting representative and two data processing representatives, one of whom was bilingual, the team for Panama consisted of two data processing representatives, the system administrator from Chile, and one Chilean clerk. All members of the Panama team were bilingual. No representative from the corporate accounting department participated on the Panama team.

The use of the Chilean system administrator and one member of the Chilean clerical staff in the Panama training sessions proved to be invaluable. These individuals were versed in the daily operation of the system and assisted the staff in Panama with many problems and questions. The data processing personnel conducted the formal training for the system administrators, but the individuals with practical experience supplied real life examples.

In Chile local management had taken no active part in the training and had opposed the system completely. By contrast, the Panamanian management insisted on participating in every aspect of the training, both clerical and system-related. In Chile the staff's first reactions were anxiety and fear over losing employment: in Panama the initial surge of interest was so large that scheduling was necessary in order to accommodate everyone at a terminal for at least part of the day.

The training of the clerical staff and the system administrators was conducted simultaneously. This was possible because of the assistance from the Chilean clerk who performed a large portion of the clerical training. She showed the clerks how to prepare their work and familiarized them with the new accounting procedures, teaching shortcuts for associating the old account numbers with the new ones.

Parallel testing was performed to ensure that the data tapes sent to the U.S. could be accepted by the corporate host computer. Although the systems in Chile and Panama were identical in function, some of the unique accounting practices accepted by the Panamanian government had to be tested. The result of this parallel test was a fully debugged system except for the items that were considered country-dependent (about 20 percent of the system). Parallel testing lasted one month although the volume of data put through almost equaled the amount that Chile processed in its two-month test.

The system went "live" two months after the initial test. The system administrators were all of equal knowledge and interest, thereby eliminating the need to single out one individual as primary. The local clerical staff was very pleased with the system and the assistance they received from their Chilean counterparts. The local management was relieved to see the implementation go so well, especially after hearing about the problems in Chile. The international division, corporate accounting, and computer services all acknowledged each other's contributions. The only difficulty was the Chilean managers' objection to the use of their personnel for training in Panama. However, this objection was quickly removed by the international division in a formal public acknowledgement of the Chilean contribution to the successful implementation in Panama.

DISCUSSION

The case study presented here affords comparisons between subsidiaries in two developing South American countries that experienced different degrees of success in implementing information technology. Obviously the implementation team learned from the problems they experienced in Chile and avoided most of them in Panama, implementing the system in far less time and with far greater acceptance. The reasons for this success cannot be traced to differences in the technology because each country implemented basically the same information system. Rather, explanation of the differences between the two settings depends upon the social context.

Social context is often operationalized as national culture, and numerous studies of technology transfer have focused on the differences among national systems of beliefs, values, and social traditions. A comparison between Chile and Panama reveals some cultural and political differences, but not of the extent that would explain the drastic differences in implementation outcomes between the two countries. It is more likely that the immediate, organizational cultures of the subsidiaries provided the context within which the meaning of the information system was interpreted. This level of culture focuses on issues such as job security, managerial power, and work efficiency. According to the model presented in Figure 1, significant differences between the organizational culture would predict difficulties in implementation.

Examining the reactions of the two subsidiaries in this light reveals a distinct contrast. In Chile the system was perceived as a threat to workers and to local management. Workers were concerned with job security from the outset, and managers perceived an erosion of their power base and possibly their stature in the local business community. These reactions were not due to the inherent characteristics of the technology but rather to the actions taken by the corporate implementation team. The team did not involve the end users, they did not provide important manuals in Spanish, they by-passed the international division, and they overruled the local management's choice of system administrator. These actions reflected the cultural assumptions of corporate accounting and signaled that they owned the system and that it would be used to control Chilean operations. Only when the implementation process was modified by the involvement of the international division did the system get redesigned and implemented successfully.

In Panama, the system was eagerly accepted, but not because it was a better system. Rather, the actions of the implementation team were adjusted to involve the international division, to involve Panamanian management in early discussions and demonstrations, to use Chilean clerical workers in the training, to avoid the conflict over choosing one system administrator, and to communicate in Spanish. The signal conveyed by these implementation tactics was that the system was a local product, embodying assumptions compatible with the business culture of the Panamanian subsidiary.

The role of the international division was particularly important because the international division mediated the relationship between the U.S. team and the South American managers. The international division had the trust and respect of the local managers and could play a credible role in facilitating the integration of the U.S. team into the business environment of Panama. The U.S. staff and the local managers were involved in social gatherings that the U.S. team initially regarded as unimportant and inefficient. However, the team learned that social functions are an integral part of business in Latin America, and they ultimately benefitted from these activities.

It is tempting to contrast this case as evidence of good and bad implementation practices rather than evidence of cultural compatibility. One might argue that no system implemented in the way that the corporate group implemented the system in Santiago would ever be successful. This criticism sees good implementation practices as universal rather than culturally bound. The research design used in this study cannot unequivocally determine whether the outcomes observed were caused by implementation practice or by the interaction of practice and culture. However, the team members approached the Chilean project in the same way that they approached similar projects in the U.S. They appeared surprised by the difficulties they encountered and admitted some bewilderment over why this standard approach did not work for them. Thus there is indirect evidence that the implementation practices only became "bad management" as a result of cultural differences.

While the case generalized beyond the specific settings, it does illustrate a basic point about implementing information systems in different cultural contexts. Implementation teams play a key role in influencing the use and consequences of new systems because their actions send signals interpreted by the members of the target organization. This symbolic behavior affects the meanings that the information system has for managers and users in the target organization. These meanings are not inherent in the technology itself; they are supplied by the prospective users. Implementation tactics, such as the printing of technical manuals in a language that the users cannot understand, convey an important social message quite apart from the system's technical features, and that message may drastically affect the success of the implementation effort. When the cultures of implementors and adoptors differ so dramatically as they did in the Chilean case, we would expect resistance and, unless corrective measures are taken, system failure.

Unfortunately, simple prescriptions for achieving cultural compatibility are not available. Rather, practitioners should respect the complexity of culture as a source of implementation problems and appreciate the need for compatibility between cultures. Although user involvement was instrumental in the success of the system in Panama, this does not mean that user involvement is always appropriate. Rather, implementors must become generally aware of their role in creating social change. They should not assume that users are resisting the technology and attempt to overcome this resistance with more extensive training, user involvement, user-friendly interfaces, or any of the other common remedies for implementation woes. Rather, implementors should try to understand the organizational context within which their actions are interpreted and given meaning. They may then see ways to adjust their actions so the signals they convey are compatible with the cultural context of the user.

In most cases this is a difficult task for people whose primary training has been technical. The case illustrates that an intermediary such as an international division can aid in raising implementors' awareness of what their actions mean. An intermediary can also assume responsibility for part of the implementation process, if "only" by providing opportunities for technicians and managers to meet socially outside of the office. To the extent that such meetings enable more effective communication between implementors and users, they can be just as important as training, testing, or even fundamental design activities.

REFERENCES

Barley, S.R., "Technology as an Occasion for Structuring Evidence from Observations of CT Scanners and the Social Order of Radiology Departments," *Administrative Science Quarterly* (1986) 78–108.

Benbasat, L., Goldstein, D.K., and Mead, M., "The Case Research Strategy in Studies of Information Systems," *MIS Quarterly* (1987) 369–386.

Deal, T.E., and Kennedy, A.A., *Corporate Cultures*, Addison-Wesley, Reading, MA, 1982.

Kedia, B.L., and Bhagat, R.S., "Cultural Constraints on Transfer of Technology Across Nations: Implications for Research in International and Comparative Management," *Academy of Management Review* (1988) 559–571.

Kiggundu, M.N., Jogensen, J.J., and Hafsi, Taieb, "Administrative Theory and Practice in Developing Countries: A Synthesis," *Administrative Science Quarterly* (1983) 66–84.

Markus, M.L., and Robey, D., "Information Technology and Organizational Change: Causal Structure in Theory and Research," *Management Science* (1988) 583–598.

Ott, J.S., *The Organizational Culture Perspective*, Brooks, Cole, Pacific Grove, CA., 1989.

Peters, T.J., and Waterman, R.H., Jr., *In Search of Excellence*, Harper & Row, New York, 1982.

Robey, D., "The Meanings of Information Technology in the Workplace," paper presented to the Society for Industrial and Organizational Psychology, 1988.

Schein, E.H., *Organizational Culture and Leadership*, Jossey-Bass, San Francisco, 1985.

Sethi, S.P., Namiki, N., and Swanson, C.N., *The False Promise of the Japanese Miracle*, Pitman, Marshfield, MA, 1984.

Smircich, L., "Concepts of Culture and Organizational Analysis," *Administrative Science Quarterly* (1983) 339–358.

Vertinsky, L., Barth, R.T., and Mitchell, V.F., "A Study of OR/MS as a Social Change Process," in R. Schultz and D. Slevin (eds.), *Implementing Operations Research/Management Science*, New York: Elsevier, 1975.

A Standard Response

SANFORD E. DOVER

THE FIRST GLOBAL QUALITY INITIATIVE, from Japan, left American manufacturing in its dust. But while the Japanese movement transformed the international economic climate, its effect on the day-to-day workings of IS departments was far less dramatic. Now another quality thrust—this one from Europe—is gathering steam internationally. And CIOs who ignore it may endanger their departments' standing within their companies—and their companies' competitive position both at home and abroad.

The new movement is embodied in ISO 9000, a quality standard published by the International Standards Organization in Geneva. Unlike the Japanese movement that crystallized for the rest of the world with the introduction of the Honda Accord in 1975, ISO 9000 does not focus exclusively on manufacturing processes. Rather, it covers 20 functions within a company that affect the delivery of a quality product or service. These functions include training, purchasing, inspection and testing, aftersales service—and information systems.

Many people are calling ISO 9000 the second global quality initiative. The standard originated in the European Community's plan to become a single market on Jan. 1, 1993. Member nations wanted assurances that products moving across their borders would meet certain quality standards, regardless of their country of origin. Although compliance with ISO 9000 is purely voluntary, European companies have acted quickly to gain the competitive advantage that goes along with certification. England is currently in the forefront, with 20,000 companies certified since the standard's publication in 1987.

At the same time that Europe was turning to ISO 9000, standards bodies in the United States and other countries were considering revising their own quality guidelines. Cognizant that such efforts would probably duplicate—without appreciably improving upon—the European-inspired standard, these bodies chose instead to adopt ISO 9000. To date, approximately 400 U.S. companies—including Eastman Kodak Co. and E.I. du Pont de Nemours & Co.—have registered as ISO-compliant, and many are beginning to demand that their suppliers also become ISO-certified. As public awareness of the standard grows, the number of certified companies may swell to the hundreds of thousands.

The overall ISO 9000 guidelines set forth three objectives. The first is to achieve and sustain the quality of products or services so as to continually meet the customer's stated or implied needs. The second is to convince company management that the intended quality is being achieved and sustained. The third is to convince the customer.

Traditionally, IS organizations have labored only on the periphery of the quality movement, frustrated by the difficulties of translating the principles of manufacturing quality into IS quality. Yet, ironically, IS has greater need for the discipline imposed by a quality standard than almost any other department. This is because, while IS executives have done a good job of managing technology, generally they have done a poor job of managing their organizations. IS staff members tend to focus on the creative aspect of their profession rather than on accountability. As a result, the rest of the company tends to think of IS as a loose cannon that cannot be relied upon to produce consistent excellence. In 1991, the ISO published ISO 9000-3—guidelines for the application of ISO 9000 to the development, supply and maintenance of software. By adopting 9000-3, IS departments can achieve discipline and uniformity without sacrificing creativity.

Coming into compliance with ISO 9000-3 usually takes from eight to 14 months for an autocratic, single-platform IS organization with 150 to 250 staff members. In the process of seeking registration, an IS organization may find that it is already in compliance. Here's what to look for:

- Does the organization have concise documentation available for procedures that affect the quality of development and support activities?

- Are those procedures being followed consistently by competent people with appropriate training?

- Is there a document-control scheme to ensure that obsolete documents are purged and current documentation is available where and when it is needed?

- Are internal audits performed by qualified assessors, and do they result in effective corrective action by management?

If these conditions do not exist, the organization will need to go through several steps in order to come into compliance with ISO 9000-3. It must first determine best practices for all procedures—unit testing, for example—that affect product quality. Those practices must then be documented and communicated to staff, who are required to follow them at all times. Finally, the results of following these practices must be demonstrated to internal and external customers, as well as to auditors.

This process will not conflict with any ongoing total-quality management program, most of which involve reducing defect rates. ISO 9000-3 is supportive of that goal, but it emphasizes preventing problems rather than correcting them after they have occurred. In addition, ISO 9000-3 is designed to work with all of the major software-development methodologies in use. The standard's flexibility recognizes that no matter how an IS organization chooses to build and implement its systems, certain things must be done well.

The importance of ISO 9000 to any company hoping to do business in Europe is obvious. But the standard's appeal also stems from the fact that it is less demanding than the Malcolm Baldrige National Quality Award. Because it encompasses only 40 to 50 percent of the Baldrige requirements, ISO 9000 is seen by many as a stepping-stone to the Baldrige.

ISO 9000 has another advantage over its more celebrated cousin. Many people have begun to decry the Baldrige Award as a lot of hoopla surrounding a one-time demonstration of achievement, rather than a permanent commitment to quality. ISO 9000, on the other hand, is entirely market-driven, a response to customers who want reassurance that a company has quality processes and can be relied upon to deliver a quality product.

Toward that end, organizations that wish to gain and retain certification must establish internal audit groups, specially trained to make sure the organization is in compliance. Internal audits take place at least once a year and are buttressed by external audits conducted by representatives of the certifying organization. These independent inspections, in effect, audit the auditors to make sure that standards are being met and corrective actions taken where necessary.

When estimating the cost of certification, organizations should budget approximately $35,000 for the initial external audit (the figure varies with the size of the department). Such external audits are required every three years, thus ensuring ongoing compliance with the standard. In other years, less-extensive external audits will be performed at an annual cost of about $8,000. In addition, organizations should take into account any fees paid to consultants who might be used to jump-start the certification process.

The CIO is in an ideal position to spearhead the pursuit of ISO 9000 within the enterprise. An IS department that takes the initiative and qualifies for certification on its own will stand out as an exemplar of constant excellence that the company as a whole would be wise to follow. It is also a sign to senior management that IS can now be counted on to fulfill its organizational responsibilities. The department's morale will be boosted by the awareness of what it has achieved. And the CIO can boast of a world-class organization that has been calibrated against the international standard for quality.

SECTION VII
Selected Cases

In this section several cases provide some real-world examples and a means to reflect on some of the issues raised in the previous readings. Some of the cases are comprehensive in nature and address an array of related issues, while others are more specific and focus on a particular domain. These cases are presented in the final section to provide added value to the section readings.

The first case, "Building a Transnational Company," focuses on the transformation of a small domestic firm into a transnational enterprise. This case supplements the Bartlett and Ghoshal readings in Section II from the perspective of a small company. The case presents the background for thinking about organizational design, corporate culture, and the development of a global communications infrastructure. The issues for discussion are myriad and can expand into several management domains.

The second case, "Unilever's Unifying Theme," addresses the challenges of integration and coordination from the perspective of a larger, diverse conglomerate with many divisions worldwide. The challenges of interconnectivity, development of a supporting IT policy, and compatibility across all facets of the organization are clearly tremendous. The case facilitates examination of the issues from various perspectives.

"Texas Instruments: A Global Capability" focuses on the firm's pursuit of a flexible and efficient telecommunications capability. Texas Instruments has pursued global connectivity for many years. The company has positioned itself as a leader in promoting emerging technologies and has established its competitive advantage through the timely adoption of technologies and a policy of acting quickly. This case provides an interesting discussion that focuses on the firm's telecommunications capability and the resulting implications for global operations.

"Global Transport" focuses on the specific application of electronic data interchange (EDI) as an increasingly necessary technology for remaining competitive in a business environment that is becoming highly dependent on electronically generated transactions and information flows. Customer demands for EDI give freight-forwarding-companies no choice but to implement EDI systems. The case provides one example of the benefits that EDI can provide through reduced complexity, time and cost efficiencies, and rapid clearance through customs.

"One Car, Worldwide, with Strings Pulled from Michigan" emphasizes the impact of information technology on product development. The issues of global design versus local country preference is a key discussion point in this case. The utilization of virtual reality in future design and implementation provides one example of the possibilities afforded by technological breakthroughs.

The final case, "A Journey East—The Making of 1-2-3 Release 2J," reflects some of the cultural constraints and language barriers that may be encountered as companies expand into unexplored markets and set up operations in new environments. This case makes the point that obstacles to doing business in other countries will likely go beyond the technical difficulties of software development and include unique issues relevant to business practices in other countries.

Building a Transnational Company

MARTHA E. MANGELSDORF

SOME TWO DOZEN MANAGERS have gathered around a conference table at Quintiles Transnational Corp., in Morrisville, N.C. They are listening to Dennis Gillings, chief executive of the 11-year-old company, give a slide presentation. It's nothing out of the ordinary—except for one small detail: Gillings is nowhere in sight.

Gillings is in Quintiles's Reading, England, office. While his slides appear in North Carolina, his narrative arrives via speakerphone.

Nobody seems disconcerted, perhaps because faceless communication plays a big part in Quintiles's business. The company, which administers and analyzes drug-testing studies that pharmaceutical companies prepare for government agencies, has grown rapidly (see chart) while remaining consistently profitable. Much of the growth has come from Quintiles's venture into international markets. Although the company opened its first overseas location only in 1987, today it has offices in five countries. Thirty-five percent of its business is now done outside the United States. Along the way Quintiles has changed from a small U.S. professional service business to a multinational growth company.

Several factors aided the transformation. Founder Gillings grew up in England, so he had British contacts and an international perspective. Also, Quintiles operates in a global marketplace: scientific reputations cross borders, most pharmaceutical research is published in England, and Quintiles's customers are mostly multinational pharmaceutical companies.

Those advantages helped Quintiles quickly become an international organization. The process began in 1986. Gillings was following the European Community's Proposal for a unified market. If Quintiles had a well-established European presence by 1992, he reasoned, it could take advantage of a market poised for growth. To do that, Gillings believed he needed to start right away, even though his four-year-old company had only 35 employees in one U.S. location. So he decided to open a European office. "I think everyone within the company thought I was verging on crazy," he recalls.

To counter such doubts, Gillings proceeded cautiously. Before opening an office in London, in early 1987 he visited about 30 major European pharmaceutical companies. On each visit, he explained that his company was considering a European office and looking for advice and business. Although it took months, Gillings got three projects for his new office through those visits.

By August 1987 he had lined up enough work to open the office. To work on the first contracts he took over four young employees eager to travel. In London he interviewed for permanent office staff. He also begun searching for someone to run the office, preferably a native European with experience throughout the Continent, since Quintiles hoped to expand further. After more than six months, he found Ludo Reynders, a native Belgian who speaks four languages and had experience in a large pharmaceutical company. Until hiring him early in 1988, Gillings commuted between London and North Carolina.

The expansion cost more than $200,000 over 14 months, but it paid off. Quintiles's British office grew rapidly. It soon moved outside London to Reading, where growth was cheaper. As Quintiles's European business grew Gillings considered opening another site, in Ireland. There unemployment runs high, and the Irish Industrial Development Authority offers generous incentives to companies like his.

Quintiles opened its Dublin office in 1990. In 1991, the company added an office outside Frankfurt, and in 1992 established one in Paris. Although Gillings followed a similar pattern—starting small, hiring a native manager—he had to overcome more difficult hurdles in Germany and France. Besides the language barriers, he discovered that German and French business law differs from the British-American legal tradition he knew. One resource he found helpful: using a U.S. accounting firm with international offices that could refer him to local business experts.

While Quintiles has been successful in growing its European offices, a joint venture started in Japan in 1990 has so far yielded only a little business there. The Japanese equivalent of the Food and Drug Administration is still reluctant to accept clinical drug-testing data submitted by contract-research organizations, according to Sara Creagh, Quintiles's executive vice president. The company, however, has Japanese customers in other offices.

In any case, opening successful offices is only the first challenge to running a global business. Gillings envisioned an international company that could serve the global pharmaceutical market, a company through which a client could, for example, have data collected throughout Europe to be processed in North Carolina for submission to the U.S. government. For that, he needed offices that communicated seamlessly.

But the new offices, separated by culture, language, and thousands of miles, developed their own ways of doing things. Soon, for example, the British office began using a method for entering data different from the one the U.S. office used. And the two offices were using different software—which didn't bode well for Gillings's dreams of international projects and databases. So he and his managers made a key decision: each office should add the other's software to its capabilities. That would force the two offices to learn from each other.

FIGURE 1

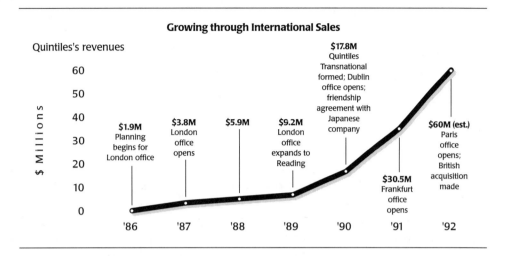

Growing through International Sales

Quintiles's revenues

As the company's international business grew, so did Gillings's efforts to coordinate among offices. In the process, he was greatly influenced by Managing Across Borders: The Transnational Solution (Harvard Business School Press, 1989). The book's authors, Christopher Bartlett and Sumantra Ghoshal, argue for a new model of international management. Instead of either a headquarters that dominates overseas offices or independent subsidiaries that have little to do with one another, they advocate a "transnational" corporation. In such a company, offices around the world work together and learn from one another. They report to an international headquarters, but the overseas offices also have specialized areas of expertise. That, Gillings decided, was the kind of company he wanted.

To create it, Quintiles in 1990 started a transnational holding company to coordinate the companywide policies among the worldwide subsidiaries. The company formed several "transnational committees," comprising the heads of a particular discipline, such as management information systems (MIS), from many of the offices. Gillings also started a management committee that included all office heads. The goal was to standardize enough policy for the company to take on multinational, multi-office projects. A number of its offices are now working together on such contracts.

That wouldn't be possible without today's technology. Everyone in the company can communicate through the electronic-mail system on his or her computer. Employees also communicate frequently by teleconferencing, voice mail, and fax, often faxing forms directly from one computer to another. Quintiles took a dramatic step early in 1992 by setting up a wide-area network to link the computers in many of its offices. Now a U.S. office can, for example, send data directly to the U.K. office without using a modem, which both speeds up delivery and improves accuracy.

No detail of the international communication is without challenges. They range from the profound (finding common terminology for a transnational committee to use) to the picayune (compensating for European and U.S. computer printers that use paper with different margins). Despite the inevitable difficulties, Quintiles today is further along than most young companies—and perhaps most companies, period—on the path to global business.

The communication among offices takes place because it's important to the company's management, and because it makes that clear. Drew Zinck, MIS director for U.S. operations, knows that from experience. During one MIS-committee phone meeting, he told his U.K. counterpart he couldn't divulge details of one of his office's marketing alliances because of a confidentiality agreement. When the meeting's minutes were routinely sent by E-mail to a number of top Quintiles managers, Zinck was besieged with E-mail messages from both sides of the Atlantic. Why was he withholding information from his colleague? Didn't he understand the importance of transnational cooperation?

Once Zinck explained, a solution was quickly found. But his experience is telling of how Quintiles uses information technology, combined with a commitment to a global way of business, to make the world a very small place indeed. After all, who would have thought two continents could seem as crowded a place to hold a business conversation as the office coffee machine?

QUESTIONS

1. According to Bartlett and Ghoshal a transnational firm is driven by simultaneous demands for global efficiency, national responsiveness, and worldwide learning. According to this definition, is Quintiles a true transnational firm? Why or why not? If not, how would you characterize the firm?

2. Quintiles's entry into international markets appears relatively simple and easy. What were the key factors for its rapid success?

3. Can a manufacturing company be equally successful by following the Quintiles strategy for global business expansion?

4. What kind of difficulties do you anticipate as Quintiles continues to expand its global business operations?

5. How critical is information technology to Quintiles's global growth strategy?

6. What factors may have influenced Quintiles's selection of its overseas office sites? Would the selection of offshore sites be different for a manufacturing firm? Explain.

Unilever's Unifying Theme

JOSHUA GREENBAUM

THE SUN NEVER SETS on the empire Michael Johnson controls from his offices near the fabled London Bridge. And considering this city's soggy climate, that's saying a lot. As head of information technology at Unilever Plc. and Unilever NV, Johnson oversees all computer and communications systems at one of the world's largest multinationals, a sprawling conglomerate made up of 350,000-plus employees in more than 500 companies, including Lever Brothers, T.J. Lipton, and Calvin Klein Cosmetics, in some 75 countries. Thousands of well-known items—from Ragu sauces to Pond's skin creams to Pepsodent toothpaste, from Wisk detergent to Faberge perfume—pour daily out of the Unilever product machine.

With $41.2 billion in sales in 1991—more than $24.1 billion Procter & Gamble Co. and $9.87 billion Kraft General Foods Inc. combined—Unilever has worked hard at being big. Since the mid-1980s, the London- and Rotterdam-based company has bought more than 100 businesses and sold nearly twice as many, averaging at least two transactions a week in an unceasing frenzy of corporate deal-making. And though some of the purchases have involved much more than small change—in late 1989, for instance, Unilever paid $2 billion for Faberge/Elizabeth Arden and Calvin Klein—cash flow has covered most of the transactions, leaving the company ample room to grow its bottom line as well. Operating margins have risen steadily from 5.6% in 1983 to 8.7% in 1991.

What's more, at the end of 1990, Unilever's current assets were 1.32 times its short-term debt, while long-term debt was just 23.6% of the company's total capitalization. And Unilever isn't done shopping yet: As 1991 began, it still had $1.15 billion cash on hand.

NEW IMPORTANCE FOR IS

In the midst of this huge corporate expansion, information chief Johnson has been given an IS mandate as broad and complex as Unilever itself: standardize the hardware and software systems of this behemoth around an open systems architecture, and bring it all together in a global network. Indeed, Johnson is out to remake virtually every sector of

---

Unilever's vast IS infrastructure, from corporate to research and development to factory management.

Considering Unilever's recent sparkling performance, it's something of a surprise that the company decided to go through with it. Historically, Johnson says, IT "was seen as irrelevant to the business. Its impact was not apparent to anybody." That attitude changed in 1989, however, when the board of directors realized that with so many companies under one roof, Unilever was drowning in technology without "getting value" from it, says Johnson. "And they wanted to know why."

The board may have been blind to the problem, but others were not. Each Unilever division, Johnson knew, was managing its own technology, oblivious to the work of other divisions. Consequently, there were redundancies galore, not to mention poorly conceived and poorly implemented systems.

Things already have begun to change. Since getting the green light from the board, Johnson has been moving at high speed. He enlisted key hardware and software partners to agree upon an open systems architecture for Unilever, and used that as the springboard for developing the global network. By the end of this year, Unilever expects to implement software based on a suite of standards—built around the Open Software Foundation's Applications Environment Specification (AES)—for systems and software development throughout the corporation.

Johnson's IT efforts come on the heels of a streamlining kick at Unilever, one that picked up steam in 1986 with the appointment of Michael Angus as co-chairman. Angus has a reputation for leanness. In the early 1980s, Angus, then regional director for North America, reportedly stormed into Unilever's red ink-plagued U.S. operations, fired dozens of executives, and put a stop to the high jinks taking place at the company's $1 million Fifth Avenue apartment. (According to corporate legend, those high jinks included at least one "secretary" on the payroll whose services had little to do with typing.) But by taking a scythe to every unit of the company that he had access to, Angus proved his point: A conglomerate as massive as Unilever has numerous benefits buried under its bureaucracy. Given sufficient leeway, a good executive can find those benefits.

That's been Johnson's experience also. In June 1990, Johnson began his attack on Unilever's IS problems by focusing on applications portability. At a meeting in a New York hotel suite, Johnson told Unilever's three primary hardware suppliers—IBM, Digital Equipment Corp., and Hewlett-Packard Co.—that his goal was to be able to build an application and "port it anywhere in the world within 10 days." Specifically, Johnson wanted to develop "competitive-edge applications in one place," send them to other Unilever companies, and install them instantly as if the recipients "had developed them themselves."

The concept was nice; making it reality was another thing altogether. Unilever's laissez-faire approach toward technology had left it with a mix of hardware and software almost as varied as its product line. Despite Unilever's stated policy to use only hardware from IBM, DEC, or HP, the company found itself facing drastic incompatibility problems. Each unit had allowed its systems, regardless of vendor, to mushroom out of control. That, of course, made it even harder to implement software portability. "You could recreate a chronological history of computing within our companies' hardware" platforms, Johnson laments.

SOLICITING COOPERATION

So, to make his plan work, Johnson had to convince the three computer makers to co-operate on a cross-vendor software architecture. That proved to be a relatively easy task. It was in the vendors' best interest to keep Unilever happy; the company is, after all, a large buyer of information technology, with an IS budget that ranks in the hundreds of millions. And since all the vendors were founding members of the OSF, hammering out a consensus was fairly simple. By the end of that meeting, the decision had been made to go with AES, a massive standards suite that includes elements of the OSF/1 operating system, the Motif interface, OSF's Distributed Computing Environment, SQL (structured query language), and Posix.

With the base environment defined, Johnson began adding other critical components. Databases from Oracle Corp. and Sybase Inc. were selected as standards, as were Lotus Development Corp.'s 1-2-3 and WordPerfect Corp.'s word processing program. Oracle's SQL Forms and Unify Corp.'s Uniface applications environment were tapped for front-end software development.

Johnson and his team then began to focus on the design of the global data network, with the idea of using AES's distributed, client-server capabilities as its foundation. Sprint International was chosen to supply and manage a pan-European data network to Unilever.

It was only last year that the company's board endorsed Johnson's plan to implement open systems companywide, but the results are already evident. For one, local technology entrepreneurship hasn't been stifled, as it often is when IT centralization occurs. For instance, Quest International, a Unilever fragrance and food ingredients company based in the Netherlands and England, is already using the AES standards, far sooner than any-one expected, to develop critical applications—so critical that it refuses to say what they are. The reason Quest has been able to capitalize on its new technology so quickly, says Alain Fastré, managing director of the OSF's office in Brussels, is that the company's relatively small size (1991 revenue: $842 million) allows it to operate on a "human scale." More importantly, it proves that Unilever's corporate consolidation does not come at the expense of individual innovation.

That kind of flexibility is in sharp contrast to, for instance, some large manufacturers that have "operations that are much more monolithic than Unilever," Fastré points out. This stunts their ability to take full advantage of technology advances.

Although Johnson's plan is nothing short of a radical overhaul, he has no intention of disrupting the company's operations while implementing it. He's taken extreme care to avoid upsetting users reluctant to switch to open systems overnight. For instance, there are still hundreds of proprietary, or legacy, applications throughout Unilever. Johnson insists that they will be "left where they are" while the company's technologists try to figure out how to make them communicate among computers.

And while the corporate model specifically excludes proprietary systems such as IBM's AS/400, several ongoing development projects at Unilever companies made it too costly to shut down those machines right away. "From a business standpoint, I just didn't want to say 'stop' to over two years of work on the AS/400," says Johnson. Instead, he's letting those companies delay the changeover, while mandating that all new software purchased or developed for the AS/400s be portable to RISC (reduced-instruction set computing) machines, one of the platforms the AES standard operates on.

It's those kinds of business decisions that make Johnson's efforts so valuable to Unilever. But his focus on the strategic corporate aspects of technology shouldn't surprise anyone. Johnson, a 31-year veteran at Unilever who had been chairman of the company's Danish operations and a senior staffer in worldwide product and quality management, is the first to admit that he has only a limited background in corporate technology. But that, he stresses, is an asset, not a liability: "We're not looking for technologically pure solutions. We really need to focus on generating business advantages."

As the technology makeover progresses, that will mean developing distributed computing and groupware applications. The idea, says Johnson, is to create a truly global company based on a "virtual team"—with software tools and the global network providing the technology to manage group projects around the world.

If Johnson sounds philosophical, he's certainly entitled. After all, he's spent the last two years laboring on a technology infrastructure for one of the world's largest companies. That infrastructure has a singular goal: to provide a common foundation for many disparate, far-flung operations. And with all the bricks-and-mortar work behind him, Johnson says, his job will really become fun. "We get to start thinking creatively about using this technology for managing the business," says Johnson. "Now we can really start changing the way Unilever does business."

QUESTIONS

1. What advice would you give to Johnson for changing from legacy systems to a globally integrated information system?

2. Do you think that the goal of building applications and "porting them anywhere in the world within ten days" is realistic? What are the benefits and challenges?

3. How should Johnson organize his IT team to ensure coordination of transnational resources without intruding on local autonomy?

4. Is it rational to continue to adapt the legacy programs to the new system or is it best to develop new software? How do you encourage information sharing between divisions?

Texas Instruments:
A Global Capability

PETER G. W. KEEN & J. MICHAEL CUMMINS

TEXAS INSTRUMENTS, whose annual revenues are close to $10 billion, makes semi-conductors, computer equipment, missile guidance systems, and other industrial electronic products. It is also widely recognized as a world leader in using telecommunications, winning several awards from trade associations and publications. *Network World*, which picked Texas Instruments (TI) as winner of its 1991 User Excellence awards, cited the "relentless pursuit of perfection" as the main reason for TI's success ("User Excellence" 1991). Its corporate telecommunications staff of around 170 people raised network availability from 99.05 percent in 1987 to 99.64 percent in late 1991. TI pushes the practical state of the art aggressively and claims to be ahead of most comparable users in technical innovation by some 12 to 18 months; it works closely with its vendors to make sure it both alerts them to its thinking and priorities and is able to be an alpha- or beta-test site for their new products. Its network spans 30 countries and links over 60,000 workstations to each other and to 23 mainframe computers, with response times of a second. The topology of the network is shown in Figure 1.

TI's success is not a matter of instant implementation. Like other firms, it has had to struggle with issues of coordination, integration, LAN-WAN incompatibilities, uncooperative PTTs, challenges of providing end-user support, and so on. The telecommunications unit explicitly focuses on service quality as its business driver, with rigorous metrics for tracking it and continuous commitment to improving performance in relation to those metrics. For example, statistics on network availability, errors, and response time are captured in a stored database and analyzed monthly. These performance figures are discussed with TI's vendors, whom it expects to offer a service well above their published guarantees.

TI's telecommunications capability evolved over a 20-year period beginning in the 1970s, when the company developed its own private global network. This development required many ad hoc and proprietary solutions because PTTs were not positioned to

---

Keen, Peter G. W., and Cummins, J. Michael. *Networks in Action* (Belmont: Wadsworth, 1994).

FIGURE 1

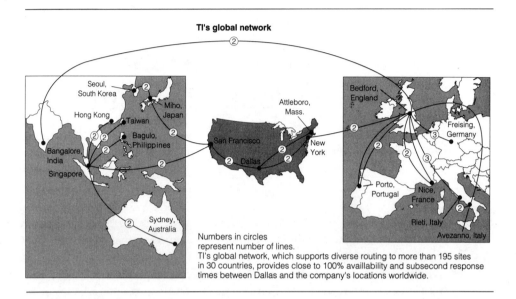

TI's global network

Numbers in circles
represent number of lines.
TI's global network, which supports diverse routing to more than 195 sites
in 30 countries, provides close to 100% availlability and subsecond response
times between Dallas and the company's locations worldwide.

provide either technology or service. Only a small subset of the PTTs would lease data communications circuits to companies. TI built a packet-switched network with a proprietary protocol for transmission over satellite links; it leased voice-grade analog lines, the only choice available.

This network was gradually migrated to a backbone network of 85 TI circuits built on IBM's Systems Network Architecture, which connects to local area networks in 25 countries. TI's manufacturing applications rely heavily on large mainframe computers in Dallas that require workstations on LANs to emulate the standard IBM 3270 dumb terminal. TI's goal is to ensure "seamlessness" across its entire geography, including being able to set up and run factories, warehouses, and design facilities anywhere in the world, with direct linkages to the Dallas mainframes, LANS, and workstations worldwide. By 1986, TI had probably the lowest unit costs for communication of any multinational firm. An electronic mail message could be sent anywhere in the world for under four cents, and a database inquiry cost less than three cents. At that time, TI's network interconnected 13,000 terminals and conducted about a million transactions a day, with a maximum response time of six seconds. The comparable figures for late 1991 were 60,000 workstations, eight million transactions a day, and a subsecond response time.

Texas Instruments's backbone global network was optimized to provide wide reach, low cost, and high reliability. The U.S. hubs are in Dallas, San Francisco, and New York; the three regional international hubs are in Miho, Japan; Singapore, and Bedford, England. These hubs are linked by pairs of TI circuits operating at 64 kbps via satellite and fiber.

Each regional hub has twin data centers, and transmission links are routed "diversely" using different physical paths to ensure protection against disasters, such as a fiber cut. (For the same reason, each hub has two data centers.) The hubs use IDNX multiplexers provided by Network Equipment Technologies. Within a region, sites link to the hubs via fractional TI, running at up to 64 kbps. The network supports SNA traffic, voice, and inter-LAN traffic. PBXs at TI locations connect to a TI multiplexer that routes voice calls through the backbone and also handles offnet calls—calls using long distance and local carriers' switched services.

Like most large decentralized firms, TI did not recognize the implications of rapid and unmanaged growth of local area networks in time to develop a strategy for ensuring integration and coordination. User departments had full freedom to build their own LAN capabilities using any vendor, product, and architecture they chose. By 1990, this uncoordinated growth had resulted in 125 LANs that used a wide variety of completely incompatible protocols, including Digital Equipment's DECnet, TCP/IP, Ethernet, Novell's IPX (Internetwork Package Exchange), and Apple Computer's AppleTalk.

As user departments began to want to interconnect these LANS, mainly to exchange files and electronic mail messages, they looked to the central corporate group for help. Initially, the network simply used point-to-point links to connect the LANS, bypassing the backbone; there were over 150 such links, a very expensive and "chaotic" solution that was replaced by a coordinated approach that succeeded mainly because TI's new "Network Interoperability Forum" (NIF) emphasized support to end-users and not central bureaucracy and control. This approach provided plenty of incentives for departments to give up much of the responsibility for day-to-day operations of their LANS. The manager for TI's communications strategy understood that "the majority of users don't want to be in the business of developing networks and will walk away from it once they know there is a corporate group that will provide quality service and cares about their needs."

Such caring and quality service rests on close interaction and coordination. The Network Interoperability Forum meets once a month and includes network support staff and end-users from every business unit. Through the NIF, TI set up a companywide requirement that all LAN operating systems must have a hardware interface to IEEE 802.3 Ethernet LANs and must be able to transmit data to a remote LAN using either TCP/IP or OSI protocols instead of its own native protocol. TI gradually adopted Cisco Systems Inc.'s line of routers, as well as concentrators from Ungermann-Bass, which became de facto standards, as did Ethernet, which is now used by 95 percent of the company's units.

TI divided the existing backbone network into two data channels; one channel is for IBM SNA traffic that is mainly to and from the Dallas mainframe computers, and the other is for LAN-to-LAN traffic using TCP/IP. The local area networks feed traffic onto the backbone through either a bridge (between local LAN segments) or a router (across LAN domains). The bridges and routers connect to the backbone through an attachment to the IDNX multiplexer.

Network management was an early priority for TI. It developed its own proprietary method of testing all its circuits on a continuous basis, logging performance data in its SAVAIL (Systems Availability) database. Specially developed software tests each SNA circuit every ten minutes, 24 hours a day. One test measures the time for a 200-kilobyte database to move end-to-end through the network and back from the Dallas host; a second test transmits the same file to terminal controllers on the network. These two figures are monitored in real-time at the Dallas network control center. Whenever performance falls outside acceptable parameters, the system generates a trouble ticket that alerts the network staff, who immediately get to work to fix the problem. Trouble tickets and their resolution are reviewed at a daily telephone conference between Dallas and Bedford.

TI meets monthly with all its carriers, which include AT&T, MCI, WilTel, local Regional Bell Operating Companies, and international value-added services. Together they review every trouble ticket for the past month to track any trends that indicate potential problem areas. The carriers trust the accuracy of the figures, and there are no arguments or self-justification. (TI's figures are more accurate and detailed than the carriers' own network statistics in most instances.) TI informs each carrier of its relative performance. Currently, Japan's NTT (Nippon Telegraph and Telephone Corporation) is the benchmark leader, with just 12 minutes of downtime for the entire year out of over three million minutes of transmission; this is over 99.999 percent availability.

Given the many and much-publicized problems that U.S. carriers have had in network failures in recent years, TI has had to take action to ensure improvement. In 1991 it set up a special quality program with AT&T as a result of a fiber cut that left it without communications to Europe for over seven hours, even though AT&T had supposedly provided physically diverse Dallas-to-London T1 routes. TI now regularly reviews circuit routes with AT&T; in turn, AT&T brings in TI's T1 experts at its own planning meetings for engineering new circuit paths. Senior AT&T network management is automatically informed if any T1 problem has not been resolved in two hours.

With its equipment suppliers, TI carries out exhaustive tests designed to find the point at which equipment fails. It looks to establish long-term relationships with suppliers and keeps them well-informed about its plans. Instead of keeping information secret for use as a weapon in negotiations, TI views sharing of information as vital. TI has a long history of cooperative alliances and joint ventures across its operations, including both its 1992 development and marketing agreement with MCI to co-market TI's EDI capabilities, which had won it the Yankee Group's EDI User of the Year award, and its many cooperative ventures with other firms in advanced computer chip development, a major area of strength for TI.

The earliest major success in TI's use of telecommunications was electronic mail. It developed its own in-house system, still in use after close to 20 years, with around a million messages a day flowing across the network. The system is host-based, with X.400 gateways used to transmit e-mail messages to locations outside the company. End-to-end delivery time is under three seconds.

Today, TI is widely seen as one of the world leaders in electronic data interchange. It began early and sustained its innovation, and it consistently wins awards for being in the top five to ten in EDI use. It links close to 2,000 trading partners in 20 countries, making over 11,000 transactions a month. It subscribes to 16 value-added networks and uses almost every established EDI standard, with EDIFACT and X12 the main ones and X.400 a key transport standard for its EDI Translator and Gateway software. It handles over 50 types of documents and can directly route them into its core business applications, including purchasing, accounting, and shipping. Close to half its purchase orders from customers are processed without a human intermediary. It has a strong consulting, training, and support group for EDI and offers EDI systems integration services.

The foundations underlying the 20-year evolution of TI's network platform have been consistent and explicit: a global window, cross-process integration and coordination, and disciplined technical innovation. The business driver has been the vital need for global processes for a global organization. According to a senior TI information systems manager, "The network is absolutely vital for TI to operate on a global basis." Such a comment has become a truism in many firms; TI, however, defined it as the priority that shaped its entire information technology plans and organization in the late 1960s. It relied on strong central planning, reflected in the design of the backbone and the use of mainframes not so much as "computers" but as libraries and shared information storage, access, and coordination points. It did not rely on the typical piece-by-piece, case-by-case, bottom-up approach to international telecommunications. The network had to serve the organizational priority of managing TI as a single entity and a "global factory." John White, the head of TI's Information Systems group, commented in 1989 that TI sees the next generation of computerization as "a global networking of machines and applications in nonlinear fashion, driven by the information-browsing users rather than being merely process-driven." White, who has headed TI's IS group since 1976, built his strategy around strong central coordination plus strong local support. The focus on service quality is at the heart of this strategy, with metrics as the key feedback mechanism and measure of progress.

Unlike almost every other company, TI thus began with a viewpoint that all telecommunications and services should be integrated. Its early development of electronic mail was intended to help project teams of designers, engineers, and manufacturing staff work closely together across three continents. The backbone network allowed TI to consolidate its financial data almost in real-time, again across three continents. Its equally early commitment to EDI was part of a business drive for process integration, not an administrative move to speed up the flow of documents. EDI is seen as part of the intelligent global factory of the future, for it links every core business process.

TI is a leading manufacturer in many areas of IT. It is at the forefront of research, development, and production of high-speed chips used in voice recognition applications, high-performance intelligent workstations, high-bandwidth multimedia applications, and programmable processors. Thus it is a natural innovator in its own use of technology.

White recommends that information systems and telecommunications organizations build close links with leading suppliers and track their innovations continuously. Information officers, in his view, need a technical awareness as well as business alertness, so that they know what is possible and where the leaders are moving. White's group takes pride in their technical expertise and is encouraged to push the practical state of the art.

One of the obvious risks in being a leader is that TI has often had to take action before standards are at all clear. This was the case in electronic mail, EDI, the almost out-of-control explosion of LANS, and TI's original development of the backbone network, and TI could easily have become spread too thin. In mid-1992, the Information Technology Group, the business unit that sells software and equipment to outside customers and that White also heads, sold off its division that provided commercial UNIX-based multi-user systems, which had performed poorly in the marketplace.

However, TI has gained many advantages of lead time over its competitors, has been able to exploit emerging technologies and applications quickly by not waiting until standards are there for all to use, and has been able to optimize its systems to provide the highest performance, often at the lowest cost. TI has the skills and experience to exploit new technology, and its general approach is to move fast and early, work closely and openly with vendors, reduce risk through exhaustive testing and monitoring, and adapt existing systems as standards and equipment for interoperability emerge.

QUESTIONS

1. What were the key business drivers that led to the development of TI's global network? How did these drivers influence the design of the network?

2. TI has the necessary resources and technical skills to actively manage its global networks. Would you recommend a similar telecommunications strategy to firms with fewer technical and financial resources? Explain why or why not.

3. TI's network evolved over a twenty-year period. How can a firm build a comprehensive global telecommunications capability in a shorter time period? Describe various options to be considered.

4. A transnational information platform can be described in terms of reach and range. Reach defines who is accessible through the IT platform. Range describes what services can be shared directly across the platform. Describe TI's network in these terms. Do you think the network is adequate to support TI's future needs? Can you suggest any improvements to the reach and range?

Global Transport

CONNIE GUGLIELMO

FOR HONDA MOTOR COMPANY, election crazed Congressmen screaming about imports is just so much noise. There are plenty of time-honored, low-tech solutions to quiet lawmakers. But getting 320,000 cars and trucks a year through the labyrinth of bureaucratic U.S. Customs clerks—now that's a job for some real technology.

Just ask The Harper Group, an international freight forwarder that uses innovative information systems as well as cargo ships, trucks, and trains to move all those Civics and Accords halfway around the world to American shores. Through electronic data interchange (EDI), Harper actually taps into Honda's computers, retrieving information required by Customs for clearing the automaker's cargo.

Here's how it works:

From its headquarters in Japan, Honda electronically sends a commercial invoice to American Honda in Los Angeles. That invoice details what's being shipped—the quantity, part numbers, tariff numbers, and value of each item. The information is then passed on to Harper's mainframe in San Francisco.

Harper supplements that data with antidumping information, visas for floor mats and other textiles used in a car or truck, and the name of the freight carrier. Harper then transmits this augmented record to U.S. Customs. Assuming the data is sufficient, Honda's shipment sails through on reaching port. If not, Harper can supply actual paperwork before the ship docks.

In a final bit of electronic interchange, Customs uses electronic funds transfer to take Honda's duty payment directly from Harper's mainframe. Harper then bills Honda for that payment, along with any expenses and handling fees.

"The whole issue is information flowing more consistently and freely between trading partners," says Steven Olson, who, as vice president of information services and chief information officer, has helped shape and implement Harper's EDI technology. "The point is to speed up the entire decision process, and for it to happen across borders. To be a global company, regardless of your business, you need EDI."

Reprinted with the permission of *PC World*. Hapgood, Fred. "A Journey East—The Making of 1-2-3 Release 2J," *Lotus*, May 1987, 101–104.

Harper is not alone in using EDI for transactions with U.S. Customs. The company says that nearly 99 percent of all 1,800 U.S. Customs brokers conduct at least some business via EDI. But Harper is unusual for the extent to which it pushes EDI across transactions and borders—delving directly into customers' computers to retrieve and deposit purchase orders, invoices, bills of lading, shipping statements, and international customs forms.

"Harper is a high-end service firm able to do what large companies require at a very competitive price," says Bruce Goedde of L.H. Alton & Company, a financial analysis firm in San Francisco.

In business since 1898, Harper does not actually own any planes, ships, or trucks. Instead, it contracts for them from providers around the world. What sets Harper apart is the way it uses available technologies to give its customers extra value. With EDI, Harper finds the cheapest, fastest, and most efficient ways to move freight. It also tracks goods through every point in an intricate pipeline that includes air, ocean, and land shippers as well as warehouses. And it smooths the otherwise arduous and error-prone customs process with international agencies.

"We must supply our customers with one source of information about their goods, no matter how many suppliers or players we add to the logistics pipeline," says Peter Gilbert, who took over this month as Harper's president and CEO.

Harper calling. For years, The Harper Group managed the flow of information about its customers' goods by creating and maintaining an elaborate paper trail. But the by-product of a paper trail is lots of paper. An EDI system, though, assumes that most of the information exchanged between clients and suppliers is generated by their internal applications. Why not keep communication at the electronic level? That's what Caterpillar of Peoria, Illinois, wanted in the early 1980s when it asked Harper to set up an EDI link between Caterpillar and Harper. But that first system was proprietary and unable to communicate with other Harper clients. "As more customers became interested in the idea, we felt we should develop a more general system," says Olson. So, from 1988 to 1989, Olson's team developed the infrastructure for Harper's current system.

The system includes an IBM mainframe at Harper's San Francisco headquarters, and 10 IBM AS/400 midrange computers at various sites throughout Europe and the Far East. For communications links, the company turned to commercial value-added network (VAN) services, which it found to be more cost-effective than creating and maintaining its own network. "We no longer have dedicated leased lines from AT&T," says Olson. Instead, the company contracts network services such as the IBM Information Network, Sears Network, Tymnet, Sprintnet, General Electric Information Service and SITA Consortium Network (for European airlines) and is participating in a European pilot project set up by Sears and Philips N.V. of the Netherlands. "The VANs have a lot of expertise in network management and it would be hard to duplicate their services," says Olson.

The EDI portion of Harper's system is a commercially available translator on its San Francisco mainframe. EDI translators are essentially data-formatting programs that convert data being sent or received into standard formats for purchase orders, invoices, or shipping notices. Several data formatting standards for EDI exist, including an early one developed by the Transportation Data Coordinating Committee: the popular N12, ratified by the American National Standards Institute; and the emerging EDI for Administration, Commerce, and Transport (EDIFACT), an international standard proposed by the United Nations Economic Commission for Europe.

But, says Olson, "The translator is the easy part. The real guts of the implementation falls to our customers, who have to develop interfaces between our system and their internal applications, such as purchase order tracking, material requirements planning, and accounting." So, when General Electric wants to know where in the world its material is, GE users access their own purchase order tracking system. The system then receives updated information, through the EDI translators from The Harper Group's computers.

"A few years ago it seemed neat to dial up information from anywhere in the world," says Olson. "Now, the main emphasis is on our computer exchanging information with their computer."

Companies developing their first EDI system can expect to pay $100,000 or more, which includes the cost of commercial translators and writing code to interface between applications. Implementing additional EDI links between shippers and suppliers costs from $5,000 to $10,000, Olson says, adding, "About 75 percent of that is testing."

3M recently made that initial investment. Before setting up its EDI links, the Minnesota company had to rekey all of Harper's reports detailing 3M's exports—no small feat, considering that last year 3M exported about $1.3 billion in goods from Post-it notes to computer optical disc subsystems. But for the past 10 months, Harper's computers have automatically logged onto 3M's internal system, electronically supplying airway-bill information, shipment logs, and export flight details. Mike West, 3M's operations analyst, says 3M no longer spends hours each day ferreting out data entry mistakes.

This benefit can be substantial. Olson maintains that typing errors can raise transaction costs by a factor of 10. If errors continue to get passed along the order cycle, they conceivably could erase "any commercial gain" from the transaction.

Customs Interface.   Life within Customs was never easy. In the old days Harper would have to manually file Customs forms that filled hundreds of pages. In turn, a Customs agent would laboriously refer to an eight-inch-thick binder of codes and regulations for each item being imported. And heaven help Harper if it had to find a shipment's status in the Customs labyrinth. That involved "dealing with forts of paper and someone at Customs saying 'You find it,'" says David Marks, vice president and director of imports for Harper.

But in 1988, Harper tapped into the Automated Commercial System (ACS), the EDI system of the U.S. Customs Service. Today Harper has automated its Customs filing procedures so effectively that it now, as a matter of policy, submits Customs forms up to five days before the customer's freight arrives, the earliest U.S. Customs allows. And using the Automated Broker Interface (ABI) to the ACS, Harper can quickly file import requests containing hundreds of pages of Customs forms, bypassing that eight-inch binder.

Those simple facts please Harper's customers, whose businesses depend on goods arriving on time. But, says Marks, with increased capabilities come increased expectations. "We have clients who measure our performance not in days but in minutes."

Which is why Harper uses ACS so extensively. The Harper Group expects to electronically file 240,000 Customs entries this year. That will give Harper 5 percent of the import-export brokerage market, making it the second largest U.S. Customs broker, behind Fritz Companies of San Francisco, which has 6 percent. (Market share is determined by number of Customs entries filed.)

"Even though ABI is not mandated right now, we'd be out of business as a broker if we didn't use it," says Marks. "Instead of a few minutes to query Customs, it would take weeks."

Other countries, such as Australia and members of the European Economic Community, are developing or have developed systems similar to that of U.S. Customs. For such international transactions, the important EDI format is the U.N.-sponsored EDIFACT. "Harper hasn't moved fast enough on EDIFACT for my taste," says Fran Warren, manager of EDI for Cummins Engine Company of Columbus, Indiana. "EDIFACT will be the language used in multiple countries. We want it widely available now, so we can set up standard processes for material movement."

In response, Olson says Harper is probably doing more with EDIFACT than any other freight forwarder. "I know some customers want us to have broader use of EDIFACT; and we expect to provide EDIFACT-formatted data to U.S. Customs sometime in the second quarter of 1992. But it was not a business benefit for us to provide that capability any sooner."

Forging relationships. A successful EDI system does not depend on technology; it relies on a strong business relationship with the client. "EDI is not, by itself, a solution," Olson points out. "It has to be truly a partnership arrangement because it involves a commitment to a long-term investment, to refining the system over time. A company shouldn't start by thinking about sending transactions back and forth: it should go back and think about the whole process, end-to-end."

That kind of commitment doesn't come easily. Today, Harper has EDI partnerships with about 20 "large-volume clients who represent about 10 percent of our revenue," says Olson. These customers include 3M; Sharp Electronics, which receives status updates on freight in transit; and Eastman Kodak, which sends commercial invoice data and also receives freight status information.

"We are a front-runner in the development and implementation of an effective IS environment, but I believe we are only at the beginning," says Harper CEO Gilbert. "We

FIGURE 1   Harper uses value-added networks to link its computers with customers worldwide.

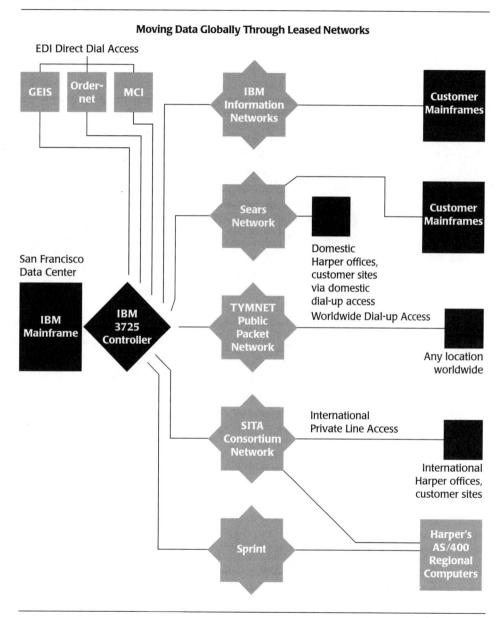

Moving Data Globally Through Leased Networks

EDI Direct Dial Access

GEIS   Order-net   MCI

IBM Information Networks

Customer Mainframes

Sears Network

Customer Mainframes

San Francisco Data Center

IBM Mainframe   IBM 3725 Controller

Domestic Harper offices, customer sites via domestic dial-up access

TYMNET Public Packet Network

Worldwide Dial-up Access

Any location worldwide

SITA Consortium Network

International Private Line Access

International Harper offices, customer sites

Sprint

Harper's AS/400 Regional Computers

have made good progress in the United States, but the truth is we have touched only a percentage, not a majority, of our customers."

That is beginning to change. Dozens of customers are gearing up their own EDI systems, says Olson, who expects EDI to boom within five years.

They call it EMI. When Harper was formed more than 90 years ago, business transactions were grounded in mutual trust built on one partner's ability to provide value to another. The Harper of today tries to provide that kind of value with communications technology.

Harper has worked with clients—such as 3M and Varian Associates of Palo Alto, California—to set up communications between customers' e-mail systems via X.400 gateways. Clients pay little for using what Olson likes to call electronic mail interchange (EMI). Fairly simple to develop from a technology standpoint, the X.400 e-mail connection lets Harper's clients send mail among themselves using their own e-mail systems.

"We use it to send correspondence, including messages forwarded from our overseas office to Harper," says 3M's West. "In turn, Harper sends us airway information, and the estimated time of arrival for an order. We forward those as early alerts to our subsidiaries. Before, we would have to wait for telexes and faxes. This is much more timely."

The benefit to Harper? "We are making ourselves a strategic partner by providing this service," says Olson. "Now if Varian is working with DEC, they can exchange messages between themselves or with other suppliers in the electronics business. We make our money on warehousing, transportation costs, documentation, and customs clearance, not e-mail. I don't know of any other logistics agency that has explored using X.400 with its clients," Olson says.

Olson sees X.400 message transmission capabilities as the future of business communications. "There is an evolution taking place. Today you can walk into any company and find e-mail. That was an exception 10 years ago; now it is expected. By the end of this decade, everyone's e-mail will communicate with everyone else's."

And, says Olson, global EMI will be expected. But companies must still figure out strategic uses for EMI. Otherwise, they may be in danger of another bout of information overload.

QUESTIONS

1. What are the benefits of EDI for Harper and its customers?

2. Explain the advantages of a common EDI standard such as EDIFACT.

3. Describe what issues need to be addressed by a company planning to use EDI for global business communications.

4. How will Harper's business change as communications links mature and customers build their own EDI systems? How can Harper respond to these challenges?

One Car, Worldwide, With Strings Pulled From Michigan

JULIE EDELSON HALPERT

WHEN THE FORD MOTOR COMPANY rolls out its new Ford Contour and the sibling Mercury Mystique this fall, the cars will have the same engines and drive trains found in Ford's new European model, the Mondeo.

Ford sees this "world car" approach to design as the key to the company's future—though it expects any new global project to cost nothing near the $6 billion it poured into developing the Mondeo family.

Seeking to shave months and millions of dollars from car design, Ford has consolidated management of its European, North American and Asian design operations into a single international network using powerful work stations based on Silicon Graphics Inc. technology linked by Ethernet networking software.

Although the Ford system has been taking shape for a half-dozen years, it was only a few weeks ago brought under a single "electronic roof," as the company refers to its new Ford Corporate Design organization based in Dearborn, Mich. The other main design sites on the network are in Dunton, England; Cologne, Germany; Turin, Italy; Valencia, Calif.; Hiroshima, Japan, and Melbourne, Australia. The circuits—satellite links, undersea cables and land lines—are purchased from telecommunications carriers.

The network enables a Ford engineer in Dunton, for example, to transmit to Dearborn massive computer files of 3-D drawings for a late-90's sedan. In Michigan, a designer can bring up the drawings on a work station, phone his English colleague and work, simultaneously with that colleague, in making on-screen revisions, even rotating the 3-D images to view them from all sides.

A few hours later, the data files might be sent pulsing through satellite or fiber-optic circuits to Turin, where a computerized milling machine can turn out a clay or plastic foam model in a matter of hours. At each of these network stops, Ford is able to take advantage of local expertise or equipment and put it toward the greater corporate good.

"It's a more efficient use of our resources," said Jack J. Telnack, Ford's newly promoted vice president of corporate design, who is based in Dearborn. "We can use any studio at the push of a button."

Mr. Telnack expects the new corporate structure to let engineers, manufacturers and suppliers worldwide get involved early in the automotive design stage, so that once a prototype hits the road, it will not require substantial alteration. Some 40 percent of development costs are due to changes that occur once a car has already been built, Mr. Telnack said.

Instead of a designer developing an idea in a vacuum, engineers can provide frequent feedback to decide if a certain type of air conditioner, say, will be able to fit within a given car. This interactive process is intended someday to cut Ford's lead time on a new car to as low as 24 months, compared with the 35 months it took to design the 1994 Mustang— already well below the domestic industry's 54-month average.

Ford is not the only auto maker to practice computer-aided design, of course. But the company says it is the first to create a single electronic worldwide system, and some auto designers are applauding the move.

"Ford has really been a leader in recognizing the value of simultaneous development," said Carl Olsen, chairman of transportation design for the Center for Creative Studies, a design school in Detroit. "Everyone will be obliged to play follow the leader."

LONG-DISTANCE DESIGN

Here is a recent example of how Ford's global design network works. (All times are United States Eastern Daylight Time.)

5:30 A.M. From a computer work station in Dunton, England, a Ford engineering coordinator transmits a 100-megabyte file to the design department in Dearborn, Mich. The file contains detailed drawings of a car planned for the late 1990's. The information is scrambled during the transmission and decoded when it reaches Dearborn.

5:45 A.M. The transmission complete, a designer in Dearborn downloads the information to a work station and begins making revisions.

8:00 A.M. The Dearborn designer dials up the Dunton coordinator and, through a voice-and-data conversation, the two make final revisions to the file. Each can view the same image and see the changes as they are made.

11:30 A.M. The revised drawings are transmitted to one of Ford's design studios, in Turin, Italy. Again, the transmission takes about 15 minutes.

1:30 P.M. The studios in Dearborn, Dunton and Italy are linked in a voice-and-data conference call. Final changes are discussed and seen by all parties.

2:00 P.M. Using the computer file for its instructions, an automated milling machine in Turin begins sculpting a clay model of the car.

But at least a few other car makers say they are unlikely to imitate Ford's move, because they believe consumer tastes vary too greatly from country to country. The General Motors Corporation, for example, has always handled its European and North American operations separately for exactly that reason, said Jerry Bishop, a G.M. spokesman.

And the Nissan Motor Company, which has been using computers to help design cars for 13 years and is able to transmit the digital instructions for clay models as Ford does, has ruled out global design, said Gerald Hirshberg, vice president for Nissan Design International Inc. in San Diego. The cultural gaps are simply too wide, he said, noting that, while Nissan's Altima and Infiniti J-30 models are thriving in the United States, they are struggling in Japan.

Ford's heavy reliance on computer models to evaluate global designs, Mr. Hirshberg predicted, "will produce horror cars."

The trick for Ford, independent experts say, will be using its computer network to facilitate the design process without letting it replace human judgment and personal interaction. But purely from a technology standpoint, Ford's reorganization is "a very brave and bold move—one that is due," said Ron Hill, chairman of the transportation design department for the Art Center College of Design in Pasadena, Calif.

It was a full 10 years ago that Ford began using its design software, the Computer Design Rendering System, developed and periodically updated for the car maker by Evans & Sutherland of Salt Lake City. But only recently have Ford executives considered hardware sufficiently advanced to let the company regard its seven international design centers as one. It all has to do with the speed at which the data can be processed and transmitted.

Creating a three-dimensional image of a car on a computer screen, one that can be moved about and viewed from all perspectives, requires complex mathematical formulas containing copious amounts of data—50 megabytes or more, which exceeds the total amount of memory on a lot of home computers. While such meaty files are mere morsels for powerful work stations, handling such data speedily—and sending it whizzing around the world—has not always been an easy task.

Thomas Jensen, general manager of Evans & Sutherland, said that computer power has been doubling every one to two years. Moreover, he said, "We are now to the point where the transmission methods are fast and cheap enough to carry the information."

Ford is using circuits capable of carrying data at speeds up to 760,000 bits per second. With data-compression techniques, a 50-megabyte file (400 million bits) can be transmitted in about $7\frac{1}{2}$ minutes. To safeguard the designs, the information is scrambled during transmission and decoded as it reaches its destination.

Tom Scott, Ford's vice president of international design, sees the day when "virtual reality" will enable a computer to recreate the look and feel of a car's interior and send this data blasting through the network so an overseas designer can slip into the virtual driver's seat. "This," Mr. Scott said wishfully, "is the next piece."

QUESTIONS

1. Why do you think it took Ford half a dozen years to develop an integrated automobile design center? What might have been the major challenges?

2. Do you think Ford's world car approach is appropriate for the world market? Explain why or why not.

3. What type of organizational issues had to be resolved in order to make the long distance design approach effective?

4. Is Ford proceeding in a rational fashion in integrating its design process? Who is correct—Ford or the other industry players? What are the benefits of Ford's long-distance design approach?

5. The next step for Ford is to achieve virtual reality. Discuss the importance and potential problems of achieving this capability.

A Journey East—
The Making of 1-2-3 Release 2J

FRED HAPGOOD

A SPECIAL VERSION of *1-2-3* Release 2 for Japan: As Lotus brass pondered the prospect in 1984, there seemed every reason to take on such a project. Japan is potentially the second-largest software market in the world. The business culture there is vast, influential, and technologically sophisticated. Perhaps most persuasive, the parallels between the evolution of the Japanese business-software market and the United States market are striking. At the time, a patchwork of competing Japanese hardware architectures was slowly giving way to a single standard. As IBM had achieved dominance in the United States, NEC seemed destined to do so in Japan. Microcomputer penetration into the Japanese business world was just beginning and no powerful integrated business software was yet available.

A fact-finding team, comprising Steve Turner, then manager of European Product Development; Chuck Digate, director of International Operations; and Stephen Kahn, manager of International Business Development, was formed. They visited Japan in November of 1984 to examine the market. They liked what they saw. Over the next six months, a development team was put together, headed by Trevor Hughes.

"Our first take," says Pamela Rathmell, one of the software developers, "was that this was going to be easy; that all we would have to do was modify *1-2-3*'s input and output routines." Before joining the Japan project, Rathmell worked on porting Lotus products to the scores of different MS-DOS computers on the market. "I was looking around for something new, heard about the Japan project, and inquired. They thought maybe they might be able to use me for three months."

Rathmell worked on the Japan project for 18 months. "I ate a lot of Japanese food," she says now, reckoning up the gains, "and developed a respect for a very *very* different culture." Dealing with those differences, integrating Western business software into the Japanese business culture, required far more than rewriting a few routines; it forced Lotus engineers and the Japanese consultants to write nothing less than the most advanced version of *1-2-3* extant, even by the standards of Release 2.01 users.

FROM A TO Z TO KANJI

The sheerest wall the development team had to climb was the Japanese alphabet, or rather, alphabets. By its very nature, *1-2-3* supports a rich and complex series of interactions with its users, and most of these depend on character recognition and manipulation. Aside from the input output routines, *1-2-3* operates directly on characters for menu selection and such essential functions as sorting and collating. Thus it was essential that the Japanese *1-2-3* be perfectly fluent in the orthographies of that country.

Such adaptations are routine in software translations and generally do not require much more than the simple modifications foreseen by Rathmell. Japan proved to be a harder case. It was not just that the Japanese write in four alphabets, but that the most important orthography, known as kanji, used in all formal business correspondence, is almost totally incompatible with keyboard entry. Kanji are enormously complex, composed of a myriad of constituent brushstrokes. A sequence of kanji looks like a row of little paintings, and there are tens of thousands of kanji. Many have tried to design keyboards from which kanji can be typed, but no one has succeeded, and to this day, most Japanese business correspondence is handwritten. Japanese software authors attack the problem with transcription programs that translate characters from one of the other alphabets into kanji. The other alphabets are phonetic. Each of these alphabets allows users to describe a character by "sounding it out." Romaji is used for the Western alphabet, Katakana is used for words borrowed from other languages, and Hiragana is used to denote the case of various parts of speech.

Kanji is decidedly not phonetic. The characters were brought to Japan from China more than 1,200 years ago, and kanji came to be used widely for all written communication. Eventually, Chinese fell from fashion, but for some reason, the Japanese went on to develop not one but two other scripts, yet retained the meanings of the Chinese characters and adapted them to represent Japanese-language sounds. By the standards of most languages, they make a poor fit. For instance, spoken Japanese uses fewer phonemes than Chinese, so there are fewer sounds to "go around" among the kanji. This means that in Japanese, 20 or more kanji might be pronounced the same way. The consequence is that the transcription programs require computer users to page through long lists of possible matches for nearly every character entered, an experience in tedium often cited as the reason behind the comparatively weak penetration of microcomputers in Japanese business. For software developers, that is not the only bad news.

There are more than 7,000 kanji recognized by PCs in Japan, and the technical problems presented by storing, sorting, and displaying them—you can't wrap in the middle of a kanji character—in a manageable space with 8-bit bytes are not trivial. On surveying these problems, many Western software and hardware companies have elected to introduce their products without making them kanji-competent. However, it was clear to the Lotus team that *1-2-3* simply had to speak kanji. A program not fluent in that orthography would not only have a small market, it would send exactly the wrong message about Lotus Development itself.

The Japanese were tired, the team had been told on an exploratory trip, of American firms bringing products to the Japanese market without learning anything about the country. Lotus had to show that it had bothered. A Japanese version of *1-2-3* would have to accept input from Romaji, Katakana, and Hiragana, allow the user maximum freedom to switch among them while working on the program, and then allow output to appear in any of the three or in kanji. "We knew we couldn't develop the conversion in this country," Steve Turner says. Kahn and Turner flew back to Japan to look for a development partner who could supply a state-of-the-art kana-kanji conversion.

The company they focused on, Kanrikogaku Kenkyucho (usually referred to as "K3," the abbreviation of their Japanese name), had written Japan's most successful word-processing program and seemed to be on the leading edge of kana-kanji technology. To Kahn and Turner, the chemistry seemed good. "We were particularly impressed that they ordered bagels and hot dogs for lunch," says Jack Plimpton, marketing manager for Japan. K3, on the other hand, didn't quite know what to make of Lotus. In Japan, American companies have a reputation for lasting a season, if that. Negotiating the K3-Lotus contract took 50 days, including one all-day session devoted to whether a specific word should appear in a certain clause. Gradually, K3 became convinced that an arrangement with Lotus might endure. "Each time we flew back to continue talking, the negotiations went a little faster," says Steve Kahn.

TOWARD CULTURAL COMPATIBILITY

Over the next several months, the K3 engineers began to tame the homonym problem by developing a conversion module sufficiently sensitive to syntactical context to eliminate many of the candidate matches on its own. The kanji storage problem yielded to a sophisticated trick that allowed the programmers to mix 8-bit bytes and 16-bit bytes together. This is done by using one bit in each 8-bit byte to signal the computer whether to read the signaling byte by itself or combine it with the next byte in line. Meanwhile, K3 engineers and other consultants educated the Lotus team in some crucial aspects of Japanese culture. For one, the Japanese keep dates in years of the Emperor; 1986, for instance, is recorded as Showa 61, the 61st year of Hirohito's reign. As even emperors don't live forever, the Lotus developers thought a provision for entering a new emperor's name would be a natural convenience. "We talked to K3 about this," Steve Turner said, "and in a very polite way, they led us to realize that we should not even dream about marketing a program that appeared, in any respect whatsoever, to question the Emperor's immortality."

And then there was the matter of the beep. Current versions of *1-2-3* sound a beep if a user types a character not appropriate to the context of the moment. The Japanese work in clustered groups, with their desks in close proximity. It was conveyed to the Lotus team that there would be some sensitivity to a feature that appeared to broadcast every fumble to the general public. The beep was made optional. The Japanese are also sensitive to the look of software, so developer Trevor Hughes overhauled and neatened up *1-2-3*'s graphics. Thicker borders were drawn around graphs, and color patterns went from solid to cross-hatched. Screen colors were made user-selectable, and new graphing conventions were added. Grid lines were introduced in worksheets to allow users to neaten up the appearance of screens, draw flowcharts, and visually track along horizontal rows more easily.

The great unknowns hanging over all this work were why microcomputers had not penetrated further into the Japanese culture, and what Release 2J might do, if anything, to address those reasons. Some said the problem was simply a lack of desk space. Real estate is extremely expensive in Japan, and enterprises squeeze themselves into the smallest possible areas. A Japanese desk with room for a machine the size of an IBM PC AT is rare. An individual office is even rarer. So plans were laid to port a version of the new *1-2-3* to laptop computers. Other authorities speculated that the problem was simply the tedium of kana-kanji conversion; the K3 team was working on that. There was an opinion that senior Japanese executives simply have a different style—that they prefer to hammer out strategies over drinks at their clubs rather than do what-if projections with a spreadsheet. Whatever the cause, if *1-2-3* were to succeed in Japan, it would have to work not only for the people who were using a spreadsheet for the first time but also for people encountering their first computer.

IMPROVING ON 1-2-3

Throughout the Release 2J project, the emphasis on ease of use was continuous. Normally, kana-kanji conversion programs are built into Japanese word processors. In spreadsheet software, however, the conversion program is external. This requires that you first suspend the application and create the characters you want to enter. These characters pass into the application when you exit from the conversion. In Release 2J, kanji conversion technology is built in so that conversions can be run from within *1-2-3*.

Other improvements include a Learn mode and an on-screen function-key template that can be used conjunction with a mouse. Release 2J users can also print graphs directly from within the program. This feature replaces the PrintGraph program. "You just press the PrintScreen key, and the program prints out three different sizes of graphs," says Plimpton. "And you can insert them anywhere in a document. This feature would make Western *1-2-3* users swoon." Also added were several new graph types (including radar charts, high-low charts, and combination stacked-bar charts) and an Edit Recall feature, which reenters the last sequence typed on the edit line.

By the fall of 1986, the manuals and Help files had been translated, office space had been secured in Tokyo—an article could be written on that alone—and the Japanese quality-assurance staff had been trained and had tested and approved Release 2J. The program disks had been duplicated and the Japanese documentation printed and bound. The NEC version was rolled out in September 1986, and the IBM version shipped two months later—a year and a half after it had been first envisioned. "The advertising and public relations campaigns were based on the theme that Lotus had bothered," Plimpton said, "that we had done our homework, that we were here to stay." There was naturally some skepticism. "They've done a good job," Kazuya Watanabe, vice president of NEC Corp., told *The New York Times*. "That doesn't mean they'll succeed," he added. But the early returns seemed auspicious. A month after its introduction, Release 2J had become the best-selling software in Japan.

For Western users, the story does not end there. It seems likely that many of the changes instituted in Release 2J may eventually show up in domestic versions of *1-2-3*. Thus, what began as an effort to fine-tune American software to the Japanese culture may end by enhancing the original program.

QUESTIONS

1. What lessons can be drawn from Lotus's Japanese experience to help with exporting applications software to other countries?

2. The Japanese alphabet presented the most difficult challenge. What other technical and organizational problems were encountered by the development team?

3. Describe the key skills needed by a team that develops and adapts software for global use.

4. Was it rational to make all the modifications to accommodate this market, or did Lotus extend beyond the call of duty? The original plan called for development to take three months; instead it took a year. How can Lotus avoid this disparity in timing in the future?